Harry Truman
and the
Crisis Presidency

BY THE SAME AUTHOR

The Cross of the Moment
The War System
American Labor in Midpassage (Editor)
Adlai Stevenson, Patrician Among the Politicians

Harry Truman
and the
Crisis Presidency

By Bert Cochran

FUNK & WAGNALLS   NEW YORK

Acknowledgment is made to Harper & Row, Publishers, for permission to quote various brief passages from *Journals of David E. Lilienthal* by David E. Lilienthal, Vols. 1 and 2, 1964.

Designed by Philip Lief

Manufactured in the United States of America

4 5 6 7 8 9 10

Library of Congress Cataloging in Publication Data

Cochran, Bert
    Harry Truman and the crisis presidency.

    Includes bibliographical references.
    1. Truman, Harry S., Pres. U. S., 1884–
    2. United States—Politics and government—1945–1953.
    I. Title.
E814.C62   973.918′090′4 [B]   72-7567

To my wife, Cynthia

Contents

1
STRUGGLE FOR THE VICE-PRESIDENCY 1

2
EARLY YEARS 22

3
ENTRY INTO POLITICS 40

4
JACKSON COUNTY JUDGE 55

5
SENATOR FROM PENDERGAST 68

6
A COCKEYED HORATIO ALGER STORY 93

7
NEW WHITE HOUSE REGIME 116

8
THE COURSE IS CHANGED 137

9
CONFLICT AT POTSDAM 158

10
TWO HALVES OF THE SAME WALNUT 176

11
FROM RECONVERSION TO TAFT-HARTLEY 198

12
THE 1948 MIRACLE 221

13
SCANDALS, NATO, PEACE TREATY WITH JAPAN 241

14
ARMS RACE AND THE BOMB 270

15
CHINA TRAUMA 291

16
INTERVENTION IN KOREA 311

17
TROUBLES ON THE HOME FRONT 333

18
TRUMANISM AND McCARTHYISM 353

19
THE LAST HURRAH 378

20
HIS PLACE IN THE PANTHEON 392

NOTES 403

INDEX 415

1

Struggle
for the
Vice-Presidency

When Harry S. Truman was handed the presidential scepter upon Franklin D. Roosevelt's sudden death, the memory of Calvin Coolidge came to the minds of many as they tried to find a parallel in American history to this incredible event. In Independence, Missouri, old Henry Bundschu, a Republican circuit court judge who had been friendly with Truman and his family since boyhood, said, "The country hasn't been in good hands since Calvin Coolidge. But it will be now." A more cosmopolitan observer, Drew Pearson, wrote in his column, "In more ways than one, Harry Truman is like Calvin Coolidge. He comes from a similar backwoods origin. He seldom gave speeches on the Senate floor. He is thrifty, remembers the day when the drugstore paid him $3 a week. But more than anything else Truman has the same brand of Coolidge political luck."

The comparison proved superficial, but it is telling that it came to many minds on April 12, 1945, when the name Harry Truman was thrust on their attention. The feeling was universal that an era had ended and that a courthouse politician had succeeded a world figure. David Lilienthal, chairman of the Tennessee Valley Authority, recorded in his journal that his response was one of "consternation at the thought of that Throttlebottom, Truman. The country and the world doesn't deserve to be left this way, with Truman at the head of the country at such a time." Edward R. Stettinius, Jr., Roosevelt's last Secretary of State, who had never met Truman, anxiously questioned other Cabinet members: "What would happen? Would there be another Harding regime?" Roy Roberts, the 375-pound, glad-handing top man at the Republican *Kansas City Star* and long-time friend of Truman, also thought that a new era was starting, but, unlike Lilienthal, he was sanguine. The new President, Roberts explained to his readers, had the "innate, instinctive conservatism in action of the Missouri-bred countrymen. The sheer fact he is the average man, understands the average man and his quality, is probably Truman's greatest asset." Roberts was confident that the country would see "the shift from personal government back to what is called, for lack of any better term, constitutional government."

Was the country witnessing the beginning—to use the hyperbole of the headline writers—of a counterrevolution because of the death of one man? Had Roosevelt been too careworn and preoccupied in his last year to realize what was afoot, as some suggested, when he consented to Truman as his running mate? The series of events that made Truman President began when the Old Fox in the White House was getting set to run for his fourth term, as the professionals had figured he would. A crisis had been provoked by the President's bid for a third term, but in 1944 there was hardly a ripple of dissent within the party. "Everyone seemed to take it for granted," said Sam Rosenman, the President's main speech writer. (George E. Allen, who like other court jesters was a shrewd one, even kidded Roosevelt about it in 1940. The President had said in Cleveland that this was his last campaign; that evening, Allen turned to Roosevelt: "Mr. President, do you remember what you said tonight, 'When that term is over there will be another President'? Well, that's going to cost us a million votes in 1944.") The organization men needed Roosevelt to win the election. The two-term precedent had been breached successfully; it no longer seemed sacrosanct. Besides, Roosevelt had a good explanation for seeking a fourth term: It was too risky to switch leaders in the midst of war.

This was a strong talking point, better than the one of 1940 that, in the crisis created by the war in Europe, only Roosevelt could be trusted to steer the ship of state to port. Roosevelt went through many moods, mostly in 1940, whether to run or not to run. But whatever his hesitations and misgivings, and whatever the crises he faced —for Roosevelt was a leader in a time of continuous crises—it was written in the stars that he would seek a third and then a fourth term once he saw that the electorate would grant him the prizes. "All that is within me cries out to go back to my home on the Hudson," he had written to Democratic party chairman Robert E. Hannegan. There was another voice that cried out with greater force. It had been given to him to scale the snowy heights of destiny, and so long as he had the choice, he was not going to retire to Hyde Park to dictate memoirs and wait for death.

The professional handlers who had his ear were all for the fourth term, although not one of them thought that Roosevelt, if elected, would live out the next four years. They did not have to read his medical charts; they could see death in his eyes. (At one point, Roosevelt's faded appearance and listlessness frightened Edward J. Flynn, the political boss of the Bronx in New York City. He had an affection for the man. In a qualm of conscience, he pleaded with Eleanor Roosevelt to prevail on her husband not to run again. "I felt that he would never survive his term.") There was a Byzantine atmosphere around the President. Politicos, speech writers, Cabinet members, handymen, relatives, were all milling around the throne, seeing the principal of the drama failing, knowing a fourth-term campaign was inevitable, pretending to themselves and to each other that all was well, that after a few weeks' vacation "The Boss" would "bounce back." The man who first saw clearly that the key to the future lay with the nominee for Vice-President was Edwin Pauley, a big, hard-driving California millionaire who had gone into politics to promote his oil ventures. From lobbying he went to electioneering because, as he told a newspaperman, "It was cheaper to get a new legislature" than to buy up the old one. At this time, he was the party treasurer and major fund-raiser.*

* Pauley was later nominated by Truman for Undersecretary of the Navy, the official with jurisdiction over oil reserves. This was blown out of the water when Secretary of the Interior Harold Ickes testified that Pauley had propositioned him to surrender federal claims to the tidelands oil fields in return for several hundred thousand dollars in campaign contributions. Several years later, the Senate Appropriations Committee learned that Pauley had made $900,000 in commodities speculation while special assistant to the Secretary of the Army, when both the President and Cabinet members were denouncing speculators for trafficking in "human misery."

The sensational Ickes exposé was actually an old story. In the midst of fund-raising for the Democratic party, Pauley since at least 1940 had directed a nationwide lobby to influence legislation—and there was no secret about it. The

Pauley began to hatch a conspiracy, as he brashly called it, to side-track Vice-President Henry A. Wallace—the wild man from Iowa and the darling of the CIO radicals, to the organization men—and secure the nomination for a safe-and-sane, feet-on-the-ground, right-thinking conservative. He sought to rally all prospective recruits to the cause with the war cry: "You're not nominating a Vice-President of the United States, but a President." At first, he related, "I found it difficult to recruit accomplices," because the people around Roosevelt "were afraid" to oppose him. His first successes were Ed Flynn, Democratic national committeeman, and General Edwin "Pa" Watson, the President's military aide. The latter was particularly important because he was able to arrange appointments for a host of picked convention delegates, national committeemen, state chairmen, and governors whose refrain was: "Mr. President, we are all for you, but we cannot stomach Wallace." For a while, according to Pauley, "these interviews made little difference in Roosevelt's thinking." But by spring, "I could sense that the President had begun to change from an enthusiastic Wallace supporter to a man who had sincere doubts concerning him. Pa Watson told me that this constant barrage was having a definite effect." All through the spring, the good work went forward. Pauley, who as party treasurer was in charge of the fund-raising dinners, used his position to keep Wallace away from the party faithful. "I very carefully planned that there would be a minimum of Wallace participation in any of these events."

This was the master plot, as Pauley and others saw it, that changed the face of American history. As is often the case in such enterprises, there were a number of subsidiary plots within the central one, consistent with the main design but possessing their own distinctive patterns and purposes. Pauley himself had his eye glued on the ball. He was out to dump Wallace, and was not too concerned with who was his replacement so long as the replacement was politically sound. Sam Rayburn, Speaker of the House, was a good man; Senator Truman was a good man; there were other good men. After Hannegan

nomination for the Navy post apparently originated with Roosevelt. Secretary of the Navy James V. Forrestal recorded in his diary on January 20, 1945: "I saw President Roosevelt today on general navy department business and talked, among other things, about his vacancy in the Assistant Secretaryship. He suggested the name of Edwin Pauley. I said that I knew Mr. Pauley only slightly and asked if Mr. Roosevelt knew him well enough to say to me that he was the proper man for the post. He did not answer directly but made the comment that Mr. Pauley had been the most energetic and successful fund-raiser of the party."

came in as the new party chairman on January 22, the charter members of Pauley's group were joined by a number of other weighty politicos. Neither Hannegan nor Flynn shared Pauley's insouciance about the vice-presidential replacement: they wanted James F. Byrnes and other contenders headed off, and the nomination assured for Truman. Flynn may have reached his position simply by calculating the odds, but Hannegan had a personal interest. His political career was closely tied to Truman's. That is why, as Pauley related, "he was afraid to push Truman openly, but did everything he could in a roundabout way."

Hannegan, like Pauley, was not a seeker of the grail. A pasty-faced, six-foot-one, 200-pound Irishman, he looked the slick courthouse technician that he was. After graduating from law school in St. Louis in 1925, he went to work as a precinct chairman in the 21st Ward of the city that Lincoln Steffens had once called the "worst governed" in the country. The Democrats regained control in 1933 after twenty-six long years in the wilderness, and then only because they rode Roosevelt's coattails; he had carried the city by a margin of better than 2 to 1. Hannegan, who had managed his associate, Bernard Dickman, into the mayor's chair, was the brains of the Hannegan-Dickman machine. His spectacular rise thereafter was owing to a fluke deal with Truman in 1934, a gamble that paid off royally for both of them.

This took place in the 1940 primary when Truman was seeking the party's nomination for reelection to the Senate, and nobody thought he had the ghost of a chance. Thomas J. Pendergast, his sponsor, was in jail; the Kansas City machine was a shambles; Roosevelt had disowned him and given the nod to his opponent, Governor Lloyd Stark. The Hannegan-Dickman machine, an offspring of New Deal popularity and dependent on the goodwill of its Washington mentors, was officially for Stark. Pendergast's decline, however, had opened the way for the St. Louis regulars to become the power in the entire state. They went into high gear with one of their own boys, the St. Louis saloon commissioner, Lawrence McDaniel, for governor. The trouble with the Stark-McDaniel ticket was that Stark was not showing the proper spirit of cooperation toward their man. Hannegan did not like the looks of it. Of what use was a Stark victory to them if McDaniel went down to defeat?

Hannegan decided the situation called for strong measures. The damaged Pendergast machine was still probably capable of churning out a bloc of votes. This, added to their own, could make up a winning combination. Accordingly, he made an undercover agreement with Truman, the low man in the three-man senatorial race. Mayor Dickman continued to wave the flag for Stark, but shortly before the primary election Hannegan called together the precinct captains and instructed them to switch their support. He demonstrated his good faith in carrying through his side of the bargain by making the announcement public two days before the election. This was the deal that saved Truman's career from extinction in 1940. He squeaked through St. Louis by 8,411 votes, and that was 444 more than his entire margin over Stark for the whole of Missouri.

Truman went on to beat his Republican opponent, but although Roosevelt carried the state by 100,000, McDaniel fell by the wayside. Hannegan did not want to give up. With the support of his Pendergast allies, he had the Democratic state committee file a petition charging fraud and irregularities in the election, and enjoining the speaker of the house from posting the count. Governor Stark denounced the petition as an attempt to perpetrate a "shameless steal," and all the major newspapers branded the maneuver. This did not deter the state legislature, controlled by the Democrats, from complying with the petition. The scheme foundered, however, when the Missouri supreme court directed the house speaker to publish the election results.

Hannegan had pressed his luck too far. He came out heavily tarnished. His statewide ambitions had been thwarted, and he had lost his patronage and power base in St. Louis. All he had was an I.O.U. note on Truman's gratitude. This he was able to redeem. Early in 1942, when the spot of collector of internal revenue at St. Louis opened up, Truman promptly recommended Hannegan for it, whereupon the St. Louis newspapers opened up on Hannegan. They called him the "most discredited boss of a discredited political machine," and described the job offer as a "disgraceful example of plum-passing." Truman was neither impressed nor intimidated. As a fervent believer in, and a dedicated practitioner of, patronage, he had no intention of compromising on a matter of principle. He told reporters what the score was without mincing words: "Hannegan carried St. Louis three times for the President and for me. If he is not nominated there will be no collector at St. Louis." After the initial appointment, Hannegan's advancement was rapid: sixteen months later, to Commissioner of Internal Revenue; three months after that, to Democratic National Chairman—in each case, on the recommendation of Truman and with the approval of Roosevelt.

As the man in charge of convention arrangements in 1944, with the added burden of pushing through his favored candidate, Hannegan had an assignment of excruciating difficulty, one that taxed the ingenuity he had learned in the 21st Ward. Theoretically, this was to be an open convention, with the delegates free to vote their choice. In practice, the President was at the controls. The front runners were the incumbent Vice-President, Wallace, and the so-called Assistant President in charge of war mobilization, Byrnes. Aside from Truman, there were no other heavies. Rayburn was not a serious contender so far as the major bosses were concerned. Senator Alben W. Barkley, as always, was "too old." Justice William O. Douglas had no strength in the party. By June, the members of Pauley's brigade thought that their labors had been successful. They had reason to believe that Roosevelt would not insist on Wallace as his running mate. But with Wallace effectively knifed, would not the nomination drop into the hot, eager hands of Byrnes? On this matter, after all, there was no unity among the conspirators. Mayor Edward J. Kelly of Chicago was thought to favor Byrnes so as to deadlock the convention in favor of his own protégé, Senator Scott Lucas. Postmaster General Frank Walker was uncertain; he had no objections to Byrnes. The same was true of Allen.

In these trying circumstances, Hannegan cast himself in the role of honest broker resolved to string Byrnes along. He did not want to expose his own candidate too early to public scrutiny, or to force decisions prematurely. On June 13 he told Byrnes (probably at Roosevelt's instigation) that he (Byrnes) was the right man for the Vice-Presidency, and that Roosevelt had expressed this opinion to him. Byrnes was all to ready to listen to that kind of talk. He was sixty-five, three years older than Roosevelt, blindingly ambitious, and this was his last chance to make the run. The press was freely speculating about a great battle at the convention between Byrnes and the regulars on one hand, and Wallace and the CIO cohorts on the other. Well, why not? If the President favored him, or was just benevolently neutral, he would have it made. Byrnes had been Roosevelt's sometime fixer in the Senate, and bore the epaulets of a virtuoso cloakroom wire-puller. His many years with Roosevelt, aside from his long experience of jugglery in politics, should have warned him at this juncture to move warily. Ambition and egotism did their work, however, and the customarily cagey Byrnes plunged rashly ahead.

It is well at this point, as the complications and the excitement mount with the approach of the convention, to inquire what the principal of the drama was doing. Was he the passive victim of Pauley and his coadjutors? It was whispered that "the boss" was not his old self, not giving leadership to the party because of his declining health. The actions of all the main actors have since been recorded in memoirs and memoranda, and while some of the accounts differ in secondary details, the essential facts are established, and Roosevelt's maneuvers stand out in high relief. His declining health notwithstanding, he knew precisely what was going on, and what he wanted out of the convention. That he went about achieving it so deviously was due not only to his ingrained habits of work, but to the nature of the balancing act that constituted the Roosevelt regime. To understand the problem as he saw it in the spring of 1944, it is necessary for a moment to turn the camera from the feverish movements of candidates and managers to the political condition of America at war.

The New Deal was the most innovative period in American history. It shook up old habits and routines, changed the mechanics of government, and introduced a new personnel, far beyond previous reform eras. But as scholars have noted, when the smoke of controversy cleared, the social and economic contours of the landscape were essentially undisturbed. The great complexes of industry, communications, and banking were in the same hands as before. That the masters of wealth turned with such fury on the national leader who had been their savior when their own standing was at its nadir was due to the feudal manner in which they had ruled over their private domains. Welfare and regulatory legislation, taken for granted in Western Europe before the First World War, were enacted here only over the savage opposition of the money aristocracy which at every stage of the legislative battle predicted disasters unimaginable.

On the electoral field, Roosevelt was, and remained to the end, "the Champ," who administered in 1936 a crushing defeat to the "economic royalists" and their dreams of turning back the clock. But "the Champ" could do little with his victory. Other sectors of government were effectively mobilized to bottle him up. His attempts to reform the Supreme Court and to eliminate a number of reactionary congressmen were described by the press lords as tyrannical usurpation, and were overcome, so that by 1938, for all practical purposes, the New Deal had ground to a halt. The panoply and circumstance of power remained, but a hostile congressional coalition had been forged which exercised an effective veto over his regime.

When the country turned to the creation of a war machine in mid-1940, there were several possible approaches. One was for the government to build its own factories, nationalize some ancillary facilities, and run the complex as government corporations. A strong case could have been made for such a procedure when military procurement began to dominate the entire scene. The traditional capitalist market was no longer operative for half the economy. At the 1943–1944 peak of the war effort, virtually half the total resources in materials and labor were used to support our armed forces and to help our allies; government spending accounted for 45 percent of the gross national product. By the last year of the war, the government had paid out of its own funds two-thirds more than the total value of prewar capital goods to finance industrial expansion. One might have thought that government operation of war industries would have been given serious consideration, since in the mythology of modern states no one is supposed to get rich out of war while the youth of the country is being called upon to risk life and limb at nominal remuneration. However, the masters of industry were not about to permit military production to be run as a gigantic TVA.

Roosevelt had no intention of trying wartime socialism. On the contrary. He was resolved to attain national unity at home, to assuage the corporation executives, to quiet the fears of the dowagers and clubmen, to mitigate the hostility of the unreconciled. That settled the method of mobilization: The corporations and banks were invited to send their representatives to Washington to man the production and procurement divisions, and contracts for matériel from airplanes to brass buttons were let out to the corporate giants as if they were risking their own funds. As will be seen in the later discussion of the Truman Committee, the businessmen descended on Washington like the Bourbons returning to Paris after Waterloo; they unceremoniously elbowed aside the New Dealers and choked the city in an atmosphere of easy money and triumphant reaction. Inside the defense agencies, the rancor between business representatives and New Dealers could be cut with a knife.

At the head of the War Department now stood Henry Stimson, partner of a leading Wall Street law firm, Cabinet member in the Taft and Hoover administrations, an elder statesman of the "internationalist Republicans." With him came a task force of high-powered graduates of Eastern prep schools and Ivy League universities who had mastered the arts of leadership in law firms, banks, and brokerage houses: Robert Patterson, partner in a Wall Street law firm, a federal judge, a demon of energy and determination, and a military martinet who wore around his waist the belt of a German soldier he had killed in the First World War; John J. McCloy, of still another Wall Street law firm, whose diplomatic talents made him the department's plenipotentiary and international operator, later president of the World Bank and proconsul for Germany; and Robert Lovett, the suave, witty, and ice-cold banker from Brown, Harriman who became Assistant Secretary of War for Air, and later Undersecretary of State and Secretary of Defense.

The Navy was likewise graced with its clan of business luminaries. The new Secretary was Frank Knox, millionaire owner of the *Chicago Daily News* and running mate of Alfred Landon in 1936. If he was a bit of a Rotarian, he had as his assistant Adlai Stevenson, fresh from a La Salle Street law firm, to write his speeches and look after his papers. The Undersecretary, to become Secretary after Knox died in 1944, was the formidable James Forrestal, the boy wonder of Wall Street who had risen to the presidency of Dillon, Read. His office, newly created by Congress, was the powerhouse for contract negotiations and procurement. His legal assistant, Charles Detmar, was of the Wall Street law firm that served Dillon, Read. For contract negotiations, there was H. Struve Hensel, partner in the Wall Street law firm of Milbank, Tweed and Hope. Working in close association with Forrestal was his former partner at Dillon, Read, Ferdinand Eberstadt, who became a major personality in the mobilization, heading the Army-Navy Munitions Board, and serving as vice-chairman in charge of materials priorities on the War Production Board.

Stimson's court biographer, Elting Morison, wrote ecstatically about the War Department's staff. "They were of the first class," he said, "and therefore they did first class work." The characterization is incomplete. For it can be said, with equal justification, that Albert Speer did first-class work. The question is, to what end? The fact is that these men, some highly gifted, some indifferent, were trained to work along one set of lines that took for granted the privileges and vested interests of their favored class. That their pretensions had not been very much tempered in the course of eight years of New Deal upheaval was seen in the fantastic if brief history of the War Resources Board. In August, 1939, when the Stalin-Hitler pact was signed, and a month before he declared a limited national emergency, Roosevelt agreed to the setting up of a board to review the War Department's Industrial Mobilization Plan. Louis Johnson, then the Assistant Secretary, and his corporation friends, thought the gates had been flung open for the business crowd to take over war mobilization precisely as it had done in the First World War. They proceeded to name a board consisting of Stettinius, scion of a J. P. Morgan partner and board chairman of U.S. Steel; Walter Gifford of American Tel and Tel; John Lee Pratt of General Motors; and General Robert Wood of Sears, Roebuck. Roosevelt's suggestion that they name a labor representative was ignored. To safeguard the "public interest," the best they could manage were two ultraconservatives, one from a foundation, the other, president of the Massachusetts Institute of Technology. When Roosevelt made it clear to the board that the War Department's blueprint was not acceptable to him, the members added to the board John Hancock of Lehman Brothers, a protégé of Bernard Baruch, and these two drafted a report that gave rhetorical satisfaction to Roosevelt's objections while retaining the plan's essentials.

The Wall Streeters were premature. A great outcry arose that effectively disposed of the board. Ickes charged that it was an oligarchy with no mandate from the people. Wallace complained that it was dominated by Wall Street bankers. Hugh Johnson, the past NRA commissar, long associated with Baruch, wrote in his newspaper column that the board was "top heavy with business executives," and privately told Louis Johnson that the government did not "intend to let Morgan and DuPont men run the war." Under fire from all sides, Roosevelt deftly changed course. He classified the board's report top secret so that even congressmen could not examine it. That was at the end of 1939. A year later business leaders were accomplishing in piecemeal fashion by tactics of infiltration and guerrilla raids what they had been unable to achieve with a frontal assault.

It was not that Roosevelt wanted to turn the show over to the money changers. He tried to continue running his administration with the techniques that had done duty in the prewar years. He played off one bloc against another; he maneuvered to be the broker between competing positions and interests; he dispersed authority and fostered competition among subordinates and agencies; he permitted jurisdictions to overlap and gave the same assignments to a number of people, all to enable him to maintain his own control over the bureaucracy and to assure his position as the final arbiter; he secreted information and kept his own counsel; he juggled, manipulated, prevaricated, improvised, switched signals, called up in crisis the vast reserves of public popularity he still commanded. The methods were the same as in the New Deal.

But the balancing act had to be performed on a different political stage. The corporation executives and their numerous satellites, who jammed the cocktail bars, hotel dining rooms and reception suites, and entertained with a lavish hand, and who with their elegantly sheathed ladies turned Washington into a composite of Louis XIV's Versailles and San Francisco during the gold rush, could and did demand that mobilization take place on their terms. They not only had the country over a barrel, as a government report put it, but, with the aid of their press associates, reversed the language of political discourse to their advantage. War mobilization was defined solely in the context of their special interests. Anyone who objected or resisted was accused of interfering with the defense effort, and the interference was ascribed to his being a New Deal crackpot or Communist dupe. Those who acquiesced were hailed in news accounts and broadcasts as far-seeing statesmen and broad-gauged patriots. When labor leaders tried to push their little bowls and tin plates in the way of the golden deluge, they were accused of sabotaging the war effort, brusquely informed that there were no strikes in the foxholes, while it was hinted that France had fallen because of unreasonable union impositions. The political scales were tipping rightward. The atmosphere reeked of hatred for all that had gone on in the past decade. Harry Hopkins, who had a propensity to shift with the prevailing winds, astonished Robert Sherwood with his outburst against an old friend who wanted to send a protest to Roosevelt: "I'm getting sick and tired of having to listen to complaints from those goddam New Dealers!"

Roosevelt retreated steadily before the demands of businessmen so as not to jeopardize their cynically conditional support. They were coaxed out of their sitdown strike in 1940 by timely surrenders: The Vinson-Tramnell Act, which limited profits on shipbuilding and aircraft production to 10 and 12 percent respectively, was suspended; corporations were permitted to write off their capital expenditures over a five-year period instead of the customary twenty years. An excess-profits tax proved more onerous in name than fact, containing a provision that reconversion expenses after the war could be used to offset the tax.

The propitiatory offerings did not dispel the miasma overhanging the capital. There was a mounting fury about the concessions Roosevelt made to the labor unions, and Congress's rage when he threatened to use his wartime powers to control prices rose to defiance when he vetoed a tax bill with the acid comment that it was in fact a tax-relief bill "providing relief not for the needy but for the greedy." The hostile coalition in Congress, become self-confident by the rightward tide and encouraged by Republican midterm victories, was completely out of the administration's control and thirsting for vengeance. Both houses overrode the veto by enormous majorities—Treasury experts said it was the first revenue act to become a law over a veto—and Barkley, who resigned as majority leader in protest against Roosevelt's harsh strictures, was treated by the press and his fellow Solons like a hero who had at last freed himself from the repulsive embrace of his overbearing master.

This was the atmosphere and these were the circumstances when Roosevelt prepared in 1944 to run for a fourth term and had to pick a running mate. He had won national unity at the price of turning over to the business crowd many agencies and departments, but he still faced an entrenched opposition in Congress and a polarization of his own party. Should he try to force Wallace again on the Democratic convention as he had done in 1940, it would precipitate the Southern split that Truman faced four years later, and many of the big-city bosses and organization professionals would sit out the election. This might not be so disastrous to his reelection chances as the professionals imagined, for they had far less influence with the voters than they wanted to believe. In his confidential memorandum to Truman in 1947, Clark Clifford called attention to what had been demonstrated in 1944: "Those alert party machines which, beginning with 1932, turned out such huge majorities in the big cities for the Democratic ticket have all through the years of their victories been steadily deteriorating underneath—until in 1944 the Democratic organization found itself rivalled, in terms of money and workers, and exceeded in alertness and enthusiasm, by the PAC [the CIO Political Action Committee]. Everywhere the professionals are in profound collapse."

The last thing Roosevelt intended, however, was to run for a fourth term as the candidate of embattled liberalism under the aegis of a truncated party controlled by laborites and New Deal enthusiasts. His type of politics required conflicting elements that could be balanced off. Moreover, any such campaign would have shattered the new alliance with the business world. The selection of a candidate for the Vice-Presidency was thus to be an exercise in *Realpolitik*. He had undoubtedly decided as far back as the middle of 1943 that Wallace would have to be sacrificed. When the bitter quarrel between Secretary of Commerce Jesse Jones and Wallace broke into public print and Roosevelt peremptorily dissolved the Board of Economic Warfare, of which Wallace was chairman, and turned its function over to

Jones's friend, Leo Crowley, it was obvious to the White House palace guard that Wallace's political career was finished. Jonathan Daniels, a White House aide, noted in his diary: "Talked with David Niles who said I could bet any money that Henry Wallace would not be the vice presidential candidate next time." The judgment was confirmed when Roosevelt, at the height of the politicking around the Vice-Presidency, shipped Wallace off on a mission to China. These were the months in which Pauley and the others labored so mightily to break through an open door. The tired, harassed President, who would not take a stand, permitted them to try to persuade him of what he had decided in his own mind months before.

The question was, if not Wallace, who? If Wallace had to be sacrificed to keep the loyalty of the professionals and the big-money contributors, the laborites and liberals could not be kicked in the teeth. They made up an important part of the coalition. Some dopesters claimed that you could take them for granted because they had no place else to go. But that was not completely valid: They could stay home. Roosevelt had to find the candidate who, as Flynn phrased it, "would hurt him least." Truman fitted the specification. His record of support of Roosevelt in the Senate was good, yet his associations were with conservative politicians and business folk. He had had labor support for his reelection to the Senate, yet he was trusted by businessmen and politicians. He came from a border state, but he had never joined in anti-Negro demonstrations in the Senate. The perfect middle-of-the-roader, in Flynn's words, "He just dropped into the slot." Roosevelt gave no thought to what kind of president Truman might make. What was exercising all the professionals did not enter into his calculations. He had decided to enlist for another four years, and apparently assumed that the Deity would have to take this into account when making His own dispositions.

With the convention near, Roosevelt proceeded to give a further twist to the elaborate charade he had been playing. At luncheon with Wallace, he continued the pretense that the convention was to be an open one, but he promised to send a letter giving Wallace a personal endorsement; he assured him he hoped it would be the same team as in 1940. A day or two later, before leaving for Hyde Park and the West Coast, he informed Byrnes, whom he had been keeping in a state of high fever with repeated inoculations, that he intended to give only a token personal endorsement of Wallace, that Wallace had no chance of winning, and that he would express no preference for anyone.

With at least two contenders set up for the convention, the party bosses, Flynn, Hannegan, Pauley, Walker, Kelly, and Allen, arrived, by invitation, at the White House on July 11 for the fateful meeting to pick the candidate. Roosevelt had asked Flynn during their canvass of the candidates the previous week to inject Truman's name into the discussion. Flynn called at Hannegan's apartment before the meeting, told him that Truman was going to be the choice, and that it was up to him to "sell" the others. Hannegan was skeptical, but he talked to Kelly and Allen and they agreed to go along.

At the White House, the guests had dinner first, at which, in characteristic fashion, Roosevelt entertained with reminiscences without once mentioning what everyone present was on pins and needles to talk about, the Vice-Presidency. After dinner, the guests, in a state of growing tension, adjourned with their host to the Blue Oval Room on the second floor where they were joined by the President's daughter, Anna, and her husband, John Boettiger. There they went over the various candidates one by one, eliminating Rayburn, Byrnes, and Barkley. No time was wasted on Wallace. To make sure that the proceedings were not too cut-and-dried, Roosevelt threw in the names of John Winant, ambassador to Britain, and Justice William O. Douglas, but these names were greeted with silence.

The conferees moved next to Truman. Flynn made the pitch; Roosevelt said a few kind words but remarked that he was a little worried about Truman's age. He asked Boettiger to get a *Congressional Directory* so they could check it. When Boettiger returned with the tome, Pauley grabbed it out of his hand and held it unobtrusively in his lap, hoping that no one would bring up the subject again. At last all agreed that Truman was the best candidate. As they were leaving, the President called out to them: "I know that this makes you boys happy, and you are the ones I am counting on to win this election. I still think that Douglas would have the greater public appeal." Flynn felt that the dinner had gone according to plan: "Everyone thought he had suggested Truman and that the President had taken his suggestion."

Downstairs, while the conferees were putting on their coats, Walker whispered to Hannegan that he ought to go back and get Roosevelt's approval of Truman in writing. All they had was a verbal agreement given in a closed room. Hannegan went back and got some kind of endorsement on a scratch pad or, according to Allen, on the back of an envelope. So masterfully did Roosevelt spread confusion over the proceedings that long after the event the participants could not be sure whether Hannegan received three notes, two notes, or just one from the President by the time of the convention vote. At any rate, the decisive note, retyped on White House stationery, that Hannegan used to line up delegates and that is now under lock and key in the Harry S. Truman Library, read: "Dear Bob: You have written me about Harry Truman and Bill Douglas. I should, of course, be very glad to run with either of them and believe that either of them would bring real strength to the ticket." (Roosevelt had agreed that Truman was the candidate to back, but Douglas had slipped in again.)

After the conference, Hannegan and Walker gave Byrnes a guarded report. This should have shaken Byrnes loose from his chimera, particularly since he was a veteran of the 1940 convention where at least half a dozen aspirants confidently informed delegates that they had received the benediction only to have Harry Hopkins lower the boom on them. But Byrnes was validating the old maxim that no one is more susceptible to a confidence game than another confidence man. Roosevelt was no longer in Washington, but Byrnes managed to reach him, by telephone, at Hyde Park. He had carefully written out his questions and took down the entire conversation in shorthand.

Why did Hannegan and Walker say that he (Roosevelt) preferred Truman and Douglas, and that either would cost the ticket fewer votes than Byrnes?

"Jimmy, that is all wrong. That is not what I told them. It is what they told me. I was asking questions. I did not express myself."

Byrnes continued his questioning. Roosevelt began a discourse on the subtleties of semantics.

"We have to be damned careful about language. They asked if I would object to Truman and Douglas and I said no. That is different from using the word 'prefer.' That is not expressing a preference because you know I told you I would have no preference. After all, Jimmy, you are close to me personally, and Henry is close to me."

After this conversation, Byrnes announced his candidacy. To guard himself against further unpleasant surprises, he called Truman in Independence, told him he had the President's support, and asked if Truman would nominate him at the convention. Truman answered that if that was so, he would be glad to. Daniels remembered the way Byrnes came to Chicago "in a marching, if not a strutting self-confidence."

The delegates began arriving to a sweltering city, and soon the hotel lobbies and bars were in pandemonium. In addition to the anticipated battle between Wallace and Byrnes, there were rumors of the candidacies of Douglas, Barkley, Truman, Paul McNutt, shipbuilder Henry Kaiser, and others. The President had achieved the chaos he wanted. Hannegan was still playing his role of nonpartisan chairman, taking Byrnes's cockiness at face value while maneuvering to put across Truman. Sidney Hillman was marshaling the CIO battalions for Wallace, at the same time letting Truman know that if the Wallace standard faltered, as it probably would, the CIO and its allies could be persuaded to support Truman. During the scurrying to and fro, Mayor Kelly took advantage of the muddle for his own byplay: He declared himself for Byrnes and tried to swing the convention to him as the President's real candidate. Flynn had to demand a special meeting of party leaders where he belabored Kelly and others about keeping their pledged word. The issue was not settled until he called Roosevelt in his private railway car en route to the West Coast. Roosevelt spoke to Walker, Hannegan, and Kelly, in turn, and the agreement was replastered. What is singular about this secret meeting, and about the previous meeting at the White House, was that at no point did anyone raise the question of the availability of Truman (who all this time was issuing statements that he was not a candidate and declaring himself for Byrnes). Were they assuming that Hannegan had it all arranged when in fact he did not? Was it true that Truman did not want the nomination and had to be pressured to accept it?

As is usual in matters relating to human motives, Truman was beset by conflicting feelings. He was happy in the Senate, where he was an established member of the inner club. He had an assured career in surroundings that were familiar and congenial to him. Why risk it? Had he not attained the pinnacle of realistic ambition? He believed, as did the Pauley coterie, that if the Democratic ticket won, the Vice-President would become President. And he had profound doubts about his ability to shoulder burdens of that magnitude. He was afraid of the Presidency. He reminded George Wallace of the *St. Louis Post-Dispatch* of what had happened to most Vice-Presidents who succeeded to the Presidency: "Usually they were ridiculed in office, had their hearts broken, lost any vestige of respect they had before. I don't want that to happen to me." That was one inner voice Truman heard, sober, temperate, shrewd.

But there was another, more compelling one. Several times, Truman had been the beneficiary of strokes of good fortune. They had come unheralded and unexpected, and he had been able to exploit each opportunity, so that he had transformed, like an alchemist, the substance of his life. After all, when Pendergast offered him the nomination for senator ten years before, it was more fantastic than the present talk of becoming Vice-President. He had no business being President. Others were far better fitted for it. Still, if the opportunity presented itself, it had to be grasped. Significantly, in his many statements denying his own candidacy, he never shut the door to accepting the nomination.

People who had worked closely with him and knew him well never put any credence in his public protestations. Victor Messall, his assistant during the Senate years, said, "I'm sure he wanted to be Vice President, but he had to pretend he didn't." George Meader, an assistant counsel to the Truman Committee who wrote speeches and magazine articles for Truman, said he thought Truman was running for the Vice-Presidency long before the convention without doing so openly. Harry Easley, a close friend from Missouri, told this revealing story: Truman called him eight days after the election in 1944 and asked that he meet him in Kansas City. Easley went to the penthouse at the Muehlebach Hotel, where there was a noisy reunion in progress of Truman's old Battery D buddies from World War I. "I stayed with him that night. He told me just lying there in bed after things quieted down that he had been lonesome ever since the day they put the Secret Service on him, and that he had not yet seen the President at all; that the last time he saw him, he had the pallor of death on his face, and he knew that he would be President before the term was up. He said he was going to have to depend on his friends. He was talking about people like me, he said. He never at any time told me that he didn't want the nomination, but he knew that he was going to be the President of the United States, and I think it just scared the very devil out of him."

If Truman wanted the nomination, why was he so resistant with Hannegan until the very last moment? His conduct was both understandable and purposeful. He showed that he was either a smarter operator than Byrnes or that, not having been personally exposed to the master's sorcery, he was able to keep a more level head. He knew it was fatuous to just decide on one's own to be a candidate. The President, and particularly a President like Roosevelt, would choose his running mate. This was supposed to be an open convention, but neither Truman nor other politicos took this very seriously. These rules of the game were all the more cogent in his own case, since he lacked the popular following of Wallace or the standing of Byrnes. He could hope to rally the majority of delegates only if it was clear that he was the administration designee.

He had received Byrnes's telephone call in Independence on July 14, and claimed later that when he agreed to nominate Byrnes, he had assumed that everything had been fixed. This is doubtful since being close to Hannegan he probably had an inkling of what had occurred. If he had any misapprehension, it certainly was dispelled in Chicago two days later, yet he continued to support Byrnes for the next three hectic days. It was a useful tactic, giving him a reason to confer with delegation heads and labor officials, a ready answer when asked what he was planning to do, and a place in the public eye. If all went well, Byrnes would have served as his stalking-horse. If the royal favor shone elsewhere, nothing would be lost.

By July 18, one day before the opening of the convention, the struggle over the Vice-Presidency took on a savagery and malevolence unprecedented in the history of contests for the second post. Hannegan thought the time had come for Truman to drop Byrnes and announce his own candidacy. Truman would not budge. Hannegan showed him Roosevelt's "Dear Bob" letter. Truman remained unimpressed. Hannegan got worried. Was his man just playing hard to get, or was it something else? Over the telephone, Roosevelt kept urging him to get Truman lined up. It was time to get moving; Hannegan's plans called for a vote on Truman just two nights later. He gave George Wallace the story that "the President would be pleased to run with Senator Truman." Next day, unable to get confirmation of the *Post-Dispatch* story, reporters were charging Hannegan with deliberately leaking fake information. He thereupon called a press conference and passed out mimeographed copies of Roosevelt's letter to him. Truman still would not make a move. Finally, on July 20, one day before the scheduled vote, Hannegan bundled Truman into his hotel suite, and he, Pauley, Walker, and Flynn began to argue. Then Flynn had a happy thought. He telephoned Roosevelt, and Roosevelt told Truman that he wanted him on the ticket with him. That was all that was necessary. Truman said quietly, "All right, Mr. President." It was done.

He then went to Byrnes's suite, gave him the sad tidings, and told him that he had to be released from his promise to nominate him. Byrnes made one last attempt to retrieve his vanished dream. He called Roosevelt at San Diego, but the President would not take the call. Byrnes's candidacy had evaporated. "In deference to the wishes of the President," he wrote Senator Burnet R. Maybank of South Carolina, he was withdrawing. He appeared to one observer "as he sat afterwards in the White House box, a small, tragic Irishman even to those who opposed him." At Barkley, who was going to make the nomination speech for Roosevelt, he growled, "If I were you, I wouldn't say anything too complimentary about him." He felt that he had been double-crossed, and left before the convention ended. A dozen years later, when writing his memoirs, the memory still rankled.

Truman had been holding out for a statement from Roosevelt that the President wanted him on the ticket. "I'm not going to get into this thing unless the President personally wants me to. I've thought it over very carefully and I've told Hannegan," he informed George Wallace. He went after the commitment he wanted with the adroitness of a papal Nuncio. He did not make telephone calls; he did not ask questions; he did not press Hannegan or the others. He just sat tight and repeated his refrain, "I'm for Byrnes."

After his talk with Roosevelt, Truman turned to Hannegan and asked, "Why the hell didn't he tell me in the first place?" Why didn't he? Some of Roosevelt's associates, in an attempt to explain his bewildering conduct, have called attention to his personal traits—that he disliked hurting friends or those who had been loyal to him, that he had an aversion to being frank when what he had to convey would make for unpleasantness. But his conduct in this case was determined by the exigencies of his intrigue, and that was contrived, in turn, to serve political aims. He had need of a running mate like Truman to keep the Democratic party from flying apart and to reassure the business community. He could win acceptance for such a choice, however, only by demonstrating that Truman was both a reasonable and necessary compromise between the extremes of Byrnes and Wallace. They had to be on the scene and appear to be representing substantial forces that threatened to seize the succession unless a compromise solution was found. Only then would the compromise candidate be palatable to most of the convention delegates and party workers. This was particularly true of the labor and liberal camp. Unlike Hillman and other labor officials who were ready to embrace Truman, the ranks were ardent for Wallace. He had become the apostle and banner-bearer of militant liberalism.

With the full weight of the administration thrown against him, Wallace was able to muster 472 votes on the second ballot, running neck and neck with Truman until the inevitable switching began. Pauley, who wanted to squeeze out for himself every ounce of credit that he could, wrote, "If a Wallace man, instead of myself, had happened to be in charge of the convention, the result might have been different." That was overstating it, but Wallace was very strong. It was his melancholy fate to be imposed on the 1940 convention where he had no support, where the feeling against him ran so high that he was not permitted by Harry Hopkins to make an acceptance speech, and to be dumped at the 1944 convention, where he had the largest following.

The Old Fox had carried it off. The convention had gone according to schedule. But the brisk-stepping politician from Missouri was to be the beneficiary of his craft.

2

Early
Years

Harry came into this world in the midst of the Gilded Age when great fortunes were being amassed. Meat packing had moved from Cincinnati to Chicago, St. Joseph, and Kansas City, and the latter was caught up in a speculative real estate boom. His father, John Truman, like other American boys, eyes dazzled by the careers of Rockefeller, Carnegie, Frick, Schwab, was convinced that one fortunate throw of the dice would put him in the ranks of the successful rich. He had caught the speculative fever, but like most, lacked the Midas touch. What saved him from disaster time and again was that there was always some land in the family's possession.

John Truman came from a line of prosperous farmers whose fortunes declined drastically during the Civil War. He was thirty when he married in 1881, at the time managing his father's 200-acre farm in Washington township. His mother had died two years earlier, and the youngest daughter kept house for father and son. John's wife, Martha Ellen Young, was of a more elevated status than her husband. Her father, Solomon Young, a full-bearded patriarch of the antebellum stripe, had accumulated means in stock raising, trading, and land speculation. For many years, as a Conestoga wagon master, he had driven great herds of cattle through wild country to Utah, Colorado, and California, leaving in May and coming back the following spring.

The Young house, which figured in Harry Truman's early life, was located at what was later called Grandview, just a few miles from the Trumans'. It was a rambling, colonial structure, originally built to house a family of nine, in addition to servants, farmhands, relatives, and guests. It was surrounded by 600 acres of choice farm land consisting of orchards, wheat and hay fields, and grazing areas for sheep, hogs, and mules. Six impressive rows of maple trees stretched for a quarter of a mile from the house to the road, providing shade in the hot summer months and lending beauty and dignity to the scene in all seasons. Although Martha had known John from childhood, she was twenty-nine—an age considered then well along for a bride— before she married him. Her life at home had been happy and comfortable, and there had been no overwhelming inducement for her to leave it.

Both husband and wife were of pioneer stock from Kentucky. Martha had gone to the Baptist College for women in Lexington, learned to play piano and to draw, was interested in culture, which was commonly conceived then in terms of a genteel avocation, and had done her share of dancing and frolicking. She was a small, compact, attractive woman, with a twinkle in her eye. She was also opinionated, and had a positive way of talking, making pronouncements, so to speak— the mark of a person who not only thought well of herself, but was at home in her milieu. These traits she bequeathed in undiluted strength to her son. Though she was supposed to have been witty, her recorded remarks show more spirit than pungency.

John, in contrast, had little formal education. Although his own father had been at one time a school director in Kentucky, John showed no interest in book learning and dropped out of rural school early. He was a small man, nicknamed "Peanuts," and, true to the tradition of small men, assertive when challenged, showing flashes of violent temper. "If my father's honor was impugned, he'd fight like a buzzsaw," his son recalled. Ordinarily, he was inclined to be taciturn. Aside from his wanting to get rich—not a unique ambition in Missouri or elsewhere—he had a hot interest in Democratic politics, was a boisterous participant in election-day encounters, and in later life became a clubhouse hanger-on.

Martha was also a fervent Democrat, but with her it was less a matter of politics than family tradition. The families on both sides, steeped in Southern sympathies, had been in the cockpit of the violent, seesawing struggle between Union and Confederate guerrilla bands. Missouri was under the control of Federal troops, but the inhabitants of Jackson County, the rural area bounding Kansas City, were mostly Southern supporters providing Quantrill's and other irregulars with sustenance and protection. The area was a staging ground for bloody raids by Bushwhackers into Kansas, and the victim of equally bloody reprisals from Jayhawkers. Early one morning in 1861, when Solomon Young was out West, the story was told and retold in the family, a filthy man with wild hair rode into the farmyard at the head of a scurvy-looking troop wearing red sheepskin leggings. He was James Lane, the Free-Soiler senator and chief of the Kansas raiders. At gun point, he forced Martha's mother to bake biscuits and fry meat for himself and his men. After their hearty breakfast, they slaughtered the 400 pigs on the farm, hacked off the hams, shot the hens, helped themselves to the family silver, and rode off. Years later when Harry came home from a trip to Kansas, Martha asked him, in grim humor, "Did you see your grandmother's silver?"

Two years after this raid, Quantrill's, Anderson's, and other bands descended upon Lawrence, Kansas, Lane's home town, reducing the houses to rubble and ashes and putting 150 of the townspeople to the sword. "Repaid the Jayhawkers in kind" were the words of Martha Truman. Lane, who had narrowly escaped seizure, demanded the expulsion of the people of Jackson and adjacent counties to deprive the Southern guerrillas of sanctuary. General Thomas Ewing, Federal commander of the Kansas City military district, issued General Order No. 11 requiring all residents in Jackson, Cass, and Bates counties to leave within fifteen days. Approximately 20,000 persons were moved off their lands, and all grain and hay remaining on the farms after the deadline was destroyed. The flames of burning barns, haystacks, and houses lighted the countryside for miles around. A Missouri artist of the time, George Caleb Bingham, immortalized the event in a painting now hanging in the reading room of the State Historical Society of Missouri, at Columbia. Missouri schoolchildren know all about General Order No. 11 to this day.

John's father had moved his family and slaves away from the area when the war started, and did not return to Jackson County until it was over. For Martha, however, Order No. 11 was part of the fiber of her being. She never forgot how as a girl of eleven, on a hot August day, with her mother and five other children, she had moved into exile behind an ox cart laden with household belongings. "I thought it was a good thing that Lincoln was shot," she would state. At ninety-two, she broke her hip and shoulder tripping over a rug. When a worried Truman visited her, she lay propped up in bed, bandaged and splinted. Before he could say a word, she snapped at him, eyes flashing, "I don't want any smart cracks out of you. I saw your picture in the paper last week putting a wreath at the Lincoln Memorial."

Martha and John settled first in the little village of Lamar, at the northern edge of the Ozarks, about 100 miles from Grandview, where John thought to make his fortune in cattle trading, the business in which his father-in-law had prospered. He bought a tiny frame house, with a big yard and barn. It was here that his first son was born on May 8, 1884, They named him Harry, and gave him a middle initial "S" standing for nothing because no agreement could be reached whether it should refer to Shippe, the paternal grandfather, or Solomon, the maternal one. Lamar was a pretty country village of 800, built around a square with a courthouse in the center. Why John picked this out-of-the-way village for his base is not clear; at any rate, his business did not thrive, and when Harry was still an infant, the family moved to a farm near Belton in Cass County, where another son, Vivian, was born. This move did not work out either, and a year later, after five years of marriage, Martha, John, the two boys, and John's father, who died the next year, moved in with Martha's parents. John bought 40 acres from old Solomon, added 80 more nearby and resumed life as a farmer. At the Young house, the third child, Mary Jane, was born.

It was a happy life for the children. The two boys had a bobtailed gray cat and a little black-and-tan dog that followed them around the farm; the long porch on the north side of the house made a great racetrack; and the two doting grandparents were there to coddle them. His grandfather Young, who was sometimes a judge of the contests, would take him to the Belton Fair. He drove a cart that had two high wheels. Harry would sit in the judge's stand, eating red and white candy and peanuts as he watched the races and had the time of his life. Harry was able to watch the wheat harvest, threshing and corn shucking, mowing and hay stacking. In the fall, peaches would be dried, and apples buried in the ground under straw and boards for midwinter making of peach and apple butter, jellies, and preserves. After the fall freeze came hog-killing time, when sausages were rolled, pigs' feet pickled, and lard rendered in a big iron kettle in the smokehouse. "Those were wonderful days and great adventures."

After four years of communal existence, John decided to strike out on his own again. He had inherited some of his father's property, and with the legacy he bought a place in Independence for $1,000 down and a mortgage of $3,000. It was a roomy frame house at Crysler and Ruby streets, with a cupola and gilded weathervane on top of it. There were ample grounds, a vegetable garden, and a strawberry bed. He was farming rented land near town with the help of a Negro employee, and again made his bid as a dealer in livestock; soon the big yard at the back of the house was full of horses, mules, goats, and cattle. He was also trying his hand at real estate with a partner under the firm name of Mindrup and Truman. Living with them at the house was their Negro cook, Caroline Hunter, her three boys and a girl, and the Negro farmhand who later became Caroline's husband.

Today Independence is a city of 118,000, boasting industries and processing plants, twelve shopping centers, access to six major highways, and its major tourist attraction, the Harry S. Truman Library and Museum. For practical purposes, it is an adjunct of Kansas City. In 1890, when the Trumans settled there, it was a delightful green town of 6,000 in rolling farm country, cooler in summer than most Missouri towns, for it sits on a high ridge between the Big Blue and Little Blue rivers. In earlier days, it was famous as the starting point of the three overland trails, the gateway to the great west. Here were the headquarters of the Santa Fe caravans, and here were outfitted the wagon trains headed for California. But the railroads disposed of the wagons, and when the Hannibal Bridge was thrown across the Missouri River at Kansas City after the Civil War, Independence fell into an agreeable somnolence scarcely disturbed by the exploits of Jesse James and his gang, who operated out of the town.

Harry had a good childhood. There had been lots of room to play in; animals to ride, befriend, and care for; cheerful and devoted households at both the Grandview and Independence places; and the security that is absorbed through the pores from living in a world that is in its proper place and is going to stay forever unchanged. This was so though this was the time when the Populists were stirring up a storm in neighboring Kansas, and the bust of 1893 sent seismic tremors through the Midwest farm country. One would not expect, of course, a boy of nine to worry his head about these matters, but these events passed over the heads of the Truman parents, and millions like them, who were not immediately affected. William Allen White, at the time a cub reporter on the *Kansas City Star*, remembered that "The young people who mingled in the society of the nobility and gentry, did not show any consciousness of the economic storm that was passing over the Missouri Valley and America. The whole structure of American business and finance was being recast before our eyes. Yet I doubt if any of us in the *Star* office, which should have been a watchtower, knew even in rough approximate what was going on."

Something did occur during this time, however, that changed the entire temper of Harry's life. That all was not serene within him had been noticeable at the Young farm when he displayed a proclivity beyond the ordinary for accidents. While combing his hair in front of a mirror one day, he fell out of his chair backward and broke his collarbone. At another time, he almost choked to death when he swallowed a peach pit, and only his mother's quick action in forcing it down his throat with her fingers saved him. A third time he fell off his little Shetland pony when it was leisurely ambling along. His father made him take the remaining half mile to the house on foot, saying that a boy who was not able to stay on a pony at a walk ought to walk himself. He cried all the way home, where he was comforted by his mother who thought he had been harshly dealt with. Now in Independence she discovered that he was unable to read small print or to make out objects that he should be seeing. He had not known that he was supposed to see better than he did. He had managed around the farm and the back lot with inadequate vision. Alarmed, she took him to an oculist in Kansas City who fitted him with a pair of thick-lensed glasses. His eyeballs were so flat that he was shortsighted to the point of blindness.

A boy of eight wearing thick eyeglasses was not a common sight in those days; glasses were worn only by old people. Harry now stood apart. He could not join in rough games with the other boys any longer, or even play ball, for the eye doctor had gone overboard in warning him about the danger of breaking the glasses and injuring his eyes. So this little Tom Sawyer, at one with his surroundings and companions hitherto, was cut off at one stroke from ready acceptance and pushed in on himself. His distress, his heartache, we can imagine. Subdued by the change in his circumstances, Harry began to act like a little old man.

He helped his mother and Caroline with the cooking and cleaning. He learned to braid his sister Mary Jane's hair and rock her to sleep. "Harry used to take me everywhere," she recalled. "Perhaps that's why I'm an old maid, because he was such a nice beau." And he became a voracious reader. For years thereafter the Independence Public Library had no steadier client for its wares between which covers he could join intrepid captains on land and sea, who overcame obstacles, hurled aside foes, fought their way to the heights, to become famous and admired.

There were further troubles in his second school year when he was nine. Diphtheria struck the household, and Old Letch, the farm worker, had hurriedly to hitch up a big farm wagon to rush Mary Jane to the Young place at Grandview. Vivian quickly recovered, but Harry's throat closed in a diphtheritic paralysis that extended to paralysis of the arms and legs. For six months he had to be wheeled around in a baby carriage, and to be lifted at home. After he recovered, he sliced off his big toe by slamming the cellar door on it. "Mama held it in place" until the local physician pressed the two pieces together with a coating of crystalline iodoform, and it stayed put and got well.

This series of misfortunes and anxieties thickened the bonds between mother and son. Martha had too strong a sense of duty, and was too completely the family pilot and protector, to show open favoritism among her children, but there was no question that her firstborn was at the center of her heart. Harry more than reciprocated the feeling, and contentedly slid into the role of mama's boy. He never wore overalls or dungarees to school, but was invariably turned out in clean shirt and tie. He never got into fights, but braved the jeers of the other boys when, music books under his arm, he dutifully went twice a week for piano lessons. His father grew irritated with him and scolded him unmercifully. He favored Vivian who would not hear of music lessons for himself ("Mama couldn't get a lasso big enough"). Vivian resembled his father physically and in his mannerisms; he was the Truman with the gun and the dogs. John took him into his cattle business when he was still at school and let him have a checking account in his own name.

During and after his presidential years there was an attempt to blur this aspect of Truman's life since it did not conform to the stereotype of the red-blooded American boy that he sought to convey and admired. When he was in his eighties, and it no longer mattered to him, he permitted himself a flash of candor. It was during one of the many talking tours for students and visitors that he conducted through the Truman Library. At the auditorium, in the question period, a small boy asked him, "Mr. President, was you popular when you was a boy?"

"Why, no," Truman answered. "I was never popular. The popular boys were the ones who were good at games and had big, tight fists. I was never like that. Without my glasses I was blind as a bat, and to tell the truth, I was kind of a sissy. If there was any danger of getting into a fight, I always ran."

Coincident with donning eyeglasses, Harry started school, and the great engine of socialization began to instill in him the mores and assumptions of middle-class America, all the more relentlessly since in a small Missouri town, it worked with the grain, merely deepening and widening the channels already cut at home. Besides grammar and arithmetic, there were readings from *Glimpses Through Life's Windows* by the Reverend Dr. Miller, designed to implant in the new generation an adequate Calvinist reverence for diligence and striving. Then there was a great favorite of Harry's, Jacob Abbot, author of biographies and the *Rollo* series. The lives struck a precise pitch of highmindedness and uplift by combining the anecdotes of the ancient historians with right morality. The *Rollo* stories insinuated a note of national pride, expounding the superiority of the American system to that of all others.

When Harry was twelve, his mother gave him a four-volume set of books called *Great Men and Famous Women*. Expensively bound, copiously illustrated, it contained over two hundred biographies ranging from Caesar and Napoleon to Edison and Livingstone. As was common in productions of this sort, the heroic was bathed in the waters of sentimentality. Harry studied the volumes, and their pieties clung to him for life. In high school, he discovered Plutarch and Sienkiewicz's *With Fire and Sword*, the blood-and-thunder epic of gallant Poland in the seventeenth century.

The problem of education in America was no simple thing: It sought to inspire high ideals of honor, truth, loyalty, in an acquisitive society where money was the measure of a man's success. The attempt to avoid cynicism and to reconcile the irreconcilable created a life style of pretense, make-believe, and a double-entry system of morality. What set off a small town like Independence from the metropolitan centers was not this contradiction between professed and actual ideals, but rather that the paucity of cultural resources and the constricted existence provided the parched soil from which sprouted the hidebound, provincial variant of self-righteous philistinism. Harry absorbed the moral code that made up in declaratory assertion what it lacked in coherence of motives or objective. When in the White House, he declared: "Truth, honor and justice are at the basis of all human relations. No really great man in history but had these attributes." He told John Gunther, "Look at Hitler. His word wasn't good, so he got nowhere, finally."

For some, religious faith filled the gap. But the powerful tide of secularism was carrying most along—including the Trumans—and reducing religion to a matter of conventional adherence. Although Martha and John were Baptists, the children went to a Presbyterian Sunday school because the nearest church was the First Presbyterian. John did not think "only Baptists have free access to heaven." Martha's father belonged to no church. When Harry once asked which church was best, Solomon Young told him: "All of them want to arrive at the same place, but they have to fight to see who has the inside track with the Almighty. When a man spends Saturday night and Sunday doing too much howling and praying, you had better go home and lock your smokehouse."

Harry received from his schooling, and from his extensive though unsystematic reading, a lasting interest in biography and in history, which for him was another form of biography. He could conceptualize events only by means of the "great man" idea of history, which he attached to a schoolboy cyclical notion that all problems had their parallels and precedents in the past. ("There is not really anything new if you learn what has gone before.") His reading—as well as his study of the Bible, begun as a child and pursued in preparing for Masonic degrees—was never internalized to give him a literary command of language. His speech remained strong in vernacular and positiveness, and weak in texture and allusion. What restricted Truman was not only a circumscribed imagination, but the excessive utilitarianism he had received from his surroundings. Everything had to have its practical payoff. Every book, every piece of history, had to have its lessons, which could be memorized and, like hognuts, be stored away for future use. He once gave a list of ten books to a law student whose career he was trying to advance, saying that these books had to be read by "any person wanting to get ahead."

No one is all of a piece, however, and it is clear that young Harry, this sober-minded, dutiful, sweetness-and-light youngster, identified himself with military heroes, ironhearted and audacious generals. There is nothing unusual in a frail youngster indulging in such Walter Mitty daydreams except that Truman's romantic addiction continued into adult life, and he made serious efforts to realize his military ambitions. In high school, his dream was to go to West Point. He received special coaching from his history teacher to prepare for the West Point entrance examination. That dream was shattered when he was informed that he had no chance of acceptance because of his poor eyesight.

At twenty-one he became a charter member of Battery B of the Missouri National Guard in Kansas City, and paid a quarter a week for the privilege of drilling and going on summer encampments to Cape Girardeau. He was very proud of his blue dress uniform. However, when he wore it on a visit to his grandmother at Grandview, she ordered him out of the house. Her objection was not to the military calling but to the uniform of the damyankees. In the First World War he finally became a soldier and officer, and saw action in France. After Pearl Harbor, when he was a senator and fifty-seven years old, he went to see General George C. Marshall, then Army Chief of Staff, about reenlisting in the Army, and was genuinely envious of his friend, Harry Vaughan, when the latter received an appointment as lieutenant colonel. Truman reminds us of another military zealot who became President, Theodore Roosevelt. Young Teddy was also a poor-sighted and frail boy who became an insatiable reader by the time he was ten; who went on thereafter to demonstrate his manhood by playing soldier; who thought that his days of dashing around Cuba were the most glorious of his life. But Harry was the plain-spoken double bass in comparison with Teddy's shrill cornet.

In spite of Truman's military aspiration, from the age of ten to fifteen he took piano lessons twice a week and practiced every morning because his mother wanted him to. In his final two years of training he went to an excellent teacher in Kansas City, but it is doubtful that either mother or son thought seriously of his becoming a professional musician. When he was fifteen, he abruptly quit. "I decided it was sissy," he explained. Later, he occasionally played duets with his sister, and music continued to be an adornment of his life. His daughter's suggestion, however, that he might have become a concert pianist should be filed with the tales of George Washington's cherry tree and Abe Lincoln's six-mile walk to return a few cents to a customer who had overpaid. His playing was that of an unsophisticated amateur while his taste in music ran to the done-to-death selections that he had learned in his studies or sentimental operetta tunes that one could whistle. He once jocularly remarked that if he had not become President, he would have probably ended up as a piano player in a bawdy house.

The decade after the Trumans moved to Independence was a period of comparative affluence for them. John's cattle trading and real estate deals were paying, and Martha had inherited a 160-acre farm from her father. After 1896 the country went into another fever of speculation; farm values and prices rose, and wheat and corn production moved westward to the Missouri Valley and neighboring states. The hunger for spoils was rampant and John Truman wanted to join the rich. He began to plunge heavily in the Kansas City grains futures market. Everything went swimmingly—until the market reversed. Then he lost everything: Martha's inherited farm, every other piece of property they owned, and about $30,000 in cash.

By the fall of 1901, after Harry's graduation from high school, his father's money was so tied up that the thought of college had to be abandoned. Instead, Harry took a job to help keep Vivian and Mary Jane in school. When John's dazzling bubble finally burst, he had to sell the house on Waldo Street where the family was living to make a down payment on a cheap little dwelling in Kansas City, and, at the age of fifty-one, to take a job as a night watchman. Two years later, thoroughly demoralized, he traded the Kansas City house for a down payment on an 80-acre farm near Clinton and moved. His troubles were not over. When the Grand River flooded that year, it washed away the entire crop of corn he had put in, and left him even worse off. The bedraggled Truman family now trooped back to the Grandview farm where Martha's widowed mother lived; not to the fine old house of before; that had burned down in an accident; but to a small makeshift one. This was supposed to serve only temporarily, but the Trumans lived in it for years. So ended for John the great middle-class dream of financial independence.

Harry got his first job when he was eighteen as a timekeeper for a contractor at $35 a month. His employer was grading for double tracking a section of the Santa Fe railroad near Independence. It was a rough initiation for a diffident youngster. He had to travel to three camps to fill out the workers' time cards, live with them in hobo tents, and eat their greasy meals. Every two weeks on Saturday nights he had to pay off the four hundred roughneck, hard-drinking gandy dancers in a saloon. It was a calling that had a reputation for choice and expressive profanity; at the Middle Border, it was a distillation of the variegated contributions of mule men, cattle men, corn and oil men, Missouri River boatmen, houn' dog Southerners, and old-country Irish. Harry acquired an enlarged and enriched vocabulary—another mark of manliness. He said later he learned "all the cuss words in the English language—not by ear but by note."

When the job was finished, he worked for a short time in the mail room of the *Kansas City Star,* then as a clerk at the National Bank of Commerce; in 1904 he landed the post of bookkeeper at the Union National Bank with pay of $75 a month. In the beginning, he lived with his father's sister, but soon moved to Mrs. Trow's boardinghouse. He was twenty, on his own, with a new life opening for him in the big city.

Kansas City at this time was a rawboned, boisterous town struggling between two elements of its inner being: the affluent reformers who were crusading to make it a city of parks, boulevards, museums, and concert halls as well as an inviting haven for real estate operators and investors, and the more sportive elements, swelled by invading legions of salesmen, cattle barons, railroad promoters, grain speculators, and other free spirits with a taste for earthier entertainment. The latter had an established tradition to build on. As far back as 1872, the leading newspaper of neighboring Leavenworth had editorialized against the "blustering, impotent Sodom at the mouth of the Kaw." Gambling was a well-established industry—the faro banks at Marble Hall and No. 3 Missouri Avenue were famous throughout the West. Wild Bill Hickok, the two-gun marshal of Abilene, Kansas, was a regular client, and Jesse James found the atmosphere relaxing and enjoyable when he lived incognito and unmolested in Kansas City. "Big Jim" Pendergast, the great boss's older brother, who was a political power by the time Harry went to work, owned two large thriving saloons and gambling places. His hotel and saloon below the West Bluff at Twelfth Street was just around the corner from Union Avenue, on which traffic moved to and from the Old Union railway station. According to William Reddig, the chronicler of Kansas City during the Pendergast years,

> Union Avenue society took a swashbuckling pride in a reputation for picturesque sordidness which was believed to compare favorably with the iniquity of New York's Bowery. Nothing was allowed to interfere with the business of making the transient's stopover at the midcontinent interchange point an interesting and instructive interval. At night the avenue leading from the depot became a midway blazing with light, tumultuous with the shouts of ballyhoo men and the cries of grays (the suckers of the day) being whisked out of sight. Booted cattlemen, silk-hatted gamblers, ticket scalpers, bunco artists, blanketed Indians, Kansas yokels and scented ladies, strolling by from Paris

and New York, mingled in this boisterous democracy. Runners, barkers and cappers employed various irresistible devices to interest the travelers in the wonders of the hotels, burlesque shows, restaurants, saloons, museums, pawnshops and barbershops along the way. The entertainment activity reached its height on West Ninth Street near the Missouri-Kansas state line. The service there became so popular that it eventually produced the wettest block in the world. It had twenty four buildings and twenty three of them were saloons.

At Fourth and Wyandotte was the famous house of Annie Chambers, who offered "the highest type girls" to a free-spending clientele. What made her famous was not her alleged descent from French nobility nor her overpriced wines, but the shapeliness and professional skills of her prostitutes. She once asked G. Van Millet, the city's leading artist, to paint portraits of her girls. He refused but later said he regretted his decision: "So many of our best citizens went down there, it would have been an excellent place to display my work. I would have had portrait commissions for the rest of my life." Annie Chambers was the madam of the aristocracy, but there were many other houses suited to more modest purses. Around 1900, there were 147 houses paying fines averaging $3,250 a month, fines being the recognized form of license fee.

When William Allen White came to Kansas City a decade earlier, he said he felt like Childe Roland in the Dark Tower. Truman was more like Dick Whittington come to London. He was too staid to be terrified, and too much the aseptically good boy to wander far from the confines of his prescribed world. He joined the Benton Boulevard Baptist Church and attended its services. He played the piano at evening songfests in the boardinghouse where Arthur Eisenhower, Ike's older brother, and two long-skirted and shirtwaisted young ladies were fellow roomers. When his folks were living in Clinton, he and Vivian would visit them on weekends. Often on Saturday afternoons he would go to vaudeville shows at the Old Orpheum, and for a while ushered on Saturdays at the Grand Theater, where he saw Eva Tanguay, the Four Cohans, Weber and Fields, Lillian Russell, and the Floradora Girls. He would butter up his superiors at the bank by inviting the chief clerk or head bookkeeper to the farm, where his mother would spread a feed of fried chicken, baked ham, hot biscuits, and custard pie. In the second year of his independence, he drilled faithfully once a week with the National Guard, and in August went to the encampment where the following year he was appointed corporal.

Were there no girl friends? Was he never tempted to taste the sweets of Babylon so lavishly offered? The records do not show. Harry was very shy with girls and remained essentially so throughout his life. His father had set the women of the family on a pedestal and would not tolerate derogatory remarks about any of them. The idealization of women went hand in hand with excluding them from the man's world of affairs. John had not consulted Martha on his grain speculations, which affected her too, but he did demand that the womenfolk be treated with respect. Harry had been trained in accordance with the Victorian code.

In later life, he placed his wife and daughter not so much on a pedestal as on a mountaintop. He did not approve of women smoking and very likely did not approve of them in politics. And there was always a certain wariness toward the opposite sex. Edgar Hinde, his long-time friend, also an officer in the 129th Field Artillery, and later Independence park superintendent when Truman was county judge, related this about him: "I've been around Legion conventions with him. He'd have his own room there, naturally. If some fellow brought a woman in there, or his wife even, I've seen him pick up his hat and coat and take out of there. He just didn't want any women around his room in a hotel." When asked about Truman's remark that he had seen the Folies Bergère when on leave in Paris during the war and that he had found the performance "disgusting," Hinde replied that Truman "never did care much for that stuff. I think Harry is one of the cleanest fellows morally that I ever saw. He never deviated from the straight and narrow so far as I know, and I was pretty closely associated with him for about eighteen or nineteen months."

That the sex urge was a weakness that had to be fought was set down in a remarkable note that he wrote to himself in a hotel room in the middle of the night after Pendergast had offered to back him for United States senator. He was fifty years old at the time, had been married for fifteen years and a father for ten: "It is 4 A.M. I am to make the most momentous announcement of my life. I have come to the place where all men strive to be. In reading the lives of great men, I found that the first victory they won was over themselves and their carnal urges. Self-discipline with all of them came first." His puritanism was accompanied by an addiction to foul language that remained with him from his days with the gandy dancers, and a taste for dunghill humor and anecdotes that relied heavily on biological functions interspersed with sexual allusions. He was a great fancier of the bawdy stories and gags of Harry Vaughan, his close companion of later years. A familiar case of bourgeois schizophrenia.

In 1906 his father asked him to come back home to help work the Young farm. Vivian had returned earlier, but stayed only a short time and eventually moved away to his own farm when he married in 1911. Uncle Harrison, Martha's brother, preferred to live in Kansas City. That left Harry. He had never done any farming before and some of the relatives bet that he would not stay at it long. They were wrong. Harry was a hard and diligent worker as well as a dutiful son. If he was disappointed in having to leave Kansas City, he never spoke of it or complained about it. For the next decade, he climbed out of bed at 4:30 A.M. in summer and at 6:30 in winter, and under his father's tutelage plowed, sowed, reaped, milked cows, fed hogs, doctored horses, baled hay, and did everything there was to do on a 600-acre farm.

His father fussed over details on the farm and on orderliness. He insisted on clean fences and fence corners and killing weeds along the edges of the farm. When the Trumans could not work the fields they would go out with their scythes and cut weeds along the roads and clean up the fences. When he became more skilled, he was accounted a progressive farmer who kept production records, followed a crop rotation plan, raised hogs and cattle, and kept dairy cattle. A legend was built up that he could plow "the straightest furrow" in all of Jackson County. Truman put the story to rest in later years in a talk to visiting farm leaders in the auditorium of the Truman Library. He recalled that he had used a four-hitch Emerson gang plow usually pulled by two horses and two mules. "You didn't have much luck in keeping that straight. You had to go the way the land goes."

The Young farmland was of superior quality, dark prairie soil excellently suited for corn, wheat, and livestock production. The entire period of Harry's farm career was one of the best in American agriculture. Farm prices rose from the turn of the century until after the First World War, and the five years between 1909 and 1914 were the golden "parity" years to which later agricultural relief legislation tried to peg prices. In good years, the farm netted the family $15,000, a respectable sum in those days. Grandma Young died in 1909, and, for her own reasons, left the farm to Martha and Harrison. Uncle Will and Aunts Ada, Sally, Laura, and Sue were not going to take this lying down. They instituted legal action that went on for a decade and led to bitter family disputations and estrangements. In the end, after she had received Harrison's share of his bequest after his death, Martha assumed a number of mortgages in order to settle with the relatives for cash in exchange for quitclaims. "The lawyers got most of it," Vivian said ruefully. "All we got was debts." This was exaggerated. The Grandview farm, considered to be worth $150,000, was encumbered with a mortgage of $25,000.

Since farming was not going to be the way to riches, and since Harry was a chip off the old paternal block, he decided in 1915 to do his share of plunging, not in cattle trading or grain futures, but in oil and mining. His father had died the year before, and he was running the farm and in charge of the household finances. He had learned from his father's experience only that one should try harder and have better luck. That year he ran into Jerry Culbertson, whom the Trumans had known before, a smooth-talking entrepreneur who had floated several unsuccessful gold mines. He was promoting a lead and zinc mine just below the Missouri border in Commerce, Oklahoma. It was his contention that an important mine, thought to be played out, actually contained rich veins that had been overlooked. Harry and a neighbor, Tom Hughes, each put up $2,000, and Harry started to commute between the mine and the farm. He found Commerce booming; lead and zinc were at a premium with the outbreak of the great war. But for all his efforts, the mine was found to be indeed played out. His investment was lost.

After this fiasco, Culbertson came around again with a proposition that Harry go into the oil business with him and David Morgan, an oil man. Culbertson would contribute his promotional know-how, Morgan 1,500 acres in eastern Oklahoma, and Harry was to put up $5,000. The midcontinental oil fields were being opened at this time, and test drilling was going on in Missouri and adjoining states. The smart talk was that oil was the coming thing because of the demand from the booming automobile industry. One lucky strike and the three would be rolling in wealth. "I was enthusiastic about the possibilities," said Truman. He turned over to his new partners five notes for $1,000 each due in ten months, signed by Martha Truman as well as himself, and the contract was set up. Morgan, the company president, was checking and leasing oil properties and directing the drilling operations of test wells. Culbertson, the secretary, was promoting stock shares. And Truman, the treasurer, was assisting Morgan and looking after the books. He had a chance to play the big businessman. The firm's bookkeeper later recalled Harry in Kansas City surrounded by salesmen, lease men, oil scouts.

The original syndicate was reorganized as a trust, and on April 1, 1917, there appeared in the *Star* an imposing advertisement by the Morgan Oil and Refining Company inviting the public to buy 10,000 of its 60,000 shares at $25 each. The notice pointed out to prospective investors that "in the event this country is unfortunately brought to war," prices for gasoline and petroleum products "will soar beyond all expectations," and with less than accuracy suggested that the firm had large holdings of "proven properties." All told, about $200,000 was raised, leases were bought in Texas, Oklahoma, and Kansas, and drilling was in progress when the country entered the war. At the time, Morgan had a well down 900 feet on a 370-acre lease at Eureka, Kansas. Either because of a shortage of funds or a loss of nerve, he and Culbertson (Truman was already in the Army at the time) decided to quit. They sold the lease and their equipment to another company that continued drilling and shortly struck what became the famed Teeter Oil Pool, one of the largest ever opened in Kansas. Morgan estimated that if he had continued drilling another 900 feet, all their fortunes would have been made. It was a familiar story told by dozens of shoestring wildcatters. Harry did not make any money on this venture, either, although the $5,000 he invested was apparently paid off from accruing income through the sale of leases and equipment. When he was in the White House, he wrote Morgan, "Maybe I wouldn't be Pres if we'd hit."

Five days after the firm's advertisement appeared in the *Star*, President Wilson secured a declaration of war against Germany from Congress, and Harry abruptly tossed aside his chances of making millions in the oil industry to join with Major John Miles in trying to put together a field artillery regiment from six undermanned National Guard batteries. When he broke the news at home, there was consternation. "It was quite a blow to my mother and sister," he said. That was putting it mildly. The full burden of a heavily mortgaged farm and the care of a sixty-five-year-old mother would fall on the shoulders of his sister. Harry was thirty-three. He had resigned from the National Guard six years earlier; he was the sole male of the Truman family on the farm; he would never have been called to service, and no one would have expected him to volunteer. What impelled him to do it?

The reasons were personal. Almost a score of years separated Truman from the owlish boy who crammed after school for West Point.

The years had taken him to sedentary jobs at a bank and then to the
flat routine on the family farm. But though the flame that had been
lighted inside him for military glory had dimmed in the interval, it
had never died. Now, with the country's entry into the World War, it
revived, all the more glowing for having been so long suppressed.
Harry, who was a joiner and an activist, was in his element rounding
up recruits, bargaining for equipment and supplies, drilling in the old
convention hall in Kansas City, marching through the streets. The
military dream was the more compelling because of other circumstances in his life. The family had always been close knit, and the
bond to his mother was tightly fixed. He had no wish to break the
strings, but at thirty-three, hankering after more independence, he
wanted to lengthen them. He had been courting Bess Wallace for
many years, and it is likely that both his efforts to get rich and his
decision now to enlist were related to his private campaign to break
down the opposition to his suit. This was successful, for Bess agreed
to marry him as soon as she learned he was joining the Army. According to his account, the marriage was postponed until after he returned from overseas because "I didn't think it was right to get married and maybe come home a cripple and have the most beautiful and
sweetest girl in the world tied down."

3

Entry
into
Politics

Truman first saw Bess—Elizabeth Virginia Wallace—at Sunday
school when he was six. She was a little girl of the same age with
golden curls and blue eyes, all properly laundered and starched, and
Harry was "smitten at once." He was too shy to dare look at her very
much. "And I didn't speak to her for five years." But from then on, he
was acutely aware of her. From the fifth grade through high school,
they were in the same classes, and both graduated in 1901. When in
high school he would go twice a week to his aunt Ella Noland's
house, across the street from Bess's grandfather's, to study Latin with
his cousins Nellie and Ethel because Bess was there. "If I succeeded
in carrying her books to school or back home for her, I had a big
day." It was a schoolboy affair, and one-sided, for Bess seemed to him
an angelic creature, far beyond the reach of a begoggled and unath-
letic boy. Besides, she came from the town's aristocracy.

Her grandfather, George Gates, after the Civil War built the house
at 219 North Delaware, which later became the Summer White
House. He was one of the founders of the Waggoner-Gates Milling
Company whose "Queen of the Pantry" flour was a brand familiar to
generations of Southern and Midwestern families. Gates got rich, and
became a pillar of the Independence social set. After high school Bess

was sent to the Barstow School for Girls in Kansas City, an upper-class institution run by two professional girl-finishers, Wellesley graduates, who came to Kansas City to instill grace and gentility in the young females of the local gentry. The school, like so many such establishments, laid great emphasis on agility and grace, and consequently on athletics. Bess, reputedly a tomboy at school, with the ability to whistle through her teeth, fitted comfortably into Barstow. She won a shot-put contest in the annual field day, and led the Barstowians to a smashing victory over an Independence girls' basketball team. After two years of higher education, she was back in Independence driving a horse and buggy, or walking her two greyhounds, all gifts of Grandfather Gates, with not a thing to do and not a care in the world, every bit the self-assured belle.

Although Harry lived in Kansas City when she was at Barstow, he never saw her. Only much later, when he was established on the Grandview farm, did he work up the courage to visit her. He rode into Independence one day, a distance of 20 miles, to see his aunt Ella Noland. That morning Bess's mother had sent a cake to the Nolands. Aunt Ella asked her daughter to return the cake plate, but Harry said he would do it, seized the plate, and rushed out. Two hours later he returned, announcing with a happy grin, "Well, I saw her." That was the beginning of the courtship that went on for six years. He saw her every time he could leave the farm, and he wrote when he could not.* In 1913, he bought a secondhand Stafford touring car for the trips to Independence. Sometimes, he and Bess and her brothers and girl friends would use the car to go on outings and picnics.

Why did the courtship move so slowly? Bess's mother was one reason. She saw herself as a lady of quality, daughter of a great industrialist and public leader, and thought it preposterous for her Bess to throw herself away on a country bumpkin without money, prospects, or education. Some described Bess's mother as "the queenliest woman Independence ever produced." Others thought her a domineering and selfish small-town *grande dame* with airs and pretensions to match.

---

* Decades later, Truman found his wife burning papers in the fireplace at home.

"What are you doing, Bess?" he asked.

"I'm burning your letters to me," she answered.

"Bess, you oughtn't to do that."

"Why not? I've read them several times."

"But think of history!"

"I *have*."

There had been tragedy in her life, but it had neither sweetened her temper nor increased her charitableness toward others.

She had married David Wallace, a tall, handsome, personable man. He had been Eminent Commander of the Knights Templar of Missouri, was for a time deputy county recorder, later had a federal job in the customs office in Kansas City. Henry Chiles, a schoolmate of Truman and sometime county treasurer, recalled him in glowing terms: "I knew Bessie's father, Dave Wallace, real well. I guess he knew everybody in Jackson County. He was the most popular man I ever knew. He was the most promising young man of the county. Led all the parades." This promising young man came home one day in 1903 twenty years after his marriage, when he was forty-three, sat in the bathtub, and shot his brains out with a pistol. He had been drinking heavily and this and the suicide were attributed by some to growing debts; marriage to a self-important lady of quality very likely added to the pressure.

Mrs. Wallace's family fortunes were thus in decline when Truman began his campaign to win Bess. Nevertheless, she was still due for a bequest when her parents died, and her opinion of her family status was undisturbed. Bess apparently did not take Harry's suit entirely seriously at first. She had become a sensible, intensely practical young woman who looked like a prim, suburban housewife of the Sinclair Lewis era. She had her mother's determination without her extravagant pretensions. She was clearly wary of marrying a man who lacked prospects. She liked Harry, or she would not have continued the association in the face of her mother's disapproval, but the ardor was all on his side.

Whether it was the magic of the uniform, or whether, at thirty-three, she had decided the time for decision was overdue, she finally gave her consent. So Harry went off to war, no longer young, yet with the energy and good health of youth. He had secured the last of the quitclaims from the relatives for his mother, and he had a promise from Bess to marry him when he returned. A nondescript, no-longer-quite-young man in soldier's uniform peers at you through metal-framed spectacles in a photograph taken at this time. One would guess from his sterilized expression that he was, in civilian life, the local YMCA secretary.

In August the 2nd Missouri Field Artillery was sworn into the Regular Army in a body to become the 129th Field Artillery of the 35th Division. The National Guard regiments lost their historic designations, but before surrendering these vestiges of state sovereignty the batteries elected their officers. Truman thought he was entitled, on the basis of his experience and his recruiting work, to be made a sergeant, but the men of his battery did better for him than that: They elected him first lieutenant. "It almost scared me to such an extent that I was afraid I'd never make good."

The 129th went to Camp Doniphan at Fort Sill, Oklahoma, for training. His mother and sister visited him there. "My mother was sixty-five years old but she never shed a tear, smiled at me all the time and told me to do my best for the country. But she cried all the way home and when I came back from France she gained ten or fifteen pounds in weight." The colonel appointed Truman regimental canteen officer, and on Truman's request Ed Jacobson was detailed to help him. Truman knew Jacobson from Kansas City where the latter had worked in a men's furnishings store. The two made such a success of the canteen, which they set up like a little department store with barbering, tailoring, clothing, and stationery supplies divisions, that the regiment's members received back a $15,000 profit on their original investment of $2,200. Truman owed his promotion to this, and was picked for the Overseas School Detail.

On his way overseas, Truman saw New York City for the first time. He bought three extra pairs of eyeglasses there, but the optometrist would not let him pay for them. He spent five weeks at the artillery school at Montigny-sur-Aube, and received additional training at Coëtquidan, one of Napoleon's old artillery camps. He read in *The New York Times* that he had been promoted to captain on April 23, and he added another bar to his shoulder insignia, although official confirmation did not come until October, and his request for retroactive pay was rejected on the ground that he had not "accepted" his commission earlier. On July 11, 1918, he was put in command of Battery D of the 129th. "I was the most thoroughly scared individual in that camp. Never on the front or anywhere else have I been so nervous."

Battery D, or Dizzy D, as it was known, was a rowdy, unmanageable outfit composed mostly of Irish from a tough neighborhood in Kansas City. When they were not fighting the Germans, they liked to brawl and to keep their commanding officers off balance. One of the sergeants said, "In those days we'd land somewhere, get into a fight and then we'd go to Mass." In his first day of command, the men staged a fake stampede of their horses, got into a fight among themselves, and sent four to the regimental infirmary. Truman called in the sergeants and corporals and said to them: "I know you've been making trouble for your previous commanders. From now on, you're going to be responsible for maintaining discipline in your squads and sections. And if there are any of you who can't, speak up right now and I'll bust you back right now."

He won the men's respect and support when the 129th moved to the front the following month. The battery was in position on Mount Herrenberg in the Vosges when, on September 6, Truman received orders to fire a gas shell barrage at the enemy. The Germans responded with a barrage of their own. Shells rained very close and a sergeant lost his head and yelled, "Run, boys, they got a bracket on us!" Truman, who had just risen unhurt after his horse had fallen into a shell hole and rolled over him, saw some men begin to scamper. From his lips came a string of expletives and maledictions learned from the gandy dancers. Father Curtis Tiernan, the regimental chaplain, recalled gleefully: "It took the skin off the ears of those boys. It turned those boys right around."

The 129th moved into new positions on November 6 and prepared for an assault on Metz. Five days later, Truman was called on the phone at five in the morning and informed that there would be a cease-fire at eleven o'clock. "The silence that followed almost made one's head ache. After that we spent our evenings playing poker and wishing we were home." It was five months before they boarded ship for the return voyage. Roger Sermon, a fellow captain in the 129th, later mayor of Independence, said, "To keep from going crazy we had an almost continuous poker game." The poker-playing habit stayed with Truman for life.

He was discharged with the rank of major in the reserves on May 6, 1919, and two days later he celebrated his thirty-fifth birthday at the Grandview farm. He said, "I didn't do anything out of the ordinary. I was not wounded, and I got no citation of any kind." He had not joined the ranks of military heroes, but his military experience was crucial nonetheless. He had been accepted by his fellow officers as a man of competence and character. He had proved to himself that he could lead a group of rough, tough men in action and win their affection and loyalty. He had made many friends. The Battery D men even gave him an engraved silver loving cup when their ship docked. He did not know it then, but this military interval opened the way to his life's course. "My whole political career," he was to remark, "is based upon my war service and war associates."

Politics was far from Truman's mind when he was mustered out. He had just left a Europe where the Bolsheviks had taken over in Russia and had cast their long shadow over the Versailles Peace Conference, where the elite of Germany was maneuvering desperately to avoid the fate of the czars and dukes, and where war losses had been placed at 10 million dead and 20 million wounded. Yet Truman, like most American servicemen, was singularly unaffected. His outlook was much the same as before the war. National pride, turned to national arrogance, made for an American provincialism remarkably immune to new impressions and ideas, and oblivious of the currents swirling through the world. He had returned to God's country after helping to clean up the mess that the Europeans had made, and he was ready to take up precisely where he had left off. When he landed on his return journey, "I made a resolution that if old lady Liberty in New York harbor wanted to see me again she'd have to turn round."

He and Bess were married in June at the Trinity Episcopal Church in Independence, and they moved into the Gates house with her mother, her grandmother, and her youngest brother. The house is a rambling white clapboard Victorian structure with multiple gables, running verandas, gingerbread details on eaves and molding, and stained glass in four narrow front windows. There were considerable grounds in an earlier day, but Bess's two older brothers built houses just below the Gates House, which looks hedged in since an iron fence had been put up around it during Truman's Presidency. Inside, it consists of fourteen high-ceilinged rooms, including seven bedrooms, an old-fashioned parlor, a music room, and a large dining room. There are three fireplaces with marble mantels, and many walls are covered with damask wallpaper. Much of the furniture is of the dainty, antique variety. When the Truman's daughter was born, four generations lived under one roof. There was no problem of space, but Mrs. Wallace was an indefatigable house manager. Floors would be periodically sanded and polished, walls repapered, trim repainted, curtains and draperies cleaned or replaced. Her two sons also came in frequently with their wives, so that the place was not precisely a haven of quiet or privacy. Beyond that, the house was not Harry's or Bess's, but her mother's. If Truman ever resented the arrangement, he never mentioned it. He had set his heart on marrying Bess, and that he had achieved.

There remained the matter of earning a living, for he had no intention of going back to farming. The successful canteen that he and Jacobson had operated at Camp Doniphan gave both of them ideas. They agreed to open a haberdashery in partnership. Truman had renounced rights to his share of Uncle Harrison's farm in return for the $5,000 his mother had raised for him to go into the oil business. He now sold the stock and equipment on the Grandview farm for $20,000, giving his mother, sister, and brother a quitclaim deed for his interest in the farm, and used most of the money for his contribution to the partnership.

Truman and Jacobson signed a five-year lease for a store in the old Baltimore Hotel at the corner of Twelfth and Baltimore, across the street from the Muehlebach Hotel. The neighborhood is still in the heart of downtown Kansas City. Now it is a center of hotels, department stores, movie houses, and restaurants. In 1919 it was the great white way of a wide-open town. In the Dixon Hotel, on the other corner, continual crap games were in progress at two gambling establishments. Prostitutes solicited on the streets and at the hotel bars. The sidewalks at all times were as crowded as New York's Times Square on a Saturday night. The firm of Truman & Jacobson stayed open till nine, six nights a week. The partners worked in shifts with a clerk to help. The store immediately became a hangout for their old buddies of the 129th Field Artillery and other veterans, who dropped in to reminisce and left with purchases.

In the first year, sales totaled $70,000, a high return on the initial investment, much of which the partners plowed back into the business. Unfortunately, while both Truman and Jacobson were good retailers, neither was a student of economic trends. They had sunk all their cash into inventory at inflated postwar prices. When the postwar slump came, their stock, which had cost them $35,000 at the start of 1921, had a value of less than $10,000 a year later. Farm prices were dropping catastrophically, people were out of jobs. Jacobson recalled, "Instead of buying, the boys came in for loans." Soon it was impossible to borrow any more to pay off creditors. Truman & Jacobson closed its doors, staving off bankruptcy proceedings only by returning the remaining stock to the creditors and promising to make payments on all balances due. These debts plagued Truman for years. He would pay off the most pressing claims in the best settlement he could get, but as late as 1934 there was an unsatisfied judgment against him for about $9,000 in favor of the Security State Bank of Kansas City. When a bank's receiver put Truman's note up for sale, he bought it for $1,000 through his brother Vivian and wiped out the last of his debts. All told, he estimated that the haberdashery business had cost him $28,000.

Truman was broke, and starting another business was out of the question. That is what turned his mind to politics. In the previous election he had supported John Miles, the man he had helped to organize the 129th, and had seen him elected county marshal. It was estimated that there were 5,000 soldier voters in Jackson County, and the veterans showed they had power when Missouri voted for a soldiers' bonus. Truman had been an early member of the American Legion and had organized a post; he was in the thick of the hell-raising at the third annual convention in Kansas City. To run for office in Jackson County, however, it was not enough to have veteran friends and to be one of the boys. One needed the support of a political machine. Colonel William Southern, editor of the *Independence Examiner*, told of Truman's asking him which political bosses he ought to see if he was going to run for office.

"Harry, what in thunder are you talking about?" asked the colonel.

"I mean to run for county judge from the eastern district," Truman told him. The county judge—in effect, the county commissioner—levies taxes, looks after roads, bridges, county buildings, and property. Jackson County elected three judges; Kansas City elected one for the western part of the county; the rural section elected one for the eastern part; and the entire county voted for a third presiding judge.

Southern advised him not to do it. "Look, Harry," he said, "I know you're discouraged over your business failure and I'm sorry, But there's no reason to be as downhearted as that. Don't mess up your whole life by going into politics. It's no disgrace to have failed in business. Many good men have done that. You'll make good at some other business. Cheer up, Harry."

When he saw that nothing would dissuade Truman, Southern agreed to talk to Nick Phelps, one of Mike Pendergast's lieutenants. Phelps passed the recommendation along to Mike, who had met Truman before the war at the 10th Ward Democratic Club. Mike's son Jim, a rising power in the organization who had known Truman at Camp Doniphan and used to drop by the haberdashery shop, also put in a good word. Harry had the qualifications they were seeking at this time in a candidate. Accordingly, Mike Pendergast drove up to the store in his big Locomobile one day and told Harry he could have the nomination. At the June meeting of the 10th Ward Democratic Club Mike made this momentous announcement: "Now I'm going to tell you who you're going to support for county judge; it's Harry Truman. Harry Truman is a returned soldier, a captain 'over there' with a fine record whose men didn't want to shoot him!" The assembled ward heelers applauded, shook Harry's hand, slapped his back, and vowed to do their all for him. Harry was launched.

That the political vocation was not rated very highly by the solid citizenry could be surmised from Colonel Southern's remarks. This was underlined when Harry called on his friend Edgar Hinde, who ran a garage in Independence. Truman walked in and asked with a grin, "What would you think if I told you I was going to run for eastern judge?"

Hinde said, "I think you're crazy."

"I got to eat," was the rejoinder.

That put a different complexion on the matter. "Okay," Hinde responded, "I'm going to do everything I can for you."

Beyond the dubious status of a second-line politico starting at the bottom of the ladder at the age of thirty eight was the uncertain position of the Pendergast machine in the rural area at this juncture, and the double-dealing involved when Mike Pendergast put up his own candidate for this particular post; all of which Harry became conversant with only after he had filed his papers and begun campaigning. The plum Mike Pendergast had handed him was somewhat worm-eaten.

Pendergast rule of Kansas City was a classic example of corrupt municipal politics. The machine had come a long way by the 1920s from the time when its founder, "Big Jim" Pendergast, opened in 1880 a hotel and saloon in the West Bottoms, a neighborhood of packing houses, railroad yards, unpaved streets, open sewers and gutters, overcrowded tenements and shanties. The causes that gave rise to a boodling officialdom and the techniques pursued were the same as those described by Lincoln Steffens at the turn of the century. In his study of St. Louis in 1902 Steffens explained how "public franchises and privileges were sought, not only for legitimate profit and common convenience, but for loot. Taking but slight and always selfish interest in the public councils, the big men misused politics. The riffraff, catching the smell of corruption, drove out the remaining respectable men, and sold the city—its streets, its wharves, its markets, and all that it had—to the now greedy businessmen and bribers. In other words, when the leading men began to devour their own city, the herd rushed into the trough and fed also."

Tom Pendergast became a virtuoso of this political brokerage. He conducted extensive welfare activities; he and his henchmen were always good for small loans to any hard-pressed constituents. At Christmas, dinners were served and food packages distributed. In the depression, as many as 6,000 men lined up for free Christmas dinners. In one ward, more than a thousand Christmas baskets a year were given away. There were gifts of bicycles and go-carts for children. Carloads of coal were distributed free by trucker friends of the machine. An unfortunate caught in the coils of the law could get the boss or one of the wheelhorses to fix the trouble or get a lawyer. Jobs were given not only to the loyal organization workers but, when available, to worthy suppliants. A Roman Catholic priest, referring to Mike Pendergast, said, "We have known him for twenty-seven years and never in that time have we gone to him in vain for aid for a needy person." Tom Pendergast boasted about it to a *New York Times* reporter: "I know all the angles of organizing and every man I meet becomes my friend. I know how to select ward captains and I know how to get to the poor. Every one of my workers has a fund to buy food, coal, shoes, clothing. When a poor man comes to old Tom's boys for help we don't make one of those fool investigations like these city charities. No, by God, we fill his belly and warm his back and vote him our way."

These welfare activities, which by the standards of a city program were picayune as well as demeaning to the beneficiaries, were unconscionably exaggerated and sentimentalized by organization hacks and newspaper reporters: the "Big Boss," under his rough exterior, had a heart of gold that bled for the deprived and unfortunate; the organization was the poor man's best friend; the Pendergast crowd was doing more for the common people than all the do-gooders combined. They had said the same thing of Tweed: "If he stole, he was at least good to the poor." The welfare program, however, did not originate in the tenderheartedness of the bosses. It was an indispensable adjunct of a corrupt political organization, and served a dual purpose of cold-blooded policy. It was a device to mobilize a mass of people behind the machine and its candidates to perpetuate the rule of the favored. And it relieved the men of property of the burden of welfare at little cost to themselves. Naturally they were inclined to view with a cynical smirk the gamier aspects of boss rule which they solemnly affirmed to be a necessary overhead cost of social order in a rowdy city.

The other side of the political brokerage business, which made the whole enterprise possible, involved the solid citizens living on the right side of the tracks. An illustration of the trade and barter constantly going on between the quality folk and the politicians was the case of the franchise of the Metropolitan Street Railway Company. The franchise was granted originally under questionable circumstances and through the years the company had built up a history of watered stock, mismanagement, and peculation. In 1914 the "Met" wanted a new franchise, although the existing one had eleven years to run, to enable it to raise its fares and pay less taxes. "Met" executives justified their grab with the explanation that only a new, more favorable franchise would enable them to extend service to new neighborhoods.

The "Met" negotiated a deal with Pendergast, who mobilized his minions and enlisted the cooperation of Republican bosses as well as rival Democratic satraps. The night before the special election, he held a meeting at his Jefferson Hotel, where 300 of the foot soldiers loaded up on free liquor and cigars that were handed out with electioneering instructions. Also attending the extraordinary session were Tom Marks, the Republican leader, and Conrad Mann, another Republican dignitary who later became president of the chamber of commerce. Next day, free drinks and silver dollars were dispensed with a prodigal hand in the neighborhoods, and the voice of the people was recorded resoundingly in favor of the company's new bargain franchise. The *Star* wrote that the franchise would never have passed without the immense vote rolled up for it in the North Side wards by the use of strong-arm tactics and money. The "Met," it said, spent thousands of dollars to gain millions.

In the late thirties, when Governor Lloyd Stark had broken with Pendergast and set out to crush him, his investigators discovered that the railroad and utilities companies had received huge tax abatements from the Pendergast-controlled city officialdom. Enormous sums of money, rightfully due the city, were turned back to the Kansas City Power and Light Company, the Kansas City Terminal Railroad Company, and the Kansas City Public Service Company. What finally destroyed Pendergast was not the use of padded voting lists and gangster tactics. These forays of shock warfare, though sensational and violent, were in the nature of supplementary operations to insure the success of the main campaign, and that was to get out the vote by means of suasion, handouts, and support in return for favors received. What finally destroyed Pendergast was the exposure of a three-quarter-million-dollar bribe he had negotiated with a consortium of eminently respectable national insurance companies in exchange for which his state superintendent of insurance would release $9 million of impounded funds.

Since business people were the modern gentry, and to be a businessman was the beau ideal, it followed inevitably that political bosses would use their strategic positions to seize some of the blessed sweets. All important politicos in Kansas City grabbed something. Tom Pendergast, the biggest boss of all, did it on a spectacular scale. In his early days, he had three saloons, but quickly branched out into the wholesale liquor business. He had an interest in the insurance business, and he teamed up with his political mouthpiece, Emmet O'Malley, whom he later installed as state superintendent of insurance, in a cigar company. This was preliminary to his entering the building supply industry, which he converted into a virtual local monopoly. After he took over the Ready-Mixed Concrete Company, the cost of concrete rose steadily in Kansas City until at one time it was as high as $3.75 a yard compared to $1.75 a yard paid on some contracts in the county. His profits from the concrete monopoly alone were estimated at half a million dollars in good years.

After acquiring power and riches, this bull-necked, 250-pound vulgarian, who was brusque and self-assured with the representatives of banks and traction companies and who treated his lieutenants like servants, began to hunger for status. This formidable freebooter, with the gross and menacing appearance of a Thomas Nast cartoon character, who was reputed to have polished off with his bare fists "Fireman" Jim Flynn, the only fighter who had ever knocked out Jack Dempsey, now discarded his derby for a homburg, shaved off his Keystone Cop moustache, smoked cigarettes in a holder, and put on spats. He wanted to be considered a social equal by the lawyers and corporation factotums who dealt with him downtown but kept him at arm's length from their homes and families.

In the pursuit of respectability and refinement, he moved his wife and children from the steaming North Side to an imposing edifice built for him on fashionable Ward Parkway. The house was of French Regency design, and the decor inside was eighteenth-century rococo. Pendergast also bought flashy sports roadsters for his daughter and son, and showered furs and jewelry on his wife. When the house was robbed in 1929, the thieves' haul included jewelry valued at $150,000, furs worth additional thousands, and 480 pairs of silk stockings belonging to his daughter.

This ostentation did little to change his relationship with the business elite, because Pendergast's position in the business community rested not on birth, cultural attainments, or the possession of a pseudo-French chateau but on political power subverted into a brokerage racket. When his boss system became too costly for the city's upper class, many of his supporters rediscovered the virtues of stern morality and scrupulous observance of the statutes, and incontinently abandoned him.

An impression grew up in later years that with the aid of hoodlums and crooked registration lists Pendergast had been able to ride roughshod over the opposition in every election, that he had been an unlimited monarch whose writ ran across party and government lines. Actually, his reign was more akin to that of a feudal potentate who had to make alliances with, or to struggle against, rival dukes and barons. His candidates lost on numerous occasions. Even after he had subdued his rivals in his last years, he was confronted with a new enemy in his own party, as well as the traditional opposition of Republicans and reformers.

Until the last decade of Pendergast's rule, the Democratic party in Kansas City was divided into two major factions, his own and that of his chief rival, Joseph Shannon, called, respectively, "Goats" and "Rabbits." Shannon was more the smooth confidence man than the gruff Pendergast. It was said of him that he could carry an armful of eels and never drop one. He was tall, well built, and some thought him distinguished looking. In contrast to Pendergast, who kept regular hours in his sleazy office at 1908 Main Street, and let everyone come to him, Shannon was a man about town; he could be seen talking to people in any part of the city at any hour of the day or night. Though a sharper in intrigue and in devising power plays, he was also competent with his fists and accompanied his bully boys to the scene of action when the need arose.

At the time that "Big Jim" Pendergast was consolidating his hold on the West Bottoms and North End, Shannon turned the 9th Ward, where he lived, into his stronghold. It was the largest in the city, with about a fifth of the city's population. From this redoubt, he concluded alliances with lesser barons, made war on the Goats, and devised the plays to seize control of the city and county. When the squabbling between the two factions resulted in the election of the entire Republican slate in Jackson County in 1900, the leaders had to compromise. The result was the famous "Fifty-Fifty Agreement." This provided that the bosses would get together before an election to draw up a common slate. Where there were differences on certain offices, and each faction put up its favorites, both agreed to abide by the primary results. Finally, regardless of the number of its supporters on the winning slate, patronage would be divided evenly.

Over the years, the two factions coexisted despite maneuvers for position, intrigues for control, and treacherous deals with Republicans. When Tom Pendergast became head of the Goats, he organized the precincts as they had never been organized before, so that by 1916 he felt that the "Fifty-Fifty" deal no longer reflected the true balance of power. When the Democratic city convention, dominated by Rabbits, voted down his candidates for mayor and alderman that year, he marched his followers out and threw his support to the Republican candidate for mayor, while running his own slate of independent candidates for aldermen in the wards he controlled. He elected his five aldermen, the Republicans took everything else, and the way was open for taking over control of the city at the next election.

Pendergast followed up this stroke by moving in on Shannon's county preserves. To weaken Rabbit control of the courthouse, he backed Miles Bulger for presiding judge. Bulger had established himself as the "Little Czar" of the 2nd Ward, and from there propelled himself to a position of wealth. He was part-owner of a cement company, and also had a big house on Ward Parkway. As presiding county judge, Bulger gained a name for running the treasury into large deficits, awarding contracts to favored parties, and building shoddy, "pie-crust" roads. Pendergast was not concerned about county deficits or "pie-crust" roads. He had even helped Bulger by sidetracking a grand jury investigation of his handling of road funds. What did upset him, and upset him badly, was the dawning realization that Bulger was an ingrate with grandiose plans to set up his own independent duchy. When it became clear that Bulger did not intend to wear the Pendergast collar, and when he supported Shannon in a dispute over the control of sixty road overseers, the Boss decided he had to go.

Pendergast left nothing to chance in preparing to crush Bulger in the 1920 primary. He offered a fifty-fifty division of the spoils to Shannon, a generous proposition since his own strength was now far greater than his rival's. He renewed a side deal with Tom Parks, the accommodating Republican boss, to get Republican support in the river wards in return for promised patronage. With this massed artillery, the Bulger ticket was blown out of the race. But this was the year of Harding's normalcy, and the Missouri Republicans saw no reason why they should not participate in the jubilant return to the public trough. The Republican candidate for governor, Arthur Hyde, promised to end the scandal of Pendergast and Shannon control of the Kansas City police department, and to bring the blessings of sound economical government to the common people. He and the other Republicans were carried into office in the national Republican sweep that year, and they won a number of offices in Jackson County as well.

Pendergast thus faced a trying situation in the 1922 elections. The Republicans had to be ousted at the same time that the Bulger machine had to be eliminated. The understanding with Shannon was that the Goats would pick the western district judge, the Rabbits the eastern district judge, and the presiding judge would be decided by competition. However, Mike Pendergast, the Boss's brother, and the leader of the 10th Ward and the rural area, had always been opposed to fifty-fifty deals with Shannon even in the days when the two factions were more evenly divided. He was an unreconstructed fire-eater who wanted it all. He therefore decided to put the eastern district candidacy up for grabs in the primary also. Whether his action was technically within the Goats' rights or an outright violation of the understanding with Shannon is not clear. At any rate, he did it, and that is how Harry Truman was catapulted onto the political arena as a tryout pugilist in a gang fight.

4

Jackson County Judge

The politics that Truman was thrust into in his first campaign was not concerned with ideologies or programs but with the scramble for spoils. It was not that candidates did not discuss matters of importance to the local citizenry, but long years of experience and conditioning had inured people to politicians' promises and declarations and had converted the electorate into a willing accomplice of its own fleecing. Politics was accepted as a low game of wheeling and dealing and of apportionment of favors to the insiders. The candidates habitually fought with an absence of scruple and regard for veracity, since they could not speak of the one subject that divided them. The 1922 primary battle in the eastern district was an especially venomous one, for the Goats were reneging on a previous commitment, and the Ku Klux Klan injected itself into the proceedings.

There were five candidates in the Democratic primary: Emmet Montgomery, a banker from Blue Springs, the Shannon man; Tom Parent, a road overseer, the Bulger man; two independents who had Ku Klux Klan backing; and Truman, the Pendergast candidate. Truman had certain assets that he exploited to the limit. He was a returned soldier and a Legionnaire; he was a Mason; he had been a dirt farmer for ten years, and this was a rural district. And his ace in the hole: "Luckily I had relatives all over the county, and through my wife I was related to many more." He drove his old Dodge roadster into every part of the district. He relied heavily on personal talks and handshaking, because his speechmaking was devastatingly unimpressive. Edgar Hinde later said, "I will never forget the first speech he made down at Sugar Creek at night. Boy, it was about the poorest effort of a speech I ever heard in my life. I suffered for him."

At one critical point he was confronted with his support of Miles, a Republican, for county marshal in the previous election. But he turned the charge to his advantage. He told the audience that he had been with John Miles in places that made hell look like a playground; that he had seen him remain steadfast at his post when Frenchmen were falling back; and that a veteran who would not vote for his comrade in these circumstances would be untrue to his country. "I know that every soldier understands. I have no apology to make for it." Nothing more was heard of this accusation, so presumably his detractors slunk away in guilty shame.

A more serious problem was presented by the growing influence of the Ku Klux Klan in the area and across the nation. From 1921 to 1924, Klan membership rose steadily until at the height of its power it was credited with over 4 million members, and that year the Klan issue tore apart the Democratic party. For a while Truman tried to duck the Klan issue, but this became increasingly difficult. Hinde urged him to join as a good political move and Truman gave him $10 for his entrance fee. According to Hinde's and Truman's account, the local kleagle asked for a meeting with Truman and, when they met at the Baltimore Hotel, demanded that in return for Klan support he pledge not to give any jobs to Catholics. When Truman refused, he was told the Klan could not accept him, and his $10 was returned to him. After this less than heroic escapade, Truman ran into trouble at home. "Someone sent my wife mean letters about what I'd been saying in the campaign. One day after she got another one of those mean letters, she said to me, 'Why don't you keep your mouth shut?'" How he was to run his campaign for county judge while doing that, Bess did not explain.

He and Montgomery ran a close race. His rival challenged the count, but the final official tabulation gave Truman a margin of 282 votes. It was a slight plurality, but he had shown strong voter appeal, for the eastern district had long been a Rabbit stronghold. His victory gave the Goats control of the county court; Henry F. McElroy was the judge from the western district, and the two could and did out-vote the Rabbit presiding judge, Elihu W. Hayes.

The two Goats proceeded to dig in. An early project was to regain jurisdiction over county institutions that the state legislature in 1919 had placed in the hands of circuit judges. They hired a well-known lawyer, John Barker, who argued the case successfully before the state supreme court on constitutional grounds. With the victory, the county judges again controlled this lush preserve of patronage. Their next move was to apportion the staff jobs of the county institutions, and the hundreds of other small jobs around the county, to their supporters. Mike Pendergast, the Rabbit-killer, was in his glory. Henry P. Chiles said that he "made Harry fire every Rabbit in the courthouse." Truman admitted as much when he recalled, "We promptly took all the jobs."

The two judges then started to bring some order into the scrambled finances bequeathed by the Bulger administration. They eliminated waste and irregularities, paid off debts, and ran county affairs in a more businesslike manner. Truman familiarized himself with the county court's procedures, problems, and responsibilities. He got to know every road and bridge, visited every state institution in which the county had patients. At this time the state Highway commission was securing rights-of-way for the construction of a state road; Truman studied the state road system and calculated how the county could best utilize the new roadway. Before the next election the *Star*, a traditional opponent of the Pendergast machine, editorialized:

> The present county court is busy paying off the debt. It paid off more than $600,000 last year. It has improved the roads. It has money in the treasury. That is the difference between county courts. The men who did this, Judge McElroy and Judge Truman, are up for renomination. Tuesday the Democratic voters of Jackson County will show whether they are interested enough in good service to renominate the men who are responsible for the remarkable showing made.

Despite their creditable record, the two Goat judges lost the election for refusing to divide the spoils. Shannon set out to do to the Goats what they had done to his Rabbits several years ago. He picked strong candidates to oppose Truman and McElroy in the Democratic primary and made a deal with the Klan. When the two, nevertheless, won the primary, Shannon and the Klan forces agreed to throw the election to the Republicans. Feeling ran high; violence was imminent, with armed supporters of both sides traveling about the district. In the end, the combination of Rabbits, Kluxers, and Republicans proved too formidable, and the two Goat judges were returned to private life.

One might imagine that all this unprincipled trading, Catholics lining up with Kluxers, and Republicans making side deals with Democrats, would lead to lifelong animosities. Not so. All adopted an indulgent attitude toward their opponents' as well as their own chicaneries. That was politics! Chiles, a Rabbit, told Truman, "I had to go out and fight you yesterday, and I hated to do it"; and Truman answered, "Don't worry about it, there's no hard feelings. You did what your gang told you, and I did what my gang told me."

Harry was again broke and out of a job. The defeat came at an especially bad time for him because his daughter Margaret had been born early that year and he was in the middle of a course at the Kansas City Law School that he had been attending at night for two years. He soon dropped the classes and went to work selling memberships in the Kansas City Automobile Club. This was the time of Coolidge prosperity, business was good, and Harry was making more as a salesman than he had earned as county judge. But there was no security, much less prestige, in that kind of job. The old flame to become a successful businessman was rekindled in him.

One day in 1926, Spencer Salisbury proposed to him that they become bankers. Salisbury, a fellow captain in the 129th Field Artillery, was a Pendergast Goat who had worked for Truman's election. Truman's association with Salisbury is important because when the two later became sworn enemies, Truman showed a capacity for vindictiveness that had not been evident, or at least, in public view, before.

In Salisbury's account, "Here was a chance to buy control of the stock of the Security State Bank of Englewood [a tiny community near Independence] for thirty thousand dollars. The beauty of it was that the bank's president was willing to take the thirty thousand dollars in notes without our paying out any cash." Arthur Metzger, constable of Independence, joined with them. Colonel Edward Stayton, a consulting engineer, and Lou Holland, president of the Kansas City Chamber of Commerce, agreed to become directors. No one seems to have asked why anyone would be willing to give up a bank without demanding any cash payment. At any rate, after they took over, the five spent a day examining the bank's books. "What we found made us ill," said Salisbury. "The bank turned out to be a Republican blind. It seems that Charles Becker, the Republican Secretary of State, wanted a bank where he could borrow money for his printing business. And this was it. All the bank's cash assets were the funds from state auto licenses that were deposited here. Becker and his friends put up notes that weren't worth a damn. The only other assets we found were second mortgages and these were shaky. We didn't have a bank—we had a bank failure on our hands." They made a report to the cashier's bonding company and unloaded their stock on other would-be bankers, getting out just in time, for the bank failed later that year.

Truman, Salisbury, and Metzger were also partners in another enterprise, the Community Savings and Loan Association, in which Truman sold the stock, Salisbury was the director, and Metzger looked after legal matters. The company did all right, permitting Truman to collect commissions on his stock promotion. He continued as president of the company after he reentered politics, but was ousted by Salisbury after their personal break. Truman relates: "In the early thirties, Salisbury, using proxies, got his own directors elected, throwing out my friends and me. Salisbury was mismanaging the association. There was not anything I could do when I found out what Salisbury was doing but report it to the Federal authorities." According to Salisbury: "I got rid of Harry in the building and loan in 1932 when he tried to turn things over to Jimmy Pendergast—when he wanted to give him a list of all the stockholders so he could consolidate with the building and loan in Kansas City which Jim Pendergast had." The two accounts, neither of them complete, are not necessarily contradictory or mutually exclusive. The break came in 1932. That year, Salisbury supported Bennett Clark against the Pendergast candidate. He was a thorn in Truman's side when Truman ran against Jacob "Tuck" Milligan in 1934. He was an active supporter of Governor Stark's investigations into election fraud, and after Tom Pendergast went to jail he stirred up the opposition. It was then—seven years later—that Truman made his retaliatory move. As senator, he sent a telegram to the governor of the Federal Home Loan Bank system in August, 1939, calling for an investigation of the Association and its manager.

The sequel was costly for Salisbury. In 1941, he was sentenced, after a plea of guilty, to fifteen months in prison for having sworn falsely when he was forced out as president that there were no lawsuits pending against the Association. At his trial, old comrades of the 129th took the stand as character witnesses on his behalf. Years later when Father Tiernan, the old chaplain of the 129th, went to the White House to plead for a federal pardon for Salisbury, Truman grimly shook his head.

Another election was coming up in 1926, and Truman wanted to get back into politics and a paying office. He had his eye on the office of county collector, which although not high in prestige, netted $25,000 a year in salary and fees. He put out a number of feelers, and then visited the great man's office at 1908 Main. He had some claims on the organization. He was a proven vote-getter and had been a faithful steward. His associate, McElroy, with a record no different from his own, had been picked earlier that year for the high office of city manager of Kansas City. But Pendergast told him no, he had already promised his support for county collector to somebody else, but Truman could run for presiding judge of the county court. This was a promotion over his previous post, although the salary was only $6,000.

Truman had stumbled into the first of the many opportunities that enabled him to mount the political ladder, opportunities that came to him by chance but that he had the energy, level-headedness, and guile to profit from. Had Pendergast agreed to his proposal for county collector, or had he shuffled him into a post in Kansas City where he would have had no independence, his political career would have been stillborn. Truman won the election easily and took over the old courthouse.

The first order of business was the parceling out of some 900 jobs and a multimillion-dollar budget. Truman met with Pendergast and Shannon to discuss the division. Before the meeting, the Big Boss said to Truman: "Now look here, Harry. They tell me you're a pretty hot-headed fellow. I want you to understand that when we are at this meeting, I don't want any fighting." Truman was astonished. He thought someone must have given the boss a false picture of him. "I won't cause any trouble, Mr. Pendergast," he said. There was plenty of arguing, shouting, and fingerpointing between the Big Boss and the lesser boss, but Truman did not utter a word. At the end, the Goats kept most of the key jobs and the Rabbits were limited to a third.

That disposed of, Truman initiated measures to make the county government more important than a dispenser of patronage and contracts and to build a reputation for himself as a resourceful and conscientious public official. He dismissed a number of jobholders who were performing no discernible functions, stopped the expense account system for road overseers, set up an inspection and audit system to verify that contractors performed in accordance with specifications, and reorganized the county's borrowing system.

The major problem before the county court was roads. Truman appointed a bipartisan committee of two, Colonel Stayton (one-time director of the short-lived Englewood Bank), a Democrat, and Nathan Veatch, a Republican, who was a leading consulting engineer in Kansas City. Their four-month survey resulted in a joint report that was a devastating commentary on the activities of previous courts. They recommended an integrated grid system of roadways, which called for 224 miles of new construction at a cost of $6.5 million. A sum of money that size could be raised only by a special bond issue.

There matters stood for another year. When McElroy offered a bond issue of $28 million for Kansas City, Truman proposed to Pendergast that a county bond issue of $6.5 million be submitted at the same time. The boss was not enthusiastic. He said county bond issues had been turned down twice before, and people would say he was going to steal the funds. Truman argued: "If I could tell the taxpayers just how I would handle their money, I felt sure it would carry." When he received a grudging clearance, he hit the evangel trail again. Up and down the county he explained the kind of system that would be built, pledging a bipartisan board of engineers to supervise the project without political favor. He promised that contracts would be granted to the lowest bidders. Whether it was these promises, or the felt need for new roads, or both, the bond issue carried by more than the required two-thirds.

Truman called in Stayton and Veatch to supervise the program, assuring them that there would be no interference from downtown. The first contract for $400,000 was awarded to the American Road Building Company of South Dakota. It was not very long before Truman got a phone call from Pendergast who told him there were several agitated contractors in his office and that he would like him to drop around. When Truman walked in, there were with Pendergast three important organization figures, William Ross, William Boyle, and John Pryor, builders of the pie-crust roads during the Bulger regime. They demanded that contracts go to local bidders, who, as local taxpayers, deserved preference. Truman wrote: "I told them that I expected to let the contracts to the lowest bidders, just as I had promised the taxpayers I would do, and that I was setting up a bipartisan board of engineers to see that specifications were carried out according to contract, or else the public would not pay for them." At that, Pendergast turned to the contractors, and said, "I told you he's the contrariest man in the state of Missouri." When the contractors left, Pendergast said to Truman, "You carry out your commitments."

What is one to make of Pendergast's behavior at this meeting, so completely at variance with his customary handling of contract matters, particularly since, as later evidence disclosed, he was, or became, a secret partner in the firms of all three contractors? It would appear that Truman actually had come to an understanding with him earlier when they took up the bond issue, and that Pendergast was just putting on a charade for the benefit of his contractor friends when he called Truman to his office. But why did he make such an agreement? We can dismiss out of hand the suggestion that some have unblushingly offered that Pendergast really admired a person of independence who was ready to stand up to him. He made compromises with people of that sort only when they had independent power, and Truman was not in that category in 1928. Pendergast could have broken him like a match stick, had he wished, as he had broken Bulger before him. Moreover, he controlled the other two Goat judges of the county court, and at his word they would have outvoted and isolated Truman, just as Truman and McElroy had outvoted and isolated Hayes. Neither can Pendergast's behavior be explained by the alleged mystique of political bosses in adhering to their pledged word. Such tales are part of the folklore of those who view history through the golden haze of antiquarian adulation and complacency.

Truman's ability to gain a semiautonomous status in county affairs was due to the special set of circumstances that existed in Kansas City at the time of his election. Pendergast had just successfully concluded a complicated maneuver. To the confusion of reformers, he had supported their panacea of administration by experts embodied in the new city charter for nonpartisan government. Shannon was amazed and proclaimed that the boss was "signing his death warrant." But Pendergast understood what the good-government liberals and Shannon did not, that social and political power took precedence over formal constitutional arrangements. A decade before Charles A. Beard had explained: "Nonpartisanship has not worked, does not work, and will not work in any major city," because the cause of parties was "social and economic."

When a primary election was held in the fall of 1925, with no party label attached to candidates' names as called for by the new charter, the two parties put up their "nonpartisan" slates. The "Beach" and "Jaudon" tickets, which everyone knew were those of the Republican and Democratic machines, easily pushed aside the independent candidates. The climax of the charter crusade was to have Albert I. Beach, the Republican, elected mayor while Pendergast placed five of his Goats in the new city council of nine. Pendergast had thus taken effective control of the city government in an admittedly honest election—that is, an election in which ballots were counted accurately. In strict accordance with the charter, he installed his henchman McElroy as city manager, and for the next thirteen years he and McElroy retained an iron grip on the government of Kansas City. Rather than eliminating boss rule, the nonpartisan charter had reinforced it.

The McElroy regime opened up limitless opportunities in a rapidly growing city. There were miles of new highways and streets to be laid out; hospitals, civic buildings, auditoriums, and parks to be built or improved; city departments and special projects to be staffed. All this called for enormous exertion and application, which reduced county affairs to a distinctly subordinate position, but the attractiveness of the city plans for expansion could be enhanced by a good record in the county.

The Truman judgeship had a lot to recommend it after Pendergast's dolorous experiences with Bulger. Truman was a loyal organization man who followed instructions on patronage and could be depended on to deliver in factional and electoral contests. His quaint notions that contracts had to be awarded to low bidders, and specifications observed, would work some hardship on organization contractors—but it was something Pendergast could live with. So for eight years—when the organization's attention was concentrated on city hall, and then on state affairs—Truman had the opportunity and freedom to carry through an ambitious program that made a reputation for him as a planner and builder. His authority increased the year after the program was started when Mike Pendergast died and Tom Pendergast turned over to him the leadership of Jackson County. When Truman's program was concluded, $200,000 of the $6.5 million bond issue had been saved and more miles of solid roads had been built than the original estimate called for. The *Star* called Truman "extraordinarily honest" and assured its readers that there was "not a suspicion of graft" in the undertaking. Truman was not one to hide his light under a bushel. He had a booklet published, *Results of County Planning—Jackson County, Missouri*, filled with pictures of farms, country places, parks, and streams beside which his highways and roads passed, and with booster copy to match. As word got around, he was elected in January, 1930, president of the Greater Kansas City Plan Association, and later that year was made a director of the National Conference on City Planning.

After the 1929 crash there was a shift in the meaning of the road program. Originally conceived as a means to improve facilities for transportation, it became a major source for jobs. After Truman was swept back into office in the 1930 election—he had by then become an institution in the county—he worked up a new bond issue for approximately $8 million; $3.5 million for additional roads, $500,000 for a county hospital for the aged, $4 million for a new county courthouse in Kansas City, and $200,000 to renovate the county courthouse in Independence. (Jackson County has its main courthouse in the city, and another one in Independence, theoretically the county seat.) This time he did not have to beg Pendergast to accede to the bond issue. Pendergast was anxious to tie the county issue to McElroy's "Ten Year Plan" to exploit the prestige of the county program for the big push in Kansas City.

The Ten Year Plan was put to the voters with all the razzle dazzle that made Kansas City the Rotarian's paragon. The bond issue called for expenditures over a decade of $32 million for city projects, plus the $8 million for the county. Everyone endorsed it: the Pendergast organization, the Shannon faction, the Republicans, the *Star*, a committee of 1,000 public-spirited citizens. The slogan "Make Kansas City the Greatest Inland City" rang in voters' ears. The bonds were approved 4 to 1 in the largest vote ever registered at a special election. Then the town celebrated with a five-day Jubilee of Progress.

The building program proved a godsend in the midst of the economic bust. It was administered honestly under Truman's direction in the county, and with maximum allowances for payoffs and loot by McElroy in the city. In both cases, it helped mitigate suffering and want, and Pendergast's Kansas City looked to many like a beacon of imaginative planning and resolution compared to the callousness and stupidity of officials elsewhere. William Allen White employed superlatives in describing it. The *St. Louis Post-Dispatch* thought it "a striking object lesson for the national government." McElroy claimed that Harry Hopkins got the idea for the Civil Works Administration from him. When early in the Depression the city faced mass unemployment, McElroy, with customary resourcefulness, proposed that $1 million be raised by the sale of water department notes to put the jobless to work building water main extensions. Wherever possible on this project, tractors and excavating machinery were dispensed with in favor of picks, shovels, and wheelbarrows. Whether McElroy was the godfather of CWA or not, Hopkins did send engineers to Kansas City to study its public works before setting up the program. CWA had the McElroy flavor about it minus the boodle: Four million men were put to work in a matter of two months. Hopkins told Roosevelt, "Well, they're at work, but for God's sake don't ask me what they're doing."

At the completion of the county's road-building program in the fall of 1932, the *Star* gave it a laudatory writeup with map, photos of the county judges and engineers, and long quotations from Truman elaborating on the complex. From the money left over in the fund, Truman threw a mammoth barbecue that produced the worst traffic jam, up to that time, in rural Jackson County.

When the Roosevelt administration began its make-work projects, Hopkins conferred with Truman in Kansas City and had him appointed as a dollar-a-year Missouri reemployment director. Later he was the individual "to be reckoned with so far as WPA was concerned," according to Harry Easley, WPA deputy administrator up to 1937. Like many politicians in the period of mass unemployment and unrest, Truman was populist-oriented. At the University of Missouri, he said, "If it is necessary to cut each working day to two hours to give everybody a job, then let's cut it to two hours and give the same wage we used to earn for a ten-hour day." That did not deter him from threatening workers with dismissal when in his opinion their demands were unreasonable or inconvenient, nor did the two positions appear to be inconsistent to him. When union members called a strike at the county courthouse, he told them that if they did not return to work, "the job will be thrown open to the employment of labor at NRA wages which are much lower than union wages."

His official duties carried him close enough to the poor to understand what was going on. He could see the lines lengthening at the courthouse door and at government employment offices. He could not escape the cries of men desperate for jobs and food. "I had seen some terrible riots in Missouri." But it was his public, not his private, problem. He was earning $6,000 a year with all his travel expenses paid. At the Gates house, all was untroubled, and the Depression seemed far away. For Christmas in 1932, he had bought his eight-year-old daughter a baby grand piano. No matter that Margaret started bawling in disappointment when she saw it, because she had wanted an electric train. It was a very expensive present for a little girl—particularly in 1932.

The acclaim and recognition he was enjoying did not alter the fact that the end of his term was approaching, and he had to decide what he would do next, since it was not customary for presiding judges to serve more than two terms. In 1933, when the state legislature was re-districting congressional seats, he lobbied to make eastern Jackson County a district. Once the district was set up, he wanted to make the run, but Pendergast again told him no. He was giving the nomination to Jasper Bell, a councilman who had made it possible for him to install McElroy as city manager. Truman had already received warning that his rating was no better than a subaltern's; the Big Boss had not named him a delegate to the Democratic national convention. Thus on his fiftieth birthday, it looked as if his political career was coming to a close. He wrote a memo to himself "that retirement in some minor county office was all that was in store for me."

Why had Pendergast passed him up? Obviously, he thought Truman was a good enough leader in the rural area, but was not cut out to be a confidant in more sensitive positions. He was a loyal organization man, one had to hand him that; but he had somewhat rigid ideas with respect to the spending of public funds. The boss, of course, had different levels of associations. With some it was an association of equals, or almost. But no one thought of Truman in those terms in the 1920s or 1930s. Even to political friends, Truman was a second-line man, able enough in certain capacities, reliable enough for certain tasks, but no earth-shaker. No one at that time put him on a par with McElroy, for example, the self-assured ex-storekeeper who was dazzling the business community with his "country bookkeeping."

Truman insisted in later years that "Pendergast never asked me to do a dishonest deed. He knew I wouldn't do it if he asked it. He was always my friend. He was always honest with me, and when he made a promise, he kept it." Truman, it has to be remembered, had picked up the habits of his trade, and did not invariably believe his own pontifications, as when he handed Edward Schauffler, a local journalist, the line that he was working inside the Pendergast organization to reform it. The statement about Pendergast, however, has the ring of truth to it. It tallies with the internal logic of the relationship between the two men. What was the dividing line between honesty and dishonesty to Truman? What was his moral code as distinct from the rhetorical pieties? The spoils system, the parceling out of posts to supporters, friends, cronies, relatives, was not only not dishonest; it was the warp and woof of democracy. He never pretended to think or act otherwise. And he was never taken aback, or felt the need to justify his conduct when caught passing out sinecures to party regulars.

If we therefore include patronage in its broadest application under the heading of legitimate political activity, what remains? The other major opportunities for dishonesty on a county or municipal level would involve fraud and violence in elections, graft and favoritism, sales of public properties and resources in return for bribes. It is probably accurate that Pendergast never proposed these to Truman. The Big Boss, aloof and guarded with outsiders, jovial, genial, and a storyteller with intimates, was a shrewd man, a judge of people. He understood Harry's makeup and his code; he knew that Harry would not fix elections or take bribes, although he had no objections to giving support to, and accepting support from, those who did; and it was not the Boss's style to press demands that would not have been welcomed.

Truman's moral code was based on the philosophy of Sancho Panza. He was not rich enough and well connected enough to be able to afford the toney morals of a parson. At the same time, he clung to a personal integrity that would enable him to walk the narrow line of middle class respectability dividing legitimacy from corruption. If the dividing line was shaky for a system of higher ethics, it was acceptable for working purposes in the knockabout world. When people asked him why he consorted with the Pendergast crowd, he looked at them in utter amazement. How could he have had a political career without the support of the Pendergast organization? Didn't they know that so many of the pious figures who at one time or another had waxed morally indignant at Pendergast had done so only after their requests for his support had been rejected? Beyond that, he was somewhat in awe of the boss, who had that authoritative quality of controlled ferocity that he lacked; he thought him a natural leader of men.

Truman's kind of public service had been not only acceptable but valuable to the machine for the past eight years. Had his usefulness now come to an end, and was the Big Boss preparing to retire him to some obscure post where he would shuffle papers and draw a salary?

5

Senator
from
Pendergast

It was in this dark hour that the god that looks after children and road commissioners intervened as he had done once before.

As happened throughout his career, Pendergast was facing another challenge in 1934, this time over control in the state. Bennett Clark, son of the Champ Clark who had lost the presidential nomination to Woodrow Wilson, had been elected to the United States Senate two years earlier as an avowedly anti-Pendergast candidate. His subsequent activities made it clear to the Kansas City strategists that he was trying to build himself up as the Missouri boss. Now, this was made explicit. Clark announced that he was backing "Tuck" Milligan, who had served seven terms in the House of Representatives, for the Senate seat held by an old mossback Republican, Roscoe Conkling Patterson, who was up for reelection. With the New Deal at its popular apogee, the Democratic nomination was equivalent to election.

It was a serious challenge, for with the swelling of the federal bureaucracy and the inauguration of immense public works programs, federal patronage had become a major prize. A city boss could no longer wield effective power if the flow were directed to a rival's quarters. The support of the solid, substantial business people was also based on the expectation that the political bosses could deliver through the state's congressmen and senators necessary favors and government awards. Control of, or a close alliance with, a state's congressmen and senators was no longer limited, as it had once been, to considerations of prestige and occasional windfalls of patronage; it had become an indispensable part of the political boss's apparatus of power.

It was consequently necessary to find a suitable candidate to repulse Clark's ambitions. This posed a problem since Milligan was an attractive candidate with a pro-Roosevelt record in Congress, and Clark was a man of large influence throughout the state. Pendergast first turned to James Reed, seventy-two and in retirement, a hard-bitten reactionary opponent of the New Deal. Reed had always been a trying, assertive associate, but he had also been a captivating orator of the old stem-winding school with an ability to mesmerize audiences and corral votes, and it was hoped that the old reprobate had enough fire and venom left to perform in a crisis. Shannon correctly predicted to William Helm, the Washington correspondent of the *Kansas City Journal-Post*, that nothing would come of it. "He's getting old. And he's comfortable. I don't think he'll run." Reed didn't. The Boss next turned to Shannon, who was sixty-seven, had a safe seat in Congress, was living in Washington, and knew that defeat, certainly a possibility, would be a cruel blow to his standing. He decided to let well enough alone, and also turned down the offer. The Boss thereupon turned to James Aylward, attorney for the Pendergast organization and Democratic state chairman. He was considered one of the organization's ablest strategists, had received his earlier political training under Shannon, and became a go-between through his ability to work with both faction leaders. Aylward, too, refused. The *Star* said that Pendergast was "backed into a corner."

It was at this point, when all the heavies on the Missouri political scale had taken themselves out of consideration, that the thoughts of the strategists turned to the cocky little road builder in Independence. When Truman was told that Pendergast had decided on him for the Senate, that the organization would back him "at least ninety eight percent," and that influential Democrats in St. Louis could be counted on for support, he was not in a position, like the other three, to weigh the pros and cons. Besides, he was given to understand that if he ran and was defeated, the organization would back him later for the gubernatorial nomination. He accepted on the spot. In an early-morning memorandum to himself he wrote, "If the Almighty God decides that I go there, I am going to pray as King Solomon did, for wisdom to do the job." Although grown thick-skinned and battle-scarred in the political wars in Jackson County, he still retained something of the diffident little boy studying the lives of great men at Central High.

Pendergast told different things to different people in explaining his choice. To Tom Evans, president of the Fifth Ward Democratic Club, who later built up a drug chain empire, he said, "I don't feel that Harry Truman has a chance." To Spencer McCulloch of the *St. Louis Post-Dispatch* he said that he had noticed that some senators represented the oil industry, others the railroads, steel, or utilities; that therefore he decided to send his office boy to represent him. After the election he was to brag, "Frankly it was a matter of pride to me to name just any man and beat Clark's candidate." Disregarding the boss's megalomania, he picked Truman because Truman was the best candidate he could find who would agree to make the run. As Shannon told Helm, "You know, Tom hasn't got a field of world-beaters to pick from." The *Star* reported: "It was agreed Pendergast had taken on a real job. To jump a man from the county court bench to a Senate nomination was quite an undertaking."

In Washington, Shannon was saying to Helm: "I'm afraid Truman's too light. He's a good mixer, a very pleasant sort of fellow. And he's clean. I suspect that was one of the chief reasons Tom wanted him. I haven't got anything against Truman; in fact, I like him. On the other hand, I haven't got much for him." Shannon then said Truman would probably spoil his chances by his habit of dancing around nervously when making a speech, which he proceeded to illustrate by going into a pantomime, described this way by Helm: "Shannon affected a grimacing grin, raised and lowered his arms rapidly like a rooster flapping its wings, and pattered around the floor in quick little jerky steps. I laughed." Shannon then remarked: "It isn't quite as bad as that, but the fellow's always grinning and he's too quick with his mouth. He talks off the cuff at the wrong time; doesn't stop to consider what he's going to say before out pop the words."

All the same, Truman was an appealing candidate. In addition to his old assets, he had his record of accomplishment and many friends around the state whom he could call upon to rally round. In Maryville, at the northwest corner of the state, he was introduced to a convention of preachers and Sunday school teachers by his old friend Colonel Southern of the *Independence Examiner*, who had a reputation as a Bible teacher throughout the state on the strength of his syndicated Sunday school column. Southern took Truman by the hand

and told the crowd: "Here is my boy. I vouch for him, and don't pay attention to what others may say of him." Having friendly acquaintanceships with all the county judges and county clerks in the state, and a good working knowledge of the operations of the courthouse crowds in many of the counties also enhanced his chances. He had the support of these second-string professionals when he went into 60 of Missouri's 114 counties, where he made six to sixteen speeches a day.

He could use all the support he could muster, because being a Pendergast candidate carried a heavier stigma in 1934 than before. No one was aware of it, but the events of that year presaged Pendergast's downfall. His alliance with Johnnie Lazia set the stage for the arrival of federal researchers and detectives to pry into the affairs of an organization that could not bear investigation. Lazia was a soft-spoken, gum-chewing gangster; personable, and a good dresser in a Hollywood gangland style, he had come out of the North End's "Little Italy." Under the slogan of "Home Rule for the Italian Community," and by kidnappings and gunplay, his hoodlums in 1928 had ousted Mike Ross, the Boss's business partner, and installed Lazia as the new czar of the 1st Ward.

Lazia was important to Pendergast because he was not just another goon, but a person of judgment, organizational ability, and presence. Lazia established a cordial relationship with the Big Boss based on mutual profit and trust. He was the recognized power in liquor, gambling rackets, and nightclubs. He furnished interested customers with the entertainment that had made Kansas City famous since the Civil War. He helped set up the Cuban Gardens, a nightclub and gambling casino that became known to the sports and free spenders of half a dozen states. At the Chesterfield Club, waitresses went from table to table dressed only in high-heeled slippers. In another downtown emporium, the customers could see four striptease acts in the course of a lunch costing less than a dollar. When they were overstimulated, members of the oldest profession were available to soothe their tensions. In the congenial climate, automobile stealing became an organized industry so that theft insurance rates rose prohibitively. Even tire-snatching rated as a separate concession.

Lazia could oversee the rackets and clubs with little police molestation because he was an accredited part of the machine, and in a sense, part of the law. The police department had been returned to municipal control by the courts, and Lazia was not only on amiable terms with the Goat-appointed police chief; he was one of three who had a voice in naming men to the force, and one of the formulators of the policy of winking at technical infractions by the owners of the night haunts so as to concentrate on the eradication of major crime. A federal agent, investigating Lazia's income, reported that when he called the Kansas City police department, Lazia had answered the phone.

Lazia was supposed to have an agreement with mobsters throughout the country that they could hide out without interference, but there would be no "rough stuff" in Kansas City. The trouble with Lazia's agreement with the gangsters was that he was not dealing with a responsible group of people in a stable industry. Out-of-towners tried to move in, at different times either to take advantage of Home Rule hospitality, or because they just could not control their high spirits while cooling off in Kansas City between jobs.

Then Kansas City was rocked by the major scandal of the Union Station massacre in June, 1933, when a trio of notorious killers attacked seven police officers who were delivering the bank and train robber, Frank "Jelly" Nash, to the penitentiary at Leavenworth, Kansas. A battle took place when the gunmen tried to free the prisoner, resulting in the death of two Kansas City police officers, an FBI agent, the Oklahoma police chief, and Nash himself. Federal agents descended on Kansas City to investigate charges of police laxity. They concluded that while Lazia had declined to furnish his own trigger men for the operation, he had known of the meeting of the three gunmen, and had furnished help to spirit them out of town.

The national publicity following this bungled and bloody action was all the more embarrassing to Lazia since two months earlier four young punks on the make had shaken the city by kidnapping and holding for ransom McElroy's daughter. Wasn't this precisely the kind of "rough stuff" Lazia was supposed to keep out of Kansas City? When Roosevelt took over the White House, the new Secretary of the Treasury, Henry Morgenthau, noted that Lazia was on the Intelligence Unit's list of men to get. Lacking evidence for other indictments, the Treasury charged him with income tax evasion. Pendergast promptly wrote Postmaster-General James Farley to fix the case. The case was pending when the Union Station massacre inconveniently made headlines throughout the country, and brought the federal agents to town.

In February, 1934, on Bennett Clark's recommendation, Roosevelt appointed Maurice Milligan, brother and law partner of "Tuck" Milligan, United States attorney for the western district of Missouri. Before the appointment, he was called to Washington for questioning by the Attorney General, Homer S. Cummings. Cummings said, "Kansas City is one of the three 'hot spots' in the United States. Chicago and St. Paul are the other two. I want to appoint as District Attorney one who has no connection with any criminally-allied political organization and who will prosecute crime vigorously." The decision was that Milligan qualified. He was not only a tight-lipped, self-righteous moralist; he also had political ambitions and wanted to make a reputation as the slayer of the Kansas City dragon.

This was the status of things when Truman started his fateful run for the senatorial nomination. The long-priced horse became a live one when the lineup revealed that in addition to "Tuck" Milligan, there was another major contender in the race. This was John J. Cochran of St. Louis, a weighty candidate in every respect. Cochran, a congressman for eight years, a noted supporter of Roosevelt, had been voted by Capitol correspondents one of the six most useful members of the House, and had the backing of the Igoe-Dickman machine of St. Louis. The general opinion was that Cochran and Milligan would split the vote that would have gone to Milligan. Who splits whose vote in a three-way race is a matter of some conjecture; there was no question, however, that Bennett Clark's man was now facing the opposition of two major political machines in the state.

There was speculation that Cochran's candidacy was a plot of Pendergast's with the purpose of spoiling Milligan's candidacy. In his private correspondence, G. H. Force, who was well acquainted with the intricacies of St. Louis politics, said that the scheme was arranged when Shannon conferred in St. Louis with Bill Igoe and Cochran, and that Igoe had a meeting afterward with Pendergast in Kansas City. Several attendant circumstances lend plausibility to this story. Whether the Pendergast-Igoe agreement—it is safe to assume that there was one—underwrote a Truman victory, or simply provided that the two bosses would unite to cut the heart out of Clark's man and support whichever candidate of the other two won the primary, is unimportant; in either case, the agreement put the "Tuck" Milligan candidacy in jeopardy.

From the start, "T.J." made it clear this was to be no mere token effort. He pushed buttons and things began happening all over the state. Aylward, from his eminence as state chairman, directed the campaign. William T. Kemper, Jr., son of a prominent Kansas City banker long connected with the boss, headed a young people's Truman-for-Senator club. Robert Holloway, secretary of the Missouri Public Service Commission, was granted a leave of absence to take charge of Truman's headquarters in Jefferson City. Governor Guy B. Park sent word down the line, and state employees were kicking in finances and lining up relatives, acquaintances, and subordinates. In one letter, Orestes Mitchell wrote to the governor that "the Grain Department and Police Department are thoroughly organized and there are few who have not fallen into line. All of we heads of departments are strong for and working daily for Mr. Truman." The *Star* reported that Jackson County employees would be assessed 10 percent for campaign funds.

What were the issues of this momentous struggle? Since all three candidates said that Roosevelt was God's gift to the American people, and pledged to support him all the way, and since none of them had any startling proposals of his own to lighten the burden of his fellow citizens, the boss issue became the axis upon which were hung the accusations, insinuations, vilifications, prevarications. Milligan and Cochran charged that Truman was "Pendergast's office boy." Milligan turned on Cochran with the accusation that if the latter were elected, the St. Louis organization would have two senators; whereupon Cochran rose up and said that if Milligan were elected, Clark would have two Senate votes. Truman was concerned that Clark was trying to become the boss of Missouri, and thought it unfair that he was "lending the weight of federal patronage to the candidacy of Mr. Milligan." Old Joe Shannon, who had told Helm in Washington that now that it was done, he would work for the Pendergast ticket, made his contribution by dubbing Cochran "ranting John" and "the office boy of the *St. Louis Post-Dispatch*."

Early in July the boss staged one of his spectaculars. Troops of the line were instructed to board trains bound for the University of Missouri campus for a gala gathering. "Kansas City just about took over Columbia," jeered the *Star*. Governor Park (whose executive mansion in Jefferson City Milligan called "Uncle Tom's Cabin") gave Truman a heartwarming introduction. Other politicians lent weight to the occasion, and on the platform sat Truman's wife and eighty-two-year-old mother. Truman stepped up to the microphones; his face wearing his trademark grin, the reflected light flashing from his thick lenses, he read a speech that was broadcast throughout the state. He didn't read it very well, although the Pendergast claque roared its approval; but he made a few cogent points for those who could understand what he was saying. He brought out, in answer to the Pendergast-office-boy indictment, that both Milligan and Cochran had two years before sought and gratefully accepted Pendergast's endorsement for their congressman-at-large candidacies. He was not ashamed to have this support either, although, he solemnly assured the audience, he was not a Kansas City man, but "a farmer by birth and experience."

Clark waxed sarcastic in his reply: "His opening speech at Columbia was attended almost exclusively by a mob from Kansas City (in fact, I am informed that the natives looked over the crowd to see if Dillinger was there), and by a lot of state employees ordered out by their superiors as a condition to holding their jobs." Milligan, accompanied by Clark, invaded Kansas City, and before a large, appreciative audience, hammered away at the Pendergast machine, ghost votes, and boss-controlled candidates. "Why, if Harry ever goes to the Senate, he will grow calluses on his ears listening on the long distance telephone to the orders of his boss."

When this educational canvass of the electorate was concluded, the tabulation read: Truman, 276,850; Cochran, 236,105; Milligan, 147,614; Truman had thus won the nomination by a plurality of 40,000. The abilities of the two machines to churn out and regulate votes was even more impressive than the final totals. In Kansas City and Jackson County the count stood: Truman, 137,529; Milligan, 8,912; Cochran, 1,525. In St. Louis the count stood: Cochran, 104,265; Milligan, 6,670; Truman, 3,742. The manufacture of majorities had become an industry. The extent of Pendergast's achievement can be gauged from this comparison: He had rolled up 39,000 more votes for Truman than he had for his senatorial candidate in 1932—approximately the plurality by which Truman won in the primary. Someone on the boss's staff was very good at mathematics.

An attempt has been made to rescue some shred of solace from the grim figures by pointing out that Truman would have won even if both the Jackson County and St. Louis votes had been eliminated from the totals. If we perform this operation, the figures read: Truman, 135,579; Cochran, 131,840. This is an interesting exercise in addition and subtraction, but has anything been demonstrated to contravene the conclusion that Truman owed his nomination to the Pendergast machine?

Truman's nomination and assured election in November brought the Kansas City Boss to the pinnacle. His power, which had encompassed Jefferson City, now radiated out to Washington. But the campaign had hurt Truman in a way he had not imagined possible when he accepted the nomination. It was not as easy to shrug off the Pendergast connection when the lights of the state and nation were shining relentlessly on him as it had been when shaking hands and chatting at picnics in the townships of Jackson County. The *St. Louis Post-Dispatch* sent the message thundering throughout the country: "Under our political system, an obscure man can be made the nominee of a major political party for the high office of United States Senator by virtue of the support given him by a city boss. County judge Truman is the nominee because Tom Pendergast willed it so." In Truman's triumph, the honey was diluted with gall, for he had been made to appear the puppet of a disreputable impresario.

Truman adopted an air of bravado and jauntiness that covered inadequately his wounded susceptibilities. He came into the Senate, as he admitted later, under a terrible cloud. He had difficulty in finding an experienced administrative assistant who knew his way around the Hill, and could advise him on how to set up his office. Aylward introduced him to Victor Messall who had been the aide of a Missouri congressman. "This is Senator Truman," said Aylward. "He wants you to work for him as his secretary." Messall declined the offer. He looked at this newcomer with his sharply creased pants and glistening shoes, and remembered that "Truman had been sent to Washington by a man criticized throughout the country as a crook. I didn't see any future in an association like that. Here was a guy—a punk —sent up by gangsters. I told myself I'd lose my reputation if I worked for him." (He subsequently changed his opinion of Truman and took on the post.) In the Senate, many shunned Truman like a leper. Bronson Cutting, the aristocratic senator from New Mexico, who had come by way of Groton, Harvard, a Long Island fortune, and the boss-ship of a tight political machine, stared through Truman as if he were transparent. Pat McCarran of Nevada said, "I never considered him a Senator." George Norris of Nebraska steered clear of him for a long time. Truman claimed later that these brushoffs did not bother him because he was convinced that attitudes would change in time. Actually, it wounded him so deeply that he always remembered with affection, and, if possible, rewarded with assignments and jobs, those who treated him with respect that trying first year in Washington when he was known as "The Gentleman from Pendergast." He said he always liked Harry Hopkins because "He was one of the few people who were kind to me when I first came to Washington."

Some or many senators were in no position to act like Presbyterian elders. McCarran, the cynical, archreactionary blowhard connected

with Nevada gambling and industrial interests, was affectionately
known by colleagues as the senator from Kennecott Copper. Kenneth
McKellar of Tennessee had been sponsored and propelled by Ed
Crump, the notorious Memphis political boss. A freshman senator,
sworn in when Truman was—and no eyebrows raised—A. Harry
Moore of New Jersey, henchman of Frank Hague, political boss of
Jersey City, who manufactured majorities no less ably and by no different a system from that of the sage of Kansas City. J. Hamilton
Lewis, the bewigged, pink-whiskered Democratic Whip from Illinois,
had not come to Washington without benefit of communion with
Mayor Kelly's Cook County "pols"—little noted for their strict adherence to Queensberry rules. Of Missouri's senior senator, Vice-President Garner offered this description: "If I were going to rob a train,
and I had to choose an accomplice from the United States Senate, I
would pick Bennett Clark." There were many others who came to
the Senate by votes that were impeccably correct, but who accumulated fortunes through their law firms by methods no different from
those employed by Pendergast in his Ready-Mixed Concrete Company.

This is why Americans, in a total confusion of values, sometimes go
sentimental over killers and crooks, because along with misguided,
misdirected, romantic, Robin Hood attributions, in their hearts they
feel that the morals of a Jesse James are intrinsically similar to those
of many senators, governors, and bankers. When Johnnie Lazia was
gunned down in front of his apartment building in true gangland
style, newspapers in Kansas City went maudlin. More recently, young
people all but made folk heroes of Clyde Barrow and Bonnie Parker
because of the movie idealizing them. Pendergast, however, after the
Union Station massacre and the "bloody election," became the national symbol of lawless, gangster-ridden political machines, so that
senators who observed the ordinary civilities with Truman were wary
of any sort of personal association for fear of getting tarred.

Truman's feeling of guilt accentuated his feeling of inadequacy.
Here he was, a farm boy who had never graduated from college, tread-
ing holy ground, one of the lawgivers in the greatest deliberative body
in the world. After a decade of rubbing shoulders with politicians
and businessmen he still felt awe for the chamber pictured in his
school civics books. When he came to Washington, he went to see
Helm, the correspondent for the only Kansas City newspaper that had
supported him. Helm related that Truman walked into the office one
day "grinning like two Chessie cats" and during their talk, referred to
himself as "only an humble member of the next Senate, green as grass

and ignorant as a fool about practically everything worth knowing." Harry was pulling Helm's leg, but not entirely. Helm sized him up as "a friendly, likable, warm-hearted fellow with a lot of common sense hidden under an overpowering inferiority complex." Joe Martin, the Republican leader in the House, described him at this time as "modest and unassuming," and added, "as we chatted, I could as easily have imagined him sitting on the moon as occupying the White House." Hamilton Lewis stopped at Truman's desk one afternoon to say to him, "Don't start out with an inferiority complex. For the first six months you'll wonder how you got here. After that you'll wonder how the rest of us got here." Harry's sense of inadequacy led to repeated attempts to improve his education. He had taken night classes at a Kansas City law school; he went briefly to a commercial college; he now planned to enter Georgetown University's night law school.

This idea was forgotten once he was caught up in Senate duties. His two major committee assignments were to the Appropriations and Interstate Commerce committees. Diligent worker that he was, he put in long hours at his office, on the Senate floor, making the rounds of government agencies, and studying records and documents. He quickly established a routine: He rose early as on the farm, read the newspapers, being careful not to mar the sports pages because Bess, a baseball fan, kept up with sports events. After dressing, he took a brisk walk. When he returned, he had breakfast with wife, daughter, and mother-in-law. Just before he left to walk down Connecticut Avenue, he called Messall who picked him up en route and drove him to the Senate Office Building.

One of his most important tasks was to call on department heads about work projects for Missouri, contracts, licenses, adjustments for Missouri businessmen, and job opportunities for worthy friends. The Pendergast reputation was a handicap everywhere. It took five months to get an appointment for a short social call on Roosevelt. When he got to the presidential office, several Cabinet members were sitting on sofas and chairs waiting for their appointments; none of them spoke to the senator. He sat silently, like a schoolboy, until "Pa" Watson ushered him in. Roosevelt continued to route patronage through Bennett Clark, though Clark was an unreliable supporter. Roosevelt cut him off two years later when Clark fought his Supreme Court proposition, but did not transfer all patronage to Truman.

Past students of these events, however, have taken an exaggerated view of the estrangement between Pendergast and the New Deal, influenced as they were by the subsequent federal prosecutions that ended with the Boss's disgrace. The ill will was thought to have originated at the 1932 Democratic convention when Pendergast supported Reed against Roosevelt. Some speculated that the Boss's grasp was slipping then in the unaccustomed surroundings. Private correspondence and papers available recently have thrown a different light on the relationship. Tom Pendergast understood completely that Reed had no chance in 1932, and that Roosevelt was the coming man.

There is the correspondence of Ike Dunlap, a Kansas City politico and former classmate of Roosevelt's, who was to be a member of the Missouri delegation at the convention. As early as the summer of 1931, he reported that Pendergast had told him: "If Senator Reed decides to enter the campaign, I would be required to support him. Secondly, and unless something unforeseen occurs, I will be for Governor Roosevelt, whom I greatly admire." A week later, Jim Farley came to Kansas City. He was ostentatiously welcomed by the organization. Aylward presided at a luncheon in his honor at the Muehlebach Hotel to which had been invited influential Democrats from throughout the state. From this time dated the friendship between Farley and Pendergast. Later that year, the Boss reiterated in public what he had told Dunlap in private. His position was clear as a morning glow: We will go through the motions of supporting Reed if the old geezer insists on running. Then, at the right time, we will switch to Roosevelt, who is going to be the winner. At the state convetion, the delegates to the coming national convention were not placed under a unit rule, although the Pendergast crowd dominated the convention. After the convention Dunlap again wrote Roosevelt: "Pendergast can be relied on." After it was all over, when Bennett Clark criticized Pendergast for backing Reed, Farley said, "Oh, Pendergast was all right. Was with us all the time. Reed had him hog-tied but I saw him every day and he was with us from the start."

That Pendergast had some claims on the new administration was quickly evident. The first favor he asked was a presidential pardon for Conrad Mann, the Republican boss who had cooperated so generously with Pendergast on many ventures. He had been convicted and sentenced to federal prison for violating the lottery laws. A charity frolic he conducted through the Fraternal Order of Eagles netted about $1.75 million, of which Mann pocketed about half a million. Mann, however, had loyal and understanding friends who campaigned on his behalf for a presidential pardon. His appeal was signed by the governors of 8 states, senators from 10 states, 81 congressmen, four national labor leaders, 17 judges in five states, and 15 bankers in four states. When neither the petition nor the appeal to the Supreme Court produced results, Pendergast decided to take things in hand himself. He went to Washington, and with Clark sought an interview with Roosevelt. The President would not see them. He sent word through a secretary that it was his rule never to take up personally questions of presidential pardons. Pendergast thereupon went to New York where he laid his problem before Farley. Roosevelt waited until Mann surrendered to the United States marshal in New York City and was checked in as a prisoner at the House of Correction, but then he did issue the pardon. Pendergast had some status. He also secured a number of federal appointments in Missouri; he was being cut in on some patronage.

When Truman arrived in Washington, relations with the administration had chilled primarily because of the notoriety of the Pendergast machine. One did not expect a political boss to smell of damask roses, but he was supposed to keep his more disreputable transactions discreetly covered and within bounds. His malodorous reputation notwithstanding, Pendergast was still the power in Kansas City and Missouri, and the national administration continued to deal with him —even if with head averted and at arm's length. What increased his hold was Clark's need to make peace after Milligan's defeat. Clark was concerned about his own reelection in 1938, which would be doubtful against Pendergast opposition. He therefore began to share patronage with Truman and joined in recommending Matthew Murray, who was appointed Missouri federal public works director.

Murray, a proven and uninhibited organization loyalist, was a tremendous boon to the machine. Through Murray, it controlled all WPA projects in Kansas City and the state. Federal funds made possible the new city hall, courthouse, police station, and municipal auditorium in Kansas City, and the control of a network of offices throughout the state. When Murray was sentenced to a two-year jail term for income tax evasion upon the machine's collapse at the end of the decade, it was estimated that $250 million had been spent on WPA projects in Missouri. At one time, 142,000 were on the payroll. (In contrast to his response to the plea of Spencer Salisbury, Truman gave Murray a full pardon after he became President.)

To Truman's chagrin, the Pendergast organization was racked by another scandal arising out of the 1936 election. Just as Lazia had been unable to discipline the hoodlums, Pendergast could not convert a rowdy association of squabbling grafters into a decorous assemblage of frock-coated vestrymen. After his downfall, some said that it was all due to his mania for racetrack gambling. In one year alone he bet $2 million and lost $600,000. The horses were responsible for his voracious greed for more and more money—and drove him, like a drug addict, to his ill-fated plot for the three-quarter-million-dollar bribe from the insurance companies. This is like ascribing the violent death of a man who habitually drove his car at breakneck speeds to his not having wiped the windshield carefully the fatal day. If Pendergast had not been tripped up by the bribe money, he would have been tripped up by something else. Belabored by reformers and the press at home, and harassed by federal investigators and prosecutors, the spoilsmen could no longer operate in New Deal America the way they had been trained to function in an earlier day. The organization was in desperate need of revising its techniques and habits. The ringleader, however, was not only incapable of putting through a reform; he did not even understand the need for it.

In truth, Pendergast had not only become more arrogant with the years; he was in a state of physical disintegration. He had gone with his wife to Europe on one of his regular transatlantic jaunts in the spring after collecting the third installment of his bribe. When he returned in June, he installed himself in his customary palatial suite at the Waldorf-Astoria in New York, and arranged to commute to Philadelphia to take charge of the Missouri delegation at the Democratic national convention. Messall, who had accompanied Truman on his visit to the suite the year before, described it as "a madhouse with ticker tape machines bringing him race-track news and results and the place was filled with jockeys and bookies. He told us that some jockeys had doublecrossed him with wrong tips and he almost killed a few of them." The Boss looked haggard and ill and complained of stomach pains when Truman brought him back to the Waldorf the first day of the convention. The doctors diagnosed it as coronary thrombosis and ordered a complete rest for six months. In late August, he was rushed to Roosevelt Hospital for an emergency operation to remove an intestinal obstruction. This required the closing of his rectum, and the use of a tube in his side for the rest of his life. "If he had died there in New York," Truman said, "he would be remembered as the greatest boss this country ever had."

In the August primary the opposing gubernatorial candidate, William Hirth, head of the Missouri Farmers Association, was making the freeing of the impounded insurance funds a major issue of the campaign. Although the city shook with the charges, the Pendergast machine cranked out by reflex action its immense ghost votes in both the primary and November elections. Federal Attorney Milligan was gathering evidence and preparing his cases. For two years thereafter, a steady stream of people were indicted for conspiracy; 259 defendants were convicted; total fines exceeded $60,000; and the more serious offenders were sent to jail for terms ranging up to four years. Throughout the drawn-out ordeal, the organization looked after its own. It provided bail money, legal staff, and other relief. Since Milligan was unable to implicate Pendergast or any other major figure in the election chicanery, it seemed at the time that it would all blow over with nothing substantially changed and the machine intrinsically unhurt.

Despite the raucous noises from the home team, Truman was establishing himself in his senatorial position. The ability to get along manifested itself in his new surroundings. Messall recalled: "He made friends easily, was going out of his way to do favors for others, and you couldn't help but like his smiling, friendly manner. This was not put on; he was that way with every one. I never heard him say a cross word to his staff, and that's a real test." After a while, Borah, Vandenberg, Hayden, Barkley, and other notables were treating him like a member of the clan; he became friendly with some of the freshmen senators, Schwellenbach of Washington, Minton of Indiana, Hatch of New Mexico, O'Mahoney of Wyoming. He was invited by Vice-President Garner to strike a blow for liberty from the private stock in his cabinet. (When the "Board of Education" gathered in his offices, "Cactus Jack" would look at the clock and exclaim with passion, "Somewhere it's twelve o'clock. It's time to strike a blow for liberty!") Occasionally, he participated in poker sessions. His game, according to some, lacked finesse. Merriman Smith, the United Press correspondent, thought he was inclined to recklessness when playing with friends. Messall said the same thing about his driving: "He always ignored speed limits and he passed cars on curves and hills. You sat there praying you wouldn't get killed."

On the legislative side, he became known in his first term as hardworking, conscientious, shrewd, a dependable supporter of New Deal measures, but an undistinguished senator, with little color or originality—a friendly, likable, grinning drudge. He rarely spoke, and when he did, his remarks appeared more weighty on the pages of the *Congressional Record* than in the presentation, and commanded more attention after he became President than at the time. Messall said: "I used to feel sorry for him. Every time he had to make a speech he'd tell me, 'I can't do it.' He just couldn't talk worth a damn in front of people and had to steel himself to open his mouth. When he finally spoke, he never did so extemporaneously but always read prepared statements." When Pathé News sent a crew to his office to record a speech, there was one retake after another, with the cameraman shouting angrily, "Senator, speak up!" On leaving, the sound man grumbled disgustedly in Truman's presence, "He ain't no Roosevelt."

His accomplishments were with the Interstate Commerce Committee where he helped sponsor the Civil Aeronautics Act of 1938 and the Transportation Act of 1940. Regulation of air carriers had been on the congressional agenda for several years. Roosevelt had canceled air mail contracts in February, 1934, after revelations of fraud, prodigality, and collusion in their letting during the Hoover administration. In June, air deliveries were returned to private companies in the Air Mail Act, which stipulated closer controls in awarding of contracts. Jurisdictional conflict between the ICC and the Post Office Department, and a growing interest in the importance of civil aviation for military air power, led to a recommendation by an interdepartmental committee appointed by the President in 1938 for the creation of a separate commission to regulate all phases of aeronautics.

Truman and Warren Austin conducted the hearings of a subcommittee when the chairman absented himself and wrote into the bill, sponsored by Pat McCarran, the administration recommendation of a separate commission headed by an independent administrative director. Once the separate commission and the air safety code had been agreed to, the only major item in dispute was who was to exercise control over the commission, Congress or the President. An independent commission boss, under presidential authority, was important to Roosevelt because the Supreme Court had disallowed his attempt to remove a member of the Federal Trade Commission whose policies differed from his own on the grounds that a commissioner exercised quasi-legislative functions. The aeronautics bill adjusted to the court's argument by vesting the administrator with ostensibly only executive functions.

McCarran, who wanted to keep his fingers in the forthcoming commission, pulled a fast one when the bill was reported out. He took it off the calendar, reintroduced it as a new bill, and had the Vice-President refer it to the Commerce Committee instead of the Interstate Commerce Committee where it originated. By this maneuver, he pushed Truman out when the conference committee was named to meet with representatives of the House. Bennett Clark shouted at

Garner and forced the inclusion of Truman, to enable him, working with Congressman Clarence Lea, the House sponsor, to get the original provision reinstated. "I kept the bill as the President wanted it," said Truman.

On the Transportation Act—Truman's major independent contribution—he spent many hours during three and a half years. It was a secondary legislative engagement whose course was determined by the changing national temper. Truman entered the Senate in an off-year election in which the administration in power increased its majorities in both houses. Precedents were shattered. Never in the history of the Republican party had its percentage fallen so low. In the Senate, the Democrats had 69 seats, better than 70 percent of the total. "This is our hour," Harry Hopkins exulted. The torment and humiliations that had accumulated for five years had been turned into a mighty engine of social ferment and populist aspiration. This Congress had members who demanded that Roosevelt proceed with less weaving, that he act more radically to stop the national paralysis. Fearful of getting outflanked on the left while losing the support of business, Roosevelt extricated himself from the conflicting pressures by pushing into "The Second Hundred Days" after the Supreme Court struck down the NRA.

It was in the interval of Rooseveltian indecision, when despite rebuffs from the conservative press he was still maneuvering to hold business support, that Senator Burton K. Wheeler of Montana introduced a resolution in the Senate to investigate railroad finances. Wheeler, the prosecutor of Teapot Dome fame, and one of the most impressive of the old liberals, was chairman of the Interstate Commerce Committee at this time when railroads, either in or on the verge of bankruptcy, were angling for Reconstruction Finance Corporation funds. Since the resolution was not administration-sponsored it was a year before the Senate voted a small budget for the investigation that Wheeler, heading a subcommittee, initiated in December, 1936. He did not name Truman to the subcommittee, but permitted him, because of Truman's interest, to sit in at the hearings. When one of the Democratic members withdrew, Truman replaced him. Then, in the spring of 1937, Wheeler and other subcommittee members became embroiled in the fight against Roosevelt's Supreme Court reform and attended few hearings. To maintain the status of the investigation, Wheeler appointed Truman vice-chairman of the subcommittee, and he presided thereafter.

The hearings did not attract much attention. For two years, railroad representatives argued abstruse questions of railroad financing and engaged in lengthy, learned exchanges with committee counsel. The plodding, long-drawn-out investigation concluded with the introduction of the unexceptional Wheeler-Truman bill. After it was watered down by the House the resultant conference bill, under the title Transportation Act of 1940, was signed by Roosevelt in October. The Senate committee's counsel, Max Lowenthal, characterized the Wheeler-Truman bill as "to a large extent a codification of earlier statutes." The act also embodied, in part, previous agreed-upon collective bargaining programs and procedures that would protect workers' existing conditions and rights as a prerequisite for approval of consolidations.

While neither the investigation nor the legislation won laurels for Truman, the experience was of decisive importance for his career on two counts. First, he established cordial, and what shortly proved to be indispensable, relations with the rail brotherhoods. The union chiefs were grateful for his and Wheeler's inclusion of their protective agreements into the government bill. Wheeler had long been intimately associated with the brotherhood officers, and these officers viewed Truman as a friend of their friend. This was validated after the railroads announced a wage cut for all employees in the wake of the 1937 recession. The President appointed an emergency board to stave off a strike; at the union's request, Wheeler cut his vacation short and returned to Washington to appear before the board, accompanied by Truman. Both of them gave effective testimony, as experts on railroad matters, against the wage cut. This was bread cast upon the waters found again when needed.

Second, his arduous labors brought Truman to a new milieu and acquaintanceships that enabled him to perfect his investigatory technique and create the image of the fair-minded, down-to-earth, unafraid, middle-of-the-road public servant that was to carry him to national prominence in his next term. Truman was in close contact with Max Lowenthal, an ideological New Dealer who had years of experience and friendships with union officials behind him. He was the de facto planner of the committee work and the author of the transportation bill. His special training as legal advocate and adviser to labor bosses, and later as technician for congressional committees, predisposed him to concentrate on the mechanics of legislation and government. He discerned and appreciated qualities in Truman that became apparent to others only later. He had heard, of course, the stories about Pendergast's office boy. He was consequently disturbed when, coincidental with Truman's taking charge, the hearings were to consider the affairs of the Missouri Pacific Railroad. He pointed out to Truman that some things would come out in the investigation that might embarrass him at home. Truman told him not to worry.

Lowenthal was impressed with the man's independence and with the businesslike, judicial manner in which he conducted the examinations. One day he asked him whether he would like to see his friend, Justice Louis D. Brandeis. The eighty-year old justice, an institution by this time, held open house weekly for his friends. On their way to Brandeis's apartment, Truman said, "You know, I'm not accustomed to meeting people like that." He went a number of times and recalled, "The old man would back me into a corner while he talked transportation to me. He was very much against the control of financial credit —hipped on a few insurance companies controlling too much of the country's credit."

It was at this period that Truman blossomed out with several startling speeches on the Senate floor, written in whole or in part by Lowenthal. In December, 1937, he informed the senators that the railroad investigations had revealed that great Wall Street law firms resorted "to tricks that would make an ambulance chaser in a coroner's court blush with shame"; "one of the difficulties as I see it is that we worship money instead of honor"; "No one considers Carnegie libraries steeped in the blood of the Homestead steel workers, but they are"; "We do not remember that the Rockefeller Foundation is founded on the dead miners of the Colorado Fuel and Iron Company"; "I believe the country would be better off if we did not have sixty per cent of the assets of all insurance companies concentrated in four companies. I believe that a thousand insurance companies with four million dollars each in assets would be just a thousand times better for the country than the Metropolitan Life with four billion dollars in assets"; "If Wall Street had dealt properly with the Interstate Commerce Commission, and the Commission had cut out private conferences with Wall Street lawyers and bankers, and not let them argue their cases in private, we might have had some sort of effective regulation of the railroads. Wild greed along the lines I have been describing brought on the depression." In an earlier report, he said that Jesse James who held up a Missouri Pacific train and seized $17,000 was a piker compared to the Tin Plate millionaires who looted the Rock Island Railroad of $70 million by means of holding companies.

What shall we make of this fusillade? Had Truman become a late convert to radical reform? Hardly, for his denunciatory rhetoric lacked adequate conclusions. He left his speeches dangling in the limbo of homilies and generalized exhortations. His was the politician's, not the zealot's, passion. The hearings brought out a record of looting by holding companies, high-handed manipulations and excessive fees by bankers and their law firms, no less sensational than the evidence that led to the utility holding company battle. But the administration was not thinking of taking on another titanic struggle, and Truman resisted any suggestions of government takeovers, or other fundamental proposals. His solution rested on thoroughgoing federal regulation through the Interstate Commerce Commission; but the ICC had been in existence for fifty years; it was supposed to prevent some of these very abuses. The hearings and exposures thus had no issue. By the time he, Wheeler, and Lowenthal formulated a bill, a conservative coalition had gained the upper hand in both houses, and any legislation would have to pass its inspection.

Again, as in aeronautics, Roosevelt appointed an interdepartment, and then another joint rail labor-management committee, after which he asked Wheeler to sponsor a bill along the lines of the committees' recommendations. With that the entire nature of the rail hearings veered from an attack on rail holding company promoters and Wall Street bankers, to a solicitude for safeguarding the investments of rail stockholders. The Wheeler-Truman bill proposed ICC regulation of other forms of transportation as well as railroads in order to realize its goal of a unified regulatory system. The water carriers thereupon set up a howl that the railroads were plotting to wreck competition. Since railroad income had declined drastically as a result of highway and water competition, and the ICC had a notorious reputation as a creature of the railroad industry, the water carriers feared manipulation of their rates to accommodate railroad interests. The major farm organizations contributed to the babel because they too feared higher costs on inland waterways. To meet this opposition, the bill when finally adopted included a long list of exemptions for water carriers. Air carriers were omitted entirely since presumably they would be regulated through the separate aeronautics law.

Though Truman's performance gained him no accolades, or even much public notice, he had worked up a powerful routine that would gain recognition in due course: He had made radical speeches in Congress, demonstrating that he was a man of conscience and vision; he had made a reputation as a great friend of labor, with the rail unions confirming his credentials as a broad-gauged liberal; and, reported two newspapermen in a *Harper's Magazine* article, "a handful of industrialists and financiers began to speak of Truman as a strange sort of politician—a New Dealer who showed no desire to persecute business." Actually, he had done better than that. Samuel Dunn, editor of *Railway Age*, thanked Truman for safeguarding the position of the railroads. A canny middle-of-the-road trimmer had got hatched.

On the Senate floor, he was a reliable supporter of administration measures, remaining true blue even when many fell away on Supreme Court reform and Executive reorganization. If there were lapses from the Rooseveltian grace, he was not the first senator who had run on a platform of "Roosevelt Forever" to wander, and he proved not the last. Two issues deserve scrutiny, however. In June of his first year, the *Star* quoted him as saying that Pendergast often sent him telegrams asking him to vote this or that way, but that he paid no attention: "I don't follow his advice on legislation. I vote the way I believe Missourians as a whole would want me to vote." Legislators and newspapermen took the statement to be self-serving humbug. Pendergast could not care less how Truman voted on the earthshaking questions of the day. He was interested in receiving appointments and grants-in-aid, and blocking hostile moves against himself and his friends. Messall could not recall Pendergast sending Truman any telegrams. "In fact, he never even sent the Senator a single letter on legislation. His demands were much more insignificant. He would tear off a scrap of paper from a grocery bag and scribble a note in red pencil asking Truman for a favor."

In 1937 he called Truman on the vote for Senate majority leader. Joseph T. Robinson had died, and a tug-of-war ensued between Roosevelt and Garner as to the replacement. Roosevelt wanted Barkley; Garner was lining up the conservative bloc for Pat Harrison. Truman was operating. As Barkley related it, "I knew the vote was going to be awfully close in the caucus. When the fight began I ascertained that Harry Truman would vote for me. But he came to me before the vote and said that homestate pressure on him was so great that he wanted to be relieved of his promise to me. I let him off the hook." Homestate pressure actually developed from another quarter. The White House alerted Farley, who asked Pendergast to line up Harry on the right side. Pendergast then called Truman, told him about the request, and asked him if he wouldn't vote for Barkley.

> I can't do it, Tom, and I'll tell you why. I've given my word to Pat Harrison.

And Pendergast said that it was all right, that it didn't make a helluva lot of difference to him, but that the White House had called him and asked him to get me on the phone and he said he would do it.

The incident, often cited to show Truman's independence, raises some questions. Why did he line up with the conservative bloc to vote for a Mississippi reactionary against the administration candidate? Keeping one's pledged word is noble, but why did he give that pledge at all? Circumstances indicate that he wanted to demonstrate dramatically to the White House that he would not be taken for granted any longer, that he expected the customary courtesies and returns due a faithful supporter. "I'm tired of having the President treat me like an office boy," he told his associates. If to drive this lesson home he had to cross over to the anti–New Deal camp, that was no more to be criticized than striking a blow for liberty with Jack Garner. The politics of principle had not been taught at the Pendergast Institute, nor was it a required course at the United States Senate.

The other issue related to the Public Utilities Holding Company bill that agitated the legislators shortly after Truman entered the Senate. Roosevelt's message to Congress in March, 1935, called for the breakup of the holding companies. In the words of William Leuchtenburg, the historian, "He shared the popular outrage at the electric power octupuses which had fleeced the consumer, corrupted legislatures, and by their elusive operations, evaded state regulations." The dissolution of these artifacts of bankers and stock promoters, long a favorite target of Brandeis reformers, took on urgency as a result of financial scandals. Thousands lost their savings when Samuel Insull's utilities empire collapsed, revealing the idolized mogul as a common swindler. The Wheeler-Rayburn bill, written by the Corcoran-Cohen team, empowered the Securities and Exchange Commission to simplify and reorder the holding company system; and provided, in what became known as the death-sentence clause, that after January 1, 1940, the SEC could order the dissolution of holding companies that failed to show economic justification for their existence.

The utilities launched a savage and expensively mounted lobbying, propaganda, and press campaign that moved, like an electric current, through the country. Wall Street's prominent attorneys and financiers, Wendell Willkie, John W. Davis, John Foster Dulles, the Whitneys, Howard Hopson, appeared at congressional hearings and on public platforms to predict that the bill would result in nationalization of the power industry and paralysis of the economy.

In his *Memoirs*, Truman made a big proposition of his intrepid stand against the power interests in the face of enormous pressures put upon him. According to him, he became the target of the opposition within three months of the time he had taken his seat in the Senate, since he was a member of the Interstate Commerce Committee that was sponsoring the bill; and representatives of the public utilities lobby descended upon him urging that he vote against the bill. But Truman was steadfast in his opposition to the utilities lobbyists because, as he told them, he was a convinced opponent of the monopolistic practices that were "squeezing the consumer to death," and he intended to take his stand with the proponents of the bill to control the utilities industry.

Next, in his account, lobbyists came out to Missouri to get the Democratic organization to line him up, but that effort failed, as well. Finally, a great propaganda campaign was financed and mounted by the utilities among Truman's constituents, many of whom held utilities securities. Truman related that he was swamped with letters and telegrams urging him to vote against the bill. But again, he said with pride, he remained true to his convictions, because he knew full well that the Wall Street "wrecking crew" was at work behind the scenes, and that this was the hidden hand responsible for placing the thirty thousand requests and demands that were piling up on his desk. Contemptuously, he burned them all, and an investigation of this propaganda barrage, aimed at many legislators besides Truman, was sponsored thereafter in the Senate.

Older biographers had assumed that Truman, in the light of his stand, had voted as a matter of course for the Wheeler-Rayburn bill. But the *Congressional Record,* curiously enough, shows that he was one of the handful of senators not voting; and in his *Memoirs*, after noting that the bill passed in the Senate by a vote of 56 to 32, he related that unfortunately he was detained on important business elsewhere and consequently did not take part in the vote. However, he had made arrangements to do so if there was any indication that the vote would be close. The explanation leaves one perplexed, since the crucial vote was not on the final bill, but on the so-called death-sentence clause, which passed the Senate by one vote!

Toward the end of his term, when he was accepted, and all was going well, his connection with Pendergast arose once more to plague him. This time, he was confronted with Roosevelt's proposed reappointment of Maurice Milligan, whose name was sent to the Senate for confirmation. The *Star* correspondent reported: "Truman returned to his office today after a trip to Kansas City and St. Louis. While in Kansas City he conferred with Thomas J. Pendergast, and they discussed the Milligan appointment. After the conference, Pendergast announced that anything to be said regarding Milligan would be by Truman on the floor of the Senate, leading to the belief that the Senator would actively oppose the reappointment." The reporter was only half right, for a White House aide had called Truman and asked him, on behalf of the President, not to invoke personal privilege in the debate on Milligan's confirmation, and Truman had said he would comply. When a senator declared the nomination of an individual to be personally objectionable, the Senate, as a rule, rejected the nominee. This time, in his effort to placate both sides, he chose the worse of both alternatives: The nomination was not blocked; and his own reputation was blackened.

When the nomination came to the Senate floor on February 15, 1938, Truman delivered a wild-swinging harangue against both Milligan and the two judges presiding over the federal court at Kansas City—Milligan had accepted emoluments in the form of fees in bankruptcy proceedings; he was morally unfit for the job; the two judges were Republicans who had axes to grind; "a Jackson County, Missouri, Democrat has as much chance of a fair trial in the Federal District Court of Western Missouri as a Jew would have in a Hitler court or a Trotsky follower before Stalin"—but having delivered himself of all this, "because the President asked for him, I have not attempted to exercise the usual prerogative to block his confirmation." The knife he plunged into his enemies had no blade.

He cast the only vote against Milligan's reappointment, and the rumors about Truman began to fly again. Judge Albert L. Reeves, one of the two federal judges, countered in a most unjudicial reply that Truman's Senate speech had been that "of a man nominated by ghost votes, elected with ghost votes, and whose speech was probably written by a ghost writer." A Fitzpatrick cartoon in the *St. Louis Post-Dispatch* was captioned, "Charlie McTruman does his Stuff." In a skit presented at the annual Gridiron Dinner of the St. Louis Advertising Club, Edgar Bergen asked Charlie McCarthy, "What is Senator Truman's relationship to Tom Pendergast?" To which Charlie answered, "I'll give you the real lowdown if it kills me. You know my relationship to Edgar Bergen. Weeell . . ." The audience guffawed.

Then a year later came the blow that destroyed Pendergast. After three years of checking and hunting down clues, federal investigators broke the insurance bribe case, and in April, 1939, indictments for income tax evasion were handed down against Pendergast and O'Malley; indictments followed of Otto Higgins, the police chief, John Pryor, Pendergast's partner in the construction business, Matthew Murray, the WPA director, and Charles Corallo, Lazia's successor as syndicate overseer. McElroy, the city manager, resigned as soon as the indictments came in, took to a wheelchair, and shortly died of a stroke. As investigators worked to disentangle his labyrinthine bookkeeping, a $20 million deficit was found in claims and accounts, $11 million of sinking-fund bonds had been diverted to other uses, other bond funds had been used to meet inflated payrolls, and the delinquent tax bill was estimated at another $10 million. With new sensations and scandals reported daily by the press, the Pendergast ship of state started to fall apart. To a reporter who informed Truman of the initial indictment, he said, "I am sorry to hear it. I know nothing about the details, nor why the indictment was voted. Tom Pendergast has always been my friend and I don't desert a sinking ship." Truman's term had another year and a half to run, but it looked as if decisions were out of his hands, and he was fated to go down with the wreckage.

6

A Cockeyed
Horatio Alger
Story

Truman's prospects looked grim at the beginning of 1940. Governor Lloyd Stark was going to run for his Senate seat with Roosevelt's unofficial blessing. The St. Louis Dickman-Hannegan machine, the state's major organization, had declared for Stark; his prestige was enormous as a result of his leadership in destroying Pendergast; he was excellently situated to make full use of his advantages since he controlled the state apparatus. He was also a millionaire, owner of a large nursery, married to an heiress, daughter of the St. Louis Transit Lines president. Every known politician in the state had received at some time a complimentary package of Stark's Delicious Apples. If all this was not more than sufficient, he was active in American Legion politics, had farm support, and was being hailed by the newspapers as the "Tom Dewey of Missouri." To all appearances, he was the coming man. Truman had written him a blistering letter when he declared for his Senate seat, reminding him that he, Truman, was responsible for his political career. But that did not alter the facts of 1940, nor induce Stark to withdraw. Roosevelt let Truman know that he was willing to appoint him to the Interstate Commerce Commission. Truman was determined to make a fight for vindication and reelection. "I sent him word that I would run if I only got one vote—mine."

Truman asked thirty friends to attend a meeting at the Statler Hotel in St. Louis. Only a few showed up, and those told him he did not have a chance. Messall said, "Truman looked stunned." He addressed the Democratic state convention meeting in St. Louis, but his reception was tepid and few delegates dropped in to see him at his complimentary Statler suite. To add to his misfortunes, he lacked organization and finances. He said to Harry Woodring, Roosevelt's Secretary of War, "I'm whipped." Woodring offered him a ride back to Washington on his plane. Messall said that Truman was crying when he left St. Louis.

Messall went on to Kansas City to see Pendergast's nephew, Jim Pendergast, who was trying to hold the organization together. "I won't keep you long," Messall said to him. "I just came from St. Louis. I want to know if Harry Truman files, will you support him?" Pendergast answered, "Tell Harry that if he only gets two votes, he will get my vote and my wife's vote." That was something. The Pendergast organization could not deliver its majorities of the past, but remnants of the organization and influence were still there. Messall then quit his job as Truman's secretary—required under the Hatch Act—to become campaign chairman. He rented an old building in Sedalia for campaign headquarters, and got the owners of the Ambassador Office Building in St. Louis to donate two floors of furnished offices for a subsidiary headquarters; he had helped them get RFC refinancing. He also sent out a fund appeal to all business firms and individuals that Truman had helped. Enough came in for handbills and posters, but Messall was strapped for funds until business friends around the state came through with sizable donations. Bernard Baruch, who contributed at the request of Byrnes and Clark, wrote: "After the election [Truman] came up to my apartment in the Carlton Hotel with Bennett Clark to thank me for my help. He told me that it had been the roughest fight he had ever waged, and that he would never forget my support."

Again, as in 1934, Truman was aided by the presence of a third candidate in the field, Maurice Milligan. It has been suggested that Truman himself inveigled Milligan into the race in order to split the anti-Pendergast vote. Milligan said, "When some of Truman's own friends asked me to run, I took that as positive assurance of the then Senator's desire to stay out of the race. How could a Pendergast man get anywhere without a Pendergast?" Whatever and whoever induced him to go in—and Bennett Clark originally was encouraging him—

he was in, and the Pendergast foes now had to choose between two candidates.

Truman and Messall worked up a campaign program that antici-pated the strategy mapped out by Clark Clifford eight years later. Truman had learned a lot from Pendergast and from his Senate co-workers. He had learned not only about deals, alliances, deceptive feints, adroit maneuvers, the traffic of favors for support; he had learned also about enunciating social issues and manipulating social blocs. He opened his campaign on June 15 with a rally in Sedalia, at which his friend Senator Schwellenbach was present to lend a help-ing hand. Schwellenbach struck the keynote that was doing duty in dozens of campaigns around the country: "Let me say that there has been no more loyal or better friend of President Roosevelt in the United States than Harry Truman." Then, in an aside meant to con-vey a humorous note, he added, "I need not tell you that Harry Tru-man is not an orator. He can demonstrate that for himself."

Stumble in his diction though he did, Truman managed, with the help of the newspapers, to get across a message. With his eighty-eight-year-old mother, who had never hauled down the Confederate flag, sitting on the platform, Harry appealed to the state's quarter mil-lion Negroes with the theme of the brotherhood of all men before law, and pointed proudly to his voting record on civil rights. His speech did not ignite the audience, or the newspaper readers the next day—they were somewhat distracted by accounts from abroad that Nazi troops had entered Paris—but the theme had been struck, and he kept pecking away at it. A Negro section was set up, headed by Dr. William J. Thompkins of Kansas City, an old-time Negro ally of Pendergast, appointed by Roosevelt as registrar of deeds for the Dis-trict of Columbia. A month later, Truman spoke before the National Negro Democratic Association in Chicago, and Schwellenbach had the speech inserted in the *Congressional Record* so that Truman could mail out the material under his franking privilege. He said in Chicago that he did not favor social equality: "The Negro himself knows better than that, and the highest type of Negro leaders say quite frankly that they prefer the society of their own people," but the Negro was entitled to justice, and the Roosevelt administration had done more "to give the Negro equal legal, economic and cultural rights than has ever been done before."

Two things should be noted about Truman's bid for the Negro vote. He was not pioneering. Arthur Schlesinger, Jr., pointed out in his history of the Roosevelt era, "The first Democratic boss to woo and win the Negro electorate was Tom Pendergast." Roy Wilkins, NAACP head, wrote similarly, "Truman was politically astute on the race question before he ever came to Washington, because the Pendergast machine was politically astute." The other thing to be noted is that this kind of declaration, which would ensure a speaker's getting hooted off the public platform today, passed as a resounding commitment of friendship and liberal dedication at the time.

Truman also courted the Jews. It was widely known that his partner in the long-defunct haberdashery business was a Jew. David Berenstein, a well-known Zionist in St. Louis, was prominent on his campaign committee. A special division was set up to concentrate on veterans, and much was made of Truman's war record, his services in the National Guard, and his vote in the Senate to advance the date of payment for the soldiers' bonus. The major achievement, however, was the corraling of the workingmen's vote, and Truman owed his ability to negotiate this to his friendship with Burton Wheeler and the rail brotherhood heads. Lowenthal got a contribution from A. F. Whitney, president of the Trainmen, and Whitney and Alvanley Johnston, president of the Rail Engineers, set up labor committees for Truman in all major terminals in the state. Ten days before the primary a special Truman edition of *Labor*, the joint publication of all rail unions, was issued. A half-million copies were distributed containing encomiums from fellow senators, and calling attention to his friend-of-labor record, his adherence to the New Deal, his support for the farmer. Rail union backing led to endorsement from William Green, president of the American Federation of Labor, who requested the secretary of the Missouri state organization to notify all affiliates of Truman's favorable labor record.

The basics of the campaign were similar to the fight in 1934. There were three contestants all clinging to Roosevelt's coattails. Since they were all dedicated and unswerving friends of the workingman, the farmer, the veteran, the underdog, etc., the debate inevitably turned, as before, to Pendergast and his doings, with the candidates making unflattering personal characterizations of their opponents. Truman said later that it was "the bitterest and dirtiest fight" he had ever been in. Considering that he was a veteran of two free-for-alls in Jackson County and of the 1934 state campaign, he was unquestionably qualified to make an appraisal. "Tom Pendergast's office boy" was now referred to as "Tom Pendergast's stooge." Stark, stung by the accusation of twisting the arms of state employees, charged that Truman had a slush fund squeezed from unwilling contractors. Truman countered by wanting to know, "How clean are the hands of Governor Stark as to slush funds? Who put the lug on state employees?"

It helped Truman's campaign that his two opponents were not political geniuses. Milligan wore out his welcome quickly. There was a big crowd at his opening rally waiting to greet the great prosecutor who had sent Pendergast to jail. They were looking for a masterful performance by a courtroom Demosthenes. Instead, they were confronted with a shouting, angry-looking, thin-lipped school superintendent, who conducted himself as if he had an appointment from Jehovah to set Missouri straight. His priggish behavior alienated audiences; when added to his lack of institutional backing, it forced him into last place. At the beginning of the campaign, the *St. Louis Post-Dispatch* ran a Fitzpatrick cartoon that showed two huge trucks, one labeled Milligan, the other Stark, in a head-on crash with Truman's little cart, captioned, "No place for a kiddycar." But the kiddycar had outdistanced one of the trucks.

The lantern-jawed, humorless, and arrogant Stark had a different trouble. He was getting delusions of grandeur. He had been a frequent guest on Roosevelt's presidential yacht, had been favored with the Roosevelt charm, and now had joined the pathetic band of hopefuls who each thought Roosevelt wanted him as his running mate. He set up a Stark for Vice-President headquarters in Chicago, passed out Stark Delicious Apples to the Democratic national convention delegates, had a floor manager bustling about, and his adherents staged the customary demonstration. But his bubble burst when Roosevelt via Hopkins passed the word that Wallace was to be the man. (Truman revenged himself on Roosevelt for neglecting him by helping to line up 28½ of Missouri's 30 votes for William Bankhead; FDR survived the blow.) The spectacle of Stark running for both Vice-President and United States senator irked as well as amused Missouri newspapermen and politicians; the St. Louis bosses, who had ostensibly declared for Stark, continued to sit on their hands, waiting to see whether he would sober down and talk business with them. Stark needed an alliance with them, but he was too self-confident to realize it.

In the final stage of the campaign, two individuals declared for Truman, and their support was decisive. Bennett Clark had been sitting on the fence. His preference had been for Milligan, but Milligan was clearly out of the running. As for Stark, Clark did not relish having this overbearing egotist as his fellow senator from Missouri. Truman, it now appeared, had a reasonable chance, and Truman was a known quantity, a politico you could deal with. Clark calculated the facts and figures and decided to add his weight to Truman's candidacy. He checked in at the Mayfair Hotel in St. Louis, got on the phone calling people throughout the state, and made several personal appearances on Truman's behalf. In what was probably a related move, Hannegan switched support to Truman, and Harry was in again—this time, by a hair. But whatever the size of the plurality, he was the Democratic nominee, and again, as in 1934, this was tantamount to election in November.

The tiny plurality should not minimize the major achievement of a Pendergast-tagged and a Pendergast-smeared candidate winning the nomination in the teeth of an anti-Pendergast gale. Truman proved that despite his wretched public speaking and pedestrian appearance, he was a powerful, resourceful candidate. His folksy, somewhat corny manner, went over well with many people. There was something about him that stirred up sympathetic waves; here was another average man like themselves, with no pretensions to special attainments or superior wisdom, trying to do the best he could in a less than perfect world. He did not inspire people because they thought he was better than they were; he drew them because they thought he was like them. To this extent, the similarity to Calvin Coolidge held; he was also liked in his day because he said what could be heard in every garage and barbershop. Not only Truman's folksiness but, his cockiness went over well. If he did his share of hand-wringing and despairing, he kept it in a small circle; in public, he maintained an air of confidence and aplomb, his friendly grin intact, while keeping up the frenetic pace of traveling, speechifying, shaking hands. Furthermore, the maneuvers of this campaign had a different quality from those of the previous one. In 1934, it was Pendergast and his coadjutors devising the plays and making the deals, working from a position of strength. In 1940, the plays and deals were planned and executed by Truman and his friends, working from a position of weakness.

The 1948 victory has been more publicized, but the campaign in 1940 is more memorable. After all, a President, even when his standing has fallen as low as had Truman's in 1948, commands national attention with every move he makes and every statement he utters; as the beneficiary of the resources of his office and of his party, he imposes his presence on the public; he has an entourage of advisers, organizers, planners, speech writers, to lighten his burdens and provide the appearance of a powerhouse of purposeful activity; his campaign, regardless of outcome, is history in the making. In 1940, Harry was alone, with only a small band of personal friends and allies scrounging for funds and pushing out mailings, to enable him to rush around the state shaking hands. Most thought his chances were nil in 1948 as well, but the eyes of a nation were upon him. In 1940, it looked hopeless, and aside from the small contingent of the faithful, who cared? Truman revealed in these difficult circumstances what were possibly his outstanding strengths: stamina and a fighting heart.

His chairmanship of the Special Committee to Investigate the National Defense Program, the Truman Committee, was the predominant achievement of his second term. It lifted him to national prominence. He became concerned with defense mobilization because of complaints from Missouri contractors that the big boys were gobbling up all the orders; other correspondents wrote about waste in the construction of Fort Leonard Wood in Pulaski County, Missouri. He inspected Fort Wood and a number of other defense projects, talked to contractors, and was preparing to make a speech in the Senate. He discussed this with Bill Helm, who advised him instead to call for an investigating committee. Helm pointed out that as the introducer of the resolution, he would be the committee's chairman, with the power of the Senate behind long-term investigations, whereas a speech would be only a flash in the pan.

Truman took the advice. He presented on February 10, 1941, what became later the well-known resolution (S. Res. 71) to set up a committee to investigate the status of the defense program and requested $25,000 for expenses. The resolution was eventually referred to James Byrnes's committee on audit and control. It stirred no great interest. It was figured that Truman wanted some additional work for Missouri contractors and a little publicity for himself—all he may have had in mind at first. When Byrnes asked him why he had introduced his resolution, Truman told him Missouri contractors were complaining that big companies were getting all the construction contracts, and that it would be a good thing to put a little fire under the War Department. "I know there isn't a chance in the world of your reporting it out. But if you did, I wouldn't conduct the investigation in a way that would hurt defense. You could count on me for that." He sent Roosevelt a memorandum later assuring him that the committee would be 100 percent behind the administration.

A few weeks earlier Eugene Cox, an anti-labor and anti-Roosevelt congressman from Georgia, had introduced a resolution in the House to investigate defense spending. Roosevelt had told Byrnes that he was concerned. "I can fix that by putting the investigation into friendly hands," Byrnes promised the President. Under its rules, he explained, the House took time to authorize an investigation; the Senate could act in hours. If the Senate authorized an investigation, the House would probably drop the matter. Roosevelt approved Truman as committee chairman; Byrnes went over to the Senate chamber when only sixteen senators were present, secured unanimous consent to bring up Truman's resolution, and won its passage without debate. As anticipated, the House then dropped Cox's proposal. Extensive investigations were not contemplated since the budget was reduced to $15,000. To guarantee party regularity, committee membership called for five Democrats and two Republicans. Outside of Tom Connally, who was selected to make sure the committee would not take off in unwanted directions, members were all relatively new senators.

Truman now displayed his skill as an organizer of a large undertaking. On the recommendation of Attorney General Robert Jackson, whose advice he solicited, he hired Hugh Fulton for committee counsel. Fulton was a beefy, balding specimen standing over six feet, with an avoirdupois in excess of 15 stone. He had a squeaky voice, wore a derby, and looked like a dissipated cherub, but there was more to him than beam and tonnage. His appearance belied his character—hard-driving, energetic, ambitious, and smart. In his mid-thirties, he had built a reputation by sending Howard Hopson, of Associated Gas and Electric, and Warren Davis, a corrupt circuit judge, to jail. Fulton took the job after Truman assured him that the investigation would be neither a whitewash nor a witchhunt, and that the committee would stand behind him in searching out the facts. Truman lacked funds to hire investigators; he managed to borrow, as the phrase went, a number of aides from downtown agencies, so that a skeleton staff was assembled.

The adroitness and no-nonsense sensibility that had impressed Max Lowenthal in the rail hearings now were asserted in more auspicious surroundings. Truman was investigating an activity at the center of the nation's concern, one that was due to continue for a number of years. His geniality and cooperative attitude gained him the unstinted backing of the other committee members. While keeping control, he did not try, like other committee chairmen, to monopolize the decisions or the limelight. Teams headed by two committee members were assigned to conduct particular investigations; other senators were welcomed at hearings and were permitted to question witnesses;

reports were withheld until there was unanimity. If to achieve unanimity meant to water down conclusions, Truman was willing to pay
the price. Except for Connally, Carl Hatch, and Truman, the members were serving their first terms and did not have important responsibilities elsewhere. Not only could they devote their main efforts to
the Truman Committee, but their work there would gain more public
and senatorial recognition for them than their standing committee assignments.

The atmosphere was informal and friendly. A lot of the work
among members, and with government officials, was conducted in
off-the-record discussions at "Harry's Doghouse," a high-ceilinged
room adjacent to Truman's office, with black leather easy chairs and
couch, its white walls covered with autographed photographs, newspaper cartoons, and field artillery maps that had belonged to the Battery D outfit. After a draft report was agreed upon, galley proofs were
secured from the Government Printing Office, and copies then sent to
every government agency, corporation, and individual affected. All
facts that were questioned were rechecked by Fulton and the staff.
Truman conducted public hearings with decorum and judiciousness;
his forte was a show of fairness, not high jinks. If exchanges became
heated, Truman acted the impartial judge, as when John L. Lewis
was testifying:

> *Senator (Joseph) Ball:* Mr. Lewis, you are not seriously
> trying to tell the committee that any large number of
> workers in the United States don't get enough to eat? That
> is demagoguery, pure and simple, and you know it.
>
> *Mr. Lewis:* If you ask the question, I will answer it. But
> when you call me a demagogue before you give me a
> chance to reply, I hurl it back in your face, sir.
>
> *Senator Truman:* Now, Mr. Lewis, we don't stand for
> any sassy remarks to the members of this committee, and
> your rights will be protected here just the same as those of
> everybody else. I don't like that remark to a member of
> the committee.
>
> *Mr. Lewis:* Senator, did you object when the Senator
> called me a demagogue?
>
> *Senator Truman:* Yes, it works both ways. I don't think
> the Senator should have called you a demagogue.

The procedures by themselves, though adroit and judicious, would
have made the committee's accomplishments no more spectacular

than those of the railroad investigation. What lifted the Truman
Committee out of the ruck was its unique role in the unfolding Washington drama. To understand its masterful maneuvering between
competing and hostile forces, attention must be directed again to the
problems facing the nation and the administration as a result of Roosevelt's decision to turn mobilization over to business. Only thus can
the pattern of behavior and the specifics of accomplishment be
gleaned from the hearings and reports that extended for eight years
to make up 43 volumes of testimony. It is necessary to disregard the
newspaper imagery of a Fearless Fosdick cracking down impartially
on malefactors, forcing all evil-doers into the paths of justice and
patriotism, and saving, in the process, carloads of money—$15 bil-
lion according to some newspaper accounts. The lines Truman spoke
and the gestures that he made have meaning only when related
to the lines and gestures of the main players on the Washington
stage.

In the first phase of mobilization, which lasted approximately to
Pearl Harbor, when the country was preparing for, but was not yet
officially at war, the business corporations wanted to move leisurely,
with minimal alterations in their economic arrangements. They
wanted to superimpose whatever percent the war orders would prove
to be on the civilian production. There was a twofold motivation for
their policy.

Business had just emerged from a long depression in which plants
had been consistently underused. Now there was a booming market,
and the industrialists were resolved to gather in all the harvest they
could lay their hands on. Most of the munitions they produced during
this defense period were in addition to, not instead of, civilian production. This prudential policy, commended by seasoned bankers and
investors, made businessmen wary, as well, of hasty agreements to expand their facilities. Many components of the politicoeconomic outlook were still unclear; we were not yet at war; no one knew whether
Britain would hold up; the volume of war goods that would be
needed could not be adequately calculated; and they feared being
burdened with overexpanded plants in the postwar period. Pell-mell
expansion would not just pose a danger later on; it could enable in-
terlopers to disturb the existing monopolies. All this called for caution.

Since the Office of Production Management, the government
agency charged with mobilizing the economy, was run by business
representatives, that was its party line as well. The result was not

only to produce war materials short of the administrative goals, but to make a shambles of the entire conversion program. Steel, rubber, tin, nickel, copper, zinc, lead, aluminum, which were to be stockpiled for the flow of armaments, were chewed up in producing automobiles, household appliances, and luxury items. Machine tools supposed to be readied for planes and tanks were churning out civilian products. New facilities to expand capacity for steel or aluminum production were not being built.

There was a bizarre reversal of customary roles. New Dealers, liberal administrators, reformers, inclined to pacifism and suspicious of the "merchants of death," now shouted: "We are not producing enough war stuff; we are too self-indulgent." Industrialists, the mainstays of the American Legion, the National Guard, and a strong Army and Navy, were saying: "Don't let's get excited. Things are moving along satisfactorily. Leave it to us." The pacifists had turned into fire-eaters, and the "merchants of death" had become guardians of the civilian economy. Since the moneyed crowd could not present its case candidly, it resorted to duplicity, public relations pap, and "stop thief" diversions. As events showed up the discrepancy between reassuring reports and the chaotic state of conversion, a series of scandals overtook the defense agencies.

There was another reason why industry could not hurry. From May to October, 1940, took place what has been referred to as capital's sit-down strike. They would not work until they had agreement for their not inconsiderable demands on taxes and profits. Roosevelt had decided to thorw to the wolves a rapid amortization for privately financed defense plants and the repeal of the Vinson-Trammel Act limiting profits, but he insisted that this must be joined in one law to an excess profits tax. The business elders shook their heads, and their henchmen in Congress kept the bill bottled up in committee. This strike had the sympathy of defense officials and newspaper editorialists. There were no outcries against the strikers for holding up the war effort; the pressure was on Roosevelt to go along. Henry Stimson, the patron saint of the Wall Street crowd, recorded in his diary:

> If you are going to try to go to war, or to prepare for war, in a capitalist country, you have got to let business make money out of the process or business won't work, and there are a great many people in Congress who think that they can tax business out of all proportion and still have

businessmen work diligently and quickly. This is not human nature.

Roosevelt was in a quandary. He had promised that there would be no repetition of the First World War saturnalia, that the defense program would not raise a new crop of millionaires. He wanted to be able to say in the coming election campaign that he had closed the door to unconscionable profiteering. Was there to be another historic clash between Roosevelt and business? Not really. The stuffing had gone out of the New Deal. It was now mainly posturing and pretense. Daniel Bell, head of the Bureau of the Budget, reported to Morgenthau that Roosevelt "told me that we must have an excess profits bill this session. I then told him that apparently the representatives of the Ways and Means Committee and the Senate Finance Committee were thinking of a face-saving bill, and not one that will really get the revenue on an equitable basis. The President then said that he did not want this bill to get bogged down because of differences between the Treasury experts and the Congressional experts. The main thing now is to get a bill through and then straighten it out next January. He said even the amount of revenue is not so important this time."

Morgenthau decided to bring the controversy to a head when he visited Hyde Park on August 5. "I can boil down what happened yesterday," he reported to his staff on his return, "inside of the room and under the robes. I got on the President's back porch and he says, 'I can tell you very simply how I feel. I want a tax bill; I want one damned quick; I don't care what is in it; I don't want to know. The contracts are being held up and I want a tax bill." He got his tax bill, and business got its pound of flesh.

The delays in defense production, the scandals, the uproar, the chaos, the contradictory reports and instructions, the feuding between agencies, all led to repeated and pointed criticism of the administration, climaxed by the demand that one man be placed in full charge of the production effort. This was the only way, it was argued, to stop wasting the country's military potential, to get the planes, tanks, guns, moving out of the factories in the quantities called for and in the time allotted.

Some joined in this crusade because they honestly believed that centralization would bring order out of disorder as surely as the Lord had brought the earth and the heavens out of the darkness and void.

They had no comprehension that differences over methods of doing things reflected conflicting interests whose resolution depended on political power balances, not on assertions of will or on charts detailing the line of command. There was no lack of bungling and miscalculation; the major disorders, however, were not due to bureaucratic stupidity, or sloppy administrative arrangements, but to the limitations inherent in organizing a capitalist economy for war under the direction of those at one with the empires of finance and industry.

Not all were disinterested in the crusade for a production czar. For many it was a handy stick to belabor the man in the White House they despised. A defense czar would satisfy their urge to drive New Dealers out, and to rid defense of unwanted supervision. When they carved up Sidney Hillman like a holiday bird, it could be discerned that their homicidal impulses had passed beyond the point of mere calculation. Hillman was the president of the men's clothing union, on leave. Though formally a codirector of the Office of Production Management with William S. Knudsen, president of General Motors, he had been relegated by the dollar-a-year men to labor affairs exclusively, and his assignment was seen as the recruiting and disciplining of the labor battalions. He had far more native ability, and a far more variegated experience, than the associates who patronized him. He was personally pleasant enough, with the manner and appearance of an accountant, although some may have found it objectionable that he was a Jew, had been born in Russia, and spoke with an accent. A pliant organization man, he had entered the defense establishment in the spirit of a soap manufacturer elevated to the House of Lords, determined to demonstrate to the gentry his reliability and loyalty. He had gone so far as to join with the corporation lawyers and Army brass to demand that troops be called out to break the strike of the North American Aircraft workers. So stern a taskmaster as Stimson wrote in his diary, "We have all tried Sidney Hillman out and felt pretty well satisfied with him." Yet the press defamation of him never stopped until Roosevelt decided that Hillman was no longer of use. No matter how often Hillman bent the knee, he was still a union official and New Dealer, and had to be axed.

The bellowing for an all-powerful defense boss left Roosevelt cold. In one of his more scintillating press conferences, he ridiculed the idea that the country's fate depended on making some one man a combination Czar, Poohbah, or Akhoond of Swat. He was aware that an economic chieftain could usurp his domestic power. As it was, the building of a defense establishment under business aegis had shifted the balance in his disfavor. To turn over to the same faction full control would be equivalent to a semiabdication. As explained in the official Bureau of the Budget history: "The issue in large measure was who was going to run the defense program."

The OPM lumbered along for eight months, absorbing the criticisms for scandals and foot-dragging. When in August it threatened to come apart, Roosevelt patched up the machinery by creating the Supply Priorities and Allocation Board, which was supposed to assign priorities and allocate resources between military, lend-lease, and civilian needs, with the OPM continuing as an operating agency under the policies set by the new board. The SPAB-OPM combination, despite its unwieldiness, set up guidelines for distributing scarce materials and made preparations for expanding metal production goals. It would have huffed and puffed up the hill for another year, if not longer, except for Pearl Harbor, which instantaneously, and to the relief of Stimson and others, brought the country into war against both the Mikado and Hitler. (Stimson despaired of mobilizing the nation until the country was at war.)

Roosevelt could no longer resist the cry for a single production director. He named Donald Nelson, who had been in charge of purchasing for the OPM and the executive head of the short-lived SPAB, as director of the newly created War Production Board, with authority to write the Executive order that established his administration. At last we had a production czar. Now all would be well. Yet within ten months, Byrnes, at the President's request, resigned from the Supreme Court to become director of economic stabilization, or, as the press christened him, Assistant President; a superczar had been appointed to oversee the deflated czar, and WPB became but another barony in the defense kingdom. True, Nelson's board presided in the period when American industry was performing prodigies of production. But this was due to America's unparalleled industrial plant, to her managerial and engineering cadre second to none, and to the fact that after Pearl Harbor, industry plunged headlong into war production. The achievements had little to do with the creation of the WPB and the appointment of a so-called czar. True, also, that Nelson brought some order into the madhouse of priorities and allocations—only after the economy was virtually paralyzed when the military, without plan or study of feasibility, hurled $100 billion of contracts on the economy on top of a previous commitment of $20 billion in the first six months of 1942. The Controlled Materials Plan was put through, however, by haggling and accommodation, if not capitulation, to the Army-Navy Munitions Board, not by a czar issuing orders.

It was an improvident way, and, as later experience proved, a dangerous way to get war supplies, but the goods were coming in. By 1942, munitions production was three and a half times as great as in 1941. When mobilization reached its peak in 1943–1944, nearly half of all resources were committed to the war effort, a degree of engagement that closely approached the national effort of Britain, whose position was more desperate and which operated through a centralized Ministry of Supply, and markedly greater than that of Nazi Germany operating under a dictator. The division of authority, however, made for interagency feuds, newspaper headlines, and congressional outcries; a mechanism that moved from one crisis to another.

When Roosevelt was again distracted from his preoccupation with the far-flung battlefronts by renewed threats of congressional intervention, he solved his dilemma by making Byrnes a supercoordinator, working directly under the President, with the establishment in early 1943 of the Office of War Mobilization. Besides being a cagey, conservative Southern politician, Byrnes was also a political friend of Baruch, the spiritual architect of the Industrial Mobilization Plan, and called him in as a major adviser; and Baruch, in turn, brought along his good friend and associate, Hancock. The War Resources Board team were back visiting at the old plantation. If the Rooseveltian jugglery did not change the power essentials of the defense program as recommended in the Industrial Mobilization Plan, it kept formal authority more scrupulously in the hands of the political directorate, and slowed the consolidation of what was known later as the military-industrial complex. That is the least and the most that can be said for the virtuoso performance.

Truman eased his way gingerly into the mobilization barrel of worms. His committee began its investigations by inspecting Fort Meade in Maryland and other cantonments. A billion dollars had been spent on camp construction; more camps were to be built; and there had been newspaper reports and individual complaints about waste, mismanagement, favoritism, and faulty locations. Truman did not start his investigation with the Army camp program by chance. He had a plan. The evidence was overwhelming that the Army conducted construction like a blind man sailing a boat. Truman thought the right initial target was to establish the committee's reputation with the least risk. He wrote his friend, Lou Holland, that he did not believe there would be any difficulty in getting funds for further investigations. "I had to justify the existence of the committee in the preliminary stage and that is the reason I stayed shy of the real controversial issues." The committee brought on record an enormous amount of incontrovertible data. Army studies had been made after the First World War, but the material had been lost, and there were no plans on hand when the defense program started. The generals did not realize there was not enough construction equipment available for a billion-dollar project superimposed on other defense construction and rented equipment at fantastic prices. Had the government bought new equipment, $12 to $13 million would have been saved on that item alone. In addition, the cost-plus-fixed-fee contracts were too costly.

The committee rounded off the record of misfeasance by including labor unions in its general indictment. This became a trademark of Truman's attempts to balance the blame. Involved were the AFL building trades unions that required all nonmember workers on a job to get union permits, often for inordinately high fees. These craft unions always restricted membership and charged high initiation fees and dues to provide insurance benefits. Confronted now with immense projects for which they could not provide the necessary work force from their ranks, and not wanting to sign up new workers to avoid overcrowding their membership when construction declined to normal, they made a petty racket out of the special permits. Truman had a case, although it was secondary compared to the contractors' potboiling. The criticism fell in with the widespread labor baiting of the period.

The investigations and hearings veered to industrial mobilization, and a kaleidoscope of exhibits of private greed and public irresponsibility were shown in profuse variety. The damning record of statistic and fact concerned shortages of basic materials, dollar-a-year men passing on contracts for each other's companies which continued to pay their salaries while they were on leave, public officials acting as guardians of private interests. The committee began an inquiry into aluminum supply in May. Stettinius had been jollying the public along with assurances that there was plenty of aluminum, but work had been halted on the Boeing bombers because of metal shortages. When W. L. Batt, then deputy production director in the OPM, otherwise head of the SKF Roller Bearing Company, was before the committee, he admitted, after much prodding and probing, that sometime in 1942 there would be enough aluminum for aircraft and direct military requirements, but none for civilian or "indirect military purposes." This was serious because aluminum did not go only into pots and pans; it was essential for transportation equipment, machinery, electrical conductors and parts, iron and steel metallurgy. Closer examination disclosed that even this calculation was overestimating supply and underestimating military demands.

Then came G. R. Gibbons, senior vice-president of the Aluminum Corporation of America, to the stand. Fulton asked whether Alcoa had anything to do with Stettinius' statement of the previous October that the country had plenty of aluminum. Gibbons first wanted to make sure that no criticism was implied of Stettinius, for, as he said, "We ought to get down on our knees and thank God for the OPM."

> *Mr. Fulton:* We are not criticizing Mr. Stettinius. I am simply asking this question. Reading that release in the light of what you have testified as to the facts which the Aluminum Company then knew, if it saw that release, it knew that release was not correct, did it not?
>
> *Mr. Gibbons:* I might have seen the release and thought it was quite correct because I might have thought the war would be over in three months, in which case there was more than enough aluminum for civilian needs. I did think, in fact, last fall, that there was a high probability of there being very much less need for defense aluminum than turned out to be the case. That was my error, but I recall distinctly thinking we were forging ahead, and where were we going to land out here. Suppose England was immediately conquered, as it looked very much as though it would be at times, and the war should suddenly subside, where would we land? I didn't know, but I thought we might land with a huge capacity here and nowhere to go, and Mr. Stettinius may have thought that, I don't know.

Only after the Truman Committee determined that production was 600 million pounds short did the OPM move to expand capacity, and then under provisions that called for a $50 million government investment to buttress Alcoa's postwar position. When Truman had lunch with Harold Ickes in October, he mentioned that Jesse Jones, the RFC head, was to appear before the committee, and that he had signed a "vicious contract" with Alcoa. The hearing brought out that Jones had given Alcoa control over the wartime rate of operations in the plants the government was financing, had exacted no penalties for failure to perform, had permitted Alcoa to retain effective control of alumina, the semifinished product into which bauxite is processed. The contract further stipulated that the new, low-cost facilities to be built would be shut down after the war, and the market turned back to Alcoa. Jones acted his usual overbearing self in the witness chair, blustering and referring to Fulton as "that whippersnapper." But the unfavorable publicity was more damaging than he had anticipated, and he negotiated a supplemental agreement that protected somewhat better the government's investment.

The investigation of aluminum was duplicated for steel, rubber, magnesium, copper, lead. The committee went into the automobile industry's reluctance to use its facilities for the $4 billion of war contracts it had received; it compiled dossiers on questionable decisions of procurement officials; it noted the concentration of contracts with the major corporations; so that by the time Truman presented the first annual report in January, 1942, his committee had been accepted by both press and officialdom as a major investigatory arm of Congress. Senators would pass on to Truman complaints from constituents. "It got so," he recalled, "Senators would ask me, 'Harry, won't you investigate this for me?'" After the first period, he had no problem getting funds.

The Truman hearings and reports tell why he won acceptance from both New Dealers and conservatives, why he was able to maintain his balance on slippery, potholed ground where so many lost their footing. The committee's exposure of the industrialists' sharp dealing and spoliation established him as a fearless tribune of the public interest. It won plaudits from liberals and laborites, and it gave the man in the street the comfortable feeling that there was an agency in government that would hunt down sinners and boodlers. At the same time, the muckraking was invariably blunted by Truman's lecturing, with equal fervor and impartiality, government administrators, military officers, businessmen, union officials, on the need for unselfish dedication to the public weal. The result, aside from the rare instances when he was able to intervene directly to good purpose, was to make of the exposés a catharsis. Conservatives realized that the thrusts did not wound because they had no special target. Such a pillar of Wall Street as James Forrestal concluded that "The Truman Committee has served a useful purpose in providing a medium for the exploration of criticism of the war effort."

The first annual report laid out that the Navy procurement men were excessively generous with public funds. Nine of the thirteen companies that had cost-plus contracts were entitled to receive amounts that exceeded their net worth. In one case, the fees were 800 times greater than the firm's 1936–1940 annual profits. In other cases, they were greater by 20, 30, or 40 times. A representative of Todd Shipbuilding testified that Navy ship conversion contracts "gave us a profit of $1.80 a day on every man we had, and I think we had around thirty-five thousand. If it hadn't been for taxes, we couldn't have handled our profits with a steam shovel." Yet Truman was never an advocate of strict excess-profits tax laws. He put his faith in the Renegotiation Act of 1942, which, like the Second Revenue Act of 1940, was more effective in quieting public indignation than in guarding the public treasury. And toward the end of the war, the committee was more concerned with suspending renegotiation altogether than in reclaiming exorbitant profits.

The gravamen of the first annual report was its assault on the OPM. The agency was not only charged with failing in its duties, but the entire system of dollar-a-year men was disqualified. "The committee is opposed to a policy of taking free services from persons with axes to grind. No man can honestly serve two masters." This pernicious system was responsible for funneling contracts to the corporation giants, for holding back the expansion of manufacturing capacities of strategic materials, for failing to require the conversion of existing facilities to defense. To this thunderous indictment was attached a recommendation that was more than acceptable to the interests that had just been excoriated. The committee associated itself with the press campaign for a new defense agency headed by a single director. The punishment did not fit the crime. It was like a prosecutor accusing a suspect of armed robbery, and asking the jury to punish him by streamlining the Mafia organization.

The solution had the further virtue for the conservatives of driving Sidney Hillman, the OPM codirector, out of the defense establishment, and ending even the pretense that labor be represented along with business. In this case, Truman dropped the sociological sermonizing and attacked his victim by name. In an earlier speech to the Senate, Truman went after him mercilessly for insisting that a contract be denied the Currier Lumber Company to avoid labor strife. "A responsible company has made a low bid, which it is prepared to perform and is capable of performing if not illegally interfered with. I cannot condemn Mr. Hillman's position too strongly. If Mr. Hillman cannot or will not protect the interests of the United States, I am in

favor of replacing him with some one who can and will." Hillman
had spent months at the start of the defense program trying to get a
ruling that contractors be required to adhere to labor laws. The policy had been approved by the President, and then largely ignored by
the military. Currier was an involuted case, since the company had
avoided dealing with the building trades unions by signing at the
eleventh hour a labor contract with John L. Lewis' catch-all conglom-
erate, District 50. For Truman to inject himself into this labyrinth of
claim and counterclaim in the supposed national interest was a piece
of cheap posturing. It did not even cost him with labor, since both
the AFL and CIO had stopped supporting Hillman when it became
clear he was a mere figurehead.

The attempt to balance the derelictions of labor with the derelictions of business was like equating the Pennsylvania Railroad and the
owner of a hack service because both were in the transportation business. It was middle-class thinking to put on the same plane the modest improvements in wages and the enormous improvements in war
profits in order to declaim triumphantly against both Big Labor and
Big Capital. Truman kept his reputation as a friend of labor although
often joining with its opponents because he exhibited acumen in
adopting the stance of a high-minded legislator standing above all
special interest groups. His apportioning of criticisms was so finely
weighed that he could point to a record of having voted both for and
against the Smith-Connally antistrike law. He voted for the bill, but
against the conference report, and against overriding the President's
veto. In the veto message, Roosevelt asked for an enabling act to
draft strikers. In upholding the veto, Truman added for good measure, "I am neither for a military dictatorship nor for drafting labor."
He was covered for all eventualities.

The one time he drifted with the prevailing tide beyond the lines
he had set might have had serious consequences. He approved a
ghost-written article that appeared under his name in the *American
Magazine* in November, 1942. It was an anti-Roosevelt harangue for a
homefront czar. "We are in danger of losing this war in Washington.
We are in danger of losing it because of red tape and bureaucratic
waste, because of conflicts between military and civilian agencies, because of overlapping jurisdictions and the failure to delegate authority." As soon as Hugh Fulton heard of it, he rushed up to New York
to try to stop the article. He was unable to take any legal action because Truman had initialed every page of the manuscript. When Roosevelt read the article, Truman went on the unpreferred list for al-

most a year. His fellow committee member, Harley Kilgore of West Virginia, a staunch New Dealer, patched things up for him by telling Roosevelt that Truman had not read the article beforehand. Roosevelt grudgingly agreed to call off the quarrel.

Truman claimed Roosevelt got the credit for setting up the War Production Board, but that his committee's report was responsible for it. He added coyly, "That was all right with me. I wanted action more than credit." Actually, there were many influences that forced Roosevelt after Pearl Harbor to discard the OPM. The committee report was one of several, and not the foremost one. As for Truman's disinterest in credit, his conduct did not confirm it. The committee's public relations officer was always functioning. Information was ground out steadily, with an eye to press needs and deadlines. Reporters were encouraged to come to the staff for information. If they missed a hearing, they could pick up a transcript or receive a rundown from a staff member. The entire operation was fashioned like a windmill to take maximum advantage of prevailing winds and press clamors. Whenever John L. Lewis cut up, the committee would suspend momentarily whatever investigation it was working on to call him in so that it could add its voice to the general hubbub, although, strictly speaking, labor relations were outside its jurisdiction. Truman was not a colorful person, nor an articulate one, but he had learned to make a virtue out of his homespun appearance and manner. He was the embodiment, he implied, of the great American mass, nothing fancy on the outside, but great strength, great character, great heart, within.

By 1943, the press lords recognized Truman's special qualifications as a senator who, in the words of Reddig, "knew the New Deal routine and yet was safe." Henry Luce began the national buildup of the man with a future. The March 8, 1943, issue of *Time* carried his picture on the front cover and gave him the very-important-person treatment: had saved the country billions of dollars; fearless; courageous; and the indispensable, unnamed Washingtonian came along to remark, "There's only one thing that worries me more than the present state of the war effort. That's to think what it would be like by now without Harry Truman." Stanley High described the committee in *Reader's Digest* as "the public's most accessible court of appeals, the sharpest prod and one of the most powerful action-getting agencies in the government." Additional testimonials followed thick and fast. When the committee first got under way, *The New York Times* wondered if it would not do more harm than good. What was called for, it held, was a bipartisan committee that would have the nation's full confidence. By the summer of 1944, it gave complete endorsement to the committee and its chairman.

It is difficult to assess the committee's accomplishments, much less put a money value on them, because the committee did not achieve any of its major objectives. It did not eliminate the dollar-a-year-man system; it did not redirect the flow of contracts to the benefit of small business; it did not relieve the military services of procurement prerogatives; it did not overturn, in the latter part of the war, the plan of the major corporations to hold up reconversion until they were ready to take over the civilian market. Even in the cases where the committee exposed indictable criminal conduct, as in the forging of inspection reports by Curtiss-Wright, or fraudulent inspection practices at Carnegie-Illinois Steel, the committee subsided when assured by the companies that the so-called mistakes had been corrected.

Truman's primary achievement—a considerable one—was to provide an authoritative public forum. The investigations and hearings made up an unsurpassed and searching review of all important aspects of the war mobilization. Defense officials and contractors carried on in the knowledge that the glare of publicity might be turned on their activities. Now and then Truman was able to bear down, as with the Alcoa contract, to force improvements. Despite his conflicts with Nelson about the dollar-a-year men and procurement, Truman cooperated closely with the War Production Board, and often, through hearings and publicity, he put pressure, as requested, on the military or on businessmen. In contrast to the Civil War Committee on the Conduct of the War, which was dominated by Radical Republicans who sought to discredit Lincoln and his border-state policy, Truman's committee was a cog of the defense establishment that brought to light the freebooting and malefaction in such a way that, on balance, it helped to maintain the social equilibrium.

In what had prompted Truman to propose an investigating committee, the complaints of Missouri businessmen that they were not getting their share of the contracts, he was notably successful, although it is doubtful that small business fared better in Missouri than in the country at large. The many efforts to integrate small business into the defense program proved useless. Maury Maverick, at the head of the Smaller War Plants Corporation created by Congress, labored for a more equitable distribution, and made some headway, but the pattern was set by the military's awards of the $200 billion of prime contracts, so that by war's end there were fewer smaller firms than in 1939, and they accounted for a smaller share of all manufacturing. Truman was instrumental in placing Lou Holland, his erstwhile fellow banker in the ill-fated Englewood venture, as head of the Smaller War Plant Division in the WPB. Working in close alliance with Holland, with J. C. Nichols, a major Kansas City realtor who had headed a division at the OPM, and other Missouri business figures, he helped in channeling contracts into the home state. Kansas City grew into an important war industries center, and by the middle of 1945 war supplies from Missouri were valued at over $4 billion.

From a politician fighting for his political existence, he had become in the short space of four years a respected national figure. A newspaperman called his odyssey a "cockeyed Horatio Alger story." An apt characterization.

7

New
White House
Regime

Truman's career as Vice-President was a short one—82 days. The job promised to be a not very onerous one since Roosevelt was not taking him into his inner family. Ahead were days of presiding over the Senate, meeting with the boys to strike blows for liberty amidst convivial cloakroom wirepulling and vote-swapping. Before the President left for Yalta, he wanted to dispose of the item he had vowed to take care of after the election, namely, to cut "Jesus H. Jones's" throat. He told Truman he was firing Jones and naming Wallace in his stead as Secretary of Commerce. With some trepidation, Truman answered that he would try to line up the senators to confirm the appointment. He got approval only after an ugly struggle and by agreeing to sheer away from the Cabinet post the key federal lending agencies that Jones had run like an overlord.° Another appointment, of Aubrey Williams, a dedicated New Dealer, and former National Youth Administrator, for head of rural electrification, was contemptuously turned back.

° In his ghost-written memoirs, *Fifty Billion Dollars*, Jesse H. Jones boasted of thwarting, at every turn, Roosevelt's policy and following his own, of conspiring repeatedly against his chief with the Southerners in Congress.

Hardly had he settled in his new post when a voice from the past called, and Harry responded—this time, without calculating whether his move would affect votes. Tom Pendergast died on January 26. As soon as Truman got the news, he ordered an Army bomber to take him to Kansas City where he attended funeral services at the Visitation Church. He said to newspapermen, "I'm as sorry as I can be. He was always my friend and I have always been his." Old Tom, Deserted by family and associates after his disgrace, died a broken man. Truman could forget neither that Pendergast had been his leader nor that he owed his political career to his support. He paid no attention to the criticism for attending his old mentor's funeral. Truman was a sentimental man, a repository of maudlin and conventionally appropriate feelings about family, friends, neighbors, schoolteachers. But these were kept severely apart from his political dealings; the one was not permitted to intrude on the other. His loyalty to friends, much commented upon in later years, was selective and not without a heavy touch of self-interest or self-indulgence. It might be thought ironical that, aside from family relations, this gesture of pure sentiment should have been reserved for Pendergast, but it was so.

Since there was not much for Truman to do, he turned to the capital's high life. In the Washington social whirl, where the job, not the person, counts, Harry became a prize catch for the social climbers. One columnist reported, "Currently, the new Vice-President is the most fed gentleman in Washington. He has guzzled at more feed troughs than Whirlaway." There were days when he and Bess went to three cocktail parties and a formal dinner. Entertaining the Trumans made Perle Mesta a society eminence, and sent her as ambassadress to Luxembourg. At a blowout given by the National Press Club, while he was playing the piano for reporters, Lauren Bacall, the screen star, climbed on the piano and displayed her long, pretty legs to the delectation of the audience and the millions who saw the photograph in their newspapers. (Bess thought it was time he quit playing the piano.) But high jinks and synthetic glamour came to an abrupt end on the historic day of April 12 when word came through that Roosevelt had died of a cerebral hemorrhage at Warm Springs, Georgia. Harry Truman, by the grace of God, was now President of the United States.

He inherited a gargantuan institution. The presidencies of even Wilson and Hoover did not begin to compare with the bureaucratic leviathan that Franklin Roosevelt had forged over the New Deal and war years. After the Reorganization Act of 1939, and the proliferation of new agencies and bureaus during the war mobilization, power had shifted to the Executive without reference to the strength or weakness of the particular White House occupant. The 1940 federal payroll of over a million was twice that of ten years before, doubled again during the war, and stayed at 2 million in 1950. Since the power to initiate laws and prepare the budget was now lodged with the President; since the warmaking powers were increasingly to become administrative decisions of the Commander in Chief; since the Senate's advise and consent was largely bypassed by Executive agreements—the role of Congress was reduced to one of amending, obstructing, or blocking presidential initiatives. "The authority that men like Lincoln and Theodore Roosevelt have exercised in times of crisis, real or assumed, has become a stable, dependable, and predictable basis for the exercise of presidential authority." There had been monarchs in the past who wielded authority as intensive, but not many.

Truman was woefully unprepared to accept the crown and scepter so suddenly turned over to him. He had expected to inherit the Presidency; yet when the day came, he was frightened. He was speaking from the heart when he said to reporters, "Boys, if you ever pray, pray for me now. I don't know whether you fellows ever had a load of hay fall on you, but when they told me yesterday what had happened, I felt like the moon, the stars, and all the planets had fallen on me." When one of the reporters called out, "Good luck, Mr. President," he turned to him and said, "I wish you didn't have to call me that." He knew that a series of accidents had brought him to the White House. He had misgivings whether he could fulfill expectations. The diffidence that he had shown on entering the Senate reasserted itself. Then, it was because of his compromising association with a crooked political boss. Now it was doubt about his own adequacy. Even in later years, when he had blown up enormously in self-esteem, he said with conviction, "There are a great many people, I expect a million in the country, who could have done the job better than I could." His humility and self-deprecation were exhibited so frequently and to so many people in the first weeks that Barkley took him aside and told him to cut it out; people would lose all confidence in him if he did not show confidence in himself. "God raises up leaders. We do not know the process, but in the wisdom of Almighty God, you have been made President."

Some have sought to reduce Truman's unpreparedness to the small change of lack of executive experience, or to Roosevelt's not having briefed him on outstanding topics. This was not the essence of the matter. Truman had been a United States senator for ten years. He had more experience, a better practical acquaintanceship with the workings of government, than Lincoln and many other Presidents before assuming office. As for being conversant with the going problems, he was no differently situated than most other Presidents, and these can be grasped, with the help of technicians, in fairly rapid order, if one has the essential equipment. In a technical sense, no man can be prepared for the Presidency in the way an architect or engineer can be said to be prepared by a decade of experience to design a building or construct a bridge. The Presidency now includes so many different functions that no man can know fully what goes on in his administration and pass on more than the most important policy decisions and appointments; even in many of these he is dependent on advisers and associates.

James Bryce, the well-known student of the American political temper, wrote that a President need not be a man of brilliant intellectual gifts, that profundity of thought or extent of knowledge, while to be desired, were not necessary for the successful discharge of his duties. "A man may lack them and yet make an excellent President. Four fifths of his work is the same in kind as that which devolves on the chairman of a commercial company or the manager of a railway." That was in the relatively simple 1880s. This formula, that had more or less sufficed for years, broke down in the crisis of 1930. What followed was a bizarre anomaly. While the administrative machinery of American government underwent a revolutionary transformation in the next decade, the method of selecting the master superintendent of the works remained unchanged. Thus, when the United States stood at a pinnacle of power greater than had been attained by any nation since the fall of the Roman Empire, it picked its Presidents, now endowed with Caesarian powers, by the same devices that had done duty in the times of Chester Arthur, Grover Cleveland, and Benjamin Harrison.

Truman's first act was to assure Congress and the nation that he would carry out the policies of Roosevelt. This was an algebraic formula at best, for Roosevelt's genius was as a conjurer and improviser, not as a planner. Even as guideline generality, the pledge was equivocal. Truman was diffident, unsure of himself in the initial period, and he had been in some awe of Roosevelt, at least at first. But psychologists have pointed out that emotions do not come singly and pure but in clusters of contradictory impulses; love is intertwined with hate; feelings of generosity are attached to drives to dominate. Truman had a sense of inferiority but he was at the same time willful and opinionated; what he lacked in depth of comprehension, he made up for in the positiveness with which he asserted his judgments.

That he was personally conservative was known to his intimates in senatorial days. This would not establish by itself his exact presidential course, for, as James MacGregor Burns showed, so was Roosevelt conservative. The modern Presidency, is not primarily a machine for self-expression. Caught in the swirl of conflicting tides, the President maneuvers and manipulates, grants concessions to this bloc or that bloc, to maintain a social equilibrium, working within the confines of basic laws, institutions, and dispensations. Truman's own views were not merely the stock conglomeration of positions and prejudices of a provincial businessman, however; like others who prided themselves on their common sense and practicality, he was suspicious of reforming liberals and had contempt for the dedicated New Dealers. He had attached himself to the New Deal when it was necessary to do so as a matter of convenience, not of sentiment.

His dislike of the Rooseveltian order was a profound thing; it went to the roots of his makeup. Clark Clifford described it several years later to David Lilienthal. Clifford told him that on coming to work for Truman, he was called in for a talk in the course of which Truman said that "most of the people Roosevelt had close around him were 'crackpots and the lunatic fringe.'" (Clifford emphasized that those were the words Truman used.) Truman said, "I want to keep my feet on the ground; I don't want any experiments; the American people have been through a lot of experiments and they want a rest from experiments." Lilienthal had previously diagnosed Truman as reacting against the vocabulary of the New Deal intellectuals because he came out of Middle West progressivism and used a different terminology. He admitted that some of the things Clifford told him went beyond what he had in mind "and may confirm the feeling of quite a few liberals that Truman does not understand the world at all, and is no liberal by any definition."

Semantics was not the issue. Truman reacted against certain words —and the people who used them—not becuase they sounded unmusical to his ears, but because he did not approve the political attitudes they connoted. "I don't know how I ever got out of that mudhole," he told Jonathan Daniels, referring to Roosevelt's Cabinet. Before three months had passed, they all went flying out except for the heads of the military services, and Wallace and Ickes, kept on as propitiary offerings to the party's New Deal wing—and they did not last long, and their exit was less than amicable. Not that the old crowd leaving was unusual; under the Presidential system, a Chief Executive picks Cabinet members who will by loyal to him. Harry Hopkins had said, "Truman has got to have his own people around him, not Roosevelt's. If we were around, we'd always be looking at him and he'd know we were thinking, 'The President wouldn't do it that way!' " What was remarkable was not that he picked his own replacements, but the kind of replacements he picked. Nor should it be thought that his choice was limited since he did not have a wide acquaintanceship outside his own political circles. High government officials are most often selected on recommendation, not through personal association; given a President's prestige and authority and the elevated status of a Cabinet position, a President's opportunities are virtually unlimited.

To take a few examples: Truman replaced Francis Biddle with Tom Clark. According to his account, Biddle had been a good Attorney General, and there was no ill-feeling between them. He had not asked Biddle to resign; Biddle's quitting was his own decision. Truman opined that that was because Biddle did not think he was going to be as liberal a President as Roosevelt. Truman then asked Biddle whom he would recommend to take his place, and Biddle suggested Tom Clark. That is not the way Biddle reported it. He said he received late in May a telephone call from Steve Early, the holdover press secretary, who told him that his resignation was accepted. Biddle, a scion of one of the most proper Philadelphia families, was outraged. "Dammit, Steve," he shouted, "I expected my resignation to be accepted sooner or later, but at least I should have the courtesy of a personal request for it from the President." Early agreed that that was the way it ought to be done, and within an hour Biddle was summoned to the White House. The business was disposed of in a formal but not unfriendly manner, after which Biddle asked if Truman minded telling him who his successor was to be. "Not a bit, General, and I know it's one you will approve of. He's a man from your own department, Tom Clark." Biddle was shocked. Clark was an amiable, reactionary lightweight from Texas who had been put into the department as a political payoff to Rayburn and Connally. His main talents lay not in the law, but in cultivating rewarding political friendships, and in breaking into the newspapers with concocted stories of alleged law enforcement prodigies. During his four-year tenure as Attorney General, as could have been foretold, the department became a byword for favoritism and loyalty obsession, after which Truman rewarded him with an appointment to the Supreme Court.

"Unhappily, Mr. President, I do not approve of your choice," Biddle said. "And I most urgently suggest that you study this matter further before making up your mind." Truman had already made up his mind. He probably had Biddle tagged as one of the lunatic fringe around Roosevelt.

Another appointment was Fred Vinson replacing Morgenthau at Treasury. He and Byrnes became the two heavies of the first Truman Cabinet. It was the kind of appointment that had been made by other administrations without eliciting passionate response for or against. Like Truman, Vinson was a complacent, border-state politician, except that he was the possessor of more impressive physical equipment: He looked like a judge or statesman. An innate conservative who played the New Deal game, he had been a congressman from his Kentucky district for fourteen years, a circuit court judge, and then followed Byrnes as stabilization director. In his year in the Cabinet, before Truman sent him to grace the Supreme Court as Chief Justice, he lent his 200-odd pounds to giving the administration a judicious Hooverite equilibrium. Under his both-feet-on-the-ground, no-far-out-schemes administration at Treasury, congressional committees were no longer annoyed and antagonized by smart-aleck technicians with visionary blueprints to equalize tax burdens. What was telling about Truman's political bent and intellectual dimension was not that he made the Vinson appointment, or that Vinson loomed as the states-man of the Cabinet, but that in a Cabinet where Truman felt he needed to have the benefit of different viewpoints, Vinson was sup-posed to represent the practical New Dealer.

Compared with his successor, though, Vinson was a flaming re-former and counselor of unlimited sagacity. John Snyder, who had been picking up Vinson's jobs as the latter moved on to higher things, was installed as mobilization head until he stepped in as Secretary of the Treasury. For the first eighteen months of the administration, he was a major influence, a prime helper in directing the President to the disastrous course of dumping controls in a pell-mell rush to nor-malcy. He had been a minor bank official in St. Louis, but his real claim to fame was his early association with Truman. The two had at-tended artillery school together in France, had roughed it on summer maneuvers of the National Guard; he had supported Truman in the senatorial campaigns, was a family intimate of Bess Truman and a welcome visitor to the home in Independence. He had Truman's non-descript appearance, but achieved it with a different combination of features and mannerisms. He had little beady eyes, was inclined to pudginess, and walked with a waddle. Humorless and prim as a deacon, his face perpetually wore a pained look so that, like Alice Longworth's description of Calvin Coolidge, one would have thought he had been weaned on a pickle. Some claimed that he loosened up remarkably at poker sessions and displayed a Legionnaire's ability for horseplay that no one discerned during working hours. How Truman concluded that this shallow, ignorant Babbit was a great financier and thinker was a mystery. The Treasury, which, as a bureaucratic entity, was one of the best departments under Morgenthau, became, under Snyder's ministrations, one of the most listless.

Truman made four appointments to the Supreme Court. The first was Vinson, who replaced Harlan Stone as Chief Justice and was supposed to unify a badly divided court. It was on his suggestion that Tom Clark was moved in, an appointment that could not be justified on any grounds until a newspaperman suggested that Vinson wanted at least one man on the bench who knew even less law than he did. He apparently needed a safe vote to buttress his center bloc so that he could dominate the opposing Frankfurter-Jackson and Black-Douglas combines. Clark did not disappoint his sponsor. In 107 cases decided during the 1949–1950 session, he differed from Vinson only twice. Truman's two other appointments showed the same predilection for conservative mediocrities. Harold Burton, a corporation lawyer who had faithfully served the public utilities, was Republican mayor of Cleveland, and then a member of the Truman Committee in the Senate. As a legal talent, he was considered to be in the Tom Clark class, but like Vinson he did look every inch the Supreme Court justice. The final appointee, Sherman Minton, had come to the Senate at the same time as Truman; the two occupied adjoining desks and became political friends when Truman was unusually appreciative of friendship. In his one term, Minton had been a militant New Dealer, but he made clear to the Senate, when his name came up for Supreme Court confirmation, that he would be reliable. He was. He joined Vinson almost as consistently as did Clark. Vinson's record on labor law, civil liberties, free speech, illegal search and seizure, harked back to the positions of the Butler-Van Devanter-McReynolds cabal. Now that he was freed from popular pressures, he could reveal, without circumlocution, his natural standpat proclivities. Truman's four appointments tilted the court heavily to the right and to the second-rate.

Truman had inherited the mammoth military services structures that had spread over Washington like jungle vegetation. Stimson stayed on until the conclusion of the war. Forrestal remained in the Cabinet for the first term. The insiders' coterie of lawyers, bankers, and military men remained as decisive policy makers and advisers in defense and state and continued furnishing from their midst the pro-consuls and plenipotentiaries to oversee America's expanding inter-ests and commitments. Patterson, Lovett, McCloy, Marshall, Mark Clark, and dozens like them went on dominating military and foreign policy, and deepening the atmosphere they had helped create, which made Washington resemble Rome under the first Augustus. Lilienthal was to become impatient with liberal criticism on this score. He noted in his journal, "As for ultra-conservative appointments, if that is one of the charges, and there is plenty to support this, who was it who put Forrestal and Harriman and Lovett into public life in the first place but FDR himself?"

This related to blue-ribbon officeholders. An administration, though, like a political clubhouse, cannot live on high politics alone. Truman took over the host attached to the Executive Office, and then, like a good organization man, enlarged it. Civil service regulations to the contrary, more than half the federal jobs are obtained through po-litical pull, not to mention more important and better-paying jobs in dozens of bureaus, divisions, and subdivisions. As soon as the word came through that Good Old Harry had struck it rich, they began to come down by plane and train. Office-seekers stood mob-thick in the big lobby of the Executive Offices. As summed up by the *Washington Daily News* in its headline, ALL MISSOURI'S HERE TO SEE HARRY. And Harry did not disappoint his cronies from the American Legion, Mis-souri courthouses, senatorial poker sessions, and 129th Field Artillery. He gathered around him a crew that Warren Harding would have found thoroughly congenial. The "Missouri Gang" was of the stuff, caliber, and life style of the "Ohio Gang." Wrote I. F. Stone, the left-liberal journalist,

> The little name plates outside the little doors began to change. In Justice, Treasury, Commerce, and elsewhere, the New Dealers began to be replaced by the kind of men one was accustomed to meet in county courthouses. The composite impression was of big-bellied good-natured guys who knew a lot of dirty jokes, spent as little time in their offices as possible, saw Washington as a chance to make useful "contacts," and were anxious to get what they could for themselves out of the experience. They were not

unusually corrupt or especially wicked—that would have made the Capital a dramatic instead of a depressing experience for a reporter. They were just trying to get along. The Truman era was the era of the moocher. The place was full of Wimpys who could be had for a hamburger.

Ed McKim, sergeant in Battery D, fellow officer in National Guard encampments, insurance salesman, and practical joker extraordinaire, now blossomed out as Truman's chief secretary. When he found White House stenographers working on the thousands of sympathy letters that had come for Eleanor Roosevelt, he fired the girls and ordered the work stopped. "Mrs. Roosevelt is no longer riding the gravy train," he announced. Truman ordered the work resumed after he received a complaint. One of the stenographers exclaimed, "My God, you'd think a Republican administration had taken over, the way they cleaned out this place." George Allen, another terrific jokesmith, had been dispatched to the Truman train during the 1944 campaign to curb the vice-presidential candidate's penchant for snappy pronouncements. He was a master at collecting lucrative corporation directorships for himself. Now he became an RFC director.

The tone of the White House inner circle was epitomized by Harry Vaughan, who became a general factotum. Truman had known him since Camp Doniphan and American Legion days; from the 1940 campaign on they had been inseparable. Truman made him his office assistant when he was senator, and his military aide when he became Vice-President, although no Vice-President had ever had a military aide. Now Vaughan was transmogrified into a brigadier general, as well as military aide; later, a major general, just like in Gilbert and Sullivan. In the plethora of court jesters, he was chief clown in residence. A big man, with a slack, vacuous, St. Bernard face, he was the proverbial, loud-mouthed Elks or Shriners delegation leader, whose hearty barnyard humor drew guffaws from the boys at the poker sessions, and discreet giggles from the ladies in the cocktail lounges. His voice could be heard booming, as he dashed in and out of the President's office, "I'm still with ya, Chief."

The sudden eminence of this "flap-mouthed dunderhead," as a columnist called him, led to a flowering of his self-expression and self-assertion. Of what use was it to be close to the President if he could not let the world know about it? In a memorable address to a group of Presbyterian ladies, he offered a succinct comparison between the Roosevelt and Truman administrations: "After a diet of caviar, you like to get back to ham and eggs." When reporters baited him to explain how he was able to afford a plush vacation, he told them to lay off because, "After all, I am the President's military aide and you guys will want favors at the White House some day." The word spread that Vaughan was one to see for favors and fixes. He used his position to intercede in all manner of cases that figured in later administration scandals. When his interventions and comments on affairs and men led to repeated embarrassments, Charles Ross, the presidential press secretary, who had been the honor student of Truman's class at Independence High School, would shake his head and mumble, "*Cherchez le Vaughan.*"

Washington had not seen such a concentration of tinhorns for a quarter of a century. They were not only self-serving; they had the reflexes of backwoods Coolidges. They thought, said Judge Samuel Rosenman, that the New Deal had been a "disastrous experience." Rosenman, who was called in occasionally as a consultant and wrote some of the President's important political speeches, found the staff hostile to him at first because of his close association with Roosevelt. The palace guard even high-hatted Hannegan. As a specialist in votes and elections, his studies convinced him that the party's New Deal wing had to be given consideration and sustenance if the Democrats hoped to hold onto office. Allen, Snyder, and Vaughan poked fun at him to the President. "Old Bob turned out to be a pinko." Who could resist a chuckle?

Social scientists have written learned accounts of Truman's and Roosevelt's different administrative procedures. Truman was an exceedingly neat, meticulous person who, like Eisenhower after him, was impressed with organization charts and line-of-command cubistic drawings. One had only to glance at the President's well-scrubbed, bandbox appearance, the starched handkerchief peeping out of the breast pocket of the sharply pressed double-breasted suit and showing the regulation four points, to realize that here was a person who valued orderliness and predictability. In line with the then prevalent opinion in Washington, Truman thought Roosevelt a poor administrator, and believed he could bring system and teamwork into the organization. He set up clear-cut staff lines, delegated authority. He expected to back up the decisions of his officials, and to resolve disputes or uncertainties when they arose. In practice, the commitment to "completed staff work" repeatedly broke down because Truman, with his politician's training, was habituated to working with people rather than through fixed procedures. In any case, whether Roosevelt's ad-

Harry Truman's parents, Martha Ellen Young and John Anderson Truman, at the time of their marriage. (Kansas City Star)

Harry and his brother Vivian at ages six and four. (Harry S. Truman Library)

First Lieutenant Truman. (Harry S. Truman Library)

Truman & Jacobson Haberdashery in Kansas City. (UPI)

Jackson County Judge Truman with Mrs. Truman and Margaret. (Harry S
Truman Library)

The freshman senator. (*Harry S. Truman Library*)

Truman with President Roosevelt before the 1944 presidential campaign.
(New York Herald Tribune)

Politicos at the 1936 Democratic National Convention. From left, Truman,
Thomas J. Pendergast, James P. Aylward, N. G. Robertson, James Farley.
(UPI)

At the Potsdam Conference in 1945. From left, General Harry H. Vaughan, Marshal Stalin, President Truman, Andrei Gromyko, James F. Byrnes, Vyacheslav Molotov. (U.S. Army)

The Truman family at the 1944 Democratic Convention. (Harry S. Truman Library)

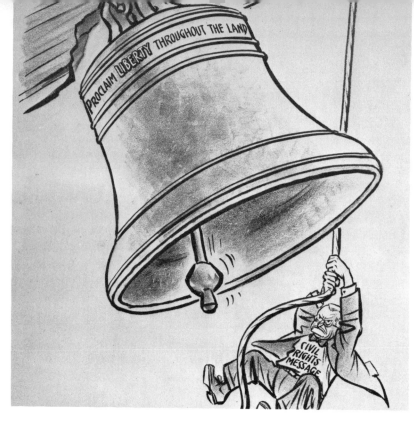

Cartoon by Herblock in the Washington Post.

President Truman reads the Japanese surrender message to Cabinet members and other officials. Seated beside him from left are Admiral William D. Leahy, Chief of Staff; James F. Byrnes, Secretary of State; Cordell Hull, former Secretary of State. Other Cabinet members are standing in background.(New York Herald Tribune)

ministrative methods were good or bad—and the opinion of scholars is veering toward the former—it was laughable to think that Truman was going to improve on the performance with his John Snyders, Charles Sawyers, and Harry Vaughans. More important than procedural and hierarchical arrangements are the quality of people, their motivations, their morale, the relationship of administration to policy.

Truman's initial humility brought on an exaggerated show of decisiveness. He was determined to demonstrate that he was no Throttlebottom. The old habit of popping opinions before he considered his position, that old Joe Shannon had detected years ago, reappeared in the new setting where public declarations reverberated like voices in a canyon. At his first press conference he snapped out answers to questions with such rapidity that reporters could scarcely write them down. Dean Acheson commented, "President Truman's mind is not so quick as his tongue. He could not wait for the end of a question before answering it. Not seeing where he was being led, he fell into traps. He thought FDR's apparent free-and-easy dialogue with the press was as easy and candid as it seemed, a profound illusion. This tendency was a constant danger to him and bugbear to his advisers. His press conferences and, even more, his early-morning walks followed by inquisitive reporters, were a constant menace." Sam Rayburn admonished him: "You don't have to give a direct answer to any and every question those buzzards throw at you." After the fiasco of his press conference in connection with Henry Wallace's Madison Square Garden speech, Ross and Clifford persuaded him never to give offhand approval of a speech until the staff could study it; to adopt the practice of saying "no comment" to questions when he was not sure of the issue.

More decisive than snap answers were snap decisions. The old cockiness could now luxuriate in the favorable climate of the Presidency. It quickly became apparent to his associates and to the press that the new Chief Executive was able to make decisions. He was not only willing, he had a positive compulsion. The question was whether this readiness was based on willfulness, nervousness, and egotism, or whether it was based on the capacity to resolve rapidly the factors relating to the problem at hand. There were times when some of his associates were not sure that Truman understood the implications of his decisions. There was the incident of August, 1946. Following the Soviet Union's note to Turkey on revision of the Montreaux Convention governing the Dardanelles, the secretaries of War, Navy, and State

met with the Chiefs of Staff and drew up position papers and a recommendation to take all necessary measures to thwart Russian demands. They went to see the President. He listened to them and then
readily agreed. What then transpired was described by Joseph Jones,
a State Department assistant:

> At this point General [Dwight D.] Eisenhower, who was
> seated beside Acheson, confided in whispers his concern
> that the President might be making his decision without
> fully understanding its importance and possible conse-
> quences. Then Eisenhower addressed the President and,
> emphasizing the gravity of the matter, suggested that
> Acheson be permitted to go over again the facts and im-
> plications of the Straits situation and the possible conse-
> quences of the decision that was being made. The Presi-
> dent agreed, and Acheson did so. When this second
> analysis was finished the President opened a convenient
> desk drawer and drew out a large map. Truman pro-
> ceeded to give a ten to fifteen minute dissertation on the
> historical importance and present-day strategic signifi-
> cance of the area, which at least one person present de-
> scribed later as "masterful." Concluding, he turned good-
> humoredly to Eisenhower and asked whether he was
> satisfied now that the situation was understood. Eisen-
> hower joined in the general laughter and admitted that he
> was.

The incident has been cited by writers to show how Truman put Eisenhower in his place, or what an expert he was on strategic matters.
That was not its sole significance. Its major significance was that
Eisenhower (and others) had reservations about whether Truman
grasped what he was agreeing to. Eisenhower happened to be mistaken,
but not because of Truman's dissertation, masterful or otherwise. For
all his impetuosity, Truman understood in a practical way the proposals he was called to pass on. The more basic question was whether
he could visualize alternatives, not only see risks and advantages
but weigh the long consequences.

8

The
Course Is
Changed

It is part of the record that Truman had a confrontation with the Russians almost immediately upon taking office; that before long, hostility between the two wartime allies was blazing, and that the Roosevelt postwar schema, one of whose cornerstones was agreement with the Russians, was discarded in favor of the Cold War. Those who have sought to deny a sharp change of course have had to admit it in their next breath. The data is there, irrefutable. What they have then argued, in effect, was that troubles with the Russians had started while Roosevelt was still alive, that had he continued in office, he would have come to a dead end in his relations with Stalin as Truman was to do, and that the alliance was never much more than a military one. This is a different thesis. It is correct in fact, and very likely correct in appraisal. There had been an ugly flareup about the proposed meeting in Bern, Switzerland, of American and British officers with Field Marshall Albert Kesselring's representatives to discuss surrender of the German army in Italy. And in the last weeks of Roosevelt's life, disagreements and arguments of increasing acerbity developed over the constitution of the Polish government.

Those who believe that history is propelled, in the first instance, by great social forces, and not by the predilections or caprices of individuals, even when highly placed, will readily conclude that such a profound disturbance as the decades-long American-Russian contest would have occurred had there been no replacement in the White House. One can surmise, knowing what a central place the United Nations held in his vision for the organization of the peace, that, had Roosevelt lived, the encounter would not have come so quickly, that he would not have brought things to a head so lightmindedly, that he would have displayed more skill in defining the terms once the struggle was joined. One does not want to carry even this speculation too far since Roosevelt had lost control of Congress, reaction had been gathering strength, Roosevelt himself was notorious for impressionability to his surroundings, and the threads of the alliance were fast coming apart.

On Truman's first full day in office, he was handed a State Department briefing paper designed to acquaint him with the background and status of the principal problems. Without any preliminaries, the report aired the charge that was to become a staple of propaganda in the time to come, that the Soviet government was not carrying out the Yalta agreements. "In the liberated areas under Soviet control, the Soviet government is proceeding largely on a unilateral basis and does not agree that the developments which have taken place justify application of the Crimea agreement." A week later Truman held what he called "an important policy meeting" with W. Averell Harriman, just back from Russia. Harriman was a tall, suave, self-assured businessman-statesman of the Forrestal-Lovett-McCloy variety. Heir to the Harriman railroad millions, former Wall Street banker, board chairman of the Union Pacific, he was, unlike most of the tribe, a Democrat. In Washington he had become closely associated with Harry Hopkins. Roosevelt employed him as an international legman. For several months he had been urging Roosevelt, in dispatches from Moscow, to adopt a more demanding policy. He had rushed back to Washington on his own decision when he learned of Roosevelt's death, and had gone into a furious round of discussions with key officials. It was immediately apparent to him that they were far more sympathetic to his strategy than Roosevelt or Hopkins had been. He realized his unique opportunity and energetically pressed his case. In truth, he did not have to proselytize. Like Leibniz developing infinitesimal calculus independently of Newton, all the key people had come to Harriman's opinion through their own ratiocinations. The atmosphere in the offices was saturated with Russophobia. Of course, this had not developed just in the week beginning April 12. It had been simmering as the Russian armies moved beyond their prewar borders. Roosevelt's death was the catalyst that set the brew boiling.

Harriman responded to the President's invitation to give his estimate about relations with Russia with a guarded exposition. The Soviet Union, he explained, had two policies that she thought she could pursue simultaneously. One was the policy of cooperation with the United States and Britain; the other was to gain control of her neighboring states. He said that associates around Stalin misinterpreted our generosity as a sign of softness. It was his opinion that we could stand firm on important issues "without running serious risks" because Russia feared any break in relations: She needed American help for reconstruction. Before Harriman could proceed, Truman broke in to say that he was not afraid of the Russians, that he intended to be firm, that the Russians needed us more than we needed them.

With that, Harriman picked up assurance and velocity. He stated that we were faced with "a barbarian invasion of Europe"; that Soviet control over any country meant Soviet interest would be paramount, and the Soviet system with its secret police and its extinction of free speech would prevail. He repeated his confidence that a working relationship could be established, but that this would require a reconsideration of our policy. Naturally, he observed airily, in any international negotiation there is give and take. Truman agreed that was so and indicated the proportions he had in mind: "I would not expect one hundred per cent of what we proposed," he said. "But I felt we should be able to get eighty-five per cent." Before leaving, Harriman took Truman aside (Stettinius, Joseph Grew, and Charles Bohlen attended the meeting), and laid it on. "Frankly, one of the reasons that made me rush back to Washington was the fear that you did not understand, as I had seen Roosevelt understand, that Stalin is breaking his agreements. My fear was inspired by the fact that you could not have had time to catch up with all the recent cables. But I must say that I am greatly relieved to discover that you have read them all and that we see eye to eye."

After a week in office, Truman had decided to shift course. Grew, who was acting as the de facto chief State Department officer, was ecstatic. A traditional Tory foreign service man, he felt for the first time since he had been Undersecretary of State under Coolidge that things were going right. To a friend he confided "what a joy it was to deal with a man who won't stand for any pussyfooting in our foreign relations." Winston Churchill commented noncommittally that it was "remarkable" that the new President "felt able so promptly to commit himself."

After he had been in office eleven days, Truman met with his chief diplomatic and military advisers to prepare for the showdown session with Soviet Foreign Minister Vyacheslav Molotov later that day. Molotov was in Washington on his way to the San Francisco conference founding the UN. Present at the presidential conference were Stimson; Forrestal; Admiral William D. Leahy, Roosevelt's chief of staff who stayed on in that capacity with Truman; Marshall, Army Chief of Staff; Admiral Ernest J. King, the naval chief; Stettinius; Harriman; General John R. Deane, head of the Moscow military mission; and Bohlen, the State Department's Russian expert.

Stettinius reported that the discussions with Molotov had been fruitless. He said it was clear that the Russians intended to foist their puppet Lublin government on Poland in violation of their pledges at Yalta. Stimson, who was to vacillate in the coming months, said that the Russians had made a good deal of trouble on minor matters so that it had been necessary in these cases to teach them manners, but on big military matters they had kept their word, and often had done better than they had promised. That is why in a major issue of this kind it was his belief that unless we probed how seriously the Russians viewed the Polish question, we might be heading into very dangerous waters. Forrestal expressed the view that the difficulty over Poland could not be treated as an isolated incident, that the Russians were under the impression that we would not object if they took over all of Eastern Europe; if they persisted, we should have a showdown now rather than later. Harriman backed up Forrestal. The real issue, he felt, was whether we were to be a party to Soviet domination of Poland. Obviously there was risk of a break with the Russians, but, properly handled, it might be avoided. Truman broke in to say that he did not intend to deliver an ultimatum to Molotov, but to make clear the American position. Stimson then remarked that he would like to know how far the Russian reaction would go to a strong position, that the Russians perhaps were being more realistic than we were in regard to their own security.

In response to a question from the President, Leahy observed that he had left Yalta with the impression that the Soviets had no intention of permitting a free government to operate in Poland, that he would have been surprised had the Russians behaved any differently. He said that the Yalta agreement was susceptible of two interpretations, and that it was a serious matter to break with the Russians. Nevertheless, he too believed we should tell them where we stood. Marshall agreed with Stimson that a break was a very serious matter, that he was concerned with Soviet military help in the war against Japan. The Russians could still delay their entry into the Far Eastern war until we had done all the dirty work. Deane answered that the Soviet Union would enter the Pacific war as soon as she was able regardless of what happened elsewhere, that if we were afraid of the Russians, we would get nowhere. Truman then declared that it was obvious that our agreements with the Soviet Union had so far been a one-way street and that this could not continue. He intended to go on with the plans for San Francisco and if the Russians did not wish to join us, they could go to hell. (Although he was aware, as he had told Harriman in their earlier talk, that without Russia there would be no world organization.)

When Molotov arrived, Truman came straight to the point. He said there was no chance of congressional approval for economic measures in the foreign field (he meant for a loan to Russia) unless there was public support, and that the Soviet government should keep this in mind when considering proposals on the composition of a Polish government. He thereupon handed him a message to be transmitted to Stalin "immediately," which stated that failure to accept the Anglo-American proposal would "seriously shake confidence" in the determination of the three governments "to continue the collaboration in the future." It was not an ultimatum, but it posed a threat. Molotov started to explain that the three governments had dealt in the past, and had to continue to deal with each other, as equal parties. Truman answered curtly "that all we were asking was that the Soviet government carry out the Crimea decision on Poland." To each further attempt of Molotov to explain his government's position, Truman snapped sharply "that an agreement had been reached on Poland and that there was only one thing to do, and that was for Marshal Stalin to carry out that agreement in accordance with his word." Molotov finally protested, "I have never been talked to like that in my life." "Carry out your agreements and you won't get talked to like that," was Truman's rejoinder. The meeting ended abruptly on that note.

Truman was intent on impressing himself and those around him with his executive stance. Whatever inner doubts he had about himself could be stilled with a display of martial assurance. Moreover, here was an issue where everything he knew and held dear reinforced his self-righteousness. He had the stereotyped notions that the Russians respected only the mailed fist, and that they mistook generosity for stupidity. All his ideological assumptions fused with his personal inclination to produce an aggressive stand. It has to be noted that the foreign policy advisers around him were not part of his Missouri crowd. Every one of them had been an important cog in the Roosevelt wartime administration. The desire for Russian assistance in the war against Japan that had determined American attitudes at Yalta was still present, as articulated by Marshall. But it had lost its urgency. Opinions were formulated and grew stronger that the Russians would enter the Far Eastern war because of their own interests, regardless, as Deane said, of what happened elsewhere.

What was decisive for settling on a symbolical showdown was the conviction that it was safe and that it would work. Truman had accepted Harriman's argument that the Russians were so hungry for American loans that they would knuckle under to political demands. The intent was not to force a break with Russia, but to force Russia to cooperate with America on the basis of what he conceived to be the true power relationship between the two. He was all for continuing the alliance provided it was clearly understood who the captain of the team was and who would call the plays. British Foreign Minister Anthony Eden was similarly convinced that the Soviet Union had to be "brought up sharply against realities." It would be a mistake to imagine that Truman's view was less sophisticated than Harriman's because he reduced the entire issue to Stalin's alleged violations of the Yalta agreement. He was aware of the weight of Leahy's remarks that these agreements could be read in different ways; he had complained privately to Stettinius that the vague wording did not give him as strong a case as he would have liked to have. He decided to fight it out on that line because that seemed the best public relations position. It also coincided with his own need to simplify political problems into easily articulated debater's points.

What were the true power balances, and why were both Truman and Churchill so insistent on parliamentary democracy for Poland when they took a philosophical attitude about dictatorships in Greece or China? We have to start with the proposition that the alliance of the United States and Britain with the Soviet Union was an anomaly forced on the Western powers by the threat of Nazi hegemony over Europe. It was an alliance that cut across the political trends of the two decades preceding the war. It lacked the political rationale of Tory England's alliance with Czarist Russia against Napoleon 150 years before. In this earlier coalition, despite the social differences between the two states, and the big power conflict that erupted after the war between them, England had a common purpose with Russia, Austria, and Prussia not only to defeat Napoleon, but to reimpose the *ancien régime* on Europe. There was no comparable common purpose between Roosevelt, Churchill, and Stalin. Beyond military understandings, and mechanical arrangements for occupation zones, there was no agreed-upon program for conquered Europe. The vacuous Wilsonian rhetoric of the wartime proclamations papered over conflicting aims rather than expressing a harmonization of different national objectives.

In liberal terminology, there was an underlying clash between the Wilsonian universalism of the Americans and the traditional spheres-of-interest viewpoint of the Russians. Russia had her fingers burned on collective security in the interwar years. Maxim Litvinov's hob-nobbing with the Western diplomats had proved an abysmal failure. It ended with the Munich Pact of 1938, as a consequence of which Russia found herself isolated diplomatically and threatened. Stalin determined to strengthen Russian security through the creation of a territorial buffer zone on her European borders. This was limited, in the pact with Hitler, to the reabsorption of the Baltic states, Finnish Karelia, Bessarabia, and territory that Poland had seized after the First World War east of the so-called Curzon Line, and this was what Stalin wanted recognized by his allies. Later, as the fortunes of war were bringing the Red armies into Berlin, perspectives and appetites increased and the sphere of influence was pushed further westward. Roosevelt and Churchill understood from the first that this stood at the top of Russian demands for a postwar settlement in Europe.

The British, because of their own vulnerability, were disposed at first to come to an agreement with the Russians. In April, 1942, Churchill wrote Roosevelt that "the increasing gravity of the war" had brought him to the view that the Atlantic Charter "ought not to be construed so as to deny Russia the frontiers she occupied when Germany attacked her." Russian demands, however, cut across the American design for the postwar world. This envisaged the realization of an idealized capitalism: free trade, free access to raw materials, freedom of capital to invest, breaking down of all political barriers to free enterprise. This glittering perspective was not confined to the sweeping declarations in the Atlantic Charter. There was an attempt to write them into contractual provisions of the lend-lease agreements. At Bretton Woods the financial institutions were founded to provide an orderly mechanism for international exchanges so as to avoid the nationalist exclusiveness and economic roughhousing of the interwar years.

The corollary of the economic open door was a political open door. It was necessary to turn away from spheres of influence, protectorates, and balance-of-power concepts; these had been responsible for the inflamed rivalries, the disorganization of mutually beneficial economic arrangements, leading in the end to wars. To pass from this dark, burdensome past to the light of a peaceful world order there would have to be a new world organization to safeguard the peace through collective security, one that embodied institutional machinery to adjudicate rival claims. In his final address to Congress reporting on the Yalta conference, Roosevelt voiced the hope that the new scheme would "spell the end of the system of unilateral action, the exclusive alliances, the spheres of influence, the balances of power, and all other expedients that have been tried for centuries—and have always failed."

The American design was bound to appear in a different light to Stalin (and, for that matter, to Churchill) than to Roosevelt. Aside from the fact that free trade works to the advantage of the economically strong, and to the disadvantage of the economically weak, the United States had a very bad record on this score, as her tariff history made evident. Her pieties customarily outran her practices. If free trade and the open door lacked appeal to a Britain in decline, one can imagine how acceptable it would be to the Soviet Union, which had a different system of state property and state monopoly of foreign trade.

In its political aspect, to counterpose an international organization to spheres of influence or exclusive alliances presupposed the existence of something that was not there. The counterposition of one to the other could have meaning only if the international organization was an authoritative government that could pass on disputes between nations and maintain public order around the globe. But humanity was as far away from world government then as it is today. Certainly no one in the councils of the Big Three considered it a topic of serious diplomacy. The world organization could be persuasive if the doctrine of collective security had potency, or even plausibility. Unfortunately, to all the expedients that had been tried and had failed, Roosevelt should have added collective security, as well. Where all the major powers are united, they might strong-arm fifth-rate countries on the verge of war to cease and desist—and even that is not always possible in a world of increasingly assertive nationalisms. Where the major powers are themselves in conflict, collective security, if invoked, becomes a formula for the organization of war, not of peace.

In the circumstances, the State Department's attempt to sidetrack Russian territorial claims on her European borders to a distant peace conference meant to Stalin that there was an attempt to cheat Russia of what her war sacrifices entitled her to. The American claim to disinterested universalism was compromised from the start by the disparity between rhetoric and conduct. Roosevelt's inveighing against spheres of influence while the United States exercised suzerainty over Latin America, the Philippines, superintendence over Nationalist China, was as incongruous as Churchill's signing of the Atlantic Charter while making it clear that it did not apply to the British Empire. What looked like a design for world cooperation to the American leaders could be interpreted by the Russians as a formula for American hegemony.*

A conflict between the two was thus implicit even in the halcyon days of Russian-American friendship. What made it acute was that Soviet ambitions inevitably widened in the wake of sensational military exploits. While the State Department diplomats were still keeping in cold storage the papers relating to the reincorporation of the Baltic states or eastern Poland into the Soviet Union, the westward sweep of the Red armies confronted the allied governments with the question of Soviet control of the entire East European heartland.

The Russian armies entered Poland, Rumania, Bulgaria, and Hungary in the spring, summer, and fall of 1944; in all cases, announcements were made that there would be no attempt to change the existing social systems. Nevertheless, the prewar elites and political leaders were in a state of uneasiness bordering on panic; a state of mind shared by the American representatives and reflected in their dis-

---

* During the UN founding conference, McCloy called Stimson to get his advice on the best legal formula for continuing American overlordship in the Western Hemisphere under a regional treaty while denying an East European sphere of influence to Russia. McCloy said, "I've been taking the position that we ought to have our cake and eat it too; that we ought to be free to operate under this regional arrangement in South America, at the same time intervene promptly in Europe; that we oughtn't to give away either asset." Stimson agreed. "I think so, decidedly. I think that it's not asking too much to have our little region over here which has never bothered anybody." This eventuated in the adoption of Article 51 by the UN, which was used as the legal basis for regional military pacts negotiated by the State Department.

patches to Washington. Much had changed in the behavior and professions of the Soviet Union since the first years of the Russian Revolution; the fierce militancy of Lenin and Trotsky had long since
ebbed; the new breed of Stalinist bureaucrats was talking in terms of
big-power realism; it had shown both interest and ability to restrain
Communists abroad; but the Soviet Union still represented an anti-
thetical system that might spread in the wake of the disorder and destruction of war. And who knew how much reliance could be placed
on the words of Stalin and his coadjutors? Would they refrain from
attempts at Communization if left to their own devices?

The way the Soviets proceeded to administer the countries they occupied convinced the Americans that their worst premonitions were
about to be realized. At the end of August, the Rumanian government, after making futile attempts to surrender to the Westerners,
signed with Russia. The armistice provided for reparations payments
of $300 million over a six-year period and restoration of Rumanian
civil administration under Soviet control. A week later Harriman told
Molotov that the United States expected to have a political representative in Rumania. Molotov made clear that representation would be
solely through the Control Commission. When the British refused to
sign the armistice until they knew what their rights would be on the
commission, Molotov stated unambiguously "that the task of the other
representatives on the Control Commission would be analogous to
the position of the Soviet representative on the Allied Control Commission for Italy." This was ominous news.

The Italian precedent to which the Russians referred repeatedly
was to plague the Western allies. It had its origin in the surrender negotiations conducted by the Anglo-American representatives with
Marshal Pietro Badoglio, appointed by King Victor Emmanuel to
head the government after the removal and arrest of Mussolini. The
Russians had not been included in the proceedings. Stalin protested
the entire arrangement and heatedly demanded the organization of a
military-political commission with representatives of the three allies
to take up all matters relating to negotiations with all governments
breaking away from Germany. Nothing was done about it since Stalin
agreed subsequently to armistice terms that provided for the appointment of a commission under the orders of the allied military commander, and Roosevelt chose to assume that this disposed of the matter. Stalin, however, returned to his proposal. The two Western heads
then agreed to the organization of such a commission while reducing
its functions to those of a liaison and advisory body. When Andrei

Vyshinsky arrived with two senior Russian officers and a staff to take his place in the commission, he was given, in Cordell Hull's words, "token representation." The Russians swallowed the affront and filed the precedent for future use. Roosevelt understood that he was storing up trouble for himself by shunting the Russians aside from policy-making in the Italian occupation. He told Harriman, who was about to go to Moscow as American ambassador, that he recognized that the Russians had the power to grasp whatever parts of Central and Eastern Europe they wanted. But he hoped to get them to abstain from doing so by a combination of warnings and concessions.

This was the "Italian formula" that Stalin was now resolved to employ on the defeated Axis allies. What had been sauce for the goose was going to be sauce for the gander. Events in Bulgaria and Hungary followed the pattern of Rumania. The governments made desperate efforts to surrender to the Westerners; they finally were brought to heel by the Russians, who imposed the same terms on them as they had done on the Rumanians, except that no reparations were demanded from Bulgaria. So far as social changes were concerned, the United States did not have too much to complain about in the first few months, but the trend of developments made her apprehensive, so that American representatives were in a state of anticipatory rage. The old ruling circles, unusually corrupt and callous, had discredited themselves by their collaboration with the Nazis. The emergence of Popular Front movements in which Communists played dominant roles made the Americans exaggerate every demand for long-overdue reforms as a Communist-takeover plot.

The truth is that the American program for Eastern Europe, to the extent that there was one, lacked relevance. In the chaos and bankruptcy of the Balkans, "open door" and "free trade" had an almost esoteric ring. American hostility to the insurgent forces, which they too simply considered mere creatures of Moscow, led them to intrigue with the scrubby political figures of the past. They thus appeared as reactionaries seeking to reimpose the unlamented interwar regimes. Had they succeeded, they would have converted the East European states not into sturdy democracies welcoming American investments and goods, but client states like Greece, claimants on American bounty and warring on their own people with the help of American arms.

It might be said that American political instincts proved sound; within the next several years, all these countries were Communized with Western influences rigorously excluded. Opponents of govern-

ment policies have countered that the dire prophecies were self-ful-
filling, that it was the Cold War aggressions of the United States that
made Stalin react by progressively shutting out Western influences in
the buffer zone. What was in Stalin's mind, or whether he was of one
mind, is impossible to say; even if and when the Russian archives are
opened, they may provide an ambiguous answer. Many things can
and have been pointed to, to demonstrate that in the initial period
the Russians did not intend to impose Communist regimes on these
countries. This has been countered with the assertion that it was simply the employment of what a Hungarian Stalinist called "salami tactics," destroying your opposition by cutting off one slice at a time.
Fundamentally, in a world riven by ideological and big-power conflicts, the Russians could not secure a protectorate zone of reliable
satellite states unless they Communized them—and, as later events
showed, even this was not an absolute guarantee of loyalty. Leaving
them capitalist, however, was to ensure their breaking loose from
Moscow's embrace at the first crisis. When the Soviet state burst out
of the war as an imposing military power, and its armies sprawled
into Eastern and Central Europe, its contest with the West was de-
creed. Whether the United States, at the pinnacle of power, which
had gone to war to block Germany's domination of Europe, would
have reconciled itself to a Czarist empire's extending its outposts to
the Elbe, is a moot question. That it would not reconcile itself to a
Soviet empire trampling underfoot private property rights in territories embracing 125 million souls was certain.

Although more time was spent haggling over Poland at Yalta than
on any other matter, the final agreement represented not a compromise, but a clouding of the differences with vaporous pronouncements. The best the Westerners were able to get was a paper stating
that the existing government in Poland would be reorganized on a
broader democratic basis, and a declaration for the establishment
through free elections of governments responsive to the popular will
in the liberated areas. After one of the sessions, Leahy remarked to
Roosevelt that the agreement on Poland was "so elastic that the Russians can stretch it all the way from Yalta to Washington without
ever technically breaking it." Roosevelt replied wearily, "I know, Bill,
I know it. But it's the best I can do for Poland at this time."

Stalin probably thought that the Polish dispute had been disposed
of, that his allies had exhausted themselves with their urgings and arguments, and that after the addition of a few new figures to the government, which would not change essentials, they would accept the

results. The declaration for free elections he assumed they needed for their home consumption. Where countries are under military occupation, elections pose problems only of logistics; results generally conform to the wishes of the authorities. Did Roosevelt and Churchill think they had won anything more substantial? It is hard to say because they were working in the heady atmosphere of military victory. The overpowering wish was to convince themselves that they were chartering the instruments to bring into being a new, beneficent world order.

This, then, was the famous Yalta agreement that Stalin was said to be violating, and the issue on which Truman decided to make a stand. It did not work out. Contrary to expectations, the Russians did not cave in. Within twenty-four hours of the meeting with Molotov, parallel messages reached Truman and Churchill accusing the two governments of ganging up on, and trying to dictate to, the Soviet Union. The only way out of the impasse, Stalin wrote, was to accept the Yugoslav precedent. There, Tito's provisional government had been broadened with the addition of members from the Yugoslav government-in-exile in the proportion of 5 to 1. The crisis deepened the next week when Molotov admitted that sixteen Polish underground leaders had been arrested for "diversionary activities" and were being held in Russia for trial. After further exchanges of messages, it was obvious the deadlock was complete. The symbolic showdown had failed.

The next step was for Truman to tighten the economic screws on his dear ally. On May 8, one day after Germany's surrender, and one day after receipt of Stalin's final rejection of American proposals, Leo Crowley, the Lend-Lease Administrator, accompanied by Acting State Secretary Grew, brought the President a draft ordering an immediate cutback of lend-lease in Europe, which he promptly signed. The order was carried out with deadly efficiency. Ships on the high seas bound for the Soviet Union were ordered to turn back, loading of ships in port was stopped, and goods already aboard ships were unloaded. Moscow immediately sent a protest, and there was public criticism. Three days later, Truman substituted a modified instruction that permitted vessels waiting for lend-lease cargoes to be loaded, while not changing the essentials of the decision.

He subsequently put the blame for his first order on Crowley and Grew, claiming that he had not read the document and that the two had overstepped their authority. This is contradicted by the understanding of other participants. Before seeing Truman, Crowley had talked on the phone to Grew to confirm his agreement. He asked Grew to accompany him when the order was explained to Truman, because he wanted "to be sure the President thoroughly understands the situation and that he will back us up." That same day Stimson was talking to the President at the White House; he thought the best approach was to eliminate the lend-lease protocol, to which Truman responded that that was "right down his alley." Stimson reported the conversation to Grew, who was "very much pleased." An immediate halt of shipments was not specifically required by the terms of the lend-lease law, as some thought at the time. Supplies were sent to Britain after the German surrender on the grounds that her contingents made available other forces for Japan. The entire incident, which was to figure in the deepening division between, East and West, showed that the second cooks had crowded in to stir and season the broth, and that the head chef was giving orders without adequate consideration of what the entire menu was going to be.

The economic squeeze produced no results either. Stalin's note of May 10 reiterated that the American attitude ruled out "an agreed decision" on Poland. At this point, Truman's advisers made it clear that they had not thought through their strategy, and Churchill, who on his part was trying to egg on Truman, revealed again that his prewar reputation in British politics as an adventurer and blusterer had been well earned. Since both the demonstration with Molotov, and the economic ploy, had not affected Stalin, the next move that Leahy, Harriman, and Grew proposed was an immediate showdown session of the Big Three. Churchill was sending urgent messages proposing the same thing, plus the additional proviso that British and American troops hold on to all the real estate they held or would hold in the next days. To Eden, who was in San Francisco, he wired that the allied armies should not move back to the lines that had previously been agreed to with Stalin until all outstanding political questions had been settled. "Nothing can save us from the great catastrophe but a meeting and a showdown as early as possible."

If a showdown session with Molotov had not budged the Russians, what would a showdown session with Stalin accomplish? What if Stalin refused to be swayed by Churchill's majestic periods, or Truman's dry Missouri twang? What was the next move? War? These great men had worked themselves into such a fever that they did not ask this question of themselves or of each other. It was assumed that somehow American pressures, threats, and bluffing would get the Russians to unbend. That they had not reacted thus far as they were supposed to, did not mean the strategy was unsound, but that it should be pursued more energetically.

Churchill had tried to agitate Roosevelt to use troop dispositions as political bargaining counters. He renewed his efforts the first week of Truman's Presidency. At first, on the advice of the Joint Chiefs of Staff, Truman rebuffed Churchill. After the tough line had been adopted, he reversed himself, overruled Eisenhower's recommendation, and he and Churchill sent messages that linked troop withdrawals to a satisfactory settlement of the Austrian issues. Both the American and British staff chiefs thought it was bad business. Eisenhower was convinced that "to start off our first direct association with Russia on the basis of refusing to carry out an arrangement in which the good faith of our government was involved would wreck the whole cooperative attempt at its very beginning." The Russians responded by recognizing the Renner government in Austria without reference to her allies, and held up joint control until the establishment of a German control commission. To the squabble over Austria was added tension with Tito over Venezia Giulia, so that a stalemate had developed on still another front. Important matters were arising every day that had to be settled by a European control commission, but no commission could be set up until the troops returned to their allotted zones.

By the second week of May, Truman began to suspect that his advisers and Churchill were pushing him too fast without a clear understanding of the pitfalls ahead. He had neither the literary effulgence nor the authoritative air of Churchill, but he could recognize a stone wall when he was in contact with one—which was not always true of his great contemporary. He decided that a tactical retreat must be made if freedom of movement to pursue basic objectives in a more realistic way was to be won. As soon as he had made up his mind, he moved with customary resolution. Without consulting the State Department or Churchill, he arranged with great secrecy to send Harry Hopkins on a special mission to confer with Stalin. Only at the last moment did he discuss it with the State Department, presumably Grew, and also with Byrnes, both of whom opposed the trip. He went right ahead, sent a wire to Stalin, who assented. In his *Memoirs* he places his first discussion with Hopkins as early as May 4, but it would appear he was trying to mist over the significance of the trip. Robert Sherwood, who got his information from Harriman and Bohlen, was probably more accurate when he said that Harriman made the suggestion to Truman in the middle of May, and that Hopkins was called to the White House a few days afterward.

It was clear that sending Hopkins, who symbolized publicly the Roosevelt policy of cooperation with the Russians, meant that Truman was prepared to make concessions. At the same time, as if to make the scenario complete, he shipped off Joseph E. Davies as his special representative to meet with Churchill in London. Any representative arriving at 10 Downing Street with the joyous tidings that the American President wanted to disentangle himself from Churchill's too fond embrace, and had in mind, in addition, to meet separately with Stalin preliminary to a meeting of the Big Three, was likely to be as welcome as a swarm of locusts at harvest time. But Truman had probably never read Davies' book, *Mission to Moscow*, or he would have realized that it was cruel beyond the call of duty to send Churchill this particular sixty-nine-year-old exponent of friendship with Russia. Davies wasted no time in telling Churchill that all suspicion must be dispelled that the two Western powers were "ganging up" on Stalin, that the three must solve their disagreements in the interests of peace. Since the Prime Minister may not have been acquainted with Kansas City politics, where you signaled a maneuver not by waving a little flag but by setting off a thunderous cannon charge, he may have exaggerated the profundity of the change from listening to Davies' lectures, which sounded almost like personal reprimands. Davies' report read:

> I said that frankly, as I had listened to him inveigh so violently against the threat of Soviet domination and the spread of Communism in Europe, and disclose such a lack of confidence in the professions of good faith in Soviet leadership, I had wondered whether he, the Prime Minister, was now willing to declare to the world that he and Britain had made a mistake in not supporting Hitler, for as I understood him, he was now expressing the doctrine which Hitler and Goebbels had been proclaiming and reiterating for the past four years in an effort to break up Allied unity and "divide and conquer." Exactly the same conditions which he described and the same deductions were drawn from them as he now appeared to assert.

The proposal for a separate meeting with Stalin was dropped when Churchill wrote that he would not attend a meeting that was a continuation of a Truman-Stalin conclave. The Davies mission was high diplomatic horseplay. If it was meant to enlighten the British as to their real place in the alliance, it was redundant, for they could not mistake their predicament when their representatives had to come to Washington hat in hand to solicit a loan.

In the serious part of the mission, the Moscow visit, Hopkins told Stalin that the past six weeks had seen a serious deterioration in relations, so that if present trends continued unchecked, the entire structure of cooperation with Russia would be destroyed, and that the anxiety was symbolized for American public opinion by the inability to carry out the Yalta agreement on Poland. Stalin countered that the reason for the failure was that Russia wanted a friendly Poland while Britain (meaning the Westerners) wanted to revive a *cordon sanitaire*. Hopkins said the United States had no such intention, that it wanted friendly countries along Soviet borders. If that was so, Stalin came back, they could easily come to terms. It was his impression that the American attitude toward Russia had perceptibly cooled once it was clear that Germany was defeated. He cited a number of instances to illustrate the changed attitude. On Poland, he said, the agreement was that the existing government was to be reconstituted, which any one with common sense could see meant that the present government would form the basis of the new—no other interpretation was possible. The Russians were simple people, but they should not be regarded as fools, a mistake frequently made in the West.

At the conclusion of the general discussion which left the matter very much where it had been left at Yalta, Hopkins went on to assure Stalin that Truman did not intend to propose any Poles, even for consultations, who were against the Yalta decision, and that he anticipated that the present Warsaw regime would comprise a majority of the reconstituted government. These were the magic words that broke the impasse. The way was now opened for bargaining. To anticipate, a dozen Poles not connected with the provisional government were invited to Moscow for consultations and carried on discussions with the Warsaw people under the aegis of the allied commission of three. An agreement was reached that of a total of twenty cabinet posts, six were to be assigned to the newcomers. Stanislaw Mikolajczyk, the most influential person connected with the London group, was to become a second deputy prime minister as well as minister of agriculture. On July 5, the two Western allies, with many misgivings, recognized the broadened provisional government. Major attention was now centered on the promised elections, which, it was hoped, would produce results that would assure the Western presence. Had anything been accomplished? Leahy, after Yalta, did not believe "that the dominating Soviet influence could be excluded from Poland, but I did think it was possible to give the reorganized Polish government an external appearance of independence." He had guessed correctly.

Meanwhile, the four commanders in chief met in Berlin to sign the joint declaration assuming supreme authority over Germany. When Eisenhower proposed the installation of the allied control commission in Berlin, Marshal Georgi Zhukov said, "No, not until your troops will have been evacuated from the areas in the Soviet zone they now illegally occupy." "Why not, then," suggested Eisenhower, "talk about both questions?" "No," answered Zhukov. "I cannot discuss the first until the second is settled." Eisenhower again advised Washington to withdraw the troops, a view concurred in by Robert Murphy, Eisenhower's political adviser. Hopkins, who met with Eisenhower at Frankfurt on his way back home, wired Truman "that present indeterminate status is certain to be misunderstood by Russia as well as at home." Truman then advised Churchill that he could not delay the pullback any longer. He sent along a text of a message he proposed to send to Stalin. "This," Churchill wrote later, "struck a knell in my breast, but I had no choice but to submit."

Hopkins disposed of another matter of consequence while in Moscow. In the midst of his discussions, he received an urgent message from Washington to take up with Stalin the veto formula for the UN over which the Russian and American delegations were deadlocked in San Francisco, a crisis that threatened to wreck the conference. To go ahead with the founding conference, as scheduled by Roosevelt, had been Truman's first decision after he took the oath of office. Although neither Stalin nor Churchill had taken the world organization as seriously as Roosevelt, they accepted it as the ostensible instrument that held the hope of ushering in a new, better international order and saving mankind from the horrors of future wars. The hopes of millions had been excited by the possibilities.

The world organization, unfortunately, was tainted at birth. The underlying mood of East-West suspicion and hostility infected most of the delegates so that they conducted themselves as if they had come for an anti-Soviet mobilization rather than to set up a universal organization. The Soviet delegates responded in kind, and much time was taken up in sordid and largely inconsequential squabbles over the admission of Argentina, the Warsaw government, who was to be the presiding officer, and in parliamentary maneuvering for petty advantage. The American press by its irresponsible and sensational reporting gave the public an impression that the Russians were an unreasonable lot bent on having their own way or sabotaging the efforts of others. James Reston in his report to *The New York Times* felt called upon to list the concessions the Russians had made in the course of the conference and to note the feeling among the delegates that American press reports had been inaccurate. The electioneering antics of the American delegation were often more appropriate to the running of a caucus at an Elks convention than what could be considered proper behavior for representatives at an international assemblage. Walter Lippmann referred caustically to the "American steamroller," to "riding roughshod through a world conference with a bloc of twenty [Latin American] votes."

The formula of big-power veto rights was thought to have been settled at Yalta: On all questions involving enforcement, there would have to be unanimity of the permanent members of the UN Security Council; that on procedural matters and those calling for a consideration of peaceful settlements of disputes, the party to the dispute would abstain on the vote. This was supposed to provide all nations the right to a hearing in the Security Council, while reserving to the major powers decisions on enforcement. Whether because the discussions in San Francisco brought out ambiguities and different interpretations of the formula, or because the Russians decided they had better seek additional protection from the American voting machine, Andrei Gromyko, who replaced Molotov as delegation head, announced that his instructions were that all permanent members had to concur for the Security Council to consider any dispute. After listening to Hopkins' explanations, Stalin told Molotov that he thought the matter was insignificant, that he could accept the American position on voting procedure.

With the immediate issues cleared away, the path seemed open for the reestablishment of cooperative relations. There was a feeling of elation in the American camp. Grew, who had cabled Hopkins, "The President, the Secretary and I send you heartiest congratulations and appreciation," reported to the Cabinet "that the international scene is a great deal brighter." For a few days, Hopkins found himself in the unaccustomed role of hero. In fact, although movement had been restored again to diplomatic relations, the principles of the conflict remained unchanged. The inevitable clash had merely been postponed.

In the course of the exchanges that had ensued since Truman took over, ideas had been adumbrated that one of the big difficulties in dealing with the Russians was that words like democracy or elections did not mean the same to them as to Americans, or that Stalin was incapable of comprehending that such matters represented principles on which we would never compromise. This was just the pseudointellectual steam that inevitably rises in the atmosphere from the heat of a protracted debate. These were not the reasons for tension. Russian dictionaries were no less comprehensive than English ones, and the Russians had the same access to the documentation of the Enlightenment as the Westerners. But conflicts of interest are real things; they cannot necessarily be dissipated by argument; in the absence of binding international law, they are not invariably settled by orderly processes. What monstrously aggravated a traditional big-power conflict was that the United States and the Soviet Union rested on antipathetic social systems whose extension tended to undermine each other's bases of strength. What made it impossible at the time to fix a modus vivendi was the American leaders' conviction that they had the upper hand, that by using the economic and diplomatic weapons at their disposal they could force Stalin and Company to bend to their will.

Thus, as Truman prepared to depart for the Potsdam Conference to meet with Stalin and Churchill, what was in the offing was not a settlement, but another deadlock. In the light of what happened, some have speculated that Truman had delayed the meeting to mid-July against the urgings of Churchill and his own advisers because he wanted to wait for the test of the atom bomb, so that he could have this weapon in hand to pressure the Russians. That the atom bomb was very much in his and in others' minds by this time will soon be evident. One can only imagine, however, that the conference date was set in accordance with a carefully designed timetable encompassing fully thought out procedures and fixed dates by ignoring the confusion, the miscalculations, the pressures, the fugitive recommendations, which enveloped a harried and inexperienced President who was making decisions on the move.

There was no real purpose in having a confrontation with Stalin when it was urged by the State Department. There was no real purpose in having one in mid-July. Truman had agreed to the date when Hopkins set it with Stalin; now he was committed to it. Had the confrontation been planned with the clear idea of pressuring Stalin with the atom bomb, then the conference was held too early. The Russians could not be pressured in any case, for, as Stimson indicated, the bomb could not affect the power realities until it "had been successfully laid on Japan." After his experiences with the initial showdown, Truman suspected before he left for Europe that not too much would be accomplished. What could be agreed on could be settled by routine diplomacy. In a letter to his mother and sister—he never neglected to send long, chatty letters home in all his years in Washington—he wrote, "Wish I didn't have to go, but I do and it can't be stopped now." He sent another letter when he was at sea: "I wish this trip was over. I hate it. But it has to be done."

Although the Potsdam meeting was not formally the peace conference, its rationale, for all intents and purposes, was as the triumphant gathering of the victors of the Second World War to settle their affairs and the affairs of much of the world at the site of the capital of prostrate Nazidom. One cannot help but contrast Truman's entrance into Europe with that of Woodrow Wilson twenty-seven years before. Wilson was received in Paris, London, and Rome amidst scenes of indescribable emotional outpouring. Massed crowds, unprecedented in number and fervor, greeted him not as a conqueror but as a savior. His prestige dwarfed, and was of a different order from the prestige of all other allied leaders. His words carried above the governments to the peoples of the defeated as well as of the victorious countries. In 1945, the arrival of the presidential party was a somber and official affair. Truman and his entourage passed through swiftly on their way to their headquarters in Berlin, like a corps of staff officers on assignment. Aside from the drive through the streets of Brussels, their main contact was with the American military and civilian occupation officials. It was as if Truman (and his two allies) were saying to the peoples that they would make the decisions for them, and the masses, on their part, harbored no excessive hopes that a brave new world was about to issue from the decisions of the victors.

More than the difference between Wilson and Truman and their standing as individuals, was the difference between epochs. Pristine faith, trifled and tampered with at Versailles and in the interwar years, could not be re-created. Even the official war rhetoric had a mechanical and labored ring. Back home, the contrast was noted by Frederick Lewis Allen, the chronicler of the decade. He said that whereas "there had been a lively crusading spirit" in the First World War, there was a minimum of it in the Second. For, as he explained, "the popular disillusionments had left their marks." A quarter century before, embattled Bolshevism had pushed Wilson to issuing his Fourteen Points, and the Big Three had labored under Lenin's threatening shadow; now Lenin's successor, at the head of a bourgeoisified Soviet Union, occupied one of the seats inside the council chamber, preparing to divide the spoils.

9

Conflict
at
Potsdam

The American headquarters, named the Little White House, was located in Babelsburg, a fashionable Berlin suburb that had been the center of the German film colony. The large stucco house set in a magnificent garden sloping down to a lake had been owned by a movie tycoon. The delegation would drive the three miles to the conference site at the Cecilianhof in Potsdam. The palace, which had belonged to the former crown prince, was a spectacular four-winged edifice overlooking immense landscaped gardens and a large lake. Each head of government had a suite of rooms for his personal use, and a conference room and offices for his staff. The main conference room, in the center of which had been placed a circular oak table, was spacious; at one end a huge window provided a sweeping view of the royal retreat. The delegates were made aware of the ruins and devastation about them only when they went sightseeing on free afternoons.

Truman's main advisers were Byrnes, Leahy, and the military people. Davies sat with the President at the plenary sessions, but had little influence. Apparently his presence was meant to keep Churchill in his place. One of the undercurrents in American councils was to keep up the Rooseveltian pretense that they were mediators between the Russians and British. Stimson, the main consultant on atomic matters, invited himself. Truman then agreed that he be close at hand when the test results were known. Harriman, who had been at Yalta and present during the Hopkins-Stalin talks, also had to propose himself. Forrestal was kept out of the delegation. He made his own arrangements to take a European trip and turned up, uninvited, at the conference site. Truman was startled when he saw him. He acted cordial, even asked him to breakfast, but paid no further attention to him. Truman had wanted to bring along Vinson, but they both agreed that a reliable person should be left to mind the store. Who was and who was not invited had to do with the pecking order in the palace guard. In the case of Harriman, it was said that Byrnes wanted to keep him out of the inner circle. That a Cabinet member and an ambassador nominated themselves, and that another Cabinet member came without an invitation, was a reflection of the weakened authority of the Chief Executive. No one had the temerity to try to crash the party at Yalta.

Byrnes, as the new State Secretary, was the senior Cabinet member. Truman had told him from the first that he wanted him at the head of State. It was decided to defer the announcement until the end of the UN conference in order not to undercut Stettinius' position there. The appointment had political value for a President who had not been elected in his own right: Byrnes had a big reputation in Congress, was generally considered a person of judgment and weight. Aside from that, Truman apparently was still sensitive about the vice-presidential scramble, in which he had not been quite the innocent bystander that he had pretended to be. In his *Memoirs* appeared the singular explanation that he thought that by appointing Byrnes it would help to balance things up.

The appointment was an unhappy one, as events were to demonstrate. Byrnes not only believed he should have received the vice-presidential nomination, but that he was better fitted by experience and ability to be President than his former fellow senator. This led to inevitable irritation between the two, which before long would lead to a rupture. The choice was not the best on another count, for Byrnes brought qualities and abilities that Truman already had, and did not contribute what Truman lacked and badly needed. Byrnes's rather comprehensive ignorance of foreign countries and cultures was wedded to an operator's mentality which transposed problems to the manageable key of maneuver and adjustment. This is not to say that fundamental policy would have been markedly different had a man of greater breadth been chosen. A course and a goal had been set, not just by the technicians in the State Department, but by the entire outlook of the government establishment.

On the way to the conference, Truman tried to bone up on the major questions to be taken up. He sailed on a heavy cruiser, the U.S.S. *Augusta,* which was led by another cruiser to make a smooth path so that neither the President nor his staff should suffer from seasickness. The State Department had provided him with briefing papers and recommendations on outstanding problems, which he proceeded to digest as rapidly as he could. The task was facilitated for him by his habit of simplifying questions into tactical exercises lending themselves to quick decisions. Byrnes held long meetings with his staff to plan the proposed agenda and presentations. Not that they devoted themselves exclusively to heavy brain work. Truman chatted with his friends and newspapermen, played cards, attended movies and concerts. He reported back home to Mama and Mary that "the trip has been most pleasant and restful. Went to church at 10:30 with officers and men. Sat around on the deck with Mr. Byrnes and Adm. Leahy most of the morning and took a nap in the afternoon. Saw a picture show that night—we have one every night."

The two major questions at Potsdam that were to determine the course of East-West relations and the future of Europe related to Germany and Soviet-occupied countries. As if anticipating that much could not be settled at the conference, Truman proposed at the first plenary session the establishment of a council of foreign ministers. The council would have the duty of drawing up peace treaties with the defeated countries, later propose territorial settlements, eventually a peace treaty with Germany. The proposal was adopted with the modification that the Chinese representative would not participate in European matters, France would not be included in East European peace treaties.

As soon as the allies moved from procedural to policy questions, the old incompatibility became evident. The American delegation circulated a statement that the Yalta Declaration on Liberated Europe still remained to be carried out, that the governments of Rumania and Bulgaria, before they could be accorded recognition, had to be immediately reorganized to conform to the standards established, and that the three powers were called upon to assist these nations to hold free elections. The gauntlet was again flung down. There was to be no peace until Stalin released his grip. In the months since Yalta, American fears had been growing. Not only were the Russians stripping occupied countries on reparation accounts; they were carrying off industrial equipment as war booty, entrenching themselves in the economies with the creation of jointly owned enterprises for which the native consortiums were required to supply funds and equities, and for which the Russians contributed as their share equipment they had seized as Nazi-owned properties. Unless, it was felt, the control commissions could be drastically overhauled, the economies as well as the governments would be converted into Soviet appendages.

The Russians rejected the American case in total and called on Washington to grant immediate recognition to Rumania, Bulgaria, Hungary, and Finland. At the same time Molotov denounced the reign of terror in Greece, and sarcastically pointed out that, despite the longer period of occupation, there had been no election held in Italy. Byrnes offered to include Italy in an international supervision of elections. Molotov demanded to know why the East European states should not all be admitted at once to the UN. They had become cobelligerents, had done more to win the war than Italy. Byrnes and Eden insisted that to admit them would be to recognize their existing governments, which, unlike the Italian, were not representative. Stalin asserted that they were as democratic as the Italian and closer to the people; they were as willing to grant access to American and British agents as Italy was to admit Russian agents. Privately he told Churchill that this was dirty pool: He had not interfered with the British in Belgium or Greece, and the Westerners had no business interfering with him in the Russian zone. The issue hung unresolved until the closing hours of the conference.

On Poland, although the reconstituted provisional government had been installed only a few weeks before, a new issue arose to bedevil the conference. At Yalta the three had agreed that Poland was to receive territorial compensation to the north and west up to the line of the Oder. It was left up in the air whether the boundary was to extend to the Western Neisse River, which included Stettin and Breslau, an area between the two lines that had been inhabited by some 3 million Germans. When the Russian troops overran the region, they turned over to the Poles civil administration of this larger area. The British had told Truman that they were opposed to going beyond the Oder, that the Russians should be told that if they would not agree, the Western allies would refuse reparation transfers from their zones. Truman upbraided Stalin for allotting an occupation zone in Germany to Poland without consulting his allies. Stalin explained his unilateral action on grounds of war necessity: The Germans had fled westward while the Poles remained; the Red Army required a local administration to maintain order behind its lines. Since Poland was to receive territorial compensation in the west, what was wrong with the conference stating its position on the western boundary, final validation being left to the peace conference?

While Truman and Churchill were joined in disputing Stalin, their tactical positions differed. Churchill wanted the line settled at Potsdam, for he feared that the more time elapsed, the firmer would become the Polish hold on the disputed areas, the greater the dependence of Poland on Russia for support of its claim. Truman was satisfied to reject the Russian position, accept no territorial settlement, even the one agreed to at Yalta, until the convocation of an undefined and undated peace conference. He felt, like Byrnes, that once the atomic bomb made its appearance on the stage, the Russians would prove to be more tractable. So, although the Poles were invited to come to Potsdam to present their case, and they lobbied assiduously, this issue, too, was deadlocked.

Inevitably the central, the crucial question that confronted the Big Three was what to do with Germany. On the answer to that hinged many of the lesser disputes as well as the fate of Europe. The American position, which over a period of two years was to make a complete 180-degree turn, had by this time changed more than halfway. Originally, at their Quebec meeting in the fall of 1944, Roosevelt and Churchill had initialed the Morgenthau Plan to dismember Germany and reduce the segments to an agricultural society. When Roosevelt returned to Washington, an agitated Stimson and a disturbed Hull put to him the consequences of such a policy in the shape of economic collapse and social convulsions in the center of the continent. Roosevelt thereupon backed away. He told Stimson he had evidently approved the plan without much thought, grinned, looked naughty, and said, "Henry Morgenthau pulled a boner."

At Yalta Stalin talked in terms of a Carthaginian peace. He wanted to dismantle 80 percent of German industry. Churchill and Eden thought his reparations demands outrageous, and, if enforced, ruinous to Europe. Roosevelt, who theoretically was mediating the two extreme positions, felt that the Germans should be made to feel in their bones the sanctions for the horrors they had unloosed. He also wanted to quiet Russian fears about a revival of German power in order to make them less grasping in Eastern Europe. After the storm over the Morgenthau Plan, he had dropped all further mention of it and had not brought Morgenthau to Yalta. Nevertheless, he still favored getting tough with the Germans, however that was to be translated into concrete decisions.

At the time there was a considerable body of opinion in the West, particularly liberal opinion, that favored a draconian policy to be applied not only to the Nazis, the generals, the industrialists, the Junkers, but for giving the entire German people a dose of their own medicine. The traditionally conservative circles, however, feared that the creation of a vast slum in the heart of Europe would make Germany either a charge on American bounty, or a breeding ground of revolution. They were already beginning to think of a reconstituted Germany to balance off a menacing Russia. In spite of Roosevelt's inclinations, he did not want to be pinned down to specifics until the armies were in occupation and the problems and possibilities were clearer. In characteristic fashion he wanted the answers to suggest themselves from the recommendations of the occupation authorities. So while Roosevelt kept nodding his head pleasantly, and while the Russians scored points in the generalized rhetoric that came out of Yalta, the major questions on Germany, aside from the approval of their respective occupation zones, were put over for future disposal. Was Germany to be one state or divided into several states? It was left open. What reparations were to be exacted? It was referred to a reparations commission, which would take the Russian proposal of $20 billion with half to be awarded to the Soviet Union as a basis for discussion. Churchill refused to accept even this vague formula, and recorded his opposition in the published protocol. What industries were to be eliminated, and what level of industry was to be permitted? No one knew.

By the time Truman headed for Potsdam, Germany was no longer seen in the light of the Yalta glow. The problem was not to reassure Stalin about his security against a renascent Germany, but to recreate a functioning, though pliable, Germany as a counterweight to Russia. Truman recorded, "We intended to make it possible for Germany to develop into a decent nation and to take her place in the civilized world." Thoughts had moved so far from Yalta that Byrnes told his staff, "Somebody has made an awful mistake in bringing about a situation where Russia was permitted to come out of a war with the power she will have; England should never have permitted Hitler to rise; the German people under a democracy would have been a far superior ally than Russia; there is too much difference in the ideologies of the U.S. and Russia to work out a long-term program."

It had now been accepted that reparations was not just another important issue, but that the decision on reparations would determine the larger decision on what Germany was going to be, what future role it would play. The tactics Truman approved were designed to permit America to carry out her new purposes. They concealed the confusion of the transition in the American camp, where bits and parts derived from the old perspective jostled in uneasy passage with recommendations derived from the new. JCS 1067, the American occupation directive to its zone commander, went through seven drafts before it was approved by Truman in May, and then it was opposed by Major General Lucius D. Clay, Eisenhower's deputy to head the military government, and the economic adviser, William H. Draper —the two people charged with administering it. Lewis W. Douglas, who had been Roosevelt's first budget director, said, "This thing was assembled by economic idiots." Eisenhower told Truman that he and Clay were convinced "that rehabilitation of the Ruhr was vital to our best interests." In practice, the zone commanders were beginning to run their regions in conformity with their social predilections and the requirements of their government bureaucracies. The American occupation officials were singling out conservative businessmen and former government officials to help them in their administration. The Russians were securing the aid of Communists, cooperating socialists and laborites, and opportunist officers to concoct Popular Front administrative formations. Each side interpreted "democratization" according to its own lights and needs.

Events were riding the government heads on the question of partition, as well. In line with its perspective, the United States was committed to a unified state. Truman's proposal to the conference that Germany "shall be treated as a single economic unit" was approved by all. Stalin had decided that his best chance for getting sizable reparations was in promoting the four-power control council. (France had been assigned a separate occupation zone and a seat on the council at Yalta.) Three-quarters of the German population, as well as of the resources, were now in the Western zones. Stalin needed Western agreement and cooperation to be able to cash in the ambiguous promissory note he had received at Yalta. Other aspects of the German settlement had become secondary to the urgent need to secure for Russia capital imports for her enormous reconstruction requirements.

The Potsdam debate over reparations, which turned into a sustained pulling-and-hauling contest arose not because of conflicting moralities, but conflicting interests. Truman and Byrnes had no principled objections to reparations; they simply were not going to permit these to undercut their basic program. Stalin, for his part, was appearing at Potsdam more in the character of the heir of Alexander I than of Lenin. The battle cry of Bolshevism in 1917 had been "No annexations and no indemnities"; the Bolshevik perspective had been an alliance of a Communist Germany with a Communist Russia. In contrast, Stalin, who had come to power with the program of "socialism in one country," had told Mikolaczyk that "Communism fitted Germany as a saddle fitted a cow." Even if we do not try to read a thesis into the remark—in keeping with his known contempt for foreign Communists and lack of confidence in their abilities to make revolutions in their own countries—his aim at Potsdam was to bleed the Germans, not to Communize them. His proposal to remove four-fifths of German industry, had there been an attempt to carry it out, might conceivably have led to revolutionary outbursts; but if it did, these would have been no more pro-Russian than the subsequent Berlin uprising in 1953, or the Polish and Hungarian uprisings in 1956.

At the first opportunity Stalin presented his due bill for $20 billion, half to go to the Soviet Union. Byrnes took the position that required imports must be the first charge against exports of current production or stocks of goods, that only the excess could be used for reparations. He rejected Molotov's contention that both reparations and imports could be paid for if German consumption was reduced. Molotov suggested a compromise. If means were insufficient to pay for both reparations and imports, both would be proportionately reduced. No, Byrnes said, if imports were too small, the Germans would produce less, and the Western powers would have to make up the deficit. When the discussion veered to what amounts would be available, Byrnes maintained that it was impossible to set any figure; conditions were too unsettled. As the deadlock was becoming total, Byrnes suggested to Molotov that it might be best if they approached the matter in a different way: Let each occupying power draw reparations from its own zone, supplemented by an accord to exchange products. Molotov pointed out that if they failed to come to any agreement, the result would be the same as under Byrnes's scheme.

The conference was grinding to a close, with no understandings on any outstanding questions. Byrnes then offered a compromise package, which, he emphasized, had to be accepted in toto or not at all. In any case, the Americans were leaving the next day. The deal was in three parts: (1) Poland would administer the territories up to the Western Neisse pending the final determination of her frontier; (2) a peace treaty was to be prepared for Italy, to be followed by her admission to the UN (the Balkan states were to remain in purgatory so far as recognition went until their status was examined "in the near future in the light of conditions then prevailing"); (3) the Soviet Union was to receive 10 percent of such industrial capital equipment unnecessary for the German peace economy that was removed from the Western zones for reparations, and could trade food and raw materials from its zone for an additional 15 percent of such equipment.

The President and his Secretary of State remembered that they were politicians, and that the American people would expect them to report some "successes." They were not yet ready to advertise a formal break in the alliance. The thing to do, in the approved Senate cloakroom tradition, was to trade off what the Russians were doing in any case in the East for what the Westerners were going to do in the West, and call it a compromise. Stalin was of a similar mind. It was clear that he was going to receive no substantial reparations, if any at all, from the Western zones. Still, it was better to have a pseudo-friendly agreement recording the power realities rather than have the conference end in acrimony. During the final heated debates, Stalin had lashed out against Byrnes's "tactics." Before the gavel fell ending the conference, he asked Truman, who was in the chair, to say a few words about "Mr. Byrnes who has worked harder perhaps than any of us. He has brought us together in reaching so many important decisions." Truman expressed the hope that the next meeting of the Big Three would be in Washington. "God willing," replied Stalin. The deal, if such it can be called, signified the abandonment of four-power administration of a unitary Germany. It meant a partition along the lines of the military occupation zones. It encouraged the creation of an irredentist movement to reclaim the lost Eastern provinces. It set the stage for the pull-devil-pull-baker struggle over Europe.

Truman had been unenthusiastic about going to Potsdam. Throughout the proceedings he exhibited impatience with the discussions, truculence in presenting American positions. The knowledge that he had the atom bomb in his hip pocket led him to give play to his brashness. In addition there was his need to overcompensate his lack of assurance with a show of brisk decisiveness. "To some of his staff," wrote Herbert Feis, "he seemed unwilling to hear them out. Nor was his memory of what he had been told always exact." He kept Davies at his side to guarantee himself against being seduced by the redoubtable British chieftain. The very nature of American-Russian relations determined that his talk with Stalin would be rigidly diplomatic, although, curiously enough, he was not only impressed by him, he liked the man. And for a special reason. Stalin reminded him of Pendergast, which, for Truman, was a high recommendation. It goes without saying that that did not affect his positions. All the more reason to show one's mettle.

When the conference was a week old, and no significant agreements had been reached, he told Stalin that "when there was nothing more upon which they could agree, he was returning home." Thereafter, the conference proceeded under the threat of imminent American departure. When Churchill and Stalin fell into a long wrangle about Yugoslavia, Truman erupted in righteous exasperation that he had not come to hold a police court hearing, that if they did not get to the main issues, he was going to pack up and go home. Stalin laughed and said that he did not blame the President for wanting to go home, he wanted to go home too. It reinforced Truman's image of himself as a no-nonsense man of action when he recalled, "I was getting tired of sitting and listening to endless debate on matters that could not be settled at this conference, yet took up precious time. On a number of occasions I felt like blowing the roof off the palace." The Big Three feted each other and went through the traditional rounds of banquets and entertainments; but the high hopes of Yalta had evaporated under the blaze of animosities bred of conflicting purposes. Possibly Harriman and Leahy were wondering, as they were leaving, why they had pressed Truman to hurry to a summit conference. The same thought may have occurred to Churchill as he nursed his electoral wounds in Chartwell.

Truman said that the most urgent reason for his going to Potsdam was to clinch Russian entry into the war against Japan. If such was the case, he displayed a surprising listlessness in trying to attain his objective. The only time he brought up the matter was when Stalin had lunch with him on the opening day of the conference, and then only as part of a rambling, informal talk in which he made no effort to press his guest for commitments. At Yalta, Stalin had promised a Russian attack on Japan three months after the conclusion of the war in Europe. In return, Roosevelt agreed to the return of positions held by Russia prior to her defeat by Japan in 1904. The bargain included a Russian guarantee to back the Kuomintang regime in China, and the American pledge to get Chiang Kai-shek to accept the arrangement. Though this secret agreement later evoked frenzied denunciations of Roosevelt's alleged sellout of American interests, at the time the entire American delegation, including Harriman, Leahy, Stettinius, Byrnes, and Marshall, thought the agreement was not only eminently reasonable, but that Russian demands, by the big-power standards that they employed, were quite moderate. The Americans were anxious to gain Russian participation in a war that they then thought would be long and costly; they understood full well that the Russians, with or without agreement, could reclaim the old Czarist possessions and more if they wanted to do so.

Prior to Potsdam, the reconsideration of attitudes toward the Russians in Europe carried over to the Far East. Notes, memoranda, proposals flew back and forth in the Washington offices, raising questions whether the Yalta position should remain operative. Truman instructed Hopkins when he was in Moscow to seek a clarification. State was worrying whether Stalin would respect the open door in Manchuria once he had a grip on Dairen and the Chinese Eastern Railway. Stalin gave Hopkins categorical assurances. "He would do everything he could to promote unification of China under the leadership of Chiang Kai-shek. He had no territorial claims against China. He agreed with America's open door policy and went out of his way to indicate that the United States was the only power with the resources to aid China economically after the war. He agreed that there should be a trusteeship for Korea." Hopkins, and even Harriman, were very encouraged. What remained then was for America to fulfill her part of the pledge, namely, to get T.V. Soong, the Chinese foreign minister, to go to Moscow and come to an understanding validating the Yalta provisions.

Soong reached Moscow at the end of June in an American Army plane. As he and Stalin ran into disagreements, it became evident that the Americans were inciting Soong, not restraining him. Soong reviewed everything with Harriman. It can be assumed he was accepting Harriman's advice. At one point, the State Department notified Harriman to inform Soong that he should make certain that the agreement protected American access to Dairen and the Manchurian railroads. On July 6, the day Truman sailed for Potsdam, Harriman received a further instruction to tell both Stalin and Soong that the United States wanted to be consulted before final agreement was concluded. Four days later, over Stalin's objection, Soong said he could not proceed further, that he would have to return to Chungking for further instructions. Truman ignored a State Department memo to invite Soong to Potsdam to continue the negotiations there.

By now Truman and Byrnes saw the situation in a different light. It was taken for granted by everybody in Washington that Russia would come into the war for its own reasons; that no agreement was needed to coax it in. Even the timing, which was exercising Marshall in April, was going to be determined, it was felt, by Russia's requirements. Consequently there was no pressure for a fast agreement. Beyond that, Byrnes was making no secret of his high hopes that the atomic bomb would force Japan to capitulate before the Russians came in. That would bypass the need for joint arrangements that were bedeviling American diplomacy in Europe. After Truman received the report of the successful atom bomb test explosion, he asked Stimson to check whether Marshall still thought we needed the Russians in the Pacific war. Marshall answered that even if Japan capitulated before the Russians came in, they could still march into Manchuria and take what they wanted. But if the Russians came in, the war would end more quickly and with smaller loss of life.

Truman accepted the advice of both Byrnes and Marshall. On July 23, two days after they had received the full report of the atom bomb test, Byrnes cabled Chiang Kai-shek: "If you and Generalissimo Stalin differ as to the correct interpretation of the Yalta agreement, I hope you will arrange for Soong to return to Moscow and continue your efforts to reach complete understanding." The purpose of the cable, Byrnes explained, was to get the Chinese to resume negotiations as soon as Stalin got back to Moscow in order to tie him up. "I had some fear that if they did not, Stalin might immediately enter the war, knowing full well that he could take not only what Roosevelt and Churchill, and subsequently Chiang, had agreed to at Yalta, but —with China divided and Chiang seeking Soviet support against Chinese Communists—whatever else he wanted. On the other hand, if Stalin and Chiang were still negotiating, it might delay Soviet entrance and the Japanese might surrender. The President was in accord with that view." That was one ploy.

At the same time, Truman and Churchill approved the report of the Anglo-American Combined Chiefs of Staff, which declared that "The Soviet Union was to be encouraged to enter the war; and such aid to its war-making capacity as might be needed and practicable was to be provided." The combined chiefs then conferred with the Soviet military chiefs to coordinate strategy. General Alexei Antonov promised that Russia would commence operations in the last half of August, the precise date depending on coming to an agreement with the Chinese. Stalin had his own contingency plans. In the end, what decided the issue was not the sly deceptions of the American, Russian, and Chinese plenipotentiaries, but the ultimate facts of military power, massive shifts in popular sentiment, and social upheaval.

Truman went to Potsdam with the great secret that the United States would soon possess a superbomb that could destroy cities, change the entire outlook of power relations. From the day he took office the thought of this dread weapon had been in the minds of Stimson and Byrnes, who communicated their exaltations and anxieties to the President. While it remained untested, it was necessary for all to restrain their ebullience for—who knew?—it might prove to be a dud. They were ignoramuses in the field of science. The scientists said it was a sure thing, but others had doubts. At one session, when Truman was being briefed by Vannevar Bush, Leahy burst out: "This is the biggest fool thing we have ever done. The bomb will never go off, and I speak as an expert in explosives."

Stimson, as War Secretary, had been in charge of the project. He had an appointment with the President on April 25 at which he took up the broader implications and problems. The memorandum he handed Truman began, "Within four months we shall in all probability have completed the most terrible weapon ever known in human history, one bomb of which could destroy a whole city." Byrnes had already hammered home to Truman the proposition that "the bomb might well put us in a position to dictate our own terms at the end of the war." Stimson now was interested less in detailing the use of the bomb against Japan—which both he and Truman took for granted— than in impressing the President with the vast problems that had to be grappled with if the bomb was not to prove a curse leading to an uncontrolled arms race. All his life he had been imbued with devotion to disinterested public service, as he understood it. He was now seventy-eight years old, on the edge of retirement, and in the twilight months of his career he felt a duty to have this country leash the monster its sorcerers had brought forth. Unfortunately, his training had not equipped him for the prophet's role. Consequently, he was forever teetering between wanting to use the weapon for military and political advantage, like Byrnes, and spinning fanciful schemes to share the bomb with the Russians in return for unnegotiable concessions.

In any case, Truman was in the market for tactics, not world statesmanship. He accepted Stimson's recommendation for the setting up of an interim committee to make proposals on the relevant issues, accepted Stimson's list of members, and added Byrnes as his personal representative. Leading nuclear scientists went into an uproar when they heard that the committee had recommended the dropping of atomic bombs on Japan. The sinister mechanism they had contrived for defeating Hitler was now going to be used to rip the world apart. They were horrified. They were outraged. A committee headed by James Franck protested, recommending as a substitute a demonstration of the bomb on a barren area. Leo Szilard, one of the world's major contributors to nuclear physics, who had induced Einstein to make the original proposal for the atomic bomb project to Roosevelt, was the leading spirit of the insurgents. Balked in his attempts to see Truman, he finally obtained an interview with Byrnes at the latter's home in Spartanburg, South Carolina.

The mutual distaste between these products of two different worlds would not have been more intense had the confrontation been between St. Augustine and Attila the Hun. Byrnes took umbrage at Szilard's suggestion that scientists be given an opportunity to discuss with the Cabinet the issues arising from possession of the atom bomb. "His general demeanor and his desire to participate in policy making made an unfavorable impression on me." Szilard was appalled by what struck him as Byrnes's ignorance, stupidity, and insensitivity. Several days later, Byrnes informed General Leslie Groves, the Army director of the bomb project, about the visit of Szilard and two fellow scientists. Groves told him he knew all about it; one of his intelligence agents had been tailing them. "The diligence of Groves impressed me," was Byrnes's comment.

The genteel, somewhat pathetic revolt of the scientists has had a greater impact on the history books than it did on the political leaders. Many of their petitions were not even read by the people in authority. Groves did not deliver some that were entrusted to him. Later an assistant prepared a memorandum of explanation for the files: Since questions of the bomb's use "had already been fully considered and settled by the proper authorities," and since the interim committee's scientific panel had provided a channel for such views, "no useful purpose would be served by transmitting either the petition or the attached documents to the White House." It would have made no difference had these been studied religiously by Truman, or his associates, any more than Szilard's remarks were to affect the thinking of Byrnes. Most of the indignation at the dropping of atom bombs on Hiroshima and Nagasaki came later. Sensibilities were numbed, emotions were brutalized, in the war. People had become inured to mass murder. Any atrocity was in order so long as leaders could justify it with the formula that "it would help shorten the war."

On July 21, five days after the Potsdam conference opened, a special courier delivered the full report of the explosion at Alamogordo. The Americans now knew the dimensions of the new weapon they had in their hands. They were in an ecstasy of elation. After Stimson read the report to Truman and Byrnes, "The President was tremendously pepped up by it and spoke to me of it again and again when I saw him. He said it gave him an entirely new feeling of confidence." Next day, when Stimson read the report to Churchill, the prime minister said, "Now I know what happened to Truman yesterday. I couldn't understand it. When he got to the meeting he was a changed man. He told the Russians just where they got on and off, and generally bossed the whole meeting." Churchill's exultation exceeded that of the Americans, if possible. Lord Alanbrooke entered into his diary: "[Churchill] was completely carried away; already seeing himself capable of eliminating all the Russian centers of industry and population. He had at once painted a wonderful picture of himself as the sole possessor of these bombs and capable of dumping them where he wished, thus all-powerful and capable of dictating to Stalin."

All the same, Stalin was still theoretically an ally who was being asked to join in the war against Japan. He had to be told something about it. The interim committee had recommended that the Soviets should be informed of the new weapon's existence before it was used. Stimson advised that the President at some point should just mention to Stalin that we intended to use the bomb against Japan and that we proposed to discuss it later in connection with the peaceful organization of the world; that if Stalin asked for details, Truman should tell him that we were not yet prepared to supply them. The communication to the Russians was thus reduced to a formality, and Truman reduced even this formality to after-dinner chitchat.

At the conclusion of one of the sessions, he sauntered over to Stalin and casually mentioned that the United States had a new, very powerful weapon, without stating that it was an atomic bomb. Stalin asked no questions and displayed no special interest. Just as casually, he said he was glad to hear of it and hoped we would make good use of it against Japan. What an exchange! A scene lifted out of the Congress of Vienna! Truman was sure that Stalin had not grasped the significance of what he had said to him. We know now that Truman was mistaken. Stalin understood perfectly what Truman was airily hinting at. The Russians were well aware of the Manhattan Project. They had set up their own atomic laboratories during the war. By the time of Potsdam, their scientists were already working to produce a chain reaction. Harriman surmised that the Russians knew all about the American project when Molotov, after both had returned to Moscow, referred sneeringly to Truman's remark to Stalin concerning the Americans' "great secret weapon."

After studying the documentation of this period then available to him, P. M. S. Blackett, the Nobel prize-winning British physicist, concluded that Truman's public explanation given three days after an atom bomb had been dropped on Hiroshima—"to shorten the agony of war; to save the lives of thousands and thousands of young Americans"—was spurious; that the action "was not so much the last military act of the Second World War as the first major operation of the cold diplomatic war with Russia." The Russians put the same interpretation on the action. "Everybody believed," wrote Alexander Werth, that the real purpose of dropping the atom bombs on Japan "was first and foremost to intimidate Russia." Blackett reasoned this way: By the time of Potsdam, it was clear to the Americans that Japan was at the end of her tether; her navy and merchant marine had been destroyed, she had lost control of the air, could not oppose American bombardment, could not prevent the destruction of her industries or cities. Moreover, the Japanese leaders were frantically seeking to get out of the war on terms less onerous than unconditional surrender. Since, Blackett argued, Russia was due to launch her attack in mid-August, and this might provide the shock, or push, that would bring the Japanese to surrender, and since American plans did not call for an invasion until November, why the haste to drop the bombs in August? Why did the Americans not wait to test the effect of the Russian attack? Because they were racing against the timetable, not of their own scheduled invasion, but of the Russian attack; because the bombs were intended to force a Japanese surrender before the Russian armies drove into Manchuria and north China.

Blackett was both right and wrong. That Truman and his chief advisers thought to use the bomb as a diplomatic weapon to overawe the Russians, that they hoped that dropping the bombs would provide the shock needed to force a Japanese surrender before the Russians came into the Far Eastern war, is told unmistakably in the memoirs and diaries of Byrnes, Leahy, Stimson, Forrestal, and Alanbrooke. At the same time, Truman was up against the uncertainties of war. No one knew whether two atom bombs would produce an immediate Japanese surrender. Truman, even when in a cocky mood, said to the press on the return voyage home, "We're going to drop an

atom bomb on Japan and we're going to end this war in less than
ninety days." Blackett overlooked something else. He disregarded the
organizational momentum, the inertial dynamism of a vast bureaucratic machine. Two billion dollars had been spent; an army of scientists had been at work for five years; goals had been approved; pins
had been inserted into maps; target dates had been set. To order that
the engines of this colossal mechanical monster be reversed would
have called for a strength of independent purpose, a vision of the future, that did not exist in the American or British camps. Formally,
Truman made the decision at Potsdam to drop atom bombs on two
Japanese cities. Fundamentally, there was no decision. Everyone involved had assumed all along that the bomb would be used if and
when it was available. General Groves explained that so far as he was
concerned, the decision simply consisted in not interfering with existing plans. He thought Truman "was like a little boy on a toboggan."
For that matter, why did we drop two bombs? Why didn't we wait
after Hiroshima to assess the Japanese reaction? Because we had two
bombs in our arsenal. Had there been two more available, we would
have dropped them also, as Grove's directive to General Carl Spaatz
provided.

The movers and shakers were aware that some scientists had raised
excited objections, but these were neither the people nor the conun-
drums that serious men of affairs paid attention to, or occupied themselves with. Truman explained, "I regarded the bomb as a military
weapon and never had any doubt that it should be used." Churchill
explained, "The decision whether or not to use the atomic bomb to
compel the surrender of Japan was never even an issue. There was
unanimous, automatic, unquestioned agreement around our table."
Blackett rejected the contention that the bomb had to be used to justify to Congress and the public the expenditure of $2 billion; he
thought the suggestion was insulting to the American people. Insulting or not, it went into the calculation. Byrnes asked Szilard during
their talk, "How would you get Congress to appropriate money for
atomic research if you do not show results for the money which has
been spent already?" Groves said that if the bomb had not been used,
there would have been an outcry: "Why did you spend all this money
and all this effort, and then when you got it, why didn't you use it?
Knowing American politics, you know as well as I do that there
would have been elections fought on that basis." Leahy, who felt that
there was no military need to drop atom bombs, and that in using
them, "we had adopted the ethical standards common to barbarians

in the dark ages," was also convinced that many "wanted to make this test because of the vast sums that had been spent on the project." Had the Russian government been headed by Rotarian free enterprisers who would have made a creditable showing at a Chamber of Commerce banquet, the American machine would still have rolled on relentlessly in accordance with its programmed schedules.

After the surrender, when the Japanese situation was more fully understood, the members of the United States Strategic Bombing Survey concluded "that certainly prior to December 31, 1945, and in all probability prior to November 1, 1945, Japan would have surrendered even if the atom bombs had not been dropped, even if Russia had not entered the war, and even if no invasion had been planned or contemplated." As for the Russians, their armies moved into Manchuria as per their schedule three days after Hiroshima, and seized the properties assigned to them at Yalta. Had there been a Lincoln in Washington, instead of Truman and Byrnes, he would have frankly confessed —as he had done—that he was not controlling events, but that events were controlling him.*

---

* Truman's public explanation for the decision to use the bomb was the best available to him in the circumstances. Since, according to the later evidence, it was at best based on a miscalculation, it would have been wisest not to go beyond, or to embellish, the argument of military necessity. Truman seemed to have been under a compulsion, however, to picture himself as the hard-bitten captain who did not flinch from ruthless decisions. Remarks better left unsaid continued to come out of him in later years: "I never lost any sleep over my decision"; "I would do it again"; "That was not any decision that you had to worry about, nothing but an artillery weapon." Churchill's moral responsibility was no different from Truman's, but he had a larger sense of the judgments of history. At a private dinner with Truman when the President was turning over the office to his successor, he said, "Mr. President, I hope you have your answer ready for that hour when you and I stand before St. Peter and he says, 'I understand you two are responsible for putting off those atomic bombs. What have you got to say for yourselves?' " Robert Lovett, the urbane banker, then Undersecretary of State, deftly shifted the conversation by inquiring politely, "Are you sure, Prime Minister, that you are going to be in the same place as the President for that interrogation?"

10

Two Halves
of the
Same Walnut

A month after Potsdam, a jaunty Byrnes left for the foreign ministers conference in London to gather in the harvest. The atom bomb had been "laid on" Japan, the invincibility of America was clear for all to see, and the script called for a more docile Russian delegation to put in an appearance. Byrnes was quickly disabused. The Molotov who arrived was the same legalistic, unbending, indefatigable Molotov. All the issues argued at Potsdam were rehashed, along with a new Russian demand for a role in the occupation of Japan. If anything, Molotov was more intractable because the cavalier American attitude that she was going to decide policy in the Far East without interference of any of her wartime allies was further chilling relations.

This is not to say that the bomb was of no consequence in the power balance. In the next period, the Russians gave way in Iran, in the Dardanelles, in Trieste. Conceivably they would not have yielded but for America's possession of the bomb. Most likely the Russians' own war exhaustion was the main determinant in shaping their diplomacy. But on their basic control in Eastern Europe, and on the Yalta-allotted sphere in the Far East, neither threats, warnings, nor blandishments would make them budge. There was no easy way of utilizing the bomb for diplomatic triumphs, like transforming potential into kinetic energy in a laboratory.

Byrnes, Molotov, and Ernest Bevin, the British laborite foreign minister, haggled for almost a month. They could agree on nothing important. Molotov brought the agony to a close by demanding the exclusion of the French and Chinese representatives. He had agreed to their attendance in contravention of the agreement at Potsdam. Apparently he hoped to bring out differences among the allies. When he found himself methodically outvoted, 4 to 1, he changed his mind. He said the conference had to be reorganized, since an error had been made at the outset in permitting China and France to participate. Byrnes would not agree; he did not want to have bad blood with the French and Chinese, who would be affronted at their ouster once they had been admitted. He took the position that while France and China might not vote on treaties with countries with which they had not signed armistice terms, they could take part in the discussions. He telephoned Truman to inform him of the crisis. Truman was at the Jefferson Islands Club and could not be reached. Byrnes described the situation to Leahy, who, because of the urgency, sent a message to Stalin in the President's name. Stalin confirmed Molotov's position. The conference had come to a dead end. At the closing, the ministers could not even agree on a protocol. Stimson, recording a conversation with Byrnes two days before the latter sailed for London, noted that Byrnes was "very much against any attempt to cooperate with Russia. He looks to having the presence of the bomb in his pocket, so to speak, as a great weapon to get through the thing." The bomb had not accomplished its mission. It had let Byrnes down.

Both as politician and career man, Byrnes was sensitive about the failure of the conference. While his policy was intransigent, he was not guilty of any of the impatience or abruptness that Truman had displayed at Potsdam. A skilled and self-confident negotiator, he was a good match for Molotov in tenacity and imperturbability. And he had more authority than Stalin accorded his man. He need not have been concerned about the effects of the failure back home. Truman was not disturbed, and the Senate Committee on Foreign Relations, to which Byrnes reported, was more inclined to encourage him to act tough than to persevere with negotiations.

Byrnes had not attained the later Acheson-Dulles rung of wisdom that negotiations were passé. The deadlock, he thought, had to be broken. Now he knew the bomb was no magic wand. Waving it would not open the locked inner doors. While reviewing the problem, he recalled that it had been agreed at Yalta that the Big Three foreign ministers should meet periodically; here might be a way to get things moving again. Accordingly he cabled Molotov and proposed a meeting in Moscow. Byrnes had assumed at London that the reason for the deadlock had been his refusal to grant recognition to Rumania and Bulgaria, that Molotov had only raised the question of a joint allied control commission for Japan as part of his war of nerves. Then Harriman had sent word from Moscow that this was very much on Russian minds. Stalin had become heated in his denunciation of American policy. The Soviet government, he said, was being treated not as an ally, but as an American satellite, and he was not going to stand for it. This introduced another discordant note. It was set American policy to keep control over Japan in our own hands. As justification, it could be said that the Soviet Union had waged war against Japan for a few weeks compared to our forty-four months. On the other hand, if the gauge was sacrifices, forces contributed, or numbers of the enemy engaged, the Western allies should have had no more than a third or a quarter share in the occupation of Germany. At any rate, the way had to be opened for renewed relations. So, Byrnes explained, "against the advice of the diplomats and the columnists, I went to Moscow."

As in the previous Hopkins mission, an American concession on Eastern Europe broke the log jam. Hungary had already been afforded recognition in November. Now a formula was devised for signing peace treaties with the other Nazi wartime satellites. Drafts drawn up by the powers would be submitted to a twenty-one-nation peace conference, which could make recommendations. The texts were to be fixed up by the same powers that had prepared the drafts and would come into force when ratified by them. The Russians, in turn, agreed that two additional representatives from the old parties would be added to the Rumanian provisional government and the newly elected Bulgarian government. Though the details varied, the agreement was essentially on the lines of the Polish compact. On Japan, the Russians had to settle for legalistic assuagement. They accepted under protest Byrnes's involved scheme for representation on an eleven-power Far Eastern Commission sitting in Washington with the right to recommend policy—which, in fact, left General Douglas MacArthur's proconsulship intact.

Byrnes returned to an unfriendly Washington. Truman was boiling mad. It was not just over the politics. There was talk in the palace guard that Byrnes was slighting him, was acting as if he and the President were equal sovereigns, or worse, as if he were dealing with a junior senator. Byrnes had neglected to keep Truman fully informed on what was going on at the conference. There was also grumbling in the press and among senators about appeasement; Leahy was frankly critical of the agreements. Leahy, it must be recalled, was an unreconstructed reactionary who had got along swimmingly with Marshal Henri Pétain when he was the American ambassador to Vichy. The drift of the times came across like an acrid odor in his diary notation that "Byrnes was not immune to the communistically inclined advisers in the State Department." Truman concluded that Byrnes "had taken it upon himself to move the foreign policy of the United States in a direction to which I could not, and would not, agree." According to his account, he had a showdown with his Secretary of State. From his desk in the Oval Room, he read out to him a letter he had written in longhand. After bawling him out for not keeping the President informed, he laid down some strictures in typical Trumanesque style:

> Unless Russia is faced with an iron fist and strong language another war is in the making. I do not think we should play compromise any longer. We should refuse to recognize Rumania and Bulgaria until they comply with our requirements; we should let our position on Iran be known in no uncertain terms and we should continue to insist on the internationalization of the Kiel Canal, the Rhine-Danube waterway and the Black Sea Straits and we should maintain complete control of Japan and the Pacific. We should rehabilitate China and create a strong government there. We should do the same for Korea. Then we should insist on the return of our ships from Russia and force a settlement of the Lend-Lease debt of Russia. I'm tired of babying the Soviets.

Byrnes denied that any showdown took place, that the President voiced any disapproval of his conduct. Had this occurred, he said, he would have resigned immediately. When he learned of the letter in later years, he wrote that it was probably fabricated for the record after he had publicly broken with Truman. The logic of the situation is with Byrnes. It is unlikely that he would have consented to remain in office after such a dressing down. That does not mean that Truman did not write such a letter at the time, and after reading it over, put it back in his desk drawer. Then, in later years, when publishing his papers, he decided—as others had done in similar cases—to take post facto revenge for having had to suppress himself. The letter, in any case, was a faithful reflection of his thinking. He had a hot-spur temperament. Though Byrnes's relations with him remained friendly on the surface, Byrnes was aware of the disapprobation of Truman's advisers, as well as senators, columnists, publishers. He concluded ruefully that "much of the criticism came from people so unreasonably anti-Soviet in their views that they would regard any agreement with Russia on any subject as appeasement." He took the experience to heart, never permitting himself to be outflanked by the Leahys thereafter. For his conduct at the conferences he attended in his last remaining year, he earned the good opinion of Forrestal, the arch Cold War warrior of them all.

It was a year of loud talk and saber-rattling. *Life* ran newspaper ads that Russia and the West could never reach agreement, under the headline, WHY KID AROUND? Russia was forced to withdraw her troops from Iran under sustained American pressure. Her oil concession was canceled by the government of the shah and the Persian landowners, with American military advisers, military supplies, and dollar credits coming in. Truman rejected the Russian proposal to vest control of the Dardanelles Straits in the Black Sea states, and, to lend emphasis to his note, sent a naval squadron to the area. Churchill's speech at Fulton, Missouri, and Henry Wallace's later rejoinder dramatized the struggle for public opinion.

The Churchill speech on March 6, like many large events in history, began on the level of banality. Who therefore was better fitted to initiate it than the President's own military aide, Harry Vaughan? It seemed that Vaughan was an alumnus of Westminister College located at Fulton, and that he had been a classmate of Frank McCluer, at this time the college president. The college had a funded program to invite famous people to address its students, and McCluer was in town with a letter he intended to send to Churchill. Naturally, Vaughan took him in to see the President, who was delighted to help out. Truman added a note to McCluer's letter, saying, "Dear Winnie: This is a fine old college out in my state. If you'll come out and make them a speech, I'll take you out and introduce you." The President accompanying Churchill to make a speech—that put a more serious complexion on the thing. Vaughan related:

> We went to Jefferson City, and got off, and it's twenty five miles up to Fulton. We drove up and had a parade through town. Mr. Churchill met the faculty and all the dignitaries; the Governor and everybody was there. Then

they took him upstairs in the president's house to one of the bedrooms so he could put on his robe and his hood, and his tam-o'-shanter, the black velvet tam-o'-shanter, a Cambridge robe I guess it is. Well, there had been quite an extent of time where Mr. Churchill hadn't had any pick-me-up, and Mr. Truman said, "Harry, you better get Mr. Churchill a drink before we go into the gymnasium," where the ceremony was going to be. So, I scouted around and it was a little bit difficult. My friend Tom Van Sant scouted around and found a pint for me. I went out to the kitchen and got some ice and a pitcher of water and a glass and went upstairs. Mr. Churchill was sitting there with his robe on and I said, "Mr. Churchill, here I thought maybe you might need a little pick-me-up before we go over to the gymnasium." "Well, General," he said, "am I glad to see you. I didn't know whether I was in Fulton, Missouri or Fulton, Sahara."

If the scene was incongruous, there was nothing provincial or hesitant about the message. Churchill belted it out like an avenging prophet calling to battle the hosts of the Lord. He wanted a British-American military alliance for a showdown with Russia before it was too late. "If the population of the English-speaking commonwealths be added to that of the United States with all that such cooperation implies in the air, on the sea, all over the globe, and in science and industry, and in moral force, there will be no quivering, precarious balance of power to offer its temptation to ambition or adventure. On the contrary, there will be an overwhelming assurance of security." Stalin hurled back his answer with even less equivocation. He said that Churchill's speech "was a call for war on the USSR," bearing in its assumption of Anglo-Saxon race superiority a striking resemblance to the racist position of Hitler. "I don't know whether Mr. Churchill and his friends will succeed in organizing a new armed campaign against Eastern Europe after the Second World War; but if they do succeed —which is not very probable, because millions of ordinary people stand guard over the cause of peace—it may confidently be said that they will be beaten just as they were beaten once before twenty-six years ago."

Churchill's speech understandably created an international sensation. A person of his worldwide prestige proclaiming publicly that Communist Russia was bent on conquest, that there was an irrepressible conflict between her and the West, that the English-speaking world was called on to push back the barbarian hordes threatening to break the dikes of civilization—people naturally assumed that a new war was coming. Some date the Cold War from this speech, although it is uncertain how much it contributed to the incitation of Western public opinion.

Truman's maneuver—accompanying Churchill to Fulton, introducing him, and applauding his sallies—was maladroit. The reaction of Capitol Hill and the State Department was critical, so much so that Truman tried to wash his hands of all responsibility with the fib that he had not seen a copy of the speech beforehand. Byrnes said he had not been consulted about the speech and that the United States had nothing to do with it. Acheson, who was scheduled to speak as the State Department representative at welcoming ceremonies for Churchill in New York, canceled his appearance, pleading urgent business. As a trial balloon to test public reaction, or a campaign to heat up the conflict with Russia, the attempt was faulty on three counts:

(1) A call to a crusade of this nature by a personality as renowned as Churchill should have been made in his own country, not as a guest at a college exercise abroad.

(2) The message, though in line with the thinking of American leaders, was encased in the armor of an Anglo-American military alliance, an alliance that they did not want or need.

(3) It was too early—only six months after the end of the war—for the call to be put in such incendiary terms. It frightened people. Middle America was seeking security, not glory.

Henry Wallace, the lone New Dealer remaining in the Cabinet—Ickes had resigned the month before—was disturbed at the turn of events. He wrote Truman the next week proposing friendly discussions with the Russians on their economic problems. Truman sent him a noncommittal reply. Four months later, Wallace tried again, this time with a longer and more critical document. He wrote he was "troubled by the apparently growing feeling among the American people that another war is coming and the only way we can head it off is to arm ourselves to the teeth." He wondered what conclusions we would draw "if Russia had the atomic bomb and we did not, if Russia had 10,000 bombers and air bases within 1,000 miles of our coastlines, and we did not." He urged again a friendly discussion with the Russians on their long-term economic needs. Truman, of course, had no use for Wallace's proposition, but thanked him for taking the time to put his thoughts on record, and sent a copy of the letter to Byrnes.

By autumn, Wallace decided to take his case to the public, and now followed one of those moments of pure farce punctuating Truman's Presidency in which the absurd and inept intertwined with the purposeful and grim. Wallace read out to Truman the policy sections of a speech he intended to make at Madison Square Garden. Truman told him it was fine, that he had his blessing. Since the speech was an implied attack on the administration's entire foreign policy, why did he permit Wallace to make it? And why did he tell him he approved it? When the smoke began to pour out, there were the usual lame explanations: The President had only thumbed through the speech, he had not read it carefully. Or, he had not approved the speech, he had only approved Wallace's right to voice his opinions.

The scribes figured that he had given his endorsement without much thought, as he had a habit of doing at times. They were not entirely correct. The President did not need to have it explained to him that the speech outlined a policy contrary to his own. He was well acquainted with Wallace's position. When Wallace approached him, however, he had something else on his mind besides the contest with Russia. He was worried about the coming contest with the Republicans. Hannegan had advised him that Wallace's support was important. As he recorded, "Wallace had a following. I realized that his appeal had some effect. If I could keep him in the cabinet I might be able to put some check on his activities." Wallace leaving the administration after the departure of Ickes might have unpleasant consequences in November. Truman's popular standing was dropping precipitately. He could ill afford to lose any assistance from whatever quarter. Where he miscalculated was in imagining that a President of the United States could get away with the juggling act that City Manager McElroy used to put on in Kansas City.

Wallace told a cheering crowd at Madison Square Garden that the "get-tough" policy would not work, that "the tougher we get, the tougher the Russians will get." He proposed a straight spheres-of-influence division. "We should recognize that we have no more business in the political affairs of Eastern Europe than Russia has in the political affairs of Latin America, Western Europe and the United States. Whether we like it or not, the Russians will try to socialize their sphere of influence just as we try to democratize our sphere of influence." With that, as Clark Clifford, by then the President's legal

counsel, said, "hell broke loose. Oh, boy, it really did." Truman compounded his original miscalculation by thinking he could brazen it
out. When reporters, armed with advance copies of Wallace's speech,
demanded to know whether he approved only one passage that Wallace had specifically noted as embodying Truman's position, or all of
it, he answered, "I approved the whole speech." To the question, "Do
you regard Wallace's speech a departure from Byrnes's policy?" he
said, "I do not. They are exactly in line."

This was too much. No one could tell what the captain was signal-
ing, or whether he himself knew. Official Washington was in turmoil.
The press excoriated him. Arthur Vandenberg, the Senate Republican
leader on foreign policy, who was working with Byrnes at the Paris
peace conference, issued a statement that he could cooperate with
only one Secretary of State at a time. The American delegation halted
activity until it knew where it stood. Truman had created a first-class
crisis for himself. For a few days, amidst mounting criticism and confusion, he tried to doubletalk his way toward the lee in the hope that
the storm would blow itself out. When he was confronted with an ultimatum from Byrnes to accept his resignation unless Wallace was
muzzled, he had no choice but to ask Wallace to get out. He did not
do it very elegantly. He had to vent his spite. He wrote out his decision in longhand and sent it to Wallace by messenger. The letter was
so intemperate that Wallace told Ross by phone that he doubted that
it would be wise that it should go into the archives, much less be
made public. Ross was of the same opinion. The outburst seemed a
reversion to Kansas City roughhouse. After the letter was returned to
the White House and destroyed, Truman asked Wallace for his resignation in a civil manner. The letter to Mama and Mary about the big
doings was as full of good spirits as ever. "Well, I had to fire Henry
today, and of course I hated to do it. He was so nice about it, I almost backed out! The crackpots are having conniption fits. I'm glad
they are. It convinces me I'm right." The man could certainly not be
faulted for a lack of exuberance or ability to rationalize.

Six months later, a grim-looking President stood before Congress to
announce the historic decision to use American resources for a worldwide struggle against Communist Russia. The crusade that had been
whispered about and acknowledged only in private notes and diaries
was to be proclaimed from the housetops. "Every nation must choose
between alternate ways of life," and we were enlisted "to support free
peoples who are resisting attempted subjugation by armed minorities

or by outside pressures." We were the virtuous, with a way of life "based upon the will of the majority" and "free institutions." The other side were the wicked, "based upon the will of the minority" relying on "terror and oppression." All were going to have to take their stand and be counted. Those who resisted the iniquitous foe could count on our support. Those who joined with him could count on our hostility. Were there people who had grievances? Oppositions in conflict with oppressive governments? "The status quo is not sacred, but we cannot allow changes in the status quo by such methods as coercion, or by such subterfuges as political infiltration."

Everyone following events recognized at once that this was not just another bombastic threat; that a portentous, formidable shift of traditional American policy was being proposed. Joseph Jones, the main craftsman of Truman's speech, a Knight Templar to whom the entire litany of the Cold War was Holy Writ, and who has supplied a blow-by-blow account of this weighty decision, said that it represented "an enduring national conversion to the role of world leadership." He and everybody else in the State Department were in seventh heaven because "a new chapter in world history had opened and that they were the most privileged of men, participants in a drama such as rarely occurs even in the long life of a great nation." *The New York Times* shared the opinion and approved the course.

That a commitment this sweeping was accepted with so little fuss or discussion was a source of amazement to Jones. He referred to it again and again. "It had all gone like clockwork. No one in government had opposed. No one had dragged his feet." Less than three weeks elapsed from the time the British had delivered their "blue piece of paper" announcing their planned withdrawal from the eastern Mediterranean to Truman's appearance before a joint session of Congress. Two months later, the measure had passed both houses of Congress by resounding majorities and was awaiting the President's signature. Considering the political situation at the time, the action appears not amazing, but unbelievable. Everything should have indicated a laborious, protracted passage through the mazes of legislative pipelines with the chances for successful emergence in grave doubt. Truman commanded little prestige with the public and less respect from the Congress. The Republicans had seized control of both houses in the November election in their greatest victory since Hoover's in 1928. They were sharpening their knives to take revenge for their years in the wilderness, and boasting of their intent to cut $6 billion from the budget. There was no great demand steaming up from either cities or prairies for Churchillian embroilments. The public, as Jones noted ruefully, was "apathetic and heedless." What were the instruments employed to yield brisk response from this ordinarily lethargic organism? The entire movement of policy toward the Soviets had been in this direction for two years, so that the proclamation of the Truman Doctrine appeared as the logical and necessary climactic step in an existent course. Every major group and institution of the elite was in the grip of imperial passion. All were convinced that history had decreed that the United States was to organize and oversee the world in accordance with her ideas and interests. This is what made for "the virtual unanimity of view" and drove the Congress to swift compliance.

Many have written then and since about the extraordinary courage the President displayed in promulgating this far-reaching policy. This is a misunderstanding. Truman showed great spunk at times, notably in his fight for the senatorial nomination in 1940 and in the presidential campaign in 1948. It took no lion heart, however, to press the Cold War crusade in March, 1947. He was moving with, not against, the tide. He was not defying, he was appropriating the Republican thunder already raised in the 1946 campaign against appeasing Communism. The main opposition to the policy came from Wallace and the bedraggled, fast disintegrating troop of aging left New Dealers. That was not an opposition that took any noteworthy courage to face —or to ignore. Had Truman set the course against the Cold War, there would have been more reason to talk of courage.

When the President met with congressional leaders to line them up for his bill, General Marshall, the new Secretary of State since the beginning of the year, explained what was at issue. Marshall, the Army chief of staff throughout the war, represented for Truman the acme of perfection. He not only gave him his full confidence and respect; he was in awe of him. He had called him in the past the "greatest living American," and it was an opinion he was never to abandon. The man epitomized for him everything he would have liked to have been: a five-star general, solidity of body, steely, craggy, of impassive appearance, an air of martial authoritativeness, a manner of curt decisiveness, of self-control suggesting enormous reserves of power. After his appointment, Marshall proceeded to organize the department on strict staff lines of procedure, the organization scheme that Army men, for reasons none to clear, considering the results in the Army, believe to be the most efficient. Until he became a target of the McCarthyites, it was almost sacrilegious to question his reputation as a public servant of unimpeachable integrity, standing outside of and above politics. He was a symbol of the rising prestige of military men in Washington.

On this august occasion he unfortunately flubbed his lines. It sounded as if the President was asking for $400 million to bail out Britain, which led, it appeared to the handlers, to such irrelevant and trivial questions as "What are we letting ourselves in for?" or, "How much is this going to cost?" The meeting was turning sour. Acheson, the real guiding spirit of the enterprise at State, agitatedly asked permission to intervene, and when the President called upon him to speak, he let out all stops. "In the past eighteen months," he declared, "Soviet pressure on the Straits, on Iran, and on northern Greece had brought the Balkans to the point where a highly possible Soviet breakthrough might open three continents to Soviet penetration. Like apples in a barrel infected by one rotten one, the corruption of Greece would infect Iran and all to the east. It would also carry infection to Africa through Asia Minor and Egypt, and to Europe through Italy and France, already threatened by the strongest domestic Communist parties in Western Europe. The Soviet Union was playing one of the greatest gambles in history at minimal cost. It did not need to win all the possibilities. Even one or two offered immense gains. We and we alone were in a position to break up the play." A long silence followed. No further "irrelevant" questions were asked. Who would dare? Vandenberg, greatly impressed, promised his support. He said to the President, "If that's what you want, there's only one way to get it. That is to make a personal appearance before Congress and scare hell out of the country."

The problem with conducting policy by scaring hell out of the country is that, as in osmosis, a diffusion proceeds between the declaratory and the substantive. Even the laboratory technicians do not have total control over the process of equalization. In the course of scaring others, people often succeed in scaring themselves as well. To what extent was this occurring inside the Truman administration? The most authoritative exposition of the thought of the State Department was George F. Kennan's paper, "The Sources of Soviet Conduct," which appeared in the July, 1947, issue of *Foreign Affairs*. He had submitted the basic proposition in an 8,000-word cable eighteen months before when he was chargé d'affaires at the Moscow embassy, and had repeated his thesis in lectures at the War College. On the strength of it, he was named head of State's Policy Planning Staff. By all accounts, it was of major importance in providing a theoretical framework for the predilections of the tacticians. It was accepted by the informed public as the motivating rationale for the Truman Doctrine.°

The major thrust of Kennan's argument was that Russia was basically a vulnerable, even an impotent nation, whose decay was far advanced. Her ideology and internal character led to expansionism, so that she moved, in the absence of obstruction, like a fluid stream to fill every nook and cranny in the basin of world power. If the Western world contained her by the application of counterforce at every point where the Russians showed signs of encroaching, they would retreat, and in ten or fifteen years, the strains would lead to either the breakup or the gradual mellowing of Soviet power.

Walter Lippmann demolished some of the assumptions in a series of articles that appeared in September. Referring to Russia's alleged inner weakness, which Kennan had said "cannot be proved, and it cannot be disproved," as well as Kennan's corollary that the strain on Russia would become unbearable if the United States showed itself as a country of spiritual vitality coping successfully with her own problems and responsibilities, Lippmann observed that one could have no confidence in a policy that relied upon wishful thinking about the collapse of Soviet power, bolstered by an extra-strong dose of wishful thinking about the United States. "Do we dare to assume, as we enter the arena and get set to run the race, that the Soviet Union will break its leg while the United States grows a pair of wings to speed it on its way?" Lippmann further pointed prophetically to the ultimate end of a policy of containment and counterforce. "The policy can be implemented," he wrote, "only by recruiting, subsidizing and supporting a heterogeneous array of satellites, clients, dependents and puppets. [It] means that we must stake our own security and the peace of the world upon [these] agents about whom we can know very little. Frequently they will act for their own reasons, and on their own judgments, presenting us with accomplished facts that we did not intend,

---

° Unaccountably, Kennan, while favoring economic aid to Greece, was opposed to the ideological tone of the Truman speech, the portraying of two opposing ways of life, the sweeping commitment to aid all who lined up with us. This was not what he was talking about at all, he insisted. In later years, he was to blame his own formulations for the misunderstanding. He had meant "not the containment by military means of a military threat, but the political containment of a political threat." One has to put down this strange reaction to his inability to understand the unavoidable implications of his own pronouncements.

and with crises for which we are unready. The 'unassailable barriers' will present us with an unending series of insoluble dilemmas."

Neither Kennan nor any other Cold War partisan had a coherent explanation for Soviet expansionism. Hence, they could not grasp its pattern, its purpose, and its limitation. There were repeated references to Marxist-Leninist "world revolution," but this was no better guide to the Kremlin's current intentions than a reference to the Declaration of Independence would have been for understanding Washington's policy in 1947. World revolution was not a doctrine, as some writers made it appear, of Russian expansionism, of Red Army movements across frontiers, or military pressures on other nations. It was a doctrine of the proletariat making independent revolutions in their own countries, with the eventual formation presumably of a world federation of socialist republics. The unfocused ranting about Soviet expansionism obscured another relevant aspect of Soviet sovereignty. Stalin had come to power as an isolationist in a struggle against Trotsky, the internationalist. The ruling Soviet bureaucracy had been preoccupied for fifteen years with industrializing its country, not extending frontiers. Its foreign policy had been characterized by caution and conservatism, as well as subversion of foreign Communist parties into instruments of its own national purpose.

Many believed that the Communists could have taken power in France after the Germans were driven out. The Communists never tried, nor did they probe the possibilities. Under Kremlin guidance, their leaders dutifully cooperated with Charles de Gaulle and humbly accepted cabinet posts in his government. In later years it became known, through the documentation of the Yugoslavs, Vladimir Dedijer and Milovan Djilas, that Stalin had put pressure on Tito to unite with the royal government-in-exile; had told the Chinese Communists that there was no chance for a revolution in China, that they had to disband their armies and join the Kuomintang government; had informed Tito's foreign minister that the Greek rebellion had to be stopped as quickly as possible. His long-standing, organic skepticism about foreign revolutions had become transformed into positive opposition to revolutions that he could not control. The realization that Stalin was not another, more cagey Trotsky dawned on the Kremlinologists as time went on. Kennan himself was to say, "From his political entourage in the world of communism, Stalin wanted only one thing: weakness. This was not at all identical with revolution. Stalin did not want other states to be communist."

Nevertheless, it was a fact that the Soviet Union had expanded in Europe and had repossessed the Czarist positions in the Far East. It was also a fact that Stalin was using his military power to put through revolutions from the top in a number of countries under Red Army occupation that were to align them socially and politically with the Soviet Union. American analysts were tardy in grasping the paradox because their commonsense approach had not prepared them for the subtleties of contradictory phenomena. Yet without understanding that Stalin was both an opponent of revolutions, as well as a Bonapartist inheritor of a revolutionary state opposed to capitalism, whose emergence from the war as a major victor made possible the overwhelming of weak nations on its European borders—without understanding this, policy makers were unable to anticipate or comprehend much of Soviet behavior. They were suspicious of Stalin's intentions when they had good reason to be suspicious. And they were suspicious of his intentions when his sellout of foreign Communists was working in their interests. This explained the flaw in Kennan's master chart. He assumed that popular insurgencies, led or abetted by Communists, were inevitably extensions of Soviet power and subservient to Soviet design. It made containment, when coupled with Truman's assertion that changes in the status quo could not be permitted by "coercion" or "political infiltration," a generalized, universal counter-revolutionary commitment. It would lead to, and, in fact, produced egregious misreadings of political realities.

The oversimplification and easy equation became a function of strategy. When in the following years government functionaries and an interested public gained a better knowledge of what was going on in faraway places, and monographs and surveys gushed from the university institutes in an unending stream, what was altered was not the strategy, but the semantics. It was inflexible purposes, not inflexible explanations, that we were wedded to . The resolve to uphold the status quo, everywhere we could, and as best we could, and to make common cause with a motley crew of factions, tribes, cliques, juntas, political racketeers, military strong men, and adventurers on the make, at a time of intense dislocation and insurgence, was a fateful one. The system of alliances with rickety, reactionary regimes did not augment our military strength; it became a claim upon it. It did not add luster to our protestations for democracy and freedom; it sullied them. It did not place us in the mainstream of the historical tide; our coalitions cut across it.

Truman explained to his Cabinet that the $400 million request for Greece and Turkey "would be only the beginning." It was understood that vast sums would have to be ladled out. Discussion of the Truman Doctrine was taking place at a time when Western Europe was prostrate, when the structure that was to be the indispensable adjunct to America in the free-enterprise world-to-be was in danger of caving in. The severe winter of 1947 was enough to thrust England into an economic tailspin. What had been the center of the world's mightiest empire was now revealed as a bankrupt little island-country too battered and exhausted to provide sustenance for its own 50 million souls, much less maintain its imperial grip overseas. "What is Europe now?" Churchill had cried out to an audience at Albert Hall. "It is a rubble heap, a charnel house, a breeding ground of pestilence and hate." This was the same Churchill who had bellicosely declaimed that he had not become the king's first minister to preside over the liquidation of the British Empire. He had not so presided only because the British voters had returned him to private life at the end of the war in Europe. His successors could not avoid the distasteful chore. India, Burma, Ceylon, Palestine had been cast adrift. The overlordship of Greece and Turkey had to be turned over to the United States. In a few more years, Egypt, Sudan, and the military bastion at Suez would have to be abandoned.

The American experts knew the facts of England's debilitation. They had also been kept informed of critical conditions on the continent. Stimson had reported to the Cabinet as early as April, 1945, that McCloy, who had made an inspection tour, had found "conditions of chaos" and "near anarchy." Such reports continued coming in to the State Department. Somehow, the full significance of these reports never registered with the President or his high officials. As soon as Japan surrendered, Truman again decided, again on the advice of Crowley and Grew, to discontinue abruptly all lend-lease operations. He explained to the press, "The bill passed by Congress defined lend-lease as a weapon of war, and after we ceased to be at war it is no longer necessary." Acheson was to remark that the statement "was untrue and the decision disastrous," that it had been made without an understanding of its consequences.

The British government, faced with impending disaster, sent a delegation to Washington headed by John Maynard Keynes and Lord Halifax. The American leaders in the negotiation were Vinson and William Clayton. Vinson thought what was involved was a straight business deal, that it was his duty not to permit the brilliant, fast-talking economist with the careless airs of a Cambridge don to put anything over on the American squares. Clayton was the ex-Liberty League millionaire cotton broker from Texas then in charge of economic affairs at State, who, like Cordell Hull, fervently believed that free trade and the open door, once permitted to demonstrate their beneficent qualities, would cure ailing Europe of her disorders. Together they drove a hard bargain. Clayton boasted in a letter to Bernard Baruch, "We loaded the British loan negotiations with all the conditions the traffic would bear." Instead of a $5 billion interest-free grant-in-aid or loan that the British wanted, they recommended a $3.75 billion loan at 2 percent attached to provisos for the dismantling of much of the Imperial Preference system and the free convertibility of the pound sterling. Robert Boothby, a Tory leader, complained that "comparable terms have never hitherto been imposed on a country that had not been defeated in war." The proud de Gaulle had had to make a similar pilgrimage, following which his experts bargained for a billion-dollar loan that they received only after pledging to curtail government subsidies for French exports.

By the time of the Truman Doctrine, the master planners on the Potomac saw the blinding light, like Saul on the road to Damascus, that after a war in which a continent had been ripped apart, the Europeans could not just clear away the debris, patch up the machinery, and start production motors whirling on the old lines of Manchester capitalism, as if nothing unusual had taken place. It was borne in on them that without a stupendous effort on a different basis, the United States might be tied to a Europe that was a basket case, or a school for revolution. Once it was clear that, while free trade and free convertibility of currency remained among the eternal verities, it would be necessary to put some meat and fat on the Europeans' bones before they could again become reliable free enterprisers and debtors, things began to move fast. Vinson was now ensconced in the Supreme Court, where he did not have to worry about Europe, and Europe did not have to worry about him. As for Clayton, the fires of free trade continued to burn in him as fiercely as a year earlier. But this two-fisted, can-do, take-charge entrepreneur had learned something. He had learned that he had to resuscitate the customer before he could hope to do business with him. Ill and on a plane to Tucson for a rest before he was to go to Geneva for a trade and tariff conference, he sent a memorandum to the department. The message was urgent: An emergency fund to succor beleaguered countries was essential to our own security; the President and Secretary of State had to shock the country into a realization of its peril. A message from Clayton carried weight. His reputation as an economic statesman was at its highest both in and out of the department.

Political dangers were intertwined with economic ones. At stake was nothing less than America's well-being at home and its grand design for a free-trade, open-door world system. America's exports, up to $16 billion annually, were 400 percent higher than before the war, but a third of this was being paid by United States government aid schemes, and another fifth with Europe's remaining gold and dollar reserves. Without a new aid program, the President's Council of Economic Advisers anticipated a catastrophic decline of exports to be followed by far-reaching readjustments in the domestic economy. Nor was this all. Caught in an economic squeeze, the Europeans were reverting to restrictive interwar practices that, unless halted, would defeat America's multilateral commercial plans. The solution, as the White House managers saw it, was a comprehensive aid program that would subsidize exports, support investment abroad, and batter down all attempts to reimpose closed trade areas and preferential arrangements.

Technicians had been at work for three months. Clayton submitted a second memorandum at the end of May which contained key components of the coming Marshall Plan. The different papers were gone over in a conference with Marshall, and the project was nailed down. One major question remained to be decided. Was the offer to be addressed to all of Europe, or the Western powers alone? "If the Russians came in," Jones explained, "the whole project would probably be unworkable. But there was a strong possibility that the USSR would never come in on the basis of disclosing full information about their economic and financial condition."

Marshall and his associates decided not to take the onus of dividing Europe, to let the Russians make the decision. "Play it straight," advised Kennan—and that is the way it was played. Marshall made the momentous offer in an address at Harvard on June 5. In the ringing words of Bohlen, who wrote the speech, "Our policy is directed not against any country or doctrine but against hunger, poverty, desperation, and chaos. Its purpose should be the revival of a working economy in the world so as to permit the emergence of political and social conditions in which free institutions can exist." Marshall's authority was such that he had not considered it necessary to clear the text with Truman, and Truman's esteem of him was so pronounced, he never thought to take exception, as he would have done with Byrnes. "I had referred to the idea as the 'Marshall Plan' when it was discussed in staff meetings," Truman explained, "because I wanted General Marshall to get full credit for his brilliant contributions to the measure."

The British and French immediately jumped to attention. Ernest Bevin and Georges Bidault invited the Russians to confer with them. Molotov arrived in Paris with a staff of eighty-nine. As the Americans had anticipated, they would not accept the terms of reference. Molotov accused the British and French of trying to create a new organization to interfere in the affairs and control the development of independent countries. When the dispute reached an impasse, Molotov predicted that the scheme would result in the splitting of Europe, with one part pitted against the other, and angrily departed. The Western press, particularly in the United States and England, rose in righteous protest and belabored the Russians for refusing to cooperate in the economic rehabilitation of the continent. Others, more cynical, made acid comments about Molotov's clumsiness in taking on himself the responsibility for the break and division.

Despite the indignation, some genuine, some counterfeit, most of it bred of Cold War fanaticism or conditioning, there was no possibility or provision for Soviet participation. The Marshall Plan was not something apart from, or a substitution for, the Truman Doctrine, as many publicists imagined or pretended. Truman, who was in a position to know, said, "They are two halves of the same walnut." Newspapers that were emptying vials of wrath on the disruption-bent Russians had been freely speculating the week before that the Marshall Plan could be used to pry Poland and Czechoslovakia loose from the Russian hold. The plan had been made to appear as coming from the Europeans, but as Clayton emphasized, this was not to be another UNRRA: "The United States must run this show." As finally passed by Congress, each recipient of credits had to enter into a bilateral agreement with this country, which provided that it would set aside counterpart funds from the sale of the products America furnished. The right to approve the way these funds were to be spent enabled the United States to oversee the budgetary policies of recipients, who were also required to make at least 5 percent available to the United States for purchase of raw materials, and to open their markets to American investors on an equal basis.

The Marshall Plan was the most successful foreign project undertaken by us in the postwar years. The $13 billion spent (to which has to be added the additional billions in NATO apportionments, and large-scale American procurement because of the Korean war) accomplished what the program set out to do. The economies of the Western European nations were rehabilitated and set to operating again on capitalist lines. The disastrous price inflations and unemployment pools of the interwar years were avoided. England, France, Germany, were not to regain their positions as powers of the first order, but Western Europe was saved as a working society, as a bastion, and as an ally. The face on the other side of the coin was more forbidding. The Truman-Marshall program institutionalized the division of Europe. Both sides proceeded to batten down the hatches for the irrevocable struggle ahead. France and Italy dumped the Communists from their cabinets and began systematically to isolate them. Russia consolidated her hold on Hungary and Poland, and Mikolaczyk, the Polish opposition leader, was forced to flee the country. The newly formed international bureau of the Communist parties announced its own version of the Truman Doctrine, and Andrei Zhdanov, Stalin's ideological commissar, called on the faithful to close ranks for the holy war.

The bloodless Communist coup in Czechoslovakia in February, 1948, was to have a more shattering effect on Western public opinion than any event since the Stalin-Hitler pact. Czechoslovakia had been the one genuine parliamentary democracy in the East European world, and its forced communization seemed to many to prove the validity of the worst accusations that had been made against Stalin. Even the Scandinavians, who had been least affected by the anti-Soviet fulminations, responded with fear and revulsion. Talk of war was so freely bandied about in the American press that Walter Lippmann thought it wise to warn that such a perspective was illusory and self-defeating. In the asymmetrical reactions evoked by the Cold War, the Communist closeup of Czechoslovakia appeared more immoral or threatening than American arming of the bloody Tsaldares regime in Greece to enable it to continue warring on its own people. The curtain had gone up on the next act of the Cold War, which was to include the repeated crises over Berlin, the carving of Germany into a Western American-style state and an Eastern Stalinized state, the hardening of the two blocs into military alliances whose forces faced each other threateningly across the demarcating lines of their respective spheres.

Truman was able to put this program through Congress because of the support of the internationalist wing of the opposition party, headed by Arthur Vandenberg. Truman needed his support even in the initial two years of his administration when the Democrats nominally controlled Congress, because effective control was in the hands of the conservative coalition. After 1946, when Vandenberg became chairman of the Senate Foreign Relations Committee, his collaboration became indispensable. That an unexceptional politico, an "Establishment invention," according to Joseph Kraft, was touted in the press and sold to the public as a major statesman, a profound thinker in foreign affairs, is a commentary on the making of political reputations. A Senate isolationist in the 1930s, his public conversion to the new internationalism, announced by a blast of trumpets, made him an ideal shepherd of the old oppositionists into the fold of bipartisanship. To his new role he brought three spectacular assets: He was an orator in the Senator Claghorn tradition, self-assured, vapid, pompous, bombastic; he was a reliable conservative from Michigan, on excellent terms with the automobile magnates; and he was at the center of the inner club that runs the Senate.

On any measure of consequence his mind immediately bore through to what for him were the essentials: Was it in line with the positions and opinions of his powerful patrons and friends? Could it be successfully piloted through Congress? What concessions could be demanded and extracted in return for Republican support? In Acheson's more diplomatic phrasing, his was "a strong and practical mind rather than a subtle and original one." In the exercise of his preeminence, Vandenberg developed a technique to carry the electorate along, while keeping the press bemused. When a program was offered, he went through an initial period of publicly viewing with alarm, of skepticism, of seeing merit in objections raised and criticisms offered. Then he would discover—again in full view of the press—a fatal flaw in the proposal, a discovery he would proceed to elaborate and belabor. This prepared the way for the ritual conversion. At the proper moment, he would introduce his own amendment, generally an innocuous addition or alteration, which thereupon transmuted the base metal into authentic gold, and constituted for the trade a Vandenberg guarantee of its purity. As soon as the State Department aides caught on to the routine, they cheerfully played their assigned roles in the buffoonery. In the case of the Marshall Plan, Truman had to agree to additional concessions: $463 million of blackmail money was included for the Kuomintang to keep Henry Luce and the China Lobby quiet; and an independent agency under, but not responding to, the President had to be set up to administer the funds, headed by a Republican industrialist.

With all this finessing, and with all the Establishment names and bipartisan politicos hammering away, Truman had to scare hell out of the country again before Congress—its mind on the 1948 election— would vote the immense funds. The Marshall Plan was adopted in an atmosphere of quasiwar crisis, thickened by the hysteria over the Czech coup, made ominous by the President's frantic call for universal military training and resumption of the draft. The managers were not immune to the frenzy they were trying to induce. On March 5, General Clay sent an alarmist telegram from Germany that war might come with dramatic suddenness—a warning, as he admitted, that could not be supported "with any data or outward evidence," but was based on a "feeling" he had. This was sufficient to send the intelligence services into a whirligig of activities, and on March 16, the CIA, having pondered over the omens—employing undoubtedly the sure techniques devised long ago by the Oracles at Delphi and Delos —made its pronouncement: A war was not probable within sixty days.

11

From
Reconversion
to Taft-Hartley

Paralleling discussions in foreign affairs, some have addressed themselves to whether Truman tried to continue Roosevelt's domestic policy or broke sharply with it. The question in this case is unreal: It is like trying to grasp one set of shadows to compare it with another set. Whether Roosevelt would have made a sustained effort to reopen a new era of reform had he lived is unknown. His steady retreat before reaction in his final years leaves ample room for doubt. That he would have succeeded, had he made the effort, in the teeth of congressional reaction and the intransigence of the business community and press, is even less likely. Fortunately for Roosevelt, and the Hopkinses, Morgenthaus, Ickeses, and Wallaces gathered around him, they were not called upon to demonstrate what they would do, or could do, in the disorderly postwar period. With his dexterity in maneuver, artistry in manipulation, ability to elicit popular response, Roosevelt would have avoided Truman's spasmodic lunges and cruder weavings. The materials for the reconversion crisis, however, had all been gathered during Roosevelt's wartime tenure, and were ready to explode with the ending of hostilities.

In line with the wartime pattern, the welfare, security, and general comfort of industry was underwritten for the transition. The wartime tax laws had thoughtfully made provision for business to use reconversion expenses to offset taxes. In July, 1945, before the war with Japan was over, Congress passed the Tax Adjustment Act raising exemptions and speeding up refunds and credits. Byrnes's wartime agency had been expanded into the Office of War Mobilization and Reconversion the year before on recommendations of Baruch and Hancock, who naturally were concerned almost exclusively with the business aspects of the changeover. Roosevelt grumbled, on signing the bill, that it ignored "the human side of reconversion." Moreover, it was generally understood that the excess profits tax would be eliminated, and in fact the Revenue Act of 1945, approved in November, did so, as well as repealing the capital stock tax, lowering corporation tax rates, and continuing indulgent carry-back and carry-forward arrangements in tax calculations. Industry was thus in the enviable position where its profits in the initial postwar period were assured even if it shut down most of its operations.

Congress was not equally solicitous of wage and salary earners. As a matter of fact, it could work up no interest on their behalf. The Kilgore-Murray bill, introduced in 1944, which called for unemployment benefits of up to $35 a week and a policy advisory board composed of industry, labor, and agriculture representatives, went down to resounding defeat. Congress would not pass this or any other legislation to federalize unemployment insurance or improve compensation schedules. The Full Employment bill, making it the federal government's responsibility to guarantee every worker the right to a job, originally introduced at the end of 1944, was passed only in February, 1946, and then in such emasculated form as to constitute nothing more than a provision to analyze the condition of the economy. (The sole piece of important ameliorative legislation adopted by Congress was the G.I. Bill of Rights, whose variegated benefits and loans helped several million returning soldiers to rebuild their lives—and that probably succeeded because it was connected patriotically with the war effort.)

The exercise by Congress of its class bias on a people far from docile assured labor turmoil in the reconversion period. The labor unions came out of the Second World War much more powerful than in 1918. They had 15 million members now, and the strikes that paralyzed industry in the months following V-J Day were designed to preserve the wartime gains in wages and conditions, not to establish the right of unions to exist and bargain, as in so many of the battles in 1919 and 1920. Because of the changed relationship, violence was minimal. Despite the extent and militancy of the strikes, employers made no attempts to operate their plants or use strikebreakers, relying on economic pressures and government intervention.

The unions made their big stand in the economic arena because they lacked leverage in the political one. They had no party responsive to their interests. The Democratic party—with which they were affiliated for practical purposes—considered labor another pressure group, even if an important one. Although, since the advent of the CIO, unions had engaged in political action more intensively than in the Gompers era, their abilities to achieve their aims were circumscribed by the feudalistic, patronage-ridden makeup of American politics. Labor had been the decisive bloc in the Democratic victory of 1944, yet labor could not translate the electoral victory into legislative accomplishments. The conservative coalition that had dominated Congress since 1938 continued in control after 1944. The political structure was weighted against labor, and its own structure made for little resiliency. It was a coalition of parochial guilds organized for limited purposes. If the membership was no longer the aggregation of Gompers' humble mechanics, bedazzled when President Wilson consented to address one of their conventions, or overwhelmed when one of their business agents was appointed to an advisory post, they were far from regarding themselves as a major political power prepared to determine the course of national affairs.

On the way back from Potsdam, Truman asked Rosenman, who was helping him prepare the conference report, to work on a speech outlining a comprehensive domestic program. Rosenman called on the appropriate agencies and departments to submit their ideas and recommendations. He then wove the responses together into what came to be known as Truman's Twenty-One Point Program, which was presented to Congress in September, 1945. It was a compendium, a laundry list, lacking specific provisions or priorities, ranging from wage incomes and unemployment compensation to crop insurance, lend-lease, and higher congressional salaries. Harold Smith, the budget director, took issue with this dispersive approach. What was needed, he told Rosenman, was a limited, specific, integrated set of recommendations designed for the emergency, to be vigorously fought through Congress. Truman disregarded the criticism. He had a different purpose in mind. Talk was common that his administration represented a conservative departure from Roosevelt's New Deal. Senator Harley M. Kilgore was threatening to outflank him on the liberal front with his own reconversion program. Truman had to stake out his claim as Roosevelt's heir. He wanted his program accepted as in the direct blood line of Roosevelt's Economic Bill of Rights. How much of it, or whether any of it, was to be adopted by Congress was something he could worry about later, if then.

The actual administration thrust was in a different direction. Truman's working program—to the extent that a series of disconnected, fitful, and contradictory decisions can be called a program—was to rapidly dismantle the wartime control agencies and permit the free market to restore proper balances. The general notion was that if wage earners could be mollified with small adjustments, price inflation could be quickly smothered by unleashing industry for civilian production. The confusion about the remedies called for in the interim was aggravated by initial fears that a new depression was due, now that war production was coming to an end. Memories of the 1930s were still green.

The dollar-a-year men of the War Production Board made a mad dash for normalcy. So expeditiously and efficiently did they junk all controls that two and a half months after the end of the war they literally as well as legally closed up shop. Equally drastic was Truman's Executive Order 9599 issued three days after V-J Day. Unions were free to bargain for wage increases, but employers could not use such wage increases as a basis to seek price increases. Where price increases were contemplated, wage increases would have to be approved by a government agency using standards that made approval more than problematic. At the same time, Truman appealed to labor to renew its no-strike pledge and continue to honor decisions of the War Labor Board until a labor-management conference he planned to call could agree on new arrangements to minimize strikes during reconversion. The official OPA history observed with judicious restraint:

> In hindsight it may appear quixotic for the administration, in the transition period following V-J Day, to have depended so heavily, on the one hand, on government price control unaided except by a few auxiliaries, and, on the other hand, on voluntary self-restraint among clashing interests. Looking back, it seems politically inevitable, once manufacturers were given free rein by the lifting of production controls and a financial stimulus by the repeal of the excess profits tax, that labor's no-strike pledge would

end with V-J Day; that without such a pledge wage controls would be inoperative—and stabilization would therefore go out the window.

It needed no hindsight. The program was a chimera from the moment of its promulgation.

Labor ranks had been restive in the last months of the war. Their officials were in no position to renew the no-strike pledge. They would have been repudiated had they tried. The War Labor Board had become an object of hatred. The Little Steel formula was viewed as a tricky, inequitable device to keep wages frozen in the face of rising prices. The restraining dikes were swept away with the end of the war when workers saw their earnings drastically reduced. Instead of 48 hours with 8 hours at overtime rates, their work week was set at the regulation 40 hours, and great numbers were downgraded to lower paying jobs. Were all the gains they had made in the war years to be taken away? Would they be pushed back to the living standards of the Depression Decade? The feeling was in the air that this was the time to make their stand, while profits were high and before mass unemployment undercut labor's bargaining power. An almost universal cry went up for 48 hours pay for 40 hours work, which, translated into rate figures, meant a 30 percent hourly wage increase.

Now that his stabilization program was in jeopardy, and the signals pointed to a storm ahead, Truman began shuffling between the two parties like a mediator. As a true broker of power, he sought to conciliate now one party, now another, and to reconcile or juggle conflicting claims. If he found himself—as the professional politico so often does—upholding the conservatives when the conflict sharpened, it was not because he was wedded to Tory convictions like a Herbert Hoover or a Robert Taft; it was that the greater power was lodged in that camp.

Government economists reported in late October that most industry could raise wages by 24 percent without raising prices and still earn profits at prewar levels. Truman appeared to side with this view. In a radio speech he pointed out that weekly earnings of many war workers had been greatly reduced, that wage increases were imperative "to cushion the shock to our workers, to sustain adequate purchasing power, and to raise the national income," and that this could be done without breaching the existing price structure. Concurrently, however, he issued Executive Order 9651, which virtually reaffirmed his previous position. Under this dispensation OPA was instructed to take unapproved wage increases into consideration in determining price ceilings, but only after a six-month test period. The theory was that, because of this proviso, industry would exercise profound caution in granting wage increases without denying some suitable adjustments, while the price structure would be protected during the most trying period of changeover.

All these fine-spun directives, like the radio rhetoric, were as chaff in the wind. The major corporations made it clear that they would not consider raising wages until they were assured they could pass on the costs to their customers. And the labor ranks were readying for a test of strength as the only way to save their living standards. The labor-management conference that met at this time was as much an exercise in futility as the one called by Woodrow Wilson at the end of the First World War. By this time, unauthorized stoppages were breaking out in many places, and unions in oil, lumber, glass, trucking, and textiles, as well as longshoremen, had already called strikes. Before the conference ended in late November, 180,000 workers in General Motors plants throughout the country manned picket lines. When they were joined in January by the CIO electrical, packing-house, and the three-quarter million employees of the steel industry, the greatest strike struggle in American history was under way. New statistical records were set that month in numbers striking and man-days lost.

With the labor-management conference unable to agree on any rule to avoid stoppages, and with major strikes in progress or in the offing, Truman sent a message to Congress on December 3 calling for restrictive labor legislation. He wanted authority to appoint boards in major disputes to ascertain the facts and make nonbinding recommendations. For thirty days, while the fact-finding machinery was in motion, it would be unlawful for unions to strike. The labor leaders were shocked by this unexpected blow. Philip Murray, the CIO president, criticized Truman for his "abject cowardice" in the face of industry's "arrogance." He predicted, correctly, "It can be but the first step for even more savage legislative repression."

On December 14, before Congress had acted on his proposal, Truman appointed on his personal authority a fact-finding board to look into the GM dispute, and asked the union to call off the strike pending the board's findings. The union rejected the request, but agreed, as did GM management, to present its case to the board. When the board, following the positon Truman had taken earlier, announced that ability to pay would be considered as a relevant although not the sole factor in making its recommendations, the GM executives declared that they would refuse to participate further in the hearings and walked out. "General Motors," they announced with a flourish, "refuses to subscribe to what it believes will ultimately become the death of the American system of competitive enterprise."

The board announced its finding on January 10 of the new year. It recommended an hourly increase of 19.5 cents, which it felt the company could pay without increasing prices, although the company was free to petition for higher prices. GM promptly rejected the recommendation as based on unsound assumptions and subscribing to faulty principles. The union was willing to accept the recommendation, but in view of the company's decision its acceptance was academic and the strike went on. The first fact-finding adjudication had broken down.

Meanwhile the bargaining in steel was coming to a dead end. In an effort to forestall a strike, Truman invited Murray and Benjamin Fairless, president of U.S. Steel, to the White House. The union agreed to scale down its demand to 19.5 cents an hour, while U.S. Steel offered 15 cents provided price increases were approved. After he received an informal report from his steel fact-finding board, Truman proposed a settlement of 18.5 cents. Again, as in the GM case, the proposal was accepted by the union and rejected by the company. Murray complained publicly that if the steel industry did not operate another day in 1946, it would still receive $149 million in tax rebates, a sum 29 percent greater than its prewar earnings.

It was not the 3.5 cents that blocked a settlement. While it appeared to be a traditional labor-management conflict, the industrialists were in effect saying to government officials: You have to grant us price increases to reflect the wage increases we grant our employees. This had been implicit from the start of reconversion. With the steel strike the issue could no longer be evaded. Chester Bowles, the OPA director, felt, for reasons best known to himself, that if government held firm, there would be a settlement eventually by the parties themselves, and the matter of prices could be dealt with separately on its merits. Truman did not agree. Two million workers were out on the streets; the economy was in a state of paralysis; he decided to give business its head. The problem was taken out of OPA's hands entirely, and he and John Snyder, head of the Office of War Mobilization and Reconversion, made a straight deal with the industry heads to hike prices $5 a ton, and still another Executive Order, Number 9697, was issued authorizing price increases to reflect higher wages. There was brave talk that this was only a "bulge" in the price line that would eventually be smoothed out, but in reality it was the beginning of the end for price control. "From this point on," reads the OPA history, "a really firm price policy was in fact no longer possible, either administratively or politically."

The settlement in steel set the pattern for labor peace—18.5 cents, with prices to be raised accordingly. The major strikes were ended on that basis, and by mid-March the numbers striking dropped to 200,-000. But then John L. Lewis, head of the coal miners, who had been such a thorn in Roosevelt's side with his wartime strikes, demanded in addition to the 18.5 cents a health and welfare fund to be financed by a royalty on each ton of coal mined. The negotiations deadlocked, and on April 1 the miners quit work. Coal supplies went down; a brownout was ordered to save fuel; some industries had to curtail operations. As pressure against Lewis rose, he sent the miners back to work in May on a two-week truce. When Truman's proposal for arbitration was rejected by both sides, he ordered Julius Krug, his new Secretary of the Interior, to seize the mines. The miners ignored Krug's appeal to continue working after the expiration of the truce. Four days later Krug gave in, the miners won their welfare fund, and coal prices began pushing upward.

Even this did not resolve all labor troubles, because a week earlier a nationwide rail strike had started. The rail unions had been asking for wage increases and rules revisions. Eighteen of the unions agreed to submit the wage issue to arbitration under the Railway Labor Act and drop their rules demands. The two key operating unions, the Engineers and Trainmen, held out, and Truman referred this dispute to an emergency board he appointed. Both boards awarded wage increases of 16 cents, 2.5 cents below the national pattern. The emergency board, in addition, recommended a few rules changes, returning the remainder to the parties for further negotiation. All the unions condemned the awards, and the Engineers and Trainmen called a nationwide strike for May 18. Truman seized the railroads on May 17, secured postponement of the strike date for a week, and made a compromise proposal for an additional 2.5 cents pay increase to accord with the national pattern. The offer, unconditional for the eighteen unions, was made conditional for the Engineers and Trainmen on their agreement to forego the rules changes already recommended by the emergency board. The two unions refused, and on May 23 the rail strike was on.

Truman now let exasperation dictate his conduct. He had had no success in convincing industrialists to use some of their swollen tax rebates to satisfy wage demands. He therefore turned with unrestrained fury on labor leaders who were discommoding him and producing doubts about his ability to conduct government. It was a case of turning on the party that could more easily be strong-armed. He had not shown anger when GM had walked out of the fact-finding hearing. He had not denounced the steel executives when they turned down his compromise. Ironically, the two rail union chiefs, Johnston of the Engineers and Whitney of the Trainmen, were the same two who had extended themselves so generously in 1940 to make possible his reelection to the Senate.

The day after the strike began, Truman told advisers he was going to address the public and then ask Congress in a personal appearance to sock labor with the stiffest law in American history—to draft strikers into the armed forces. When Attorney General Clark wondered if such a measure was constitutional, he brushed the question aside. "We'll draft them first and think about the law later," he snapped. For the speech over the radio, he drew out of his pocket a bundle of twelve small sheets on which he had written out his remarks. Ross convinced him that the speech had to be toned down. It is unfortunate that, though the speech was revised, the original was not consigned to the furnace like his letter to Wallace. There is no blinking the fact that when he was crossed or frustrated, his instinct was to lash out like a madcap bar room brawler. The original speech was nothing less than a call to veterans to organize themselves into a vigilante mob for the purpose of cleaning up traitors on the home front: "Every single one of the strikers and their demigog [sic] leaders have been living in luxury, working when they pleased and drawing from four to forty times the pay of a fighting soldier. Now I want you men who are my comrades in arms, you men who fought the battle to save the nation just as I did 25 years ago, to come with me and eliminate the Lewises, the Whitneys and the Johnstons, the Communist Bridges and the Russian Senators and Representatives and really make this a government of, by and for the people. Let's put transportation and production back to work, hang a few traitors and make our own country safe for democracy."

Even in its toned-down delivered version, the speech was a blockbuster. The workers, Truman declared, were striking not against management but against the government; unless they returned to work the next day, he would call out troops to break the strike. The next day he appeared before a joint session of Congress and, as good as his word, proposed the most punitive law against unions and strikers since the days when a labor combination was held to constitute a conspiracy. He asked for the power to declare a national emergency whenever the government had seized a facility, after which a strike would be unlawful; any striker failing to return to work would lose his employment rights and be subject to induction into the army; union officers failing to call off the strike could be fined or imprisoned. After Truman began reading his speech, Clifford got word that Johnston and Whitney had signed the agreement at the final moment. He raced over to the Capitol and scribbled a note on a scrap of paper: "Mr. President, agreement signed, strike over," which he gave to Leslie Biffle, the Senate secretary. Biffle dashed into the House chamber and placed the note on the rostrum from which Truman was speaking. Truman halted in the middle of his remarks to announce with a grin, "Gentlemen, the strike has been settled." The chamber burst into clamorous applause. But he went right ahead with his speech and his proposal.

For the moment he was the hero of the conservative coalition and the press. The *Los Angeles Times* likened him to Grover Cleveland, who sent troops to Chicago in 1894 over the protest of Governor John Peter Altgeld to break Eugene Debs's Pullman strike; "Cleveland's capacity to hew to line" was what was needed in the White House. Other papers chimed in to praise his "courage" and his championing of the "people's rights" against the "labor bosses." "If he rose to heights of greatness in the critical hour it was because he spoke from the heart of the American people," said the *Philadelphia Record*. The House rushed through Truman's proposal that same day in an orgy of self-congratulatory bravado by a vote of 306 to 13. It was due to Senator Taft—Mr. Republican himself—that the hysterical onrush was sidetracked. The bill, he said, violated "every principle of American jurisprudence." *

When John L. Lewis tried to break through for further gains, Truman reacted as he had done with the rail workers. In late October, Lewis accused government officials of having violated the vacation and welfare fund provisions of his contract and threatened, unless a settlement was reached, to call another strike on November 20. Truman was vacationing in Key West. As the deadline came near, he summoned a number of his aides and asked them to work out the best available strategy to slap down Lewis hard. He and his advisers

---

* At the time, the Republicans were pushing the Case bill, whose chances were superior for withstanding a court challenge.

acted as if Lewis' aggressive tactics—whether they were well advised is another matter—were a personal affront to the President. Years later Clifford said of the battle: "I think you can put your finger on winning this showdown with Lewis as the moment when Truman finally and irrevocably stepped out from the shadow of FDR to become President in his own right." Truman said the same thing of his Twenty-One Point message: The date he sent it to Congress symbolized for him his assumption of the office of President in his own right. Apparently, it was something that had to be proved again and again.

The strategy devised called for disregarding the Norris-LaGuardia anti-injunction law. The government took the position that the contract could not be reopened; it petitioned for a restraining order. Two days before the scheduled strike, Federal Judge T. Alan Goldsborough issued a temporary order restraining union officials from calling a strike until there was a judicial review. When Lewis refused to withdraw his termination notice and the miners walked out, Goldsborough found Lewis and the union guilty of civil and criminal contempt, denounced the strike as "an evil and monstrous thing," fined the union $3.5 million and Lewis $10,000, and granted the government a preliminary injunction. In March the Supreme Court upheld the conviction, although it reduced the fine to $700,000 on condition that the union purge itself of contempt. The justices wrote five different opinions; the decision that an injunction was permissible under the Norris-LaGuardia Act was made by a 5 to 4 vote. Lewis retreated, and Truman won his victory and presumably became President in his own right.

The President's triumph resolved neither his own predicament nor the controversy itself. In late March Lewis made use of the Centralia disaster, when eleven miners were killed in an explosion, to proclaim a six-day Holy Week as a memorial to the dead. The catastrophe shook the public, ruling out any reprisals against Lewis for his defiance of the Supreme Court. Before a Senate investigating committee appointed to determine if there had been government laxity at Centralia, Lewis berated Krug—"this great modern Hercules, with a No. 12 shoe and a No. 5 hat"—for permitting the miners to die "by negligence in action and by a dishonorable violation of his own agreement." When the mines were returned to the owners at the end of June with the expiration of the Smith-Connally Act, Lewis negotiated a new contract raising wages and doubling the royalty payments to the welfare funds. The government pyrotechnics, dictated by extraneous considerations, had merely delayed a settlement.

Truman knew that his punitive forays had estranged the liberal wing of his party. He made an effort to keep a semblance of balance. But the makeup of his Cabinet and the utilitarian, courthouse approach of most of his aides militated against his ability to arouse an independent public response against a hostile legislature. When in January, 1946, he reintroduced his Twenty-One Point program by rearranging and combining the most important of them, and went on the radio to appeal for public support, Robert Sherwood wrote Rosenman that the speech fell dead, that there would have to be aggressive leadership if the lagging spirits of the liberals were to be revived. When the Case bill, an assortment of labor-restrictive provisions many of which found their way into the later Taft-Hartley Act, was adopted by both houses and sent to him, Snyder and George Allen tried to persuade Truman to sign the bill because labor could not shift to the Republicans; it had no place to go. In any case, the unions represented only one out of every five workers, and the independents would be lost if the President vetoed the bill. Truman rejected the advice, and managed to get his veto sustained in the House by a bare five votes. The veto message was incongruous, however, coming from a President who several weeks before had called for drafting strikers. The signals were further confused when he immediately afterward signed Section Seven of the Case bill, which he had criticized in his message but which Congress passed separately as the Hobbs bill, making unions subject to antiracketeering provisions in interstate commerce.

A sense of direction, of coherence, was conspicuously absent. Harold Smith, the budget director, candidly laid it on the line to Truman in a conference in February. He said, "While you yourself are an orderly person, there is disorder all around you, and it is becoming worse. For one thing, you need good, continuous, organized staff work, and you are not getting it." Truman interrupted to say, "I know it, and the situation is pretty serious."

Smith went on, "I will give you just one example, but I could give you many others. Not more than three or four weeks ago top people in Agriculture were making speeches which indicated their worry about a possible food surplus in this country. Now you are issuing a statement about black bread. If this sort of thing continues, Mr. President, the people of the country will think that the Administration has gone completely crazy. Frankly, I don't know who does what around here, and that is a rather dangerous situation for all of us to be in. You would be interested in my recent wisecrack that the top people in the government are solving problems in a vacuum and the vacuum is chiefly in their heads."

With his legislative scoreboard registering defeats for all his welfare proposals, Truman determined to dig in for a battle royal on extension of the Price Control Act, due to expire at the end of June. Labor leaders and liberals jousted mightily with the National Association of Manufacturers. Liberals in Congress exchanged hot words with conservatives. Millions of dollars were spent on newspaper, magazine, and radio advertisements. Housewives from across the nation marched up to Capitol Hill to demand a year's extension of OPA "without crippling amendments." The President heroically vetoed one bill because, as he said, it offered the choice between "inflation with a statute and inflation without one." He protestingly consented to sign a revised bill no better than the first because it was the best he could get. This titanic battle, in retrospect, was like a star whose light shines most piercingly when it is already extinct.

By the summer of 1946 it was a matter of rearguard skirmishes, fixing the blame, and courting public opinion. When in the fall OPA tried to reimpose a ceiling on meat prices far higher than the one of June 30 but lower than what was then being charged, the industry created a meat famine by withholding livestock from the market. Thereupon Truman gave up all pretenses and ordered the abandonment of meat controls. With that, the entire program collapsed. In the last six months of the year consumer prices shot up 15 percent, with food prices leading the way at 28 percent—a record for this short a period—and the postwar inflation continued to rage throughout Truman's Presidency.

Many have criticized Truman's reconversion record. Some criticisms came from people who think anything can be patched up by bureaucratic fixing, clearer directives, or rhetorical uplift. The consequential criticism was that controls were eliminated too soon, that had an adjustment of the Little Steel formula been made while price rises were held to their wartime tempos, the chaos of the year after the war would have been avoided or largely mitigated. Whether such a course could have been maintained against an obstreperous manufacturers' association, bellicose farm organizations, a hostile Congress, a belligerent press, no one will ever know. That it should have been attempted, and that it would have been, had Truman and Snyder not been in the grip of a laissez-faire mystique, both logic and subsequent experience indicated. It would be fatuous to pretend, however, that inflation would not have come in any case once controls were lifted.

Many factors ensured it: The war had been financed largely by deficit spending and commercial borrowing; the tax laws had placed enormous sums in the hands of business firms; a huge pool of private savings had been created; cashable-on-demand government securities held by banks and other institutions made their funds highly liquid; tax relief and easy credit added their pressures.

At midterm election time, Truman was considered a failure. His fears at the 1944 convention that he might become another Millard Fillmore, if not another Andrew Johnson, were being realized. His leadership of the pack in the confrontation with the Russians did not add to his stature or redeem his bumbling. The wounding jokes were beginning to go the rounds: "To err is Truman"; "Don't shoot the piano player, he's doing the best he can"; "I wonder what Truman would do if he were alive"; "Why had the President been late to today's press conference? He got up this morning a little stiff in the joints and had trouble putting his foot in his mouth." Wrote a liberal columnist, "Poor Mr. Truman, an object of pity." The Republicans, with the help of an advertising agency, summed it all up in a catchphrase that became their winning campaign platform: "Had enough?"

The Republican landslide was explained by some as akin to a process of nature, like the movement of the tides: There is a flow, and then an ebb. There was war-weariness, there was frustration over high prices, black markets, strikes. A swing to normalcy was inevitable, made more pronounced by the ineptitudes and inanities of an accidental President. The explanation can be made more specific. The surge to reaction came about not because a mass of the Democratic electorate passed over to the Republican camp but because it did not bother to vote. Daniel Tobin, then head of the Teamsters union, who had been prominent in all four Roosevelt campaigns, had publicly warned Truman that if the average worker saw no difference between the parties he would not vote at all.

That is precisely what occurred, and not only in the case of workers. It was not that 8 million Democratic voters—the margin of Democratic failure—decided that they preferred Republican normalcy to Truman normalcy; it was that these 8 million Democratic voters could not see enough at stake to warrant making a special trip to the polls. Truman had reduced the liberals and laborites to apathy and despair; and he had not gained the approbation of conservatives, for the business community and its sympathetic press generally preferred the avowed and consistent Republican spokesmen. Despite the attempt of the media to make it seem so, there was no popular stampede for McKinleyite pastures. Many had simply lost their motivation to vote. Apathy, we are told, is a natural defense against dangers one feels powerless to do anything about.

It was thus a funereal scene when the President with Bess and Margaret returned from Independence. As told by Acheson, "It had for years been a Cabinet custom to meet President Roosevelt's private car on his return from happier elections and escort him to the White House. It never occurred to me that after defeat the President would be left to creep unnoticed back to the Capital. So I met his train. To my surprise and horror, I was alone on the platform where his car was brought in, except for the station master and a reporter or two."

The Republicans flocked to Capitol Hill in the spirit of the Cavaliers foregathering in Whitehall at the Restoration, except that the Republican leaders lacked the forebearance of the pleasure-loving monarch. The conservative coalition had run things at the previous Congress, but now the Republican chieftains took over the committee chairmanships and offices and, chortling with anticipatory glee, let it be known that heads would fall and the pendulum begin its long swing to the right. While Vandenberg, by common consent, was the oracle in foreign affairs, the man who called the signals on all other matters, one who incarnated the inner spirit of the party, was Robert A. Taft.

As unprepossessing and crusty as Calvin Coolidge, and totally lacking any of the gifts popularly associated with the political gladiator, Taft put his impress on the Republican Congress by his professional competence and single-minded dedication to the task at hand. Son of a President and a scion of one of America's political and financial dynasties, he had watched over the trusts and estates of Cincinnati's upper class for over a quarter of a century as a successful corporation lawyer. What made this dry, brusque, sober-minded curmudgeon the plumed knight of reaction was that he was a true believer among opportunists. Surrounded by sycophants, lobbyists, and acolytes of big-business interests, here was a moral and upright man trying to raise an assortment of laissez-faire shibboleths to the status of a moral philosophy. He had opinions on most questions of the day and, unlike others, disdained to conceal them. Although politically ambitious, and a seeker of the presidential nomination since 1940, he displayed no hesitation in bucking overwhelming public opinion, as he did in the case of the Nuremberg trials. The aristocratic Whig peered every so often out of the drab garb and awkward mannerisms of the middle western politico. He lacked oratorical talents or graces, but spoke lucidly and intelligently. He had no need for the customary campfollowing of ghost-writers and memoranda-briefers. His associates knew that they could count on him to get the facts and generalize them for legislative purposes; that the gray, pedestrian figure would rise from their midst when needed and, speaking extemporaneously, make the necessary arguments; that their leader was a political mechanic, not an artifact of public-relations technicians. Among papier-mâché statesmen, he showed up as an authentic figure, if an unexciting one.

Taft was called an isolationist in his world views, but the designation had become a general-purpose term of opprobrium and abuse, conveying a false impression of the congeries of notions, prejudices, and precepts of a significant part of the American business community. Like so many of this milieu, he had doubted the need of going to war with Germany, had seen Russian Communism as a greater threat than German Nazism. He had supported the Truman Doctrine and Marshall Plan grudgingly and with reservations, and had raised grave objections to the military alliance with Western Europe. At the same time, he took for granted this country's suzerainty over Latin America, and became positively jingoist and uproariously imperialist where the Far East was concerned. The liberal terminology that contrasted isolationists and internationalists was, in Taft's case, not only inexact but misleading. The difference was over ways and means, and where lay the center of gravity of America's big power interests.

Taft's major leadership, however, was not in foreign but domestic affairs. As the intellectual and working leader of the congressional party, he rang up all the catchwords and phrases—states' rights and keeping government close to the people, living within one's budget, cutting down on bureaucracy, righting the imbalance between labor and capital, halting the interference and meddling of government in activities of freeborn Americans—that became the totemic objects of worship of the American Right for the next generation. This or that specific act of the Eightieth Congress or position paper of Taft's cannot be justly appraised if not seen in the context of the generalized set of beliefs and purposes that animated the business mind. There was the conviction that the New Deal system of extended government, its proliferation of bureaus, its assumption that it was government's duty to underwrite the nation's welfare, its consequent commitment to government spending, high taxes, and debt—all this had established a calamitous trend toward a planned economy and a collectivist society. That trend, unless reversed, would lead to socialism, which by definition, was unworkable, dictatorial, and destructive of all those virtues that had built this country and made it great. Business had realized, after the humiliating rejection of the Liberty League and its sponsors, that the electorate could not be returned to the glories of the past in one forced march, that a protracted campaign of education, pressure, guerrilla attacks, and piecemeal counterreform had to be waged before ground could be regained and the heights of Mount Pisgah were in view. The grand objective, nevertheless, was to disparage the New Deal, to make it a thing of obloquy and shame, and stigmatize and eventually to drive all those associated with it out of public life.

The counterreform faced a number of inherent difficulties. For one, the argument that a program of mild reform was a way station to totalitarianism was unpersuasive, except to laissez-faire fanatics. Nor was it likely that Roosevelt, the hero to multitudes, could now be unmasked as a collectivist villain. Moreover, any idea of returning to limited government, low taxes, minimal regulation, and balanced budgets while at the same time building an enormous military force, maintaining bases and dependencies around the globe, and pursuing a Cold War with another superpower, had to be a mirage. Most of the welfarist reforms of the New Deal had become part of the pattern of American life. To eliminate them would have meant social turmoil on a larger scale than the business community was prepared to accept. Taft's inconsistencies, acrobatics, and accommodations were thus less attributable to his intellectual limitations than to the grotesque, inflated character of the program to which both he and the great corporations were dedicated, at least polemically. If that were not sufficient, Taft, like a true upper-class Whig, also had a trace of noblesse oblige; he recognized that at least some reforms for the benefit of the disadvantaged were indispensable for the stability of the system.

To a generation that has grown accustomed to labor unions as complacent adjuncts of the status quo, it seems strange that Taft and the Republican Congress should have seen their taming as the first order of business, and that the Taft-Hartley Act was viewed by Taft as his foremost legislative accomplishment. The *entente cordiale* between unions and corporations resting on the twin pillars of labor conservatism and inflation was to be an achievement of the subsequent decades. At this time, the memories of the CIO sitdown strikes, of the siege of the Ford River Rouge plant, of the comeback in Little Steel, of the wartime coal strikes, were still fresh and rankling, and the reversal of the New Deal was in the first instance conceived of in terms of shackling labor.

The Taft-Hartley Act was not the resurrection of the American Plan that followed the First World War. The unions had attained such strength that an attempt to mount an open-shop assault would have led to a struggle dwarfing the 1945–1946 strike wave. At the same time, the legalization and encouragement of state right-to-work laws, the reimposition of injunctions in labor disputes, and the act's other harsh provisions represented a threat. No one knew at the time whether this might not be the first stage of a campaign to emasculate unionism, and had the unions begun to disintegrate under the blow it would likely have been followed by further punitive efforts, legislative or extralegal or both. The hostile purposes and consequences of the law were not controverted by the fact that unions proved strong enough to weather the attack—nor by the fact that they were in need of reform.

That the unions were unimpressive as a progressive social movement only labor apologists would deny. They were dictatorially run; they wasted funds and energies on jurisdictional and internecine squabbles; most of their leaders lacked social vision; many were less than adequate in promoting the immediate interests of their memberships; many discriminated against blacks; all rode roughshod over oppositions and dissenters; in some unions, there was outright corruption and embezzlement of funds. The several hundred newspapers issued by the international unions, central labor bodies, and local organizations, and mailed to the millions of homes of members, were tawdry and spiritless house organs devoted more to inflating the concocted reputations of union officials than to formulating policy and enlisting the loyalties of the dues-payers to a movement of social aspiration. But it was vain to seek reforms from congressmen whose interest was not in making the labor movement more democratic or socially full-blooded, only more docile and legally constricted. The employers' multimillion-dollar propaganda efforts succeeded in muddling these categories.

The argument that carried most weight with the public, inconvenienced as it was by strikes and often antagonized by the parochialism and pugnacious small-mindedness of union officials, was that the labor bosses had grown excessively powerful and that it was time to redress the balance; that just as the Wagner Act had been necessary to restrain corporations become too arrogant, so now it had become necessary to restrain labor unions become too irresponsible. According to a Gallup poll conducted after the election, two-thirds of those questioned favored laws to control unions. The precise place and rights one wants to assign to labor unions in a capitalist democracy depends on one's political philosophy; the precise position taken in a strike, on the specific circumstances of the dispute. In any case, this premise for restrictive labor legislation was based on a misreading of the American reality. Businessmen had regained during the war much of their reputation lost in the bad days of the Great Depression when bankers were referred to as banksters and corporation heads as economic royalists. Now they were convincing a large part of the public that they were the aggrieved party being pushed around by power-hungry labor bosses.

Truman vetoed the Taft-Hartley bill on June 20 and went on the air that evening to explain his stand. Taft replied in a similar nationwide broadcast. Next day, 43 minutes after the veto message was read to the House, over half the Democrats joined the Republicans to override the veto. Two days later in the Senate, almost half the Democrats joined with the Republicans to override the veto. Eric Sevareid called it the most important victory of Congress over the Executive since Roosevelt's setback in the Supreme Court fight. This was only the first of repeated overridings of vetoes—of a "rich man's" tax reduction bill, of bills excluding new categories of workers from Social Security, exempting railroads from antitrust laws, removing the Employment Service from the Labor department. The Eightieth Congress cut appropriations for welfare agencies, buried fair employment and antilynching legislation, refused funds for public housing and aid to education, refused to act on national health, on raising minimum wages, on higher unemployment benefits. TRB summed up the liberal reaction in *The New Republic:* "This Congress brought back an atmosphere you had forgotten or never thought possible."

To Clark Clifford it was obvious after the 1946 defeat that, unless Truman revamped his administration, he had no political future. The defeat, he said, "pointed up more clearly than anything else could that there just was no clear direction, no political cohesion to the Truman program. And it pointed to two more years of frustration and final defeat." He and Oscar Chapman, Undersecretary of the Interior, Oscar Ewing, Federal Security Director, Leon Keyserling of the President's Council of Economic Advisers, and several others took to meeting together to discuss domestic issues "to try to plot a coherent political course for the administration. Naturally, we were up against tough competition. Most of the Cabinet and the Congressional leaders were urging Mr. Truman to go slow, to veer a little closer to the conservative line. They held the image of Bob Taft before him like a bogeyman. We were pushing him the other way, urging him to boldness and to strike out for new, high ground. He wasn't going to pacify that Republican Congress, whatever he did. Well, it was two forces fighting for the mind of the President."

Clifford, probably the most impressive and influential member of the White House staff, was a chance find. Jake Vardaman, a wealthy St. Louis businessman of doubtful reputation, whose shoe company had been involved in a financial scandal, brought Clifford along as his assistant when he was named naval aide to the President. Clifford had handled Vardaman's legal affairs in St. Louis and got a commission in 1944 as a Navy lieutenant on a desk job with Vardaman's help. Born into a well-situated middle-class family, he had been a successful trial attorney before the war, a patron of the St. Louis Opera, an accredited member of the city's social set. Six-foot-two, with smiling blue eyes, shining teeth, and wavy golden hair of a matinee idol, the sleekness, polish, and self-assurance of a courtier, Clifford had the precise talents needed to gain the President's confidence. "The whole relationship between the President and me," he explained, "was a highly personal one. It developed because there was a vacuum in the White House. We were both from Missouri. He was comfortable with me." Clifford was a cool customer with more than a touch of the icy calculation of the Renaissance Florentine. In the setting of the Truman White House, he appeared a liberal, but it was a liberalism of the professional journeyman who had figured the odds, a liberalism drained of passion and ideas. Politics was a chess game to him, a vehicle to exercise his considerable abilities. After he left Truman and went on to build the most lucrative practice of any Washington lawyer, he applied himself to devising strategy for the great corporations with the same energy and cold-bloodedness he had displayed in the White House, and probably with as little personal commitment.

The liberal cabal carried the day with Truman in the case of the Taft-Hartley bill. Clifford wrote the slashing veto message that was to become the basis for the later election campaign. By the latter part of 1947, Truman accepted Clifford's general analysis of his situation and adopted the strategy outlined in a Clifford memorandum: "The administration should select the issues upon which there will be conflict with the majority in Congress. It can assume that it will get no major part of its own program approved. Its tactics must therefore be entirely different than if there were any real point to bargaining and compromises. Its recommendations—in the State of the Union message and elsewhere—must be tailored for the voter, not the Congressman; they must display a label which reads 'no compromise.'"

Discarded were the attempts to ingratiate himself with individual congressmen, or to win over waverers by displays of moderation and sweet reasonableness. Everything he had learned in Kansas City convinced him that Clifford had the right idea, that his only chance for survival was to reenact the old reliable melodrama of the plain people against the interests. When he called Congress back in the fall of 1947 for emergency appropriations prior to the definitive enactment of the Marshall Plan, he also tossed in a ten-point program to halt inflation, including wage and price controls. His State of the Union message in January, 1948, called for a "poor man's" tax reduction, the ten-point anti-inflation program, an extensive housing program, extended Social Security, and national health insurance. A month later he unloaded on Congress another ten-point civil rights message in which he pledged an executive order to insure nondiscrimination in the federal establishment. The slogan at the White House was "hit 'em every Monday." Congress was peppered with special messages, rebuked for its derelictions, lectured on its duties.

Nor did Truman neglect to play for Jewish votes and campaign contributions. For two years he had been backing and filling between the State Department and Zionists while the struggle between Jew and Arab mounted to a climax in the Near East. Marshall, Lovett, Loy Henderson, like their counterparts in the British Foreign Office, were maneuvering to keep friendly relations with the Arab rulers. Forrestal was mobilizing sentiment inside and outside the administration for a pro-Arab policy, called for, in the opinion of bankers and oil corporations, by both imperial and economic requirements. Truman was personally sympathetic to the Zionist cause, probably influenced by his earlier cordial associations with Jacobson, his partner in the haberdashery business, and with Jewish supporters in St. Louis. Now he felt there were pressing reasons to corral Jewish support for his administration.

At a conference to discuss the question of recognition of Israel, attended by both Marshall and Clifford, Marshall protested: "Mr. President, this is not a matter to be determined on the basis of politics. Unless politics were involved, Mr. Clifford would not even be at this conference. This is a very serious matter of foreign policy determination." "He said it all," Clifford recalled angrily, "in a righteous God-damned Baptist tone." Truman closed the matter by saying "We must follow the position General Marshall has advocated."

Afterward, Lovett began wavering on the pro-Arab course. He had several talks with Clifford and came around to his way of thinking. When State officials reversed themselves, Truman approved Clifford's proposition that the United States be the first to tender recognition to Israel. In May, when the British mandate expired, the United States extended de facto recognition—sixteen minutes after the official proclamation of the new state. (It was a typical Truman performance, however. De jure recognition was still withheld, and the arms embargo that the State Department had instituted was not lifted. Numbers of liberals, among whom pro-Zionism was intense, considered his oscillations reprehensible. Eleanor Roosevelt wanted to resign as UN delegate. Dorothy Schiff, owner of the *New York Post*, refused to support him in the election because of his shiftiness on this question.)

Clifford's many successes notwithstanding, Truman was not easily rehabilitating himself with the liberal-labor constituency. There were too many conflicting impulses in his administration to make the struggle with Congress entirely convincing. It was difficult to portray the Executive branch, loaded with complacent politicians on the make and spoken for by conservative Establishment figures, as a knighthood of populist zealots. The shuffling and jobbing had produced, in the phrase to be applied in another era, a yawning credibility gap. At the very time that the air was rent with the debate on Taft-Hartley, Truman issued an executive order setting up loyalty investigations of federal employees. His appointments continued to outrage liberals, as when he dumped James Landis, the New Dealer who, as head of the Civil Aeronautics Board, had tangled with the airlines over monopolistic control and safety measures, and substituted for him an Air Force general; or when he replaced Marriner Eccles with Thomas McCabe, an ultraconservative Republican, as chairman of the Federal Reserve Board. The big scandals that beset his administration did not break until his second term, but the shape of things to come was visible when the public learned in January, 1948, that Pauley, then special assistant to the Secretary of the Army, and Brigadier General Wallace K. Graham, Truman's White House physician, had made a killing in commodity speculation. Nor were most labor leaders assuaged by his veto of the Taft-Hartley bill. The odor of his earlier onslaughts still lingered.

Consequently, when the time approached for the Democratic convention in the summer, there were few who wanted Harry Truman to continue as the party standard-bearer. Jacob Arvey, the Chicago boss, William O'Dwyer, mayor of New York, Frank Hague, mayor of Jersey City, James and Elliott Roosevelt, most of the leaders of Americans for Democratic Action, Claude Pepper, the voice of liberalism in the Senate at its most unrelenting—joined, for their own reasons, by Southern bourbons—were sending off letters, issuing public statements, rushing to and fro, in a desperate effort to induce Eisenhower to accept the Democratic nomination. None was disturbed by his ignorance of where Ike stood on the political questions of the day, any more than were the Republicans four years later. Noted *The New Republic*, "Democratic politicians are not concerned about Eisenhower's views. What they want is a winning candidate who will carry local candidates to victory." Practically all the important labor leaders were opposed to Truman. "That squeaky-voice tinhorn; I want nothing to do with him," said Daniel Tobin. Others held the same opinion without expressing themselves that inelegantly. It was only at the end of August, after Eisenhower had refused to be considered, after Justice Douglas had proved unavailable, after all attempts to find a substitute candidate had collapsed, that the CIO executive board endorsed Truman.

The eleventh-hour hunt for a new candidate was futile. Once Truman decided to seek vindication, his control of the convention assured him the nomination. Even were another candidate available, to have repudiated Truman and the Democratic administration would have guaranteed not only defeat but a party holocaust. Only the despair and disorganization in the Democratic camp could account for the spectacle of seasoned politicians lending themselves to the illusion.

The delegates that gathered in Philadelphia in July, 1948, for the Democratic convention did not so much nominate Truman as become reconciled to going down to defeat with him. Very few Democrats would have disagreed with the judgment of the *St. Louis Post-Dispatch* that Truman lacked "the stature, the vision, the social and economic grasp, or the sense of history required to lead this nation in a world crisis," or with the Roper and Gallup polls, which showed him losing to Thomas E. Dewey.

12

The
1948
Miracle

It was not all work, decisions, pressure, and jeers and taunts. The Presidency gave scope for relaxation and play. Truman's annual salary and expense account by the second term was $150,000. He had a private Pullman car, with radio and telephone, bedrooms, kitchen, and dining room; a yacht with a crew of 100; an airplane; a fleet of automobiles; a rent-free house on 16 acres with swimming pool, tennis courts, riding horses, and a retinue of servants. There was free medical and dental care for himself and his family; free concerts, movies, and other entertainments—with the greatest talents available for command performances. According to compilations of a magazine staff, the perquisites of the office would cost a private citizen $3.5 million a year. Despite its bourgeois pedestrianism and obeisance to democratic simplicity, it was a style of living that a maharajah need not have disdained.

Truman brought to his playing the same restless energy that he did to work. He was blessed with a harmonious and balanced biological mechanism with reserves of apparently inexhaustible vitality. His temperament was unusual: Although impulsive and given to quick-tempered eruptions of anger and spite, he moved along with equanimity on a steady keel of routine, carried himself with poise through his difficulties without agonizing or despairing. Through the vicissitudes of two terms, he displayed a cheerful self-possession. His ability to slough off mistakes, never to brood about decisions made, to fall into a sound sleep once his head hit the pillow, was proverbial. Whether due to a lack of depth or to a well-ordered and self-protective disposition or both, he emerged from the White House after eight years as a crisis President with health and optimism unimpaired. His appearance at midpassage was not much changed from wartime senatorial days, the gestures as vigorous as before, the manner more authoritative and assured. Though the hair was now dull gray and receding at the temples, and he had acquired jowls and a little paunch, the skin was still clear and glowed with health, the chin firm, the expression alert, the mica glint in his eyes, essentially the same brisk, compact figure accoutered in a sharply pressed double-breasted suit.

If congressmen accepted his friendliness as part of the politician's working equipment, it was valued by his aides and servitors and bound them to him. Richard E. Neustadt said that "he was worshipped by his household staff and by his secret service agents as no President in memory before him." His aides made a point of commenting on his consideration and courtesy. U. E. Boughman, the Secret Service chief, wrote, "Many of my men on the White House Detail still speak of him with real emotion, of his unfailing kindness and generosity." Where Roosevelt was too preoccupied and busy to take notice (except during the celebrated Christmas parties when everyone working at the White House was treated to an individually marked and wrapped gift and a handshake), and Eisenhower treated the staff as he would soldiers at sentry posts, Truman talked to everybody as he walked through the White House. Nor was Truman one to neglect the ceremonial duties. In steady procession came strawberry queens, Indian chiefs, chamber of commerce dignitaries, eagle scouts, disabled veterans, little girls with poppies. Whatever the weather, political or atmospheric, the photographers were brought in, a grinning, relaxed Truman posed with the visitors, and after a quick handshake that group was ushered out to make way for the next.

These ceremonial duties, practiced by all Presidents to one extent or another, were for Truman merely preliminaries for truly Lucullan feasts of delight. Six months after taking office, during the reconversion crisis, he made a five-day trip to the small Missouri town of Caruthersville for the American Legion state convention, where, according to one newspaperman, he "did everything except have himself shot from the mouth of a cannon." He held court on the porch of the town's rundown hotel, gossiped with farmers, politicians, and inebriated veterans, performed the traditional rite of spitting into the Mississippi. By noon of the first day, he had pinned medals on a troop of boy scouts, accepted membership in the Lions Club, attended church services, received a custom-built hat from the local clothier, shaken hundreds of hands, and given equal numbers of autographs. After lunch, when frolicking Legionnaires drove up to the hotel in a miniature locomotive, he and that other good-timer, John Snyder, raced to the street and took turns yanking the bell cord of the locomotive to the delight of the photographers and citizenry. That evening, at a dinner served by the Methodist Church ladies, Truman pounded out Paderewski's *Minuet* on a battered piano, and at the finish, turning himself around on the piano stool, announced, winking at the ladies, "When I played this, Stalin signed the Potsdam agreement." Everyone applauded. Here was democracy at work and history in the making. He topped off the heart-warming events of the day by staying up half the night playing poker with his buddies.

Poker was more than a diversion; it was an avocation. Unlike Harding, he never permitted card-playing in the White House. But he regularly attended stag poker sessions at his associates' homes, and it was staple recreation on yachting trips and Key West sojourns. One of Boughman's entries reads: "Truman played cards at Attorney General Howard McGrath's house, joined by Stuart Symington and Secretary of the Treasury [Snyder] till ten minutes to four in the morning." Several weeks before Caruthersville, while holiday-making at a Democratic jamboree on the Chesapeake—the time Byrnes could not reach him from the London foreign ministers conference—he finished up the day sitting on the front porch of a cottage decked out in the garish sportswear he loved for off hours, playing stud poker in full view of the crowd. As with so many straight-thinking, feet-on-the-ground, conformist men of affairs, there was a gaping hole inside him demanding to be filled, and he fed it the only way he knew.

He was a strict family man. Ross attested to what people knew: "Harry Truman never had a Mrs. Peck." * He not only was passionately devoted to his wife and daughter; his overprotectiveness had an intensity that shattered precedents in literature as well as history. His suspicion that the blue bloods around Washington were patronizing

---

* Mrs. Mary Peck had been a friend of Woodrow Wilson since his Princeton days. There was a whispering campaign before the 1916 election that she would act the jilted paramour if he married Edith Galt, who became the second Mrs. Wilson.

the homespun Trumans of Independence made him rage at any fancied slight. By a process of association and transposition, he converted criticism of his wife or daughter into disrespect for the office of the Presidency. At one time, the combination of sensitivity and willfulness pushed him close to creating an international incident. On the afternoon of the first annual diplomatic dinner of his administration, Stanley Woodward, the protocol chief, was informed by the Russian mission that Ambassador Nikolai V. Novikov had been taken ill and would be unable to attend. The State Department quickly discovered the reason for the illness—which was entirely diplomatic. By an oversight, the arrangers had also invited the envoy of Lithuania, which had been reabsorbed by the Soviet Union. When Acheson and Woodward came the next morning at the President's summons, they were prepared, Acheson reported, "for a good wigging for sloppy work." They were not prepared for an order to tell the Soviet ambassador to clear out because he had been inexcusably rude to Mrs. Truman. "We threw ourselves into the breach, explaining Novikov's dilemma, proclaiming our own ineptitude, warning of the serious consequences of such a step and the dismay of even our best friends abroad." The President remained adamant. It was only after his wife telephoned from upstairs and agreed with Acheson that he was willing to drop the matter. After the call, Truman picked up an old-fashioned gold filigree photograph frame, opened it and handed Acheson a snapshot of a young woman. "I guess you think I'm an old fool," he said, "and I probably am. Look on the back," he added. Written was a message dated 1917: "Dear Harry, May this photograph bring you safely home again from France—Bess." He then exclaimed, "Any — — – —— who is rude to that girl is in trouble with me." As Acheson and Woodward were leaving, he called after them, "Tell old Novocaine we didn't miss him!" One is tempted to say that the incident is made up, a scene out of a faded Victorian novel. But then it is impossible to make up things like this.

Previously he had banned congressman Adam Clayton Powell from the White House because Powell had had the temerity to call Bess Truman "the last lady" when she attended a tea given by the Daughters of the American Revolution after their refusal to permit Hazel Scott to give a concert at Constitution Hall. Powell was not only protesting racial discrimination; he also had a wife to cherish and shelter. He was married at the time to Hazel Scott. An even worse contretemps involving his daughter, Margaret, did not threaten to set in motion a clash of empires, but neither did it help Truman's prestige.

Margaret gave a concert at Constitution Hall on December 5, 1950. She was trying to establish herself as a professional singer. Paul Hume, music critic of the *Washington Post,* wrote a devastating review. When Truman read it the next morning, he dashed off one of his wrathful handwritten letters before leaving for his office: "I have just read your lousy review buried in the back pages. You sound like a frustrated man that never made a success, an eight-ulcer man on a four-ulcer job, and all four ulcers working. I never met you, but if I do you'll need a new nose and plenty of beefsteak and perhaps a supporter below. Westbrook Pegler, a guttersnipe, is a gentleman compared to you. You can take that as more of an insult than a reflection on your ancestry."

Truman's friends have explained that he was under unusual emotional stress at the moment: His press secretary, Ross, had died the day of the concert, and he had been locked in conferences with Clement Attlee, the British prime minister, who had rushed to Washington when Truman threatened to use the atom bomb in the Korean war. Unfortunately, this is a case where explanations redound to the benefit of the prosecution. Truman could not get it through his head that his wife, as First Lady, was a public figure, accountable for her conduct; that his daughter, in giving public performances, invited the views of critics and the public. Some of the society reporters' comments did consist of catty gossip to the effect that Bess Truman's clothes were dowdy or that Margaret had thick ankles and a sloppy figure. Since the Trumans were grasping the roses, they were not well situated to complain of the thorns.

Truman's bumptiousness extended to protecting cronies. When Drew Pearson attacked Vaughan for accepting a medal from Juan Perón, the Argentine dictator, and suggested that Vaughan ought to be separated from the staff, the President resented such meddling in his affairs. At a dinner given by the Reserve Officers Association to honor Vaughan, he made these extemporaneous observations: "I am just as fond of and just as loyal to my military aide as I am to the high brass, and I want you to distinctly understand that any SOB who thinks he can cause any of these people to be discharged by me by some smart-aleck statement over the air or in the paper, he has another think coming." Arthur Krock took cognizance of Truman's "expanding self-assurance" in the second term. He concluded from some of the President's speeches and his bearing that he had arrived at a credo: "He is right and all opponents are wrong, spiritually and factually; he can beat any politician or set of politicians at their common trade; he is boss and intends to assert it; the American majority and most men and women of good will support him down to the item; and if his friends are criticized, with or without good basis, it is a virtue to make a blanket defense of them and to keep them in the places to which they are assigned." Although Truman's nature had little of the demonic, the devil of pride brought him close at times to damnation.

This combative man, called by Herbert Agar "more willful than any President since James K. Polk," was said to be henpecked in his own home. The evidence is there that the little woman whom he so compulsively sought to shield from gibes and malice tried to cure his excesses in decorum, and that he would become concerned, if not cowed, by her displeasure. She had made a scene about his speech to the Reserve Officers Association. When William Hassett, his correspondence secretary, told him that a Washington rector had averred that under similar provocation he might have said the same thing that Truman had, he answered glumly, "I just wish that the rector would go talk to my wife." After he was out of office, he informed an audience in San Antonio during the 1960 campaign that any Texan who voted for Nixon ought "to go to hell." Richard Donahue of Kennedy's staff found him afterward, white-faced, pacing his hotel room. "The Madam," he explained to him, had heard his speech on television and said flatly to him, "If you can't talk politer than that in public, you come right home."

The Bess Truman that the public came to know in the presidential years was a short-bobbed, gray-haired, frozen-faced provincial figure, lumpish in appearance, with the pebble eyes of the matriarch. She carried out her public functions dutifully and correctly, displaying neither zest, flair, nor pleasure. She had not sought the role. If it had been her choice, she would not have gone to the White House. She did not want her daughter to be a First Lady; and if she had had a son, she would not have brought him up to be President. When the term of office was finished, she wanted her husband to return to Independence, because that was home. Her dearest friends had been and remained the ladies of the Independence bridge club. She brought them all to Washington for a four-day splurge, when they ate in the State Dining Room, sat in the presidential box at Constitution Hall for a concert, went sailing on the Potomac in the presidential yacht, visited the President's office, and sat in on a press conference—a tourist's dream come true. She had regularly attended the altar society meetings at the Episcopal church where she had been married, and she resumed her membership when the Washington days ended. Her limited horizons and provincial preoccupations notwithstanding, she was a robust, strong-willed, clear-headed, no-nonsense woman, given neither to sentimentality nor self-deception. If there was little verve or glitter, there was strength of character. If her distaste for the synthetic bonhomie of politics sprang from conventional gentility, it marked a determination to cling to a world where she belonged. In a city of four-flushers and social climbers, she knew who and what she was, and ruled over her own lilliputian domain with sense and tranquillity.

The family stayed close-knit through all the vagrant movements of Truman's public career. When he was away he called Bess regularly as he had since their marriage began. When he was in Florida, and Margaret was in New York, he rang up the White House promptly at six, and Margaret would be connected with them for a three-way conversation. If the telephone interview that Margaret conducted with her parents on Edward R. Murrow's *Person to Person* show was any example of the three-way talks—and Margaret said it was typical—then any discussion of them would be a mistake. What was important about the stilted, inhibited expression of family interests and sentiments was the underlying feeling. Talking together conveyed more than what was said.

Truman was heavily dependent on the family relationship. Margaret Truman related that "In spite of my enthusiasm for departing Washington, both Mother and I always hated to go off and leave Dad, who was capable of the most abysmal loneliness when we were out of town. He looked so forlorn when he saw us off that we were ready to turn around and go back, knowing he would be eating dinner in solitary state and wishing for us." Here, from Truman's diary, is how one of these dinners proceeded:

> Had dinner by myself tonight. Worked in the Lee House office until dinner time. [Since the White House was undergoing extensive repairs for most of the second term, the Trumans were living at Blair-Lee House, the elegant mansion diagonally across Pennsylvania Avenue used traditionally as a guest house for foreign dignitaries.] A butler came in very formally and said, "Mr. President, dinner is served." I walk into the dining room in the Blair House. Barnett in tails and white tie pulls out my chair, pushes me up to the table. John in tails and white tie

brings me my fruit cup, Barnett takes away the empty cup. John brings me a plate, Barnett brings me a tenderloin. John brings me asparagus, Barnett brings me carrots and beets. I have to eat alone and in silence in candlelit room. I ring. Barnett takes the plate and butter plates. John comes in with a napkin and silver crumb tray—there are no crumbs but John has to brush them off the table anyway. Barnett brings me a plate with a finger bowl and doily on it. I remove the finger bowl and doily and John puts a glass saucer and a little bowl on the plate. Barnett brings me some chocolate custard. John brings me a demitasse (at home a little cup of coffee—about two good gulps) and my dinner is over. I take a hand bath in the finger bowl and go back to work. What a life!

It is startling to discover that a President of the United States, in the eye of the world's storms, surrounded by advisers, assistants, coadjutors, flunkeys, guards, should be in terror of being by himself for a few days, or that, with all his poker-playing cronies in the vicinity, he should be dining alone when his wife and daughter were away. Propinquity is clearly not the equivalent of communion. As John F. Kennedy once remarked, in politics there are no friends, only allies.

In the interval between the Democratic convention and the November election, as eight years before, Truman fought desperately for his political life and honor. (His mother-in-law could not for the life of her understand why he was running against such a nice man as Dewey, and was not bashful about broadcasting her opinion.) His battle strategy was set when he accepted the Clifford thesis and declared war on the Eightieth Congress. He fired the first round of electoral grapeshot at the convention. As the climax to his fighting speech delivered to a wilting assemblage at two o'clock in the morning, he announced:

> On the twenty-sixth of July, which out in Missouri we call "Turnip Day," I am going to call Congress back and ask them to pass laws to halt rising prices, to meet the housing crisis—which they are saying they are for in their platform. At the same time, I shall ask them to act upon other vitally needed measures, such as aid to education, which they say they are for; a national health program; civil

rights legislation, which they say they are for; an increase in the minimum wage, which I doubt very much they are for; extension of the social security coverage and increased benefits, which they say they are for. . . . Now, my friends, if there is any reality behind that Republican platform, we ought to get some action from a short session of the Eightieth Congress. They can do this job in fifteen days if they want to do it. They will still have time to go and run for office.

The unsigned memorandum that Clifford had handed Truman advocating this tactic (it had originated with different people) carried the admission: "This course may be hazardous politically, but we cannot shut our eyes to the fact that President Truman faces an uphill fight to win the coming election." Clifford explained, "We had to be bold. If we kept plugging away in moderate terms, the best we could have done would have been to reach midfield when the gun went off. So we had to throw long passes, anything to stir up labor and to get the mass votes of the great cities." The hazard of the special session proved slight. The Republican stalwarts were dizzy with success. Herbert Brownell, Dewey's political fixer, later Attorney General in Eisenhower's Cabinet, conferred with congressional leaders, urging them to pass two or three measures that the Republican platform favored so as to deprive Truman of the issue. He was up against a stone wall. Taft informed him sententiously that a principle was involved on which there could be no compromise, namely, Truman's misuse of a presidential prerogative. When Vandenberg suggested some bills that he thought might profitably be adopted, Taft was laconic: "No, we're not going to give that fellow anything." The special session saw the passage of some inconsequential legislation, a Southern filibuster in the Senate on a poll-tax proposal, and lengthy statements of denunciation between the Republican leaders and the President. The tactic had worked: It had focused attention on the attitude and record of the Eightieth Congress.

Aside from his bleak prospects, political developments were pushing Truman to a more radical course than he would have adopted ordinarily even under the Clifford battle plan. His civil rights message to Congress in February was considered by liberal standards to be audacious and advanced, beyond any position that Roosevelt had adumbrated. According to the Clifford dope sheet, this was safe to do since the South would stay in camp no matter what Truman advocated. "As always, the South can be considered safely Democratic. And in formulating national policy, it can be safely ignored." But the bourbon reaction was more intense than had been anticipated. Governors of seven Southern states recommended that electors not vote for any candidate favoring civil rights for blacks, and there was rumbling that Mississippi and Alabama might bolt the party convention. Said Governor Ben Laney of Arkansas, "The Democratic Party doesn't want to run the race with a politically dead Missouri mule." True to form, Truman worked his familiar balancing act. On the grounds that Congress would reject legislation that he recommended, he admitted that he did not plan to submit a civil rights bill. And nothing more was heard of his pledge to issue an executive order. A. Philip Randolph threatened—as he had successfully threatened Roosevelt in the mobilization days—to lead a campaign of mass civil disobedience unless Jim Crow was abolished in the military. Truman made temporizing gestures, but resisted the demand. At the convention the decision was taken out of his hands.

The administration henchmen at Philadelphia, guided closely by Clifford, wanted to get the civil rights issue out of the way by inserting in the platform the innocuous plank of four years before. It was not to be. The ADA'ers, unable to nominate a more appealing candidate, vowed a do-or-die stand on this front to salvage something. When the platform committee, after an acrimonious debate, approved the administration proposal, the minority announced that the fight would be taken to the convention floor. Their incendiary amendment that the Truman regulars feared might split the party called upon Congress "to support our President" in guaranteeing "the right of full and equal political participation," "equal opportunity of employment," "security of person," and "equal treatment in the service and defense of our nation."

Unexpectedly, fresh converts joined the cause before the presentation of the two reports to the delegates. Influential Northern bosses, convinced that the national ticket was a lost cause, were less concerned with Southern diehards bolting than with solidifying the Negro vote behind their local and state candidates. Henry Wallace was making a powerful appeal to this constituency in major cities. Any spectacular demonstration of the Democrats as resolute defenders of Negro interests that would head off a Wallace threat was to be welcomed. Ed Flynn came over to Hubert Humphrey and Andrew Biemiller who were waiting for the debate to start. "I hear you kids have a minority plank on civil rights," he said cordially. "That's what we need to stir up this convention." He then sent runners down to the floor to fetch Arvey, Hague, and David Lawrence, mayor of Pittsburgh and Democratic chief in Pennsylvania. All reaffirmed support for the minority plank.

In quick order the convention adopted the minority plank; the Alabama and Mississippi delegations withdrew from the convention; the Dixiecrats met in special convention two days later at Birmingham to launch a rebel party ticket. A hole having been blown open in his strategy, Truman proceeded to strengthen his opposite front by issuing the executive orders that he had promised in February. Thus a border-state politician intent on pursuing an ambiguous racial policy had the torch of civil rights unexpectedly thrust into his hands. Once it was evident that he was going to lose the electoral votes of at least four Southern states, the original strategy to outbid Wallace became more exigent. Wallace had been drawing exceptionally large crowds and making inroads among the Democratic faithful. Without winning a single electoral vote, he might throw the victory to the Republican candidate in half a dozen key industrial states. Consequently, the same reason that had propelled the bosses to embrace civil rights was pushing Truman to adopt militant liberal positions all along the line.

None of the tacticians, promoters, and organizers, including the redoubtable Clifford, was sanguine when the seventeen-car, armor-plated presidential campaign train (originally built for Roosevelt by the Association of American Railroads) pulled out of Washington before Labor Day for Michigan. One thing Clifford could be thankful for was that the Snyders, Allens, and Vaughans had been left behind. The working team on the train was made up of sturdy forward-lookers, though, of course, none was of the "crackpot" variety that Truman could not abide. On hand were Jonathan Daniels, William Batt, the research head, David Niles, the minorities expert, Charles Ross, his press secretary, Rosenman, Clifford, and others of the same ilk. Chapman as advance man, Ewing and Charles Murphy (legislative assistant, later legal counsel after Clifford left) as anchor men in Washington, were in constant communication with the train, all convinced that the chief's only chance of coming in was to "throw long passes" or, as Clifford explained in another winged metaphor, "We've got our backs on our own one-yard line with a minute to play; it has to be razzle-dazzle." One could be reasonably confident, therefore, that the strategy would not be undercut by the home guard. Was their man cut out for this assignment? No one had ever mistaken him for a spellbinder. Leonard Reinsch, a radio expert, had put in long hours with him since vice-presidential days to slow down his riveting-gun pace and impart some intonation and rhythm to his delivery. The results had not been dazzling.

Still, Missouri audiences had responded to Truman's bantam-rooster sass. It occurred to his aides that his natural style might be the most effective on the platform rather than trying to make him over into a Bryan. In April he had read a radio address to the American Society of Newspaper Editors in the familiar, dreary, twanging monotone with its onrush of garbled phrases. Once off the air, he gave an extemporaneous off-the-record talk that was lively, real, and caught the audience's attention. The surprised editors gave him a round of hearty applause. The extemporaneous talk had, in fact, been prepared; Truman spoke from detailed notes arranged in outline form by Murphy. The new technique was tried again and pronounced satisfactory by his aides. Then they all had a trial run in the two-week warmup "nonpolitical" tour that Truman took in June to the West Coast to deliver a commencement address at the Berkeley campus of the University of California. At first the crowds were undemonstrative, often sparse, and the party was beset by mishaps, botched lines, wrong cues, and near disasters, all gleefully reported in the press. By the time the train reached the West Coast, the crowds were immense and cordial, and Truman had developed a campaign style, folksy, corny, angrily polemical, that was going over. So when the campaign formally got under way in September, Clifford and the others knew that at least their candidate was in fighting trim and could put the strategy to a fair test.

In fact, he did his handlers proud. As in 1940, he bloomed in the sunless, Stygian zone where the air was thick with contempt and ridicule and his own aides were oppressed with feelings of hopelessness. Here were all the polls predicting an overwhelming Republican victory, their results repeated as gospel by all the pressmen and broadcasters, bookies giving odds of 15 and 20 to 1, some of his own Cabinet members negotiating surreptitiously for new jobs after the election—and through it all he moved unruffled, self-confident, assured, his cheerfulness intact, his nerve unimpaired, a sixty-four-year-old man with the steady energy of a commission salesman, the aplomb and brashness of a riverboat gambler. No one knew whether he was the supreme actor or mad enough to think that he could win. Even Bess Truman asked Clifford, "Does he really believe that he'll be elected?"

As soon as the bell sounded, he rushed to the center of the ring, shouting imprecations, his two arms moving like an electric pump. He told workingmen that the Taft-Hartley Act was "only a foretaste of what you will get if the Republican reaction is allowed to grow"; that a Republican victory meant a resumption of boom and bust: "The boom is on for them and the bust has begun for you"; that the Republicans wanted to roll up people "into one big company union and run it for the benefit of the National Association of Manufacturers." In Dexter, Iowa, he reviewed for the farm audience how the New Deal had saved farmers from the disasters of the Great Depression; now the Republicans were back at their evil machinations. "This Republican Congress has already stuck a pitchfork in the farmer's back." Farmers had been forced to sell their wheat at less than support prices because of a shortage of storage bins due to the Eightieth Congress' failure to vote necessary funds. "These Republican gluttons of privilege" had hurt the farmer by cutting funds for soil conservation, by killing the International Wheat Agreement. Everywhere he announced "a crusade of the people against the special interests, a crusade to keep the country from going to the dogs." There was an all-purpose peroration: "When I talk to you here today about Republicans, I am talking to you about the party that gets most of its campaign funds from Wall Street and Big Business. I am talking to you about the party that gave us the phony Wall Street boom of the nineteen twenties and the Hoover depression that followed. I am talking to you about the party that gave us that no-account do-nothing Republican Eightieth Congress." He stayed clear of civil rights, but symbolically went up to Harlem in the final week of the campaign to make a generalized pledge of his continuing devotion to "the goal of equal rights and equal opportunities."

Foreign affairs did not figure importantly in the campaign, although the Berlin crisis was raging, because Dewey was committed to Vandenberg's bipartisanship. At the end of June Truman had ordered all planes of the American command in Europe to ferry in supplies to the beleaguered city to break the Russian blockade. There were the usual outcries. General Clay proposed smashing the blockade by sending in an armored column. Others wanted to break off diplomatic relations. Despite his sustained leadership in the Cold War, Truman was not averse even at such a time to snaring the peace vote that Wallace was courting. He seized the idea of two of his speech writers that a new mission to Moscow would offer a profitable diversion. Chief Justice Vinson reluctantly accepted the assignment to confer

with Stalin for unspecified purposes. On teletype, Truman informed
Marshall in Paris. Marshall objected vehemently; a special mission,
he said, would cut the ground from under his negotiations at the UN
where the Security Council was considering a resolution to condemn
Russia for the Berlin blockade. Crestfallen, Truman agreed to drop
the project. He had not completely decided, though, when he summoned Arthur Vandenberg and Tom Connally to the White House
that evening. Neither senator gave him encouragement. After they
left, Vandenberg said to Connally, "He must be feeling desperate
about the campaign." When word of the proposed trip got into the
newspapers, there was a clamor of criticisms and contradictory explanations. The Dewey experts thought the incident was highly damaging to their rival. Clifford and Murphy expressed consternation as
well. Truman, with a twinkle in his eye, said to them, "I don't think
it's that bad." He obviously believed that a lot of people would conclude that, despite the difficulties the State Department was making
for him, he was a man of good intentions who wanted peace.

The final count made fools of all the dopesters, pollsters, and wise
men. Truman was reelected by a plurality of over 2 million. He
polled 49.6 percent of the popular vote to his rival's 45.1 percent,
amassing 303 electoral votes to Dewey's 189. In the many postmor-
tems, some maintained that Dewey had snatched defeat out of the
jaws of victory. Undoubtedly, he had not been an appealing candidate. A gopher-faced, hard-driver who had clawed his way up the
ladder after establishing a reputation as a relentless district attorney,
to become the undisputed boss of the New York party and a wheel-
er-dealer for the Eastern establishment, he gave the impression of a
cold, ruthless character. Walt Kelly, the creator of the Pogo comic
strip, showed him as a pint-sized robot-computer with a human head.
A familiar quip went, "I don't know which is the chillier experience
—to have Tom ignore you or shake your hand." This somewhat forbidding candidate and his advisers decided to employ a campaign
strategy in line with the advice that Nicholas Biddle had given the
Whig managers of General Harrison, the hero of Tippecanoe, a
hundred years before. The watchwords were: blandness, platitudes,
homilies. "We know the kind of government we have now," Dewey
pontificated across the country. "It's tired. It's confused. It's coming
apart at the seams. It cannot give this nation what it needs most—
what is the real issue of this election—unity." His advisers repeatedly
counseled against halting the bromidic stream as Truman drew increasingly large and responsive crowds. It was the nearly unanimous

opinion of the commentators that the strategy was masterful. Drew Pearson was typical when he wrote that Dewey had "conducted one of the most astute and skillful campaigns in recent years."

What made the strategy appear more fatuous than it was, was the air of omniscience with which the Dewey forces moved to an assumed victory, and how hollow their vaunted expertise proved to be. The mistaken polls and his misguided overconfidence aside, Dewey had two fundamental alternatives, the Republican party being what it was: He could conduct his campaign by transcending the mundane conflicts and problems with a dialectical synthesis encompassing unity, managerial professionalism, efficient political engineering, all the while keeping his distance from Taft and fudging Republican opposition to the New Deal; or he could launch into an unabashed defense of the Eightieth Congress and an equally intrepid assault on the New Deal. It was a familiar dilemma that had plagued the Republicans since Roosevelt's ascendancy, whether to run a "me-too" campaign or to offer "a choice, not an echo."

Dewey had followed the former strategy four years before against a powerful candidate in an election conducted in the midst of war, and had propelled it with savage personal thrusts, innuendos, and asides that sent an exhausted Roosevelt to tour New York City in a downpour of rain and freezing winds and reduced his popular margin to the narrowest since Wilson's hairbreadth victory over Hughes in 1916. Now the formula should suffice against a weak, discredited candidate to whom, he felt confident, he could contemptuously give the back of his hand. The Republicans' dilemma stemmed from the political reality: Liberalism had become the dominant national ideology; the conservative coalition consequently was ruling the legislature not in accordance with the majority will but by "rotten borough" devices, political concoctions, and alliances with the avowed racists and reactionaries of the South. It was not until the Republicans four years later bemused the public with a military hero who identified himself with the resentment over "Truman's war" in Korea that they could outflank the old Rooseveltian battle line and forge a new presidential majority. Communism could not yet be transmuted into electoral gold. Dewey had tried with small effect in 1944. It was a stronger talking point in 1948 because newspapers had carried sensational testimony of ex-Communists; still, Communist spies and spy-hunting did not become a national mania until later.

Did the personalities of the opposing candidates figure in the election results? A postelection survey found that many voters thought

Dewey patronizing, superior, cold. A candidate's personality, however, cannot be abstracted from the political complex of which it is part. People who think they are voting against a candidate because he antagonizes them are responding to many programmatic dislikes or suspicions that they have not conceptualized. The same Dewey with the same appearance and mannerisms was reelected governor of New York two years before under different circumstances with the largest majority in the state's history. In another way, Truman's performance was no less patronizing than Dewey's; his populist vituperation was taken with large doses of salt by many who applauded him and voted for him. When the *Progressive* said his courage "was born of desperation, not conviction," it echoed the sentiments that were commonplace among Democratic supporters.

After the election, Truman said, "Labor did it." Others credited farm support in the Midwest. An NAACP analysis showed that seven out of ten Negroes in twenty-seven cities had voted for Truman; had they not furnished this balance in California, Illinois, and Ohio, Dewey would have had the prize. In an election won by a narrow margin, with three key states carried by a handful of votes, it is easy to point to this or that group without whose support the results would have been reversed. If we focus our attention instead on the major blocs that supplied Truman with the bulk of his 2 million plurality, without which all accretions would have had no consequence, we can see that great impersonal developments were at work to reconstitute the disrupted Rooseveltian coalition.

The fundamental threat to Truman was that massive numbers of the labor-liberal camp would desert him, either by not voting or by supporting the Wallace insurgency. The fundamental reason Truman surmounted the threat was that the Wallace movement rapidly disintegrated, so that instead of the 5 to 10 million votes that had been anticipated, Wallace finally polled only about 1 million. Innumerable articles have discussed Wallace's mistakes, stupidities, suicidal propensities. The way the press tore to shreds the reputation of a courageous and attractive American progressive, standing head and shoulders over most politicos of his day, was a minor scandal incident to the Cold War. Wallace made many mistakes, but the fundamental mistake from which flowed all others was launching an independent party when he did. The movement came at least a year too late. It had to count on enlisting the support of a sizable part of labor-liberal forces, and these, in the main, had already departed for the Cold War preserves. One of the tasks the Clifford memorandum had set was to pin the Communist label on the Wallace movement—equivalent in the Cold War decade to the kiss of death. This proved no problem since Wallace made an outright alliance with the Communist fellow travelers. Once the decision for an independent candidacy was made, he had little choice: The Communists were the only ones who would furnish the organizers and trained personnel. Nobody else would talk to him. Their common stand on the Cold War forced New Dealers and labor officials to shun Wallace and line up behind the man with whom they had only recently broken. Even old Ickes went on the radio to announce his reconciliation. (Privately he remarked, "I am supporting as my candidate for President a man who is as fully equipped for that office as would be Adam's off ox.")

The Cold War, necessitating as it did winning mass support for the holy cause, led to horrendous consequences at home as well as abroad. As soon as it became the central issue of contemporary history, the fumes that it gave off felled one section after another of American society. First affected were the politicized intellectuals (to the importance of whose pens Clifford called Truman's attention in his memorandum). Their community was turned into a warring camp —anticipating by four years the McCarthyite rage. Living in a specialized world where questions of politics fused with the passions of morality, where sensitivity to coming trends combined with a compulsion to articulate and justify them, intellectuals had elaborated a formidable sociology, devised the rationale, coined the catchwords, and lent their names and pens to the stirring up of public opinion months before the promulgation of the Truman Doctrine. Because the tone was often set by ex-Communists turned anti-Communists, the campaign took on the violence that is associated with the apostate who turns on the old faith in which he has become disillusioned. Communists were declared by definition to be moral lepers and fifth columnists; it therefore followed that all who associated with them were either fellow travelers in treason and totalitarianism or naïfs beyond the point of redemption—in either case, to be excommunicated.

One of the ringleaders of the enterprise was Reinhold Niebuhr, called by George Kennan "the father of us all," a prominent theologian who had traveled the familiar route from leftism in the early 1930s to anti-Communism at the close of the decade. His prestige and authoritative style made him a leading ideological influence. From the same heights of Pauline and Lutheran orthodoxy from which he had excoriated liberalism in favor of Marxism, he was now impugning Communism in favor of the Western open society. As important as his influence in reconciling the Cold War with Christian morality was his role in bringing intellectuals together with New Dealers and laborites to form the vital center of Cold War liberalism. He chaired the conference held in Washington in January, 1947, to form the Americans for Democratic Action, which became the fountainhead of post-Rooseveltian New Dealism. All through that year the war of extermination against those who wanted to perpetuate the Popular Front of Communists and liberals spread from the intellectual circles to the liberal associations and the CIO unions, so that when in January, 1948, Wallace decided to proclaim his independent candidacy, rather than forming a new rallying center for liberal allegiance, his initiative completed the split in the liberal camp.

Unfortunately for Wallace, it was a split where all the big names, all the decisive influences, were against him. He was condemned by the Roosevelts, by all the New Deal luminaries, by all the liberal columnists. Even *PM* in New York opposed the new party, its editor, Max Lerner, recording in sorrow that Wallace was "a potentially great leader who has allowed himself to become isolated from the large mass of independent progressives." He fared no differently with Negro leaders, who in a general way were aligned with the Cold War liberals. The NAACP heads, despite their repeated clashes with the Democratic administration, preferred Truman to any available alternatives. A. Philip Randolph, considered at the time to represent a more militant tendency in the black community, would have no truck with Wallace or his associates, and said so publicly. In the labor movement he lost all status. Philip Murray condemned the insurgency as a Communist plot that could only help the Republicans. Lee Pressman was forced out as general counsel of the CIO; the Amalgamated Clothing Workers withdrew from New York's American Labor Party; by the time Truman's candidacy was validated, the entire labor officialdom, AFL, CIO, Railway Brotherhoods (aside from John L. Lewis and a few unimportant fellow travelers) had lined up behind the Democratic ticket, including A. F. Whitney of the Trainmen, who had threatened after the rail-strike debacle to spend his union's entire treasury to defeat Truman.

Not only that; it was demanded that everyone stand up and declare himself. Support for Wallace was taken as ipso facto proof that the culprit was a fellow traveler or Communist dupe. Some twisting of arms lent emphasis to the verbal persuasion. In at least six colleges and universities, professors declaring for Wallace found themselves out of jobs or otherwise penalized. In West Frankfort, Illinois, the

Wallace senatorial candidate was refused police protection when stoned by a mob. Wallace backers in labor unions were treated as pariahs. This is not to say that Wallace's early hopes for a huge protest vote were entirely chimerical. His candidacy had evoked palpable responses from the more militant in Negro communities, in some labor unions, in the ranks of those fearful of war. Politicians were amazed by the immense crowds who paid admission fees all over the country to hear him. The editor of La Follette's old *Progressive* wrote that he had never received so much mail to take issue with his condemnation of Wallace. But these ranks could not stand up under the steady pounding of recognized and respected leaders. In the end, "Gideon's army" was whittled down to the irreconcilables and diehards.

Thus it was that before he took to the campaign trail, Truman was the beneficiary of the realignment of labor and liberal forces along Cold War positions. The strategy he pursued, beginning with the veto of the Taft-Hartley Act, facilitated the rallying of these battalions behind his banner. His electioneering set the tone and provided the themes of a fighting, quasipopulist campaign. His radical rhetoric undercut Wallace's message. The realignment originated nonetheless from the need of liberals and laborites to break with popular-front alliances and attitudes contracted in the New Deal and war periods, to present themselves to the American public in the changed circumstances of the day free from any taint of association with the country's officially pronounced enemies. Labor was more fully engaged in the campaign than in 1944 since the AFL had by this time set up Labor's League for Political Education, its counterpart of the CIO-PAC that Hillman had directed in the earlier effort. But these tens of thousands of volunteer workers concentrated their main efforts on behalf of local and state candidates, who generally ran well ahead of the presidential candidate.

Despite Truman's and labor's gusto in getting out the vote, only 51 percent of those eligible went to the polls, a smaller figure than four years before when millions were overseas and many others were unable to register because of residence changes, and appreciably smaller than in 1940 or in the subsequent elections of the 1950s. Samuel Lubell, the political analyst, argued that Dewey's victories in the industrial East were due not to new Republican adherents but to the apathy that kept some of the old Rooseveltian adherents at home. Had they come out, Dewey would have suffered a more crushing defeat. He also maintained that the Wallace and States' Rights defections actually strengthened Truman; while some votes were siphoned off, they buttressed his overall position by neutralizing the Communist issue and reinforcing his appeal to blacks. The analysis is incomplete, however, unless the proviso is included that this gave Truman the election instead of throwing it to his rival because the Wallace movement aborted.

The day after the election, Vandenberg said to his staff, "You've got to give the little man credit. There he was flat on his back. Everyone had counted him out, but he came up fighting and won the battle. That's the kind of courage the American people admire." The enthusiastic receptions for Truman resembled less the congratulatory acclaim accorded Roosevelt after his victories than the hero's welcome tendered to the local boy, disdained by the gentry, who made good. He had told "them" off. He had shown "them" up. Three-quarters of a million people lined Pennsylvania Avenue from the railroad station to the White House for his triumphal reentry into Washington, many shrieking, "Hiya, Harry," and the bands blaring "I'm Just Wild about Harry." On January 20, after the inauguration, came the biggest parade in people's memories—cadets, drum majorettes, Missouri mules, members of the old Battery D. When the band struck up the familiar tune, Truman, on the reviewing stand, performed a little jig to the music. Margaret Truman said, "We really did have fun that week."

One person who unexpectedly stood aside from the merriment, to whom the victory brought no elation was its architect, Clark Clifford. There was still work he had to do on presidential messages and matters, but as soon as he could he intended to clear out. He told David Lilienthal that he was tired out psychologically. "He spoke in a worried tone—quite unusual for him—about the conflict within the President's own family about future policy; of the awful exhibition one sees around the White House of self-seeking, etc., and seemed rather depressed by it, not as if it were something new but that he was getting his fill of it."

13

Scandals, NATO, Peace Treaty with Japan

Presumably the road was now clear for Truman to drive through his welfare program under his own trademark, the Fair Deal. He was President in his own right, both houses of Congress were under Democratic control, liberalism could spread its wings. That is not the way it worked out. He had not mentioned in the campaign that the Democratic-controlled Seventy-ninth Congress was no more receptive to reform than the no-account, do-nothing Republican Eightieth Congress. No sooner had the smoke of the electoral battle cleared than the same conservative coalition took over. Some names were different, and the committee chairmanships changed hands, but the political orientation of the Eighty-first Congress was as conservative as the preceding one. Nor was the political cast of the Cabinet and the White House guard of the second administration markedly different; the Snyders, Sawyers, Allens, Vaughans, John Steelmans, were as evident as heretofore. The only major piece of social legislation adopted was the Housing Act of 1949, and this owned its passage to Taft's aristocratic eccentricities, and as with much liberal legislation, promise exceeded performance.* If to the act are added higher minimum wages

* The act provided for the construction of over 800,000 units in six years—one-fifteenth of what the experts figured was needed to replace broken-down housing.

and unemployment benefits, and increased funds for reclamation and public power, that about exhausts the list. In retrospect, the role of the Truman administration—once history smoothed out the inconsistencies, provided a purposefulness that the confused and contradictory movements did not always disclose, and draped a discreet cloak of statesmanship over the opportunist motivations of so many of the fuglemen—was to blunt the reactionary attack on the New Deal's economic reforms. Truman institutionalized these reforms, updated them, and pointed the way to their extension.

That Truman should be rebuffed and forced into rearguard actions immediately after his victory will astonish only those who attribute to public opinion sovereign powers that it does not possess. Public opinion is not only a desirable mistress to be courted and pleased, but a capricious creature to be manipulated, influenced, distracted, frightened, and cajoled, if need be. Public opinion can self-confidently order its votaries into action when it has leadership and well-placed allies, but it suffers a humiliating rout when it is attacked by implacable opponents and lacks institutional supports. Public opinion gave Roosevelt his unprecedented mandate in 1936, but immediately afterward watched, bewildered, helpless, torn by the propaganda barrage, when he was put down by Congress in his attempt to prepare for a new period of reform by reorganizing the Supreme Court. Was it surprising, therefore, that Truman's welfarist requests were ignored after his narrow reelection?

When Truman was unable to redeem his campaign pledges, the refrain was sounded that little Harry had no bugle note. Liberalism, which demanded inspiration from the President, was not itself very inspiring. The Cold War shifted liberal interest from defending the public against the abuses of Big Business and conservative politicians to defending Western civilization from Russian Communism and expansionism. It coincided with the takeoff of the American imperium, the long postwar economic boom, and the general improvement of living standards. Liberals metamorphosed from critics of the system to its eulogists and lyricists. By the end of the decade and into the 1950s, they provided the ideological fodder for the American Celebration—an all-national indoor game of self-congratulation, Rotarian boosting, and mutual admiration.

In the three and a half Truman years after the passage of the bill, only 60,000 units were actually built. Private industry, using generous federal handouts, accounted for most building going on, which was for the higher-income market.

David Riesman found that everyone and no one had the power in American society and that the problem had changed from economic betterment to leisure satisfaction. John K. Galbraith wrote about the affluent society in which countervailing powers prevented any single class or aggregate from imposing its will or pushing its interests too far. Adolf A. Berle, Jr., who had been troubled by the unchecked power of corporation managers, now saw the corporation as having developed a social conscience. David Lilienthal, who had been a follower of Brandeis' antimonopoly school, became like Berle a convert to the big corporation with its putatively matured sense of social responsibility. The labor leaders, after their initial burst of postwar combativeness, settled into the business unionism routine of negotiating periodic wage raises to keep up with the recurrent inflation. This was not an atmosphere in which a reform movement could thrive. Truman was a more authentic governmental representation of the ADA than their spokesmen could admit. Not only was reform a poor relation at the national jubilee; the more thoughtful sensed that a mere extension of reforms of the New Deal kind would not strike at the center of the country's ailments and concerns. Roosevelt's National Planning Board, before it was interred by Congress in 1943, had outlined some of the major postwar problems, but as Emerson said of Walt Whitman, instead of writing the epic of America the liberal planners wrote its chapter headings. The union of campus and letters was barren of programmatic fruit—until liberalism was to scramble to new ground to avoid being inundated by the rising tide of youth rebellion and contempt.

The air of decadence and drift was aggravated by the tawdriness of the administration. In his second term, Truman was beset by scandals and revelations of corruption that brought back memories of Harding and Grant. What was dubbed the "mess in Washington" by the Republicans became a major issue of the 1952 campaign; it contributed to tearing holes in his reputation so that by the spring of that year his rating, according to the public opinion polls, was even lower than it had been in the spring of 1948. It was inevitable that scandal should follow the crowd of moochers and chiselers that Truman brought to Washington. Although these were generally small-time operators compared to Albert Fall, who turned over a vast government oil empire to Doheny and Sinclair for a $400,000 payoff, some were his intimate assistants and friends. Equally damaging was the nonchalance with which he received information of malfeasance, how his efforts were bent to shield his associates, his habit of trying to brazen it out. Unlike Harding, he did not panic or suffer nightmares. His Kansas City experience had taught him that these mishaps were the stuff of politics and had to be taken in stride.

The professional politician has a philosophical attitude toward financial irregularities or jobbery. He is no less a churchgoer than the businessman, and often more responsive than the latter to the cries of the injured. But his daily experiences convince him that the line separating the righteous from the unclean in an acquisitive society is ambivalent and shifting. He is cynical about congressmen or public figures who cry out against corruption, only to ask officials in bureaus and departments for special favors for constituents and then accept campaign contributions in return for favors obtained. He sees officials who refuse gifts, cashing in IOU's received, after leaving office, in law firms or corporations whose goodwill they had previously cultivated. The politician has neither the ability nor the interest to formulate a moral philosophy; he has a working one in which collusive arrangements and friendly fixes are the indispensable oil that keeps the machinery of politics operating, in which there is much hypocrisy in the official pieties and pretensions—and in which everyone, according to his own circumstances, trades on his influence and position. The employment of a crew of hungry jobholders in agencies wielding enormous power in the booming postwar decade guaranteed that standards would be unexacting, that the appointees would consider themselves as having prebendary rights to the largess dispensed by industry lobbyists. What made the hustle particularly squalid and paltry was that most of the upstart bureaucrats lacked the ability to command jobs of comparable importance and pay in private employment. They therefore had to make the best of their opportunity while it lasted.

By 1949 scandals broke around the head of the ineffable General Vaughan. It seemed he had not confined himself to making speeches and running errands for the President. The Senate Hoey subcommittee investigating "5-percenters" brought out that he had been a veritable ambassador of goodwill for importuning business clients. He had used his influence and White House stationery to secure overseas passage for a Chicago perfume manufacturer before facilities for civilian travel were available. He fixed up John Maragon, a sleazy operator from Kansas City who finally wound up in jail, with a high-priority rating to travel for the same perfume concern, and then got him a job with the American Mission to Greece. Maragon was moonlighting on his private employment, and continued to draw pay from both jobs. After his forceful intervention on behalf of perfume, Vaughan moved on to molasses. Harold Ross, president of Allied Molasses Company, had exceeded his authorization for molasses by 771,000 gallons in a shipment to Pepsi-Cola and had consequently been cut off from further allocations. A relative by the name of Milton Polland met Vaughan and Maragon at a brewery party in Milwaukee and immediately discerned that Maragon was a party you could do business with. Polland gave him $1,000 and promised him $2,000 more if he got an allocation. When Vaughan called up Herbert Hathorn, an attorney in the Agriculture Department and explained the matter to him, Hathorn suggested he take it up with the Assistant Secretary. Vaughan berated the attorney and "ended up with a statement that he was very close to the President and that a friend in the White House could mean an awful lot for a man in one of the governmental agencies, and also that he could get my job or get a job." After this outburst, the indefatigable Vaughan took up the problem with Joseph Elvore, assistant director of the sugar branch. The next day Allied Molasses was given permission to convert a tank car of inedible blackstrap into edible products. When it came out that the molasses was higher-grade refiner's syrup, the authorization was withdrawn, but Ross used the molasses anyway.

Another case Vaughan figured in was that of the Tanforan racetrack. He was drawn in through his collaboration with a Colonel J. V. Hunt, who traded on his friendship with Vaughan to run a lucrative influence-peddling agency. Here again the problem for enterprising businessmen was to get around government regulations on scarce materials. In October, 1947, several operators plus Maragon met in the office of the Housing Expediter. They had bought the Tanforan racetrack near San Francisco and wanted the lifting of an injunction against construction that had been handed down by a federal judge. They were told that even if the injunction was lifted, no materials could be allocated for racetrack construction. At the end of the month a new Acting Housing Expediter was appointed who apparently owed his advancement to Hunt and Vaughan. After Vaughan asked him to hurry things along, a permit was granted for $150,000 worth of building materials. So far as was ascertained, the only returns for Vaughan from all these transactions were campaign contributions to the party coffers, and half a dozen frozen food lockers distributed to officials including Vaughan and Mrs. Truman and immortalized by cartoonists and columnists. When Vaughan offered to resign at the time that the subcommittee hearings were providing the newspapers with a Roman holiday, Truman, he said, "got up and walked over and put his arm around my shoulder. He said, 'Harry, they're just trying to use you to embarrass me. You go up there and tell 'em to go to hell. We came in here together and God damn it, we're going out together!' "

These were only the blossoms; the berries were still to come. By the fall of 1949, rumors were flying that all was not well with the Reconstruction Finance Corporation. The RFC had been set up by President Herbert Hoover to bail out bankrupt firms. It was used by Roosevelt in the war years to stockpile scarce materials and set up defense industries. It continued in the postwar years as a welfare agency granting loans for speculative or shaky ventures that no commercial bank would touch. The Senate Banking and Currency Committee authorized a subcommittee under William J. Fulbright to look into the allegations. After a year's leisurely investigation, he and Senators Douglas and Tobey related to the President a scarifying tale of favoritism and political manipulation. Truman told them not to worry about it, whereupon Fulbright made public the subcommittee's report. It seemed that Donald Dawson, Truman's assistant in charge of personnel—the administration patronage man—was actually overseeing affairs at the agency through subservient directors who owed their appointments to him; that the Democratic National Committee was making recommendations; and that wholesale corruption reigned in the granting of loans. The RFC had become a cornucopia for transferring cash to the party coffers, feathering the nests of grafters, and floating an array of dubious enterprises.

Truman's initial response was to brand the report "asinine" in public and Fulbright "an overeducated SOB" in private, and to pull all sorts of wires and threaten reprisals to make the senators back away. Fulbright countered that he would hold public hearings to show "that the report we issued was not an asinine report." When Fulbright wanted to call Dawson in, Truman refused to let him appear on the ground of Executive privilege. The public uproar made it unwise to maintain this position, and on May 10 Dawson was sworn in. His testimony proved even more damaging than the Fulbright report. The sordid account introduced to the public and eventually to prison officials another Missourian on the make, E. Merl Young, who as an RFC examiner helped put through a loan to the Lustron Corporation in 1948. The day the loan was approved, he resigned to go on the Lustron payroll at $12,000 a year. That summer and fall he worked away at the Democratic National Committee as assistant to William Boyle to get Truman reelected, with his salary and expenses taken care of by Lustron. Later in the year, Harley Hise, chairman of RFC, said to Carl Strandlund, Lustron president, that he would like "to see Young get something out of it," so Strandlund promoted him to vice-president at $18,000 a year, apparently for his fine work at the Democratic party office. Young also went on the payroll of F. L. Jacobs Company, another RFC debtor, for an additional $10,000, and hooked up as well with a Washington law firm representing loan applicants to the RFC. Young had become the coordinator in the influence ring that included Dawson at the White House, Boyle at the Democratic National Committee, the majority directors at RFC, and Colonel Joseph Rosenbaum, the head of the law firm representing the suppliants. Under Rosenbaum's aegis, Young was cut in on a variety of business ventures and payoffs, the least of which, although the most highly publicized, was the gift of a $8,500 royal pastel mink coat for Young's wife.

The subcommittee investigation of influence peddling uncovered the success story of still another Missourian, William Boyle, who had inherited his fervor for machine politics from his mother, an active Pendergast precinct worker. He had moved up steadily in the ranks to become Kansas City police commissioner and eventually prosecuting attorney. He took over as Truman's secretary when Vaughan went off to the wars; afterward, he opened his own law office, capitalizing on his closeness to the President. He had devoted long hours to the 1948 campaign; in April he was put on a $30,000 salary and presumably withdrew from private law practice. In August he was elected National Committee chairman. Evidently he continued to share in the law business whose clients included firms soliciting government loans. The revelation that blew him out of his position came in connection with the American Lithofold Corporation of St. Louis. Its application for a $500,000 refunding loan was turned down at all levels in the St. Louis office and by the RFC review committee in Washington but approved by the directors after Boyle was hired and paid a retainer of $8,000. Boyle tried to ride out the storm, defended by Truman to the last, but he had become a heavy liability and three months later resigned "for reasons of health." The Republicans waxed eloquent against these lapses from public morality. Senator Richard Nixon (whose secret slush fund was to be exposed in the 1952 election) denounced Boyle's manipulations. But the investigation also disclosed that Guy Gabrielson, Boyle's counterpart on the Republican National

Committee, had intervened with the RFC to get an extension of a big loan to the Carthage Hydrocol Company, of which he was president. In the end Truman had no alternative but to adopt the Fulbright recommendation that he had ridiculed.

By this time scandals were enveloping the Internal Revenue Service, and the King subcommittee of the House Ways and Means Committee joined the Senate investigators. Before these scandals were laid to rest, the tax organization was churned up from one end of the country to the other. Sixty-six individuals were dismissed and nine went to jail. Truman repeated to friends the anguished protest of Harding twenty-eight years before that he had been "sold down the river" by people he had trusted.

The cream of the jest came with the professed cleanup. Truman said he was going to set up a White House commission to look into the entire question of corruption in government and recommend necessary changes. Then he announced that the cleanup leadership would be turned over to Attorney General J. Howard McGrath. Since the Justice Department was itself suspect in the tax scandals, the appointment was not an unalloyed triumph for clean government. The House Judiciary Committee responded by voting to investigate McGrath. Truman's riposte was to appoint as special counsel, Newbold Morris, an upper-class Republican reformer and New York attorney, described by his Washington mentor, Harold Seidman of the budget bureau, as "a bit of a dope who didn't want to make any decisions," and was hungry for publicity so he could run again for New York Mayor. Morris's exact status was left up in the air. He thought he was a free agent answerable only to the President. McGrath took the position that, as a special assistant to the Attorney General, he was working for him. Congress refused him independent subpoena powers and he was called before a Senate committee to explain his law firm's role in an allegedly illegal sale of government-surplus oil tankers to a foreign government. When Morris announced that he had prepared an elaborate questionnaire (provided by Seidman) that he intended to have filled out by all higher-paid federal employees, including Cabinet members, in departments under investigation, and that a grand jury was to be impaneled to provide Morris a substitute for subpoena power, McGrath curtly informed him that he was fired. Whereupon Truman picked up the telephone to inform his Attorney General that he too was fired. It was bruited about that the burlesque had been set up by the President himself. He had told McGrath to go ahead with dismissing Morris, and then, to McGrath's astonishment, had axed him. What began as high drama came to a creaking halt as low farce.

Americans expect crookedness in their politicians but get indignant when their expectations are realized. They see the reality but are not reconciled to it. They keep hoping for something better. If it is true, as some have averred, that historians will cast a more indulgent eye on this aspect of the Truman Presidency than did his contemporaries, then it can only be because historians will have succumbed to complacency. Favors and payoffs are at the root of the political system, and disreputable activities in Truman's administration were not as unusual as Republican editorial writers made them out to be, or quantitatively greater, probably, than in the subsequent administrations. Some of the unsavory scramble for funds developed because the major corporations' fat cats were traditionally contributors to the Republican camp. Nevertheless, on grounds of public professions of political morality norms, it will be held against Truman that he loaded Washington with a crew of carpetbaggers and tried to shield them when they were found out.

It seemed at first that the second term would be a continuation of the first in basic characteristic; a stalemate on the welfarist side, and unity on the international scene—until the interaction of the domestic and the foreign blew up bipartisanship and set the country careening wildly at the mercy of a government mechanism out of control. The new field marshal directing the international front was Dean Acheson, probably the most distinguished Secretary of State since Elihu Root. Son of an Episcopal bishop and a whisky heiress, he had traveled the road of Groton, Yale, and Harvard Law School to become a partner in Washington's leading corporation law firm, Covington, Bierling and Rublee. He had been Undersecretary of the Treasury in Roosevelt's first year, but had resigned because Roosevelt was not a hard-money man; he then briefly flirted with the Liberty League. He had reentered the administration as Assistant Secretary of State for economic affairs when the Eastern Establishment rallied behind Roosevelt's interventionist policy. He was Undersecretary during Byrnes's and part of Marshall's tenures, and then took over the secretaryship at the beginning of the second term when Marshall left because of ill health. In truth, he had been the anchor man at the department in Byrnes's two years since Byrnes was out of the country half of the time, and the major architect of the Truman Doctrine and Marshall Plan.

He was not just another intelligent patrician dignitary pushed forward by powerful and prestigious associates; he was a shining specimen of the upper-class species, physically and intellectually. Tall, broad-shouldered, well set up, he had the erect bearing, bristling reddish-brown moustache, beetle eyebrows, and impeccable dress of a St. James's Street hussar. When he was photographed with Anthony Eden, he looked like the British foreign minister and Eden appeared as the effete socialite younger brother. Possessed of an orderly, precise, adroit legal mind rather than a luminous one, he was impatient with historical excursions or theoretical ratiocinations; he drove straight for the strategic objectives of policy. He had the trial attorney's attributes of presence and quickness of reflex, and made his strong-willed personality felt in all his undertakings. Although a skillful, even a brilliant diplomatist and negotiator, he was such an implacable proponent and practitioner of political warfare against Russia that there was little to negotiate about with the other superpower. To the elaboration of the going policy he was able to bring caustic wit, a cultured phraseology, personal charm, and a debonair air so that his performance glistened with an elegance lacking among his immediate predecessors or successors.

This impressive personage who epitomized the aristocratic clubman was able to set up a virtually idyllic relationship with Truman. He had learned from Byrnes's mistakes, and never permitted himself to take any material step without consulting and clearing with his chief. When he was abroad at a conference or for a negotiation, he would send daily detailed cables keeping the President abreast of every development; at home, he conferred with him two or three times a week. The President, in turn, had such confidence in his Secretary's loyalty and judgment that the State Department became the planner and executor of the country's foreign policy as it never was under Roosevelt or in subsequent Democratic administrations. The relationship between these two unlikely associates blossomed exotically under the benign influences of identical views and mutual trust. Truman, as a gesture of support and goodwill, would often come to the airport to see Acheson off when the Secretary left on a journey. In his memoirs Acheson was effusive about Truman to whom he owed a great debt of gratitude for standing behind him through the years when he was the butt of unprecedented and scurrilous attacks. The surface of Acheson's suave narrative is rippled now and then when touching on other people by some furtive, pikelike movements in the depths, giving an intimation of unspoken thoughts and opinions best not expressed. He could not quite bring himself to say that Truman was a great President or a great man, but settled for the proposition "that if he was not a great man, he was the greatest little man the author knew anything about." Beyond his obligation to the President, he had real affection for the man who could roughhouse with the political regulars and had no qualms when making big decisions.

The accession of an eminent Secretary of State enjoying the trust of his President and exercising wide authority changed fundamental policy little. The country's basic foreign policy was a continuation and elaboration of what had gone before. The course had been set after the war by the combined efforts of the country's business and political elites and could be changed only if confronted with insurmountable obstacles, stupendous failures, or new power dispositions at home. When the Republicans came in with Eisenhower, and when another formidable, if less elegant, Secretary of State, formulated policy, he proved more resourceful in devising novel slogans and war whoops than fresh ideas. As Louis Halle put it, "The policy of the Republican administration was essentially a continuation and development of the policy it had inherited from the Democratic administration, just as the policy of the Democratic administration that was to take office in 1961 would, in spite of certain nominal disguises, be essentially a continuation and development of the policy that its Republican predecessor had followed."

Once the crisis managers had committed the country to a worldwide struggle, developments proceeded with a logic of their own. The Marshall Plan had only fairly launched the economic entente with Western Europe when it was followed by the project to convert it into a military bloc. NATO has since been apotheosized as the centerpiece of the network of alliances crisscrossing the globe to succor Western civilization and secure God's Word, so that when in 1971—a quarter of a century after the end of the war—a modest proposal was offered in the Senate to cut in half American occupation troops in Europe, the aged cadre that had pioneered the Cold War, from Acheson on down, rallied from the law offices and banking houses to which they had long since retired to repulse this heresy. At the time, however, the elders found it hard to explain the purposes of this unprecedented peacetime military alliance. It has to be kept in mind that a Cold War precipitates an arms race and disqualifies other modes of thought in favor of military logic. It produces its own atmospheric medium compounded of hysteria, war scares, exaggerated interpretations of the opponent's thrusts and counterthrusts, as well as downright mendacity and misrepresentation on the part of those with a vested interest in the enterprise—and it is within this medium that policies have to be discussed and adopted.

On the public declaratory level, all was clear and well ordered. America had demobilized; Russia had not. But for the American monopoly of the atom bomb, the Russian hordes would have long since swept over Europe to the English Channel. It was necessary to build up Western military power in one mighty alliance to deter the aggressors from pushing westward, and, in the event they made the attempt, to defend every member of the alliance. Acheson later outlined the rationale with his own version of Kennan containment: The Soviet system, by its very nature, had to exploit the existence in the non-Communist world of large areas of weakness. These presented irresistible invitations to fish in troubled waters. To urge the Soviets to agree not to fish was as futile as talking to a force of nature. One cannot argue with a river; it is going to flow. One can only dam it or deflect it. Hence, the need to build situations of strength.

This sounded eminently reasonable except that the managers did not believe the Russians had any intention of marching. It was a proposal to arm against an attack no one was planning. Said John Foster Dulles to a congressional committee: "The information given me publicly and privately by our own government and by heads and leaders of European governments, does not indicate that the Soviet Union now contemplates open military aggression in Europe. Direct military aggression is not the preferred weapon of the Communist Party that controls the Russian government." Kennan, already dissatisfied at the turn the Cold War was taking with the promulgation of the Truman Doctrine, saw no need for NATO, deploring "a general preoccupation with military affairs to the detriment of economic recovery and of the necessity for seeking a peaceful solution to Europe's difficulties." Later he recalled, "It was perfectly clear to anyone with even a rudimentary knowledge of the Russia of that day, that the Soviet leaders had no intention of attempting to advance their cause by launching military attacks with their own armed forces across frontiers."

According to the statistics used at that time, the Western powers had some 12 divisions scattered in a number of countries confronting 25 fully armed Russian divisions in Central Europe, part of a total Russian force of 175 divisions. This made the West appear all but helpless before the Soviet juggernaut, but like many figures used in the arms race, then and thereafter, they were selective and partial, caricaturing rather than analyzing the comparative positions. In 1949, the Soviet armed forces had a total strength of some 3 million, as against American forces of 1.5 million, and British and French combined strength of 1.4 million. In Central Europe, in numbers and probably effective strength, the Russian armies had the advantage, although the ratio was nowhere near the 8 to 1, or 6 to 1, figures then bandied about. But it was fatuous to imagine that Russia had superior or even comparable military power to the United States. It is sufficient to recall that America still had the nuclear monopoly, that it had a large fleet of long-range bombers supported by tanker aircraft, that it was already building its comprehensive system of bases around the world, that it had the world's foremost navy, including thirty aircraft carriers. At the time, Russia had no atom bomb, no modern navy, no strategic air force, no bases. Beyond that, it was a devastated, bleeding country that had suffered 20 million dead and had not yet time to bind up its wounds, facing an America at the height of her industrial and financial power. Consequently, it did not dare use its ground superiority, as was demonstrated during the Berlin crisis when it would have been child's play for the Red Army to expel the American forces from the Western sector of the city.

Since Stalin had no intention of moving westward beyond the sphere of influence he had carved out, why the push for this elaborate and expensive entangling alliance and the escalating armaments usually associated with preparations for war? The military doctrine underpinning the venture did not make sense. The NATO armies were supposed to perform the function of a "trip wire," which, in challenging the Soviet armies on the ground, would dramatically establish the *casus belli*, touching off the alarm that would set the American strategic forces into motion. If that was the role of the NATO forces, why could not border patrols, armed with nothing more expensive and complicated than regulation rifles, serve equally well? Of course, this was only the rhetorical setting enclosing the shining jewel. As Professor Robert E. Osgood, the authority on NATO, has instructed us: "NATO was not created to marshal military power, either in being or in potential, in order to deter an imminent attack on Europe. Like Russia's huge army, it was intended to provide political and psychological reinforcement in the continuing political warfare of the cold war. There was no significant fear of a massive Russian invasion."

It was Acheson's perspective that by piling up armaments and allies, NATO would in time provide the "preponderance of power" that Byrnes had hoped would come from the atom bomb, forcing Russia to disgorge its postwar dependencies or even leading to the collapse of the Kremlin regime. To talk seriously of making Western Europe a military powerhouse meant rearming Germany—and Acheson wasted no time after NATO was ratified in putting the proposition bluntly to the British and French. An Atlantic Community anchored in a military alliance against Russia was the indispensable instrumentality to reestablish Germany as a military power in violation of the solemn vows of all the allies. German rearmament and the dispatch of a permanent American occupation army, the first of which was to lead to a long wrangle with the French, and both of which were to lead to uneasiness and disagreement at home, were blandly disclaimed at the legislative stage of the operation. When Acheson was asked at the Senate hearings whether the administration was thinking of raising a German army, he replied, "We are very clear that the disarmament and demilitarization of Germany must be complete and absolute." When asked whether the plan was to send in American troops, he said, "The answer to that question, Senator, is a clear and absolute 'No.'" If the Europeans would not have the manpower to resist attack, was NATO then aimed at preventing revolution? Acheson thought the possibilities for successful subversive activities were "remote." Harriman was more informative when he explained that without NATO there would be "a strengthening of those that believed in appeasement and neutrality." As in so many of these explanations, one must listen not merely to the arguments of the officials, which are often contradictory and not frankly expressed, but to the counterpoint and the cadences, if one is to understand what they are saying.

NATO, with its American-led command structure, was for us, among other considerations, the necessary concomitant of the Marshall Plan to keep our esteemed European allies safely within our own orbit, to isolate any European politicians who might be drawn eastward, to discourage any flirtation with neutralism or any temptation to play off one superpower against the other, and to cut short any radical oppositions that might arise. In later years, de Gaulle put it somewhat emphatically: "An American protectorate was set up in Western Europe under cover of NATO." The European leaders never harbored misunderstandings on this score. For the French, whose unstable and transitory governments confronted a powerful, indigenous Communist movement and whose overseas colonies were in revolt, and for the British, whose political structure remained intact but who faced bankruptcy at home and a disintegrating empire abroad, the prospect of binding the United States to their own fortunes, with the promise of a continued flow of goods and military supplies, was a bargain whatever the price.

There was calculation in fashioning the alliance and selling it to Congress and the public, but the calculation occurred in the context of hysteria. In waging diplomatic warfare, the planners expect the intended victim to make a riposte, but when he does, they react with shocked amazement and righteous indignation. His counterblows prove how right they were in their suspicions, and how necessary it is to step up the scale of operations. As the exchanges become more savage, rhetoric grows unrestrained, judgment is distorted, and decisions are prompted by primordial fears and pathological dissociations. This was the atmosphere, as described by Kennan, in which NATO was conceived. When he was shown Clay's telegram predicting that war might come "with dramatic suddenness," he immediately sent his remonstrances. "But by this time it was too late. Washington, particularly the military establishment, had already overreacted in the most deplorable way to the combination of Clay's telegram and the Czech coup. A real war scare ensued." Truman had come before a joint session of Congress, he told the lawmakers, because "the grave events in Europe were moving so swiftly," and to assure all concerned that we would "extend to the free nations the support which the situation requires." He said that "one nation was blocking all efforts for peace"; that its "ruthless course of action" stemmed from a "clear design" to subjugate the remaining free nations of Europe; that we must "meet this growing menace" because "there are times in world history when it is far wiser to act than to hesitate." He later explained that it looked "like the beginning of a Russian 'big push.'" Kennan insisted "that both of the events that threw official Washington into such a dither—the consolidation of Soviet power in Czechoslovakia and the inauguration of the attempt by the Russians to force the Western allies out of Berlin—were defensive reactions on the Soviet side to the initial success of the Marshall Plan initiative and to the preparations now being undertaken on the Western side to set up a separate German government in Western Germany. This reaction was something I had always expected and taken into account." But he concluded ruefully that he had been naive "in the assumption that the mere statement on a single occasion of a sound analysis or appreciation, even if invited or noted or nominally accepted by one's immediate superiors, had any appreciable effect on the vast, turgid, self-centered, and highly emotional process by which the views and reactions of official Washington were finally evolved."

That decision-making was conducted in a less delirious atmosphere in the Kremlin may be doubted on the evidence of recent memoirs and our knowledge of Russian government under Stalin. What defeated the long campaign to mobilize the Western European masses against the American program was not so much mistaken assumptions or miscalculations, however, as the character of the Stalin regime. The spasmodic efforts to rally the German people were repeatedly smashed on the rock of Russian nationalist assertion. How could Stalin win German hearts against Western machinations when his own purpose was to squeeze out enormous reparations and dismember their country? His contemptuous use of the foreign Communist movements as expendable pawns of his diplomacy facilitated Western efforts to isolate the big parties of France and Italy. It would have been one thing to ask Western Communists to conduct propaganda calling attention to the uneleemosynary aspect of the Marshall Plan, but to lead French and Italian workers into general strikes, in effect, against badly needed American aid, was guaranteed to bring discredit. The momentary disruption of the French and Italian economies was small compensation for the branding of these movements as subservient agencies of a foreign power. Above all, what made Communism abhorrent to broad publics in the democracies, and limited the effectiveness of its peace and related campaigns, was the repulsive Russian image—the frame-up trials, the midnight knock on the door and whisking away of countless victims to slave labor camps, the imposed conformity—and the forcing of similar police regimes on the satellite states. The Stalins, Molotovs, and Zhdanovs were not well placed to rally peoples against the injustices of capitalism when they had converted their own utopia into a chamber of horrors.

NATO sealed and resealed the division of Europe. Acheson's labors brought to fruition the Byrnes-Clay design of reconstituting Western Germany as a powerful capitalist state firmly placed within the American orbit. Dulles completed Acheson's initiatives by twisting France's arm to accept the building of a German army and to permit Germany's inclusion in NATO. As could have been predicted, Russia countered with the Warsaw Pact—the NATO of the East—and a massive rearmament of her own and satellite forces. What had been accomplished? The threshold of violence had been raised with the ratio of capability unchanged. NATO represented a colossal waste of funds and energies, and the courting of dangers unimaginable, to increase the figures of an equation without altering the relationship of a military standoff.

From the vantage point of 1960 or 1970, we see that NATO did not push Russian influence back from the Elbe, did not weaken or disrupt the Kremlin regime, did not impose unification of Germany on Western terms, did not prevent the rise of Gaullism in France, did not eliminate interallied conflict in the Suez crisis, did not advance Western positions in the wake of Eastern difficulties. The Communist sphere was rent by repeated convulsions from the breakaway of Yugoslavia to the revolts in Hungary, Poland, and Czechoslovakia. Rumania and, to a lesser extent, all the satellite nations won a measure of autonomy. But these developments took place because of internal dynamics or corruptions within the Soviet sphere, made harder, not easier, by the continent's conversion into two armed camps. American leadership of Western Europe was established by Europe's needs and America's colossal economic strength. The Marshall Plan was a resounding success in the terms of its organizers' aims, since it led to an economic resurgence, and the dominance in the crucial 1950s of the Catholic parties in France, Germany, and Italy. That the rodomontade of a vast military buildup, with the stationing of a permanent American army of occupation, was a necessary adjunct has been disproved by subsequent history.

In checking Truman's and Acheson's memoirs for their estimations, we find ourselves treated to American-style agitprop, flat and didactic in the case of the President, garnished with quotations and pop-philosophical asides in the case of the Secretary of State. The politican and patrician meet on the common ground of adulation of the monuments they jointly erected. Acheson, not without justice, invokes the shades of Castlereagh and Metternich; opines that wisdom lies in continuing along the course he laid out. We are invited to ponder on "the immortal sentence" of William the Silent, Prince of Orange: "It is not necessary to hope in order to act, or to succeed in order to persevere." Is the Cold War a mystic grail? Isn't there some empirical test to judge whether a treatment was a success or a failure? We are in the hands of a physician who assures us that, if we are feeling bad, we would be feeling ten times worse but for his ministrations.

The program to undo and reverse the politics of the Second World War in Europe had its inevitable counterpart in the Far East. Japan, like Germany, had to be rehabilitated and fitted into our system of al-

liances directed against the USSR, even before the Communist takeover of China converted Japan into the pivot of our position in the
area. After Japan surrendered, we moved in, arrogantly pushing aside
both the Soviet Union and our other allies. In Europe we had had to
proceed in rough partnership with England, and the main blows
against the Nazis had been delivered by Russia, but in the Pacific
American power had reduced the enemy, and Russia had come into
the war only in the last few days in order to seize the spoils assigned
to her at Yalta. Truman said that very early he had made up his mind
to cut out Russia. He told the American officials during the Potsdam
Conference that he was determined that the forthcoming occupation
of Japan was not to follow the lines of the German one. He did not
want divided control or separate zones. The Russians were not to be
given an opportunity to assert special rights or roles as they unfortunately had in Germany and Austria. The country was to be shaped up
in such a way that it could be restored to its place in the world order.

Stalin and Molotov bickered with Truman and Byrnes (while the
English and other allies grumbled more discreetly), but in the end
they had to settle for two talking shops, the thirteen-nation Far Eastern Advisory Commission meeting in Washington, and the four-power
Allied Council in Tokyo. The commission had less power or effectiveness than a UN assembly; after some years of futile complaining,
the Soviet representative withdrew. The council was the forum for
angry exchanges between American and Soviet spokesmen and
quickly became moribund. What made the American position over-
weening was that the supreme allied commander in Japan was General MacArthur. In assuming the imperial mantle, we took on some
problems of the Roman Empire. Already General Clay had been accused by Walter Lippmann of becoming a proconsul in Germany
with whom the State Department negotiated but to whom it never
presumed to give orders. But Clay was a discreet public servant compared to MacArthur, who publicly conducted himself not like a plenipotentiary but like an independent power autocratically ruling over a
conquered domain. A few weeks after the Japanese capitulation he
announced a reduction in the number of occupation troops without
bothering to consult with Truman or other Washington authorities.
When Acheson, whose nomination for Undersecretary of State was
awaiting confirmation, made a statement in agreement with Truman,
or at his behest, that in carrying out American decisions in Japan "the
occupation forces are the instruments of policy, and not the determi-
nants of policy," Senator Kenneth S. Wherry insisted that he had in-

Cartoon by Jim Berryman in the Washington Evening Star.

Cartoon by Karl Knecht in the Evansville (*Indiana*) Courier.

Reunion of the 35th Division in Omaha, Nebraska, in 1948. President Truman leads the parade. (Harry S. Truman Library)

An exultant President displays the Chicago Tribune *announcing his defeat by Thomas E. Dewey, November 3, 1948. (UPI)*

Mrs. Truman, Margaret Truman, Mrs. Alben Barkley, Vice-President Barkley, President Truman leaving Blair House for the Inauguration, 1949. (Washington Evening Star)

The presidential party at the Little White House in Key West, Florida, 1949. From left, back row: Commander William M. Rigdon, David Stowe, Dr. Wallace K. Graham, General Harry H. Vaughan, Clark Clifford, Admiral Robert L. Dennison, General Robert B. Landry, George Elsey. Seated: Matt Connelly, John Steelman, President Truman, William Hassett, Charles Ross. The men in front are unidentified. (U.S. Navy)

Top: President Truman accompanied by his press secretary, Charles Ross, at Key West, 1949. (U.S. Navy)

Right: President Truman on the bridge of the presidential yacht Williamsburg. *(U.S. Navy)*

Below: cartoon by Jacob Burch, Field Enterprises, Inc.

Meeting aboard the Williamsburg *with Anthony Eden, Dean Acheson, President Truman, and Winston Churchill, 1952. (Harry S. Truman Library)*

The Trumans with Princess Elizabeth during her United States visit in 1951. (Harry S. Truman Library)

Cartoon by Parrish in the Chicago Tribune.

President Truman greeting W. Averell Harriman, Mutual Security Adminis-
trator; Secretary of State Dean Acheson; and Secretary of the Treasury
John Snyder, arriving from a NATO meeting in Paris, 1952. (Chicago Sun-
Times)

Former President and Mrs. Harry S. Truman waiting for train on the Missouri Pacific. (Kansas City Star)

sulted the general and tried to have the nomination recommitted. Edwin Locke, later vice-president of the Chase National Bank, who was sent out the next month with an economic mission to China and stopped off in Japan for a talk with MacArthur, reported to Truman that, in the general's opinion, policies on Japan should be made in Tokyo rather than in Washington.

American occupation policy in Japan was from the first more lenient than for Germany since it was held that she could more easily be fitted into the American scheme. When Americans entered Japan, the old elite was discredited for having led the nation to disaster. By disbanding the military staffs and forcing disarmament on the country, the American occupation had the effect of completing the bourgeois revolution that had been put through partially by bureaucratic, Bismarckian methods at the time of the Meiji Restoration. The new constitution not only inaugurated a system of parliamentary government on British lines, a parliamentarianism that had had only rudimentary beginnings in the 1920s; it also unleashed the liberal, labor, and radical forces that had been stultified earlier by the dominant aristocratic and military establishment gathered around the imperial throne. The old so-called liberal parties that had been financed by the industrialists flowered in their association with the occupation authorities, without having to defer to the military and nobility. Laborism and radicalism went into a period of stormy growth. By 1949, over 6.5 million employees were enrolled in labor unions, many of them led by political radicals. Marxism became a major intellectual current among university faculties and in periodicals and newspapers. The Teachers Union of employees in primary and secondary schools was headed by leftists. The Socialist party, successor to the earlier Social Mass party, was able to poll more than a third of the total vote.

In the first flush of democratization, there had been efforts to break up the great industrial concentrations in the hands of the *zaibatsu*. As Cold War considerations came to the fore, these efforts were abandoned as well as the earlier decision to transfer industrial plants to neighboring countries as reparation payments. The occupiers became less concerned with reforming Japan, and more concerned with redirecting Japan for the new diplomacy. Labor unions were restrained, government employees were prohibited from striking, other strikes were suppressed, the business community was given free play, conservative politicians solidified their old commanding positons. The purge of military officers, high-ranking bureaucrats, Diet members, and *zaibatsu* executives was discontinued. In any case, the younger men who had taken the places of their dismissed predecessors differed from their elders only in rank and seniority, and soon reinstatement of the purged leaders began. The country was being readied to become a bastion of the new world lineup. By the time of NATO, plans were far advanced to end the occupation and introduce Japan as our junior partner in the Far East. The shift was formalized after Kennan visited MacArthur at the end of February, 1948—a mission he described as "like nothing more than that of an envoy charged with opening up communications and arranging the establishment of diplomatic relations with a hostile and suspicious foreign government" —and most of Kennan's recommendations were accepted by the National Security Council and approved by the President. (Acheson, against Kennan's advice, was moving for a peace treaty from the summer of 1949, a decision apparently hastened by his conviction that it was the only way to end MacArthur's private sovereignty.)

Dulles was appointed special adviser to carry on the negotiations in recognition of the fact that the Pacific was a special Republican preserve. Dulles was the Wall Street corporation lawyer who had represented the internationalist Republicans in every major government venture from the start of the Truman tenure. He was the authentic establishment expert in bipartisanship as Vandenberg was its senatorial rhetorician. His public personality was the meeting ground of a sanctimoniousness and big power ruthlessness. To his virtuosity in advocacy and legal jugglery he added a talent for forensic inflation animated by Christian piety that suggested a more crafty, devious, pettifogging Woodrow Wilson. In the fall of 1951, in the midst of the Korean war, he and Acheson rode roughshod over the objections of our Western and Asian allies to complete the peace treaty, signed in San Francisco by the United States and forty-eight other nations— not including Russia, Communist China, or India. Despite the international trappings, it was an American show. "Never was so good a peace treaty so little loved by so many of its participants," said Acheson. The North Pacific islands, held by the Japanese under a League of Nations mandate, had been transferred formally to the United States as a UN trusteeship territory in 1947. In the peace treaty, Japan further agreed to renounce claims to the Ryukyus and Bonins and to support their remaining in United States possession under the same formula. On the same day that she signed the peace treaty, Japan also signed a bilateral treaty with the United States for the continuation of American bases in Japan. In order to quiet the trepidation of Australia and New Zealand concerning the anticipated rearmament of Japan, the United States entered into still another treaty guaranteeing the security of these two countries—in the process invalidating another Acheson pledge. At the time of NATO, in answer to a question from Senator Henry Cabot Lodge, Jr., he had given assurances that the administration planned no further regional arrangements. Despite Truman's earlier protestations that this country had no territorial ambitions, we had come a long way toward materializing Chauncey Depew's vision of the Pacific as an American lake. We had effective possession of the entire chain of Pacific archipelagos and islands, preferential rights and military bases in the Philippines, and Japan had become, in Dulles' words, the linchpin in an iron noose of American containment in Asia.

Thus, by the end of the Truman Presidency, the basic architecture for America's new world position and for the attempted isolation of the Soviet Union had been completed. From the military missions to Greece and Turkey, on through the Marshall Plan, NATO, and the Pacific alliances, the awesome tower had risen tier upon tier, until it became for the Cold War's true believers a sacred object of worship, every line and section of which was indispensable, as in a masterpiece of art, to the inner spirit of the creation. When Stalin in 1952, in fear of a rearmed Germany tied to America, reversed his previous positions to propose to the three Western powers a peace treaty establishing a united, independent Germany with its own national army and membership in the UN, but neutral between East and West, Acheson simply scoffed at it. It was, he said, the "golden apple" thrown by the Goddess of Discord into the Western "wedding party." He, for one, was not fooled by the Soviet "peace offensive." Acheson was waiting (as Dulles was to wait) for the happy day when the crackup came in the enemy camp and a triumphant America gathered in the golden harvest. The Cold War created a miasma that had a hallucinatory effect on even its most cold-blooded devotees.

14

Arms Race
and
the Bomb

America's assumption of Britain's nineteenth-century global hegemony, accompanied by the attempt to isolate and overawe a rival superpower, meant an arms race, and that led to grave domestic
dislocations. The country's much-advertised antimilitarist tradition
was no hindrance. It had always been contradictory and confused.
The historic suspicion of the military had been coupled with a propensity for elevating victorious generals to the Presidency; it had not
stood in the way of an expanding navalism at the turn of the century.
In any event, the peacetime consolidation and entrenchment of the
powerful military caste built up during the Second World War held
no terrors for business and political leaders. A consanguineous relationship had been established between the three elites so that they intermingled and exchanged places freely in the direction of the country's affairs and viewed the country's interests and needs through the
same preconceptions.

General Clay, before becoming proconsul in Germany, was deputy
to General Brehon B. Somervell who virtually ran the Army-Navy
Munitions Board. "In this capacity," he related, "I was fortunate in
being able to assemble a staff which included some very able executives from the business world." Clay, who after his tour of duty be-

came board chairman of Continental Can, and then a senior partner in Lehman Brothers, accounted for "the improved standing" of military men "in the increased association with the business and industrial world resulting from the major role of defense spending." The passage of generals and admirals to major positions with the corporations became commonplace in the 1950s and 1960s. Recent figures show 2,072 retired officers of the rank of Army colonel or Navy captain and higher employed by the 100 top defense contractors, three times the number employed ten years earlier. What is important in this context is not whether military men seek to curry favor with corporations, but whether a caste, encompassing the alumni as well as the current staffs, has been hardened with a vested interest in the perpetuation of a large military establishment.

The military began infiltrating civilian phases of government in the Truman days. An Army chief of staff became Secretary of State. Ten of the twenty men ranking as executive officers in the State Department were brought in from the military services. General John Hildring was named Assistant Secretary for occupied areas, and he brought with him twenty-six assistants from the Army. Military men took on major ambassadorial assignments, as General Walter Bedell Smith to Russia and Admiral Alan Kirk to Belgium and later to China. The newly created Central Intelligence Agency was directed and largely staffed by them. The National Security Council was dominated by them. At the end of 1947, Hanson Baldwin, *The New York Times* military analyst, thought there was a trend to "the militarization of our government and of the American state of mind," and three years later Walter Lippmann wrote that a big chunk of the conduct of foreign affairs had been moved into the Pentagon to make for "a rather serious imitation of what in any other country but this freewheeling democracy would be militarism." The growing role and assertiveness of the military—what might have been considered a transitory development in Roosevelt's wartime regime—was getting institutionalized in the postwar administration.

It had been the great good fortune of this country that for 150 years it had avoided the building of a major military establishment. Civilian rule gave strength and continuity to constitutional government. Despite the schemes and ambitions of General John Pershing and other martinets to keep a mass military machine after the First World War, the armies were disbanded and the small corps of professionals went back to peacetime routines. There remained a great Navy, more than equal to Britain's; but the civil power found it easier to control its navies than its armies and to focus admirals' ambitions on their professional domains. The experience in that war reinforced the traditional belief that the country's favorable geographical position and industrial prowess were the sure guarantors of its security. The war reimposed some sort of European power balance, or so it was thought, and in any new challenge we could again expect to find allies to absorb the initial blows while our factories and mills were churning out the goods to raise and equip the mass forces to deliver in good time the knockout strokes.

By 1945 the old sense of security and certainties had been blown away. Not only was America's grand design being thwarted by another aspirant of the first magnitude, not only were the old European imperiums reduced to second-rate powers dependent on American bounty, but the revolution in technology was about to demolish our traditional security and make obsolete our time-honored strategy. For the first time in our history the ocean barriers had shrunk, and our cities and homes could be reduced to nuclear ash. The bewilderment and apprehension, the absence of battle experience in the new weaponry, the overturn of previous concepts of war, the bedlam of conflicting assertions and claims—all contributed to give the specialists in the black arts of violence the status of soothsayers and medicine men. Either one of the new elements, the international confrontation or the revolution in the military arts, would have impelled this country to build up a military machine. Because the two came together, militarization appeared demonic and insatiable, and there was extruded a permanent military caste alongside the constitutional directorates to disarrange historic balances.

Important writers of various political persuasions have discounted this development. They doubt that there has been a significant change in the power dispositions. Walter Millis argued that "the stage was filled with civilians more militaristic than the military, and with military men more 'civilistic' than the civilians. It was no longer clear that the substitution of a politician or businessman for a professional soldier at any given post of command would necessarily affect the course of policy." Gabriel Kolko said that "the nature of global conflict and means of violence are so thoroughly political and economic in their essential character, so completely intricate technologically, that it is probably more correct to argue the case for the declining importance of the military in the decision-making structure." William Domhoff concluded that "the role of the military remains a subservient one within the American context." Irving Janowitz similarly maintained that "Civilian control of military affairs remains intact and fundamentally acceptable to the military," although he blurred his case by adding that "the military have accumulated considerable power, and that power protrudes into the political fabric of contemporary society."

The same data is used by different scholars to prove opposing theses. Where one thinks the squabbling of the military services demonstrates that they believe their corporate position is so secure that they can afford to air their disputes publicly, another believes that their lack of unity makes it impossible for them to dictate to civilian authorities. Where one cites the growing number of retired officers occupying executive positions in corporations to demonstrate the growing influence of the Pentagon, another holds it proves the dominance of the businessman over the military. Where one points out that the military lobby is today the most powerful of all lobbies in Washington, another counters that these lobbying activities are financed by corporation dues and advertising in the business journals.

The controversy occurs not because the data are inadequate for an evaluation but because of the nature of the problem. The military is not proceeding in opposition to, but in harness with, political and business leaders. It is not trying to impose some military program on the nation that violates the civilian program of the constitutional authorities; rather, its entrance on the scene as a power coincided with the main drift of our society. Its relations with the politicians and the Executive are intimate and cordial. It is honored, not execrated, in the business world. Its relationship with the major defense contractors is practically incestuous, Pentagon officialdom and leading supply corporations having carved out a vast economic domain of "military socialism" in which cliques of congressmen have been cut in. In many cases service conflicts have rocked Congress and the nation because of competition between rival manufacturers pushing their favored wares. Moreover, some of the decisive steps in the creation of the monster military machine were taken by civilians: It was Acheson and Paul Nitze who engineered NSC-68 to lift the military budget from $15 billion to $50 billion; a succession of corporation lawyers, bankers, and big-business executives have headed the Defense Department; civilians in Defense and State were prime movers in some of the more militant decisions, from threatening Russia over Iran to the bombing of North Vietnam.

Nevertheless, there is a quality of academic hairsplitting about the controversy. The militarization of American society is acknowledged by all students of the question. One would have to be deaf and blind not to be aware of it. When a country spends astronomical sums year in, year out, to maintain a war-ready establishment, and that is proclaimed part of the necessary order; when crises and emergencies are defined as the new norm under which our society will have to carry on; when official doctrine makes peace hinge on a constantly escalating balance of terror; when the military extends its influence over research organizations, universities, and publishing houses, and maintains immense public relations divisions; when over half of our scientists and engineers work directly or indirectly for the Pentagon; when the jobs of some 4 million industrial workers are dependent on military budgets and at least a dozen states would face economic disaster if military contracts were terminated—then that nation has constructed a militarist state.

The further question is this: Has a caste solidified that has a vested interest in the perpetuation of the military power, that defines national issues in terms of military logic, whose voice is becoming more forceful in the councils of government? It can be argued that most of the elite have succumbed to the military logic, and consequently it is artificial to make a distinction between soldiers and civilians; the two have become so intertwined that where divisions occur they do not take place along military-civilian lines. There is a distinction, nevertheless, subtle yet substantive, between the Achesons, Lovetts, Harrimans, McCloys, and the military bureaucrats and arms contractors. Not that one group is more cautious and the other more bellicose. The distinction is this: The militarized civilians favor the swollen military establishment because they view it as necessary for Cold War politics and global aspirations. Their own careers are not tied to it, but to their law firms, banks, or corporations, which are only partially and indirectly tied to the military sectors. The professional soldier and military contractor, on the other hand, are fused with the military business. They are partners in a conspiracy to keep pumping out new weapons systems for an ever-expanding military WPA. It is not that pugnacious generals and admirals are elbowing aside pacifistic lawyers and financiers to make the telling decisions, but that in the councils of government members of an association with a professional interest in the promotion of an arms race are called upon to pass judgments on the national destiny.

Is there such a thing as a military ethic counterposed to a businessman's ethic? Military ideology generally has been no more than a sophomoric mélange of schoolboy maxims and Social Darwinist vulgarizations. There is, nonetheless, such a thing as a military mind and a military tradition, based on very real principles: (1) relations between nations seen in terms of military force and the settlement of conflicts by the threat or practice of organized violence; (2) an authoritarian-aristocratic concept of organization in which decisions are made by the leader, to be obeyed unquestioningly by the ranks, with a rigid apportionment into hierarchical divisions fixed by status, gradation of command, and perquisites. Since the birth of parliamentarianism in the West, the military establishment has been an authoritarian enclave within democratic territory. Hence the militarist's traditional impatience with the temporizing and evasions of democratic governments, his contempt for the politician who in his eyes was a demagogue pandering to the mob. Hence, too, his bewilderment and frustration when complex problems did not lend themselves to solution by his rough-and-ready methods, and his conviction that he was being betrayed by conniving and unscrupulous civilians. In the history of the standing armies in the European democracies, it was part of the professional code of the military staffs to reduce civilian control of their establishments to a formality. They were honored in their own guild for their deception of government officials.

This country has never faced a military crisis on the scale of the Dreyfus affair in France, or the blackmailing of British parliament in 1914 when officers threatened to resign en masse if the government enforced its grant of home rule for Ireland. The absence of a hereditary military aristocracy made more tangible American civilian control. The "admirals' revolt" of 1949, which arose out of interservice rivalry and the determination of the Navy to get a piece of the atom bomb, was quelled with the dismissal of Admiral Louis E. Denfeld and the enlarged role assigned to the Navy in the subsequent rearmament. MacArthur's dismissal following his defiance of Truman—the most serious challenge to civilian authority since General McClellan's resistance to Lincoln—became a short-lived national crisis only because the Taft wing of the Republican party and its sympathetic press rallied behind the general; the Pentagon staffs stayed loyal to the government. Unless the country is torn by a basic split in its ruling circles, the embryonic tendencies of a military establishment to become the nation's political arbiter will remain embryonic. But in accordance with an ancient law of organization, the bigger and richer it grows, the more pervasive becomes the spread of its authoritarian concepts and military mystique.

Stimson had been ruminating about the atom bomb for months before and after the Potsdam conference. In his last days before retiring, he changed his mind again and decided there must be an approach to Russia if a catastrophe was to be avoided. One month after Hiroshima, he took to the White House a memorandum in which he made the momentous proposal for three-power control of the bomb. He argued that the attempt "to maintain an Anglo-Saxon bloc" against the Soviet Union would lead to "a secret armament race of a rather desperate character."

An inconclusive and somewhat acerbic discussion took place at the special Cabinet meeting called to consider the proposal, and that was the last anyone heard of it until it was transmogrified into the Baruch Plan and unveiled at the UN. The tide was already running heavily in an opposite direction so that those who had doubts or reservations or simple amendments were swept along with the all-outers and intransigents. Byrnes told McCloy he was against any negotiations looking to international control of atomic energy. General Groves was instructed to move full speed ahead with the manufacture of atomic bombs. We were the only ones who had the secret and we were going to make the world dance to our tune and like it. Call it the American Century, or Pax Americana, or that we had come of age and were ready to assume our world responsibilities—what came out at the policy end of the funnel was the same. Truman told a visitor "that the Russians would soon be put in their places; and that the United States would then take the lead in running the world in the way that the world ought to be run." The scientists had been saying that Russia would cover the ground we had traveled within a matter of five years, but the politicians would have none of it. They decided on evidence best known to themselves that it might be as many as twenty years before the American monopoly was broken. (When the Russians exploded their atomic bomb four years later, Truman informed the American public—but he did not really believe it.*)

At the same jamboree in early October, 1945, where he charmed the Methodist ladies with a rendition of Paderewski's *Minuet*, the correspondents were invited for a press conference to the lodge on Reelfoot Lake in Tennessee, just across the state line from Missouri, where

---

* Admiral Robert Lee Dennison met with him in 1949 to advocate work on a hydrogen bomb. As an argument for his proposal, he pointed to the Russians' success with the atom bomb as proof of their capabilities. Truman told him he agreed with his proposal, whereupon Dennison and his colleagues gathered up their papers and started to leave. As they reached the door the President gave them the parting shot, "But I still don't believe it."

the President was relaxing. The reporters resembled some of the Cabinet members who had participated in the consideration of Stimson's memorandum. All they could focus on was: Were we going to give our "secret" to the Russians or anybody else, or were we going to hug the "secret" to our own bosoms? In answer to a question, Truman explained, "The scientific knowledge that resulted in the atomic bomb is already worldwide knowledge. It is only the know-how of putting that knowledge practically to work that is our secret." When the reporter wanted to know, "Would it apply to letting them in on the know-how?" Truman told him, "Well, I don't think it would do any good to let them in on the know-how, because I don't think they could do it, anyway. You would have to have the industrial plant and our engineering ability to do the job." On this matter Truman was the incarnation of the dominant American spirit in the high noon of its vainglory. Others may be great with theory. But we're the only folks who know how to put it to work. We have come up with a product no one else has got. Now the smart thing to do is to cash in on our advantage. Nor was the reaction uniquely American, Midwestern, or Missourian. The British aristocrats and laborites displayed equal smugness, all the more pitiable since they were cavorting at somebody else's wedding. To repeat the platitude of our times, the atom was split before mankind was ready for it. It was appropriate that Truman should make his pronouncement on this world-shaking question in the setting of a rustic lodge, surrounded by his good-time cronies, with his remarks interrupted by an exuberant follower at the other end of the porch bellowing, until he was quieted, "Tennessee for Truman." Nothing had daunted us in our history up to now, and there was no reason why an atom bomb should make us change our habits.

The British (and Canadians) had worked with us on the Manhattan Project, and under the Roosevelt-Churchill understanding reached at Quebec in August, 1943, a combined policy committee, consisting of three Americans and three Britons, had been set up for a free interchange of information. Upon reading of the President's press interview blazoned in headlines: TRUMAN SAYS U.S. TO KEEP ATOMIC BOMB SECRET, the British were perturbed and pressed for an early meeting. Before Truman met with Attlee and Mackenzie King in early November, the State Department sent him a paper arguing that the exchange of information had referred to scientific research and development, but that "information concerning manufacturing know-how" applied only to bringing the wartime project to "speedy fruition."

Truman wrote in his *Memoirs* that he was also of the opinion that "the nature of the partnership had to be readjusted." What he did, though, was to initial at the conclusion of the conference a memorandum drawn up by Vannevar Bush, the Director of Scientific Research, to continue the wartime cooperation between the three nations. Groves, on Truman's instruction, made an agreement to provide the British with help for the construction of their own plant.° Attlee and King then accepted the American proposition of dumping the matter of international control into the United Nations (which Stimson had warned against if an agreement with the Soviets was really desired). They instructed the still-uncreated UN Commission that the plan it offered would have to "proceed by separate stages, the successful completion of each one of which will develop the necessary confidence of the world before the next stage is undertaken"—all of which was incorporated in the Truman-Attlee-King declaration.

Byrnes was to leave for Moscow at the end of the year. He was given an interdepartmental memorandum in line with the three-power declaration; this he intended to use to secure the Russians' agreement for the creation of a UN commission to consider international control. That was when his trouble with Truman and others really started. The atomic fever was rising all along the Potomac. Generals, admirals, congressmen, Cabinet members, were working themselves to a pitch. General Groves, upon learning of the memorandum, protested vigorously. Although no one could claim better Cold War credentials than Byrnes, Forrestal joined forces with Groves. Senators Connally and Vandenberg were equally agitated lest Byrnes give away secrets in order to induce the Russians to participate in the work of a UN atomic energy commission. When Byrnes read to a senatorial group a draft of the proposal he intended to make in Moscow, Vandenberg said they were all shocked. "We are opposed to giving any of the atomic secrets away unless and until the Soviets are prepared to be 'policed' by UNO in respect to their prohibition. We consider an 'exchange' of scientists and scientific information as sheer appeasement because Russia had nothing to 'exchange.'" Since Byrnes refused to take their

° When after several months the Americans did not carry out their pledges, British representatives met with Acheson, who told them "it was quite impossible to fulfill the obligation of the arrangement. If a secret arrangement were carried out, it would blow the administration out of the water. They must just resign themselves to the fact that although we made the agreement, we simply could not carry it out; that things like that happen in the government of the U.S. due to the loose way things are handled."

fears seriously, the delegation arranged to meet with the President the following morning. The senators were shocked all over again after Truman read to them his directive to Byrnes, which listed the consecutive steps that Byrnes had read off the day before. Although Vandenberg made it clear that the directive would make it possible for Byrnes "to prematurely give away, while in Moscow, at least half of all our 'trading stock' when we seek essential controls," the President "for some inscrutable reason" failed to grasp his point. Vandenberg went into his Indian war dance again when he read the communiqué issued at the conclusion of the Moscow Conference containing the same innocuous homily that for him had a sinister connotation.

On January 16 of the new year, Lilienthal made the following entry in his journal:

> Saw Acheson. He talked frankly and in detail: Those charged with foreign policy—the Secretary of State and the President—did not have either the facts or an understanding of what was involved in the atomic energy issue, the most serious cloud hanging over the world. Commitments, on paper and in communiqués, have been made and are being made without a knowledge of what the hell it is all about—literally! The War Department, and really one man in the War Department, General Groves, has by the power of the veto on the ground of "military security" really been determining and almost running foreign policy. He had entered into contracts involving other countries (Belgium and their Congo deposits of uranium, for example) without even the knowledge of the Department of State. Finally realizing that this could not go on, Acheson was able to persuade the President and Secretary to do something about it. [Byrnes appointed a committee, headed by Acheson, to work out the American position for our UN representative, and Acheson, in turn, got Lilienthal to head an advisory panel to canvass the field.]

Out of the mill came the recommendations known as the Acheson-Lilienthal Report, in the main the work of J. Robert Oppenheimer, former director of the Los Alamos Laboratory and often referred to as the father of the atom bomb. It was a bold and far-reaching plan; indeed, a revolutionary one. An international agency was to take over ownership or the lease of all mines containing atomic materials, all stocks of uranium and thorium, was to operate all plants that produced atomic materials either for weapons or for peaceful uses, was to direct all research and development, was to inspect and license all activities in the field. This grandiose project was to be put into operation in a number of stages already outlined in the Truman-Attlee-King declaration, so that until the final stage, when the manufacture of atomic weapons was discontinued and existing bombs disposed of, the United States was to remain in possession of her stockpile, the only country with the right to carry on arms production.

Despite the revolutionary character of the concept, the plan violated the first essential of disarmament proposals, where seriously intended: In any multistage proposal, the relative positions of the parties have to be protected throughout the progression. It cannot be demanded that Power A destroy 50 percent of its stock while Power B is to destroy only 5 percent of its stock at the initial stage, because Power B pledges to destroy a far greater percentage at a later stage some years hence. What if during the interval between the first and final stages the two powers decide to war on each other? What if one of the powers decides that changed conditions make it impossible to continue the agreement, and resumes its arms buildup? The plan, as the report was at pains to emphasize, protected the favored position of the United States, should there be a breakdown in the course of the transition. It did not similarly protect the position of Russia. At the very first stage, she would be giving up her nuclear raw materials, her development laboratories, and handing over a virtual target map of her territories, in return for the promise that at the very last stage, five or six years later, the United States would turn over its factories and stockpiles to the international authority. Beyond other inequities that critics pointed out, the entire plan was a chimera. It was a proposal to set up a world government over atomic energy at a time when the two superpowers were at daggers drawn, and to have this world government run by an American-dominated majority, in which the Soviet Union would be relegated to a minority position. Even in the surrealistic world of international diplomacy, this was too far-out.

There can be little doubt that hard-boiled operators like Acheson and Lilienthal looked on the plan as an exercise in political warfare, although consideration must be given to the charged atmosphere in which all the managers were working at the time, when it seemed that history had made this country the trustee of mankind and the keeper of the sacred seals of civilization. Years later, Oppenheimer testified that he never expected the Russians to accept the plan because some of its provisions, if carried out, would lead to a collapse of their system. P. M. S. Blackett related that, in 1946, Lord Inverchapel, the British ambassador to Washington, told him the same thing. Publication of the plan set off the familiar division between "liberal-internationalist" and "conservative-isolationist" groups, illustrating again the unreality and irrelevance of so much American public debate. Acclaimed by the liberal press as a document of great vision and profound statesmanship, and enthusiastically endorsed by the American Federation of Atomic Scientists, the report was as strongly damned by the conservative press, Republican politicians, and service officers for its starry-eyed idealism and its offers to give away America's vital secrets.

The conservatives proved right in one respect: The Acheson-Lilienthal plan was too "idealistic" to survive the political gauntlet. The first intimation came when Byrnes told Acheson that he would recommend to the President that Baruch be appointed as the American representative and entrusted with the task of whipping up the Acheson-Lilienthal proposals "into a workable plan." Acheson protested the choice, and Lilienthal, when he heard about it, wrote, "I was quite sick." But that is the way it was, and control over the American position and presentation was turned over to the deaf, seventy-six-year old ex-speculator and his Wall Street crew. Innumerable meetings followed between the Baruch and Acheson groups. Aside from semantic and secondary changes—Baruch had the Vandenberg disease in acute form—the main alteration introduced into the plan was to provide punishments for any violations not subject to the UN veto. In vain Acheson and others tried to demonstrate that this provision would rule out any conceivable Russian agreement; that the elimination of the veto added nothing to American security; that if Russia, after accepting an international authority, decided to violate the procedures, the provision for penalties outside the veto simply gave the United States the privilege of waging war on Russia, a privilege we already enjoyed. Baruch was adamant. The revised plan was given to the President, who promptly initialed it. Even in its revised form, it was meant only for Baruch's guidance. It was not a directive. "I want you to have authority," Truman wrote in a separate letter he gave Baruch, "to exercise your judgment as to the method by which the stated objectives can be accomplished."

Truman's real opinion of the provision to eliminate the UN veto in atomic sanctions, or whether he cared one way or another, is not clear. He had appointed Baruch, he later admitted, because Baruch had a considerable following in Congress. He hoped that Baruch's association with the administration would help ease the opposition to the McMahon bill for civilian control of atomic energy. In his *Memoirs* Truman claimed that he had to make clear to Baruch that he did not intend to have anybody infringe on his prerogative to determine policy—a claim that Baruch denied and that Truman's letter to Baruch belied. Lilienthal recorded on a later occasion that he had heard of Baruch's having some disagreements with the administration and asked Clifford about it.

> The chief trouble, Clifford said, was that the President hadn't consulted Baruch. He was advised that he should, but he decided against it. "He said, 'I'm just *not* going to do it. I'm not going to spend hours and hours on that old goat, come what may. If you take his advice, then you have him on your hands for hours and hours, and it is *his* policy. I'm just not going to do it.'" Clifford was amused by this, but admitted that it was causing some members of the cabinet who depend on the old boy some considerable time and sweat.

The resultant Baruch Plan was so blatantly one-sided that some have speculated that the purpose of its authors was to sabotage all possibilities for international control. Since the same purpose would have been served by the supposedly more idealistic original version of the plan, it may be concluded that the Baruch clique's insistence on sanctions and the elimination of the veto had additional explanations. Already at the time of Byrnes's departure for Moscow to propose the UN atomic commission, it was apparent that the prevailing feeling of omnipotence was accompanied by symptoms of anxiety neurosis. The success of the atomic scientists in making the public aware of the doomsday aspects of atomic warfare set into motion contradictory responses. Fright and suspicion combined to pressure politicians and bureaucrats to take control of the bomb out of the hands of the military and to seek international agreement for its quarantine. They also led to the demand for complete, assured security—a security that by the nature of the situation was no longer obtainable. The quest to regain this lost Eden—the premise of all projects—made inevitable the surrender to the military mystique and the appeasement of the militarists and their allies. The only politically realistic measures were those acceptable to most of the effectives that made up the Cold War brigade. The demand for the elimination of the UN veto on atomic questions, meaningless for the reinforcement of the American position, was part of the required theater to dispel suspicions and allay apprehensions that the United States would permit itself to be seduced.

In mid-June Baruch presented the toughened plan to the UN commission in the portentous rhetoric of his publicity writer, Herbert Bayard Swope, a member of the Baruch entourage since World War I. "We are here to make a choice between the quick and the dead"; "The people want an international law with teeth in it"; "Condign punishments set up for violations"; "Before a country is ready to relinquish any winning weapon, it must have more than words to reassure it. It must have a guarantee of safety not only against the offenders in the atomic area, but against the illegal users of other weapons—bacteriological, biological, gas—perhaps—why not? against war itself?" To lend emphasis to his words, the United States conducted an underwater atomic test at the Bikini atoll two weeks later when a bomb as powerful as the one dropped on Nagasaki was exploded 50 feet below sea level.

Andrei Gromyko, the Soviet representative, as could have been anticipated, responded with a counterproposal the essence of which was a convention to prohibit the production and use of atomic weapons and the destruction of existing stocks. This was to be followed by organization and measures for the observance of the convention, and the use of sanctions against unlawful use of atomic energy, with the unanimity rule governing the UN Security Council to remain intact. The Soviet proposal derived from the same principle as the American one, except that since she was the weaker party, she sought to cut down the American advantage. Both sides introduced some secondary refinements in the course of the protracted discussions, but essentially the debate revolved on propounding the merits of conflicting schemes, and got nowhere. It was not a negotiation but an appeal to public opinion. At one point, Molotov sought to shift the discussion to a comprehensive consideration of general disarmament—something the Russians succeeded in doing later on—but the public-relations advantage was with the Americans in the initial confrontation.

The Western press bombarded the public with declarations of eminent figures describing the Baruch Plan as the most generous offer in history, which the Russians persisted in rejecting either out of malevolence or unreasoning addiction to secrecy. Most people had neither the time nor the opportunity to wade through the documentation or technical details. The impression that came through was that the American offer was not only equitable but magnanimous. Here were the Americans, sole possessors of the bomb, offering to turn over their blueprints and stocks to an international body, asking in return only a system of international ownership and authority so that their own generosity would not be abused by any would-be aggressor; and here were the Russians, unreasonable, uncooperative, nihilistic, repeating their familiar anti-Western tirades, standing in the way of international understanding. Something ought to be done about it. The bolder spirits—and there were many—called for preventive war, a sentiment succinctly summarized by George Earle, former Democratic governor of Pennsylvania: "Every nation must permit inspectors, or be atom-bombed."

The Russians countered by pounding away on their proposition to ban the bomb (climaxed in 1950 with the Stockholm peace petition). Inside the UN, they drew the Western representatives into involved, interminable technical discussions, giving ground on details, playing for time, until their own atomic progress would balance the scale. Marginal agreements made more glaring the basic deadlock. Although the bogus negotiations dragged on for almost two years, in the final period they were of interest only to the social scientists and second-string reporters at the UN. The posturings of the principles had taken on the character of a stylized puppet show to distract attention from the arms race in progress.

At the end of the war the military establishment was in a state of transition marked by strategic muddle, interservice conflict, and bureaucratic chaos. The Army and Navy had historically developed as separate sovereignties. They could be made to cooperate, even under the iron imperatives of a great war, only by the introduction of such expedients as a joint chiefs of staff working directly with the President (bypassing the civilian secretaries), autonomy for the Army Air Force, and overall theater commanders. Before the Normandy invasion, Stimson and others had said the only way out of the confusion was to unify the armed forces. By October, 1945, when the Senate Military Affairs Committee began hearings on various unification plans, the need for reorganization had become acute to meet the Army Air Force's insistent claim for independent and equal status. There was a general feeling that modern warfare, with its integrated land, sea, and air operations, necessitated an overhauling of the antiquated, uncoordinated organization rather than a simple addition of one more independent service. In the American context this was no easy matter. There was the bureaucratic rivalry of three services, each allied with major corporations profoundly concerned about organizational decisions affecting budgetary allocations for one or another weapon system. And above and beyond the bureaucratic rivalries, the atom bomb had shattered previous concepts of warfare, so that for years to come the face of war was to be an enigma.

As the war ground to a halt the only thing the chieftains could agree on was their desire to maintain the services on a war footing, before any enemy had yet been identified, before anybody knew what dangers a wartime establishment was supposed to forestall, or what diplomacy it was meant to bolster. They were not to realize their objectives all at once. For the first few years they had to curb their appetites. First came an irresistible momentum for demobilization. Immediately after the cessation of hostilities the cry to bring the boys back home and return them to civilian life became so compelling, so overwhelming—indeed, there were near-revolts among the troops in Europe and the Far East when they heard that there were plans afoot to keep them in uniform—that Truman had no alternative but to order the rapid mustering out of the draftees. The leviathan of 12 million men quickly shrank to about 1.5 million. Then the military was frustrated in its attempt to get a lien on the country's youth through permanent peacetime universal military training. The campaign for UMT, despite its intensity and unscrupulous efforts to exploit the nation's fears, ran up against two difficulties: People were suspicious of the military's intentions; and the notion prevailed that, since atomic bombs and the delivery planes constituted the heart of our military strength, there was little need for huge standing forces or reserves.

The military's problems were compounded by the lowered financing available to them in the early postwar years, the budgets of 1947, 1948, and 1949 running at approximately $14 billion, $12 billion, and $13 billion. Writers have described these budgets as "skimpy," "starved," "inadequate," "paltry," "parsimonious," not realizing how their language betrayed the seeping of militarist bias into their bloodstreams. Things were not that desperate, comparative figures make it clear. After the First World War, the level of postwar military expenditures was three times higher than prewar expenditures; the order of the increase after the Second World War was eight times higher (in constant dollars). In 1939, when the European powers were rushing their armaments in anticipation of the coming war, Germany's military budget was about $4.5 to $5 billion, and Britain's under $2 bil-

lion. Even if we double these figures to take into account the price inflation in the interval, they are still well below the initial postwar
American budgets. Nor were the increases to be explained by the
higher costs of atomic techniques. Once the research was completed,
atomic weapons were relatively cheap. In short, in any meaningful
comparisons with the past, the first Truman peacetime military budgets were fabulously high.

What was at issue to some, however, particularly the military, was
not comparisons with the past but whether these budgets were adequate to ensure our security and, what was more cogent, to carry out
our new-found world responsibilities. But if $12 to $14 billion was not
enough, how much did we need, and how were we going to spend
the larger amounts? Viewed as a device to make others bend to our
will, the employment of the military establishment was severely circumscribed. Byrnes with his atom bomb monopoly could not subdue
Molotov at the London Foreign Ministers Conference. Chiang Kai-
shek, dependent on American support, could not be made to obey our
wishes. If a $12-billion military host gave us x power, it did not nec-
essarily follow that a $24-billion host would furnish us with $2x$ power.

What held down the budgets in the first postwar years was not
doubts about the military mystique—that was to come a few administrations and internal crises later—but economic conservatism. Truman was a hard-money, balanced-budget man, stoutly upheld in his
views by Snyder and James Webb, then his budget director. When
the Joint Chiefs tried to take advantage of his inflammatory March
17, 1948, speech (in which he blamed one nation for holding up
peace) to press for supplemental multibillion-dollar appropriations,
his Economic Council chairman, Edwin Nourse, warned him that
more military spending would aggravate inflationary pressures, pose
the need to "set aside the free market practices" dear to both their
hearts, and "substitute a rather comprehensive set of controls of materials, plant operation, prices, wages, and business credit." Truman answered that he was on the right track: "We must be careful that the
military does not overstep the bounds. Most of them would like to go
back to a war footing—that is not what we want." At a news conference that fall, he said it was his hope that the international situation
would soon permit a reduction of the military budget, "for the country could not go on spending fourteen to fifteen billion dollars a year
for defense."

A similar stand was taken by the Eberstadt Committee, part of the
Hoover Commission nonpartisan investigation of the executive

branch of the government. Its report on national security stated that current military costs were "unduly high"; that they were "already imposing strains on the civilian economy and on the underlying human, material, and financial resources on which effective military strength depends." This conviction was inevitably transposed into Cold War epistemology—all questions from civil rights to the need for more college scholarships were to be discussed in this framework —that the Russians had a plot to bankrupt this country. Congressman George H. Mahon explained to the House that his committee was not considering the higher military estimates of the Joint Chiefs because "Nothing would please a potential enemy better than to have us bankrupt our country and destroy our economy by maintaining over a period of years a complete readiness for armed conflict." Forrestal, the Savonarola of the Washington crusaders, and the first Defense Secretary after the passage of the 1947 unification act, was torn between conflicting allegiances. On the one hand he was intriguing with the military to circumvent the White House limitation on military spending. On the other hand, his banker's mind clicked the same way as Eberstadt's and Hoover's. He wrote to his friend, "Ham" Andrews, chairman of the House Armed Services Committee, at the end of 1948:

> Our biggest headache at the moment, of course, is the budget. The President has set the ceiling at 14 billion 4 against the pared down requirements that we put in of 16 billion 9. I am frank to say, however, I have the greatest sympathy with him because he is determined not to spend more than we take in in taxes. He is a hard-money man if ever I saw one, and believing as I do that we can't afford to wreck our economy in the process of trying to fight the "cold war," there is much to be said for his thesis of holding down spending.

The budgetary restrictions, added to the resolves of the Army and Navy not to be pushed into inferior positions by the Air Force, led to intense rivalry breaking out into ferocious internecine battles. In time, military outlays tripled and quadrupled; we arrived at the blessed "age of atomic plenty" in which the technologists were turning out atomic weapons that could be fired through cannon, carried by light planes, delivered by rockets; the Navy turned the tables by devising an atomic submarine equipped with nuclear missiles; and all three services carved out assured positions for themselves in the lethal enterprise. The rivalry, though not eliminated, became regularized. While developments were uncertain, competition for the military dollar was fierce, and each service clung to its own exclusive strategy which assigned the central position to its own organization and weaponry.

Truman's concern that military outlays would disrupt the economy was not ill-founded, as later events were to prove. It was better founded than the inane prognostications of the neo-Keynesians, hypnotized by their comparisons of military budgets with a rising gross national product. But the managers were unrealistic in thinking that they could continue with banker's principles at home while undertaking the role of world policeman abroad. When the incompatibility of the two was forcibly impressed upon them, they threw caution to the winds and resolved the dilemma the way Forrestal had more timorously tried to resolve it earlier. The grand reconsideration got under way when it was learned in September, 1949—three years earlier than had been anticipated—that the Soviets had exploded their own atomic device.

The year had begun with the news that our ally in China had suffered a disastrous defeat at the hands of the Communists, followed soon by their occupation of Peking and Tientsin, the crossing of the Yangtze, and Chiang Kai-shek's ignominious escape to Formosa. This fearful development coincided with the Alger Hiss trials, in which were aired accusations that a high State Department figure had turned over government documents to a Soviet agent. It was in this atmosphere, tense and ominous, that Truman issued his directive at the end of January for a crash program to produce the hydrogen bomb, at the same time instructing the State and Defense secretaries to conduct a study reassessing foreign and military policy. The hydrogen bomb leaped into officials' minds as the way to stay ahead the minute it was learned that Russia had broken the American atomic monopoly.

There had been disagreement among the technicians. It was not established at the time that a hydrogen bomb was technically feasible. A crash project would interfere with the successful program that was building up the atomic stockpile, raising the power of the bomb to twenty-five times the energy of the Hiroshima bomb, and developing entire families of lesser atomic weapons. What was the purpose of a megaton monster? On strictly military grounds, neither need nor prudence spoke in favor of a crash program. The advisory committee of experts voted against it, supported by three out of five members of the Atomic Energy Commission. Albert Einstein went on television to state that "radioactive poisoning of the atmosphere, and hence annihilation of any life on earth" was within range. But the logic of the arms race overbore and overrode all other considerations and objections. If we did not build a hydrogen bomb, the Russians would or might build one—and then where would we be? For Truman, that settled it. No further consideration was necessary. Earlier, when they were working on the international control report, Acheson had brought Oppenheimer to the White House. The physicist startled Truman by blurting out, "Mr. President, I have blood on my hands." Truman and Acheson had little patience with that kind of talk. "Don't ever bring that damn fool in here again," Truman told Acheson afterward. "He didn't set that bomb off. I did. This kind of sniveling makes me sick." Acheson averred that it made him sick also.

Acheson and his new planning head, Paul Nitze, now took the lead in driving through a recommendation for a heightened arms program in what became known as NSC-68. The document, worked out in the course of six weeks' meetings with representatives of Defense, posited the Manichean struggle adumbrated by the President in his Truman Doctrine speech. It identified the Kremlin as the source of evil, and drove home the idea that if peaceful means failed we must be ready and willing to fight for our way of life. It rejected the possibility of negotiations except on the basis of power, refused to countenance the concept that the Soviet Union could be contained by mere economic pressures, and eliminated any line of differentiation between national and global security. The crisis was to be understood not as of the moment, or of a short period, but as the fundamental shape of international relations. The conclusion was a call to action: a massive armaments buildup beginning with the United States and radiating outward, to surpass that of the foe, so that the West could respond to each challenge promptly and unequivocally.

Acheson and the others decided not to spell out the precise costs of this program, although the paper did state that 20 percent of the gross national product could be devoted to security without bankrupting the economy. In their private discussions, the Acheson planners estimated that the buildup they had in mind would require an annual military budget of $50 billion. Kennan and Bohlen had serious objections to parts of the paper. They objected to the description of the nature of the Soviet threat. Kennan was opposed to the emphasis on preparing for general war. Acheson gave short shrift to both them and their objections. So far as he was concerned, the side with the biggest battalions would decide the issue. He was not interested in the niceties, and he refused to become tied up in disputations of conflicting strategies. "The task of a public officer, seeking to explain and gain support for a major policy," he wrote, "is not that of the writer of a doctoral thesis."

NSC-68 was still under consideration when the Korean war started in June. How extensive the armaments increase would have been but for that is unknown. With the war as the spur, restraint was cast aside. The four-year statutory limits on manpower ceilings were suspended and supplemental budgets rained down on the military. The 1951 budget, which had originally been submitted for $13.5 billion was ultimately authorized for a total of over $48 billion. The feverish mobilization for the Korean war did not decelerate arms movements to Europe or for general purposes. Like a mighty locomotive engine, it carried every conceivable auxiliary, Pullman, and caboose, after it. Although almost all Air Force calls in the Korean war were for ground-support fighters, the major expenditures for expansion were going for a mightier strategic armada. Although the initial request for NATO military support was for $1.2 billion, in July it was augmented by a supplemental appropriation of $4 billion. In NSC-68/4, which Truman approved at the end of the year, the guidelines for fiscal 1952 were set for a war-ready military establishment: the target date for overall rearmament advanced from 1954 to 1952. George Humphrey, Eisenhower's Secretary of the Treasury, was to say that "two more years of Truman budgets would have meant Communism in America." Eisenhower expressed the same thought with less hyperbole: Such huge military expenditures were an "intolerable burden" that would destroy "civilian morale." Yet defense costs continued to average $44 billion in his eight years at the White House.

The sorcerer's apprentices had learned how to turn it on but not how to turn it off.

15

China
Trauma

While Acheson was skillfully piloting NATO through the legislature, the pivot of our position in the Far East collapsed. Kennan could declare offhandedly not to worry about it. "Japan, as we [in the Planning Staff] saw it, was more important than China as a potential factor in world political developments. I considered then, and hold to the opinion today, that if at any time in the postwar period the Soviet leaders had been confronted with a choice between control over China and control over Japan, they would unhesitatingly have chosen the latter. We Americans could feel fairly secure in the presence of a truly friendly Japan and a nominally hostile China—nothing very bad could happen to us from this combination." But his reassurances demonstrated that he, and others in the State Department who thought like him, had an inadequate understanding of the new power configurations that were forming. The United States government could not take a breezily philosophical attitude to the Communist triumph in China.

In a major sense, this was what the war in the Pacific was about. Had Roosevelt and Hull consented to a Japanese suzerainty over China, an accommodation might have been worked out between Imperial Japan and ourselves on other matters in dispute. It was the

American insistence that the Japanese get out that forced the Emperor's advisers to the choice of giving up their main imperial ambitions or taking us on. Our government's intractability was not because of sentimental and philanthropic ties with this ancient civilization, or because of our undeviating principle to make war on all aggressors. We had no difficulty in containing our disapproval in other circumstances. Nor was it because of enormous economic interests; American investments in China in the 1930s were less than a quarter of a billion dollars. Our trade with China amounted to 5 percent of our total trade. We were doing far more business with Japan. Our determination to push Japan out of China, and bind China to us, originated not from sales charts but from our reading of the future.

For a hundred years, the imaginations of traders, investors, missionaries, and government officials had been fired by the possibilities for amassing incalculable advantages and riches in China. For a hundred years, we had been piling in with other imperialist powers to force unequal treaties on Chinese governments. We had censored British imperialism while participating in its benefits—like the Austrian empress who joined with Frederick the Great in the partition of Poland, weeping as she grabbed. With the passing of our own frontier, we established a new one across the ocean. After the war with Spain, we had acquired the Philippines and Guam, annexed Hawaii, seized part of Samoa, enunciated the Open Door for China. Over the years, individual trading companies and investing consortiums had built great fortunes in the China market, but it had not become a major field for American economic expansion. China's internal disorganization, revolutions, and warlord depredations, the wrangles of competing imperialists, and the poverty of the Chinese masses had thwarted the hope. But the vision of an immeasurable future haunted the makers of our foreign policy from the dark days of the Stimson Note of 1932 after Japan occupied Manchuria to Hull's final peremptory demands preceding Pearl Harbor.

We had fought a long, sanguinary, and costly war to smash Japan. We had made the Chiang Kai-shek regime dependent on our favor, and had put up the scaffolding for a new world order in which China was to be accredited as one of the four major powers and our assured ally. We were ready to realize the dream of Admiral Alfred Mahan, Theodore Roosevelt, Albert Beveridge, John Hay. Then, suddenly, the fruit of our exertions was snatched from our grasp by a foe more contemptuous of our political and property rights than the Japanese empire-builders. Is it any wonder that Congress and the press felt that China had been stolen from us and looked for scapegoats? But this calamitous upset of our plans for the Far East was not due to incidental mistakes; it was due to the untenability of the entire design. It was not a case of an inexperienced Truman reversing or bowdlerizing the policies of a wise predecessor. Truman followed the line chalked out by Roosevelt, to the extent that one was discernible. The policy had collapsed during Roosevelt's tenure, but in his customary manner he patched it with bits of string and paste, trusting to get it fixed once the war was won.

The essence of the China problem for the American global strategists was that the Nationalist regime was decrepit and palsied. It showed neither disposition nor ability to fight the invading armies; the Japanese invariably cut through Chinese formations with surgical finality. The only thing that stood in the way of their definitive conquest was the immensity of the country, the indomitable national spirit among the people, and, after Pearl Harbor, American aid. The government was a façade for the Kuomintang, which by the late 1930s was the decayed remains of Chiang's 1927 counterrevolution. To keep the peasant in harness while loading him with the crushing burden of wartime taxation and the expense of maintaining a larcenous regime required systematic repression. A regime that had been semi-fascist in its halcyon days took on the character of a racketeer operation under the grim pressures of war and isolation.

Chiang's troops were little more than a medieval mob of marauders, useless against the Japanese but pitiless despoilers of their own people. The Chinese masses dreaded them as much as the Japanese taskmasters. The army was the concentrated expression of a gangrenous society in an advanced state of putrefaction. The Americans on the scene were disconsolate. They had a war to win and an ally to shape up for the exalted role assigned her. It was apparent to them that unless drastic changes were put through, the Chinese theater would collapse, and large investments of funds and matériel lost. What made them frantic was that while forces were unavailable for the most pressing needs to hold off the Japanese, 450,000 of Chiang's picked troops were blockading the Chinese Communist forces in the north. Eager to get on with the job of "fighting the Jap," they wanted all the Chinese to unite their efforts for the common cause. The Chinese Communists were no longer the ragged bands who, after the incredible 6,000-mile Long March from Kiangsi in 1934, had settled with their 20,000 survivors in China's northwest. They now, according to reports, commanded an army of 900,000 regulars and a reserve militia of 2 million, and ruled an area of 300,000 square miles inhabited by 95 million. They had expanded into Shansi and Hopei, had outposts at the Great Wall and the approaches to Manchuria, and were conducting aggressive guerrilla raids against the Japanese armies in the four northern provinces.

When in May and June, 1944, American correspondents and later a military observers mission were permitted to visit Yenan, they were favorably impressed. The correspondents found the people better fed and more energetic than in other parts of China. The once barren land of North Shensi had been transformed into a flourishing region of intensive cultivation and stockbreeding. The troops were self-supporting; they had no need to live off the peasantry. The Communist armies, the reporters avowed, would make valuable allies. The military observers were equally impressed. They found high morale everywhere. The people had a sense of mission; there was no bureaucracy. John Stewart Service, a political adviser attached to theater commander Joseph W. Stilwell's headquarters, reported that the Chinese Communists had matured and would not be easily destroyed. He advocated American aid to serve a twofold purpose: enlisting effective support against Japan, and forcing the Kuomintang to compete with the Communists for the backing of the people.

Representatives of the Democratic League, a federation of small, middle-of-the-road parties and liberal figures, had been urging our embassy officials to demand from Chiang democratic reforms and a coalition with the Communists in exchange for continuing American support. Otherwise, America would be arming and reinforcing a corrupt, reactionary regime that would plunge the country into civil war. This tallied with American opinion, and the Kuomintang leaders were belabored with advice and suggestions along these lines—without avail.

Military events now intervened to bring about a showdown between China and America. In April, the Japanese launched a new offensive, code-named ICHIGO, to knock out American air bases and secure a solid line of communication from Tientsin to Canton. As her forces swept westward from the Yellow River to the gap in the Peking-Hankow Railway, the thirty-four Chinese divisions in Honan melted away before the assault, leaving the province in chaos. In their wake, Communist units from neighboring Shansi filtered in. In June, ICHIGO's second phase opened with a drive from Hankow toward the American bases in the east. It was then learned that the Chinese general staff had made no plans for their defense. On June

18, Changsha, the key to the railway and the richest rice-producing area, fell, and the economic, social, and military crisis became more unmanageable. Service said in another widely read report that, while the regime would probably survive for a while, its collapse was only a matter of time.

The Americans were aroused by the prospective loss of their air-fields, built at enormous cost, and of their planes, which had been diverted from more active fronts. On June 15 Clarence Gauss, our ambassador, met with Chiang on instructions from the State Department to urge on him once again an agreement with the Communists to free troops on both sides for the struggle against Japan. A few days later, Henry Wallace met with the Generalissimo to go over the same weary ground. Roosevelt had shipped Wallace off to China at this time to get him out of the country while the vice-presidential nomination was being decided. He had told him that for the first time he was worried that China would not hold together to the end of the war. At this point, the Joint Chiefs of Staff came up with their solution to the China crisis. Roosevelt was to request the Generalissimo in plain soldier language to make Stilwell, the hard-driving, outspoken commander of the American forces and Chiang's chief of staff, supreme commander of all Chinese forces "charged with full responsibility and authority for the coordination and direction of the operations required to stem the tide of the enemy's advances." The situation in China was "so desperate" that "radical remedies" had to be "immediately effected," for "the future of all Asia is at stake." Marshall handed the red-hot draft to Roosevelt, and Roosevelt, at wit's end, sent off the letter.

It is not clear whether Marshall and Roosevelt understood fully the implications of their demand on Chiang. For Chiang, in his shaky position, to hand authority over his armed forces to an American general, one already in control over dispensing lend-lease, might have toppled him from power. Were the consequences not that extreme, Chiang would have been reduced to a puppet of the Americans. Even had he been on good terms with his chief of staff instead of having running fights with him over the years, there was no chance of his capitulating to this incursion on Nationalist sovereignty. The Nationalists may have had a death wish, historically speaking, but the hard-bitten Kuomintang chieftains had no intention of stepping aside while they held levers of power. Chiang was in no position to turn down the proposition in the way he would have liked, but weeks went by while he temporized, stalled, spun out discussions with Washington.

By September the military crisis had become acute. After a month's rest, the Japanese resumed their drive into Kwangsi. Theodore White, covering the campaign, reported that the Chinese Sixty-second Army disappeared in five days of fighting. The troops of a relief army, the Ninety-third, had starved while marching down from the north. When they arrived in Kwangsi, their first act was to raid the rice dumps at the railway station. The commander promised the American liaison group attached to him that he would hold the position to the last man. When the Americans were awakened at night by the sound of marching feet, they found that the Ninety-third was abandoning the pass before a shot had been fired. "Such incidents happened again and again in the campaign."

By this time, American strategy in the Pacific had veered so that China was no longer the important war theater of before. In mid-June, when Gauss was still trying to persuade Chiang to mend his ways, U.S. Marines and Army ground troops invaded Saipan in the Marianas, and in a fierce three-week battle took the island. Construction of airfields for B-29s started almost immediately. After the Democratic convention, Roosevelt met with MacArthur and Admiral Chester Nimitz at Pearl Harbor and approved the campaign to retake the Philippines. An air and sea assault on Japan from the Pacific islands was in prospect. At the second Quebec Conference between Roosevelt and Churchill, the decision to center activities next on the Philippines and other islands was confirmed; within weeks, the Joint Chiefs voted that no American landing would be necessary either on Formosa or the Chinese coast; and Harriman and Deane were to take up with Stalin and General Antonov Russia's participation in the war against Japan, subsequently agreed upon at Yalta.

From a strictly military viewpoint, therefore, China's inability to repulse the Japanese was no longer decisive for American battle calculations. China had proved a military cipher, and Pacific strategy had taken that into account. Chiang's military forces had to be maintained for a holding operation, but that was all. The telling blows against the enemy were to be dealt by other forces. Politically, shoring up the rickety regime and coming to some arrangement with the local Communists was more pressing than ever. The climactic phase of the Pacific war was approaching. A firm Chinese government had to be at hand when Russian armies began driving into Manchuria and north China if disastrous consequences were to be avoided. Marshall, bitter that the air transport furnished China to no purpose possibly cost an extra winter in Europe, produced another cutting near-ultimatum to Chiang, which Roosevelt again approved. If Chiang withdrew behind the Salween, which he had threatened to do, "we will lose all chance of opening land communications with China and immediately jeopardize the air route over the Hump. For this you must yourself be prepared to accept the consequences and assume the personal responsibility. I have urged time and again in recent months that you take drastic action to resist the disaster which has been moving closer to China and to you. I am certain that the only thing you can do now to prevent the Jap from achieving his objectives in China is to reinforce your Salween armies immediately and press their offensive, while at once placing General Stilwell in unrestricted command of all your forces."

The full force of this outburst was blunted by the representations of Patrick Hurley, the President's personal emissary, whose presence reassured Chiang that he could count on continued American support. Hurley was a tall brigadier general-millionaire lawyer out of Oklahoma. With his mane of white hair, stiff gray moustache, beribboned uniform, and flow of stump oratory, he appeared a plenipotentiary extraordinary out of Gilbert and Sullivan. He had been Hoover's War Secretary and, as a tame Republican, a useful international envoy for Roosevelt. Although shrewd and worldly, he was out of his depth in the China maelstrom, his vision further obscured by his wanting to be ambassador to China and to accomplish what had eluded Americans heretofore. Some of the foreign staff personnel nicknamed him "the Paper Tiger"; Kuomintang officials gave him a more poetic sobriquet, Ti Erh Ta Feng, "the Second Big Wind." He arrived in early September with Donald Nelson, whom Roosevelt sent to China for a similar reason that he had dispatched Wallace: to get Nelson out of Washington when Nelson's feud with Charles E. Wilson was splitting the War Production Board. Whatever its deficiencies as a war machine, China was invaluable as a tourist haven for our failing politicians and administrators.

Chiang now turned the tables by demanding Stilwell's recall. He pretended to be willing to appoint an American to command the Chinese forces, but not Stilwell, who had been insubordinate and was not competent for the high post. Through all the ensuing haggling and intriguing, Chiang remained obdurate. Marshall wanted to continue the struggle, but Roosevelt had had enough. The limit of pressure had been reached. Unlike some junior embassy advisers who were willing to risk the Nationalists' fall, he saw no alternative to Chiang's government. He gave Marshall direct and explicit orders to get Stilwell out of China without delay. When Stilwell heard of this by the grapevine, he wrote his wife: "If old Softy gives in on this as he apparently has, the Peanut [Stilwell's private name for Chiang] will be out of control from now on." *The New York Times* broke the news with a sensational article by Brooks Atkinson. Stilwell's recall represented the "political triumph" of a regime described as "moribund," "antidemocratic," "unrepresentative," "autocratic," "coldhearted"; the act had committed the United States to continued support of an "unpopular and distrusted" crew. He called Stilwell the ablest field commander in China since "Chinese" Gordon. Stilwell would not adopt "a reverential mood toward the Generalissimo," but even had he been a diplomatic genius, he could not have overcome Chiang's "basic unwillingness" to risk his armies against the Japanese. The article opened the flood gates, and correspondents told the sordid tale they were not permitted to publish through the years of the China buildup. Joseph Harsch of CBS said it was "the bursting of a great illusion."

Our officials in China came to understand that the troubles with Chiang arose out of disparate aims. The Americans wanted Chiang to enlist the Communist forces in the common cause of fighting Japan. Chiang wanted to husband his military forces for the day when he could resume his fight to wipe out the Communists. He had said, "The Japanese are a disease of the skin; the Communists are a disease of the heart." What was military logic to the Americans was the counsel of death to Chiang. The attendant proposal that he liberalize his regime to win more popular support for the war effort sounded like a gallow's joke to him. Did not the Americans understand that bringing Communists and anti-Kuomintang liberals into the government would dislodge his already precarious hold? His strategy was based on the ancient dictum for dealing with militarily stronger alien powers: "Use barbarians to control barbarians." Let the eager, pushy, rich Americans defeat Japan; he would then use the armies he was refusing to expend, and the resources he was holding in reserve, to crush the Communists and reassert his rule over China.

If Chiang had no intention of accepting American advice, did Roosevelt have no other alternatives? Service had returned to the United States to make another plea for utilizing and arming the Communist forces, without reference to the Nationalist government, as Churchill had cooperated with the Tito forces while recognizing the royal Yugoslav government. The American political context made it impossible to play with such adventures. A McCarthyite-type outburst would have broken over the country had the attempt been made. Roosevelt evinced no interest; he ignored offers of the Communist leaders to come to Washington for discussions. Aid to the Communist forces was dependent on their subordination to the Nationalists in an inclusive government. There was confusion in government circles as to precisely what the Chinese Communists were—a confusion due more to ignorance of their history than to their own propaganda. But whether they were "margarine Communists" or "radish Communists" (red outside, white inside) as Stalin described them to Harriman, or "agricultural reformers," as some thought, or "so-called Communists," as Roosevelt referred to them, neither he nor others who mattered were about to equip and set loose armies whose allegiances were unclear and who might be disposed to start a revolution once the Japanese had been defeated. Power in China had polarized to two political extremes—the Kuomintang and the Communists. Given its aims and design, the United States saw no alternative to the alliance with Chiang.

When in February the embassy's political officers, exercised enough to violate protocol and go over Hurley's head (who by then had his ambassadorship), sent a joint telegram reopening the question and renewing their proposal, Roosevelt upheld Hurley against his staff, who were all reassigned to other posts. Hurley remained under instructions to prop up the Chiang regime—and continue to work for unification of Nationalist and Communist forces. How this was to be accomplished was not specified and no one knew. For months thereafter, pointless negotiations went on with Hurley shuttling between Chungking and Yenan. His reports to Washington were without focus, and the answers he received would have been more suitable as pulpit sermons where no immediate results are looked for than as instructions to an envoy. The discussions continued out of inertia. There was no way of reconciling the irreconcilable. This, then, was the dolorous China legacy that Truman inherited.

Events continued to move on their foreordained course. In April, T. V. Soong, Chiang's foreign minister, came to Washington to collect $200 million, the outstanding balance of a $500-million loan or gift made in 1942. He told Truman he wanted to use the money for gold purchases to ease the inflation raging in China. Truman referred him to Treasury, where the request stirred up a storm. Staff officials produced statistics to demonstrate that gold sales would aggravate rather than reduce prices. They also drew up a memorandum on how the previous loan had been used to line the pockets of the Soong family and other government insiders. Soong answered Morgenthau's counterproposal of a stabilization fund in the usual style of Nationalist bargaining: a combination of blandness and blackmail. China needed the loan to strengthen her hand for coming negotiations with Russia, and he referred to his country "as a volcano which may erupt at any moment." Morgenthau's aides then pointed out to their chief that the justification for the loan was not economic, "it was going down the drain," but there was a political consideration: "We do want to maintain this particular government." Soong got his money. As anticipated, the gold hoard did nothing to abate inflation. From China Hurley reported that the gold policy "has given rise to vicious speculation and much unfavorable publicity." To the Communists, the loan was more eloquent testimony of American purposes than the movements of our peripatetic ambassador, particularly since their own request for a small loan for arms was ignored.

In the summer, Mao Tse-tung publicly attacked Hurley for making the Chiang regime more reactionary by his outright endorsement, "creating a civil war crisis." Although the military situation had stabilized, armed clashes between Communist and Nationalist troops were becoming more frequent. It is remarkable how American officials were able to slither over the incipient civil war that could tear to shreds all their plans and projects and center on traditional preoccupations of big-power politics. At Potsdam, Harriman was agitating Stimson about the Open Door for Manchuria, and Stimson, in turn, was trying to agitate the President to make Stalin nail down a firm commitment. Stalin had already given a sweeping commitment to Hopkins in the Moscow pourparlers, but Harriman and Stimson wanted another, probably in writing. Next, Harriman and Byrnes were maneuvering with Soong to make Stalin write into the treaty with China that Dairen was to be a "free port," claiming that Stalin was making demands that went beyond the Yalta Agreement. It was probably they who were trying to constrict the agreement, which stated that "Dairen shall be internationalized, the preeminent interests of the Soviet Union in this part being safeguarded"—a traditional imperialist formula for special privileges.

Harriman and Byrnes were also fretting that Stalin, despite his agreements and assurances at Yalta and thereafter, would support the Chinese Communists and set up protectorates in Manchuria and north China. His bona fides should have been accepted by them since his sellout of the Communists in Greece, but they were still identifying Russia with revolution. They did not understand that this revolutionist-turned-bureaucrat had an innate skepticism of revolution, that he believed Chiang was fated to retain power, that he was advising Mao to submit to Nationalist authority. Stalin's vision extended no further than a re-creation of the old, warlord-ridden, stagnating China, with Russia reestablished in the Czarist conquests lost in the earlier war with Japan. Capitalist and Communist were alike in their lack of comprehension of the underlying, irrepressible theme of the China passion.

The next act started with Japan's capitulation. Truman immediately promulgated General Order No. 1, investing the Supreme Allied Commander, General MacArthur, with control over the Japanese surrender everywhere. Japanese commanders in China, Formosa, and Indochina were instructed to surrender only to Chiang and his representatives; in Manchuria, North Korea, and Karafuto, to Soviet armed forces; in the southeast and Malaysia, to the British; in Japan, South Korea, the Philippines, and elsewhere, to the Americans. Stalin was entirely agreeable to shutting out the resistance groups throughout the Far East, but he had a sharp exchange with Truman over his own territorial ambitions. He demanded that Soviet forces receive the surrender in the Kuriles, which had been assigned to the Soviet Union at Yalta, as well as in the upper half of Hokkaido, the northernmost of the four major islands of Japan. Truman would agree to the Kuriles provided the United States received military-commercial air bases on some of the islands. Hokkaido, he told Stalin, was out. All forces in Japan would surrender to MacArthur. Stalin answered that he was amazed at the American attitude, that the claim for bases in the Kuriles had not been made at either Yalta or Potsdam, that "demands of such a nature are usually laid before a conquered state," in which category the Soviet Union could not be included. The disagreement, with its undertone of animosity, was permitted to drop away in favor of the more important bickering over occupation policies in Japan.

The Chinese Communists, not waiting on Stalin, lost no time in asserting their own interests. As early as August 10, Chu Teh, the Yenan military commander, ordered the Japanese to surrender to his forces in the liberated areas under threat of destruction. "Our troops have the right," he announced, "to enter and occupy any city, town, and communication center occupied by the enemy or the puppets." He followed this up with identical notes to the American, British, and Russian governments demanding the right to participate in the surrender and control of Japan. Chiang answered forbidding Chu Teh to take any independent action and commanding him to await orders. Washington answered that the United States, Russia, and Britain had agreed that Chiang was to receive the surrender of Japanese forces and hoped the Communists would cooperate with him. General Albert C. Wedemeyer, who had replaced Stilwell, had already been directed to help the Nationalists move their troops to key areas, give them the support they needed, and accept Japanese surrenders on their behalf. But true to Washington's habit of playing hide-and-seek, he was also instructed not to become embroiled in the civil war by taking sides.

Hurley had arranged for the resumption of negotiations. While Mao Tse-tung and Chou En-lai were holding pseudofriendly discussions with Chiang in Chungking, and again Washington received hopeful reports from her ambassador, the race was on for occupation of the surrendered areas. During September and October, American planes and ships moved large Nationalist armies to east and north China, while 50,000 American Marines secured ports and airfields at Tsingtao, Tientsin, Peking, and Chinwangtao, and occupied the Peking-Shanhaikuan railway system. Communist forces were deployed north and west of Peking in a position to cut north-south rail communications; other troops were moving into Manchuria. By November clashes were mounting in number and involving more men, and American forces had to back off from landing at Chefoo after a Communist warning. Wedemeyer, in pressing for a clarification of his conflicting orders, said the following propositions had to be understood: It was impossible to unify China and Manchuria with American assistance without becoming involved in the civil war; and it would be impossible to do so, in any case, unless forces and shipping were provided "far beyond those now available or contemplated in the area."

American help was not getting Chiang reinstalled in the northern provinces. His military weakness reflected his lack of popular support. Wrote Edmund Clubb, American consul general in Peking, "The restoration of Nationalist rule over Japanese-occupied territory was accompanied by one of the biggest carpet-bagging operations in history." Nationalist generals reached for the fleshpots. The swarm of civilian officials was less interested in government duties than in grabbing anything movable. Roofs, paneling, and plumbing of residences and office buildings disappeared, tools of workshops and equipment of hospitals were looted and vended on the streets. When General Hsiung Shih-hui, Chiang's proconsul for Manchuria, arrived by American aircraft at Changchun with five hundred of-

ficials and conducted himself like the traditional warlord, the population turned hostile. As soon as Communist forces infiltrated the
area, an opposition local government was set up and the Hsiung
mission had to beat a hasty retreat. Similar stories were told in all
parts of Manchuria.

There were accusations that Stalin was merely going through the
motions of helping to reinstall Nationalist rule while actually helping
to arm the Communists. It is doubtful that Kremlin instructions to its
commanders went that far. The Soviet generals in the area did not interfere with the movements of the insurgent bands; they took the position that the conflict was an internal Chinese affair in which they
would not intervene. They left no heavy military equipment on departing, but did not prevent local Communist forces from acquiring
Japanese stockpiles of light ordnance and munitions. Kremlin instructions were clearly more explicit in plundering Manchuria. Chiang
was informed that enterprises that had serviced the Japanese military
would be regarded as "war booty." Gold in the banks was confis-
cated. Great stocks of commodities were bought with so-called "Red
Army notes" to be redeemed by the successor government. Plants
were stripped of machinery and parts. The area that had been built
up by Czarist and Japanese investments into the most industrialized
center of China was ravaged. With less excuse than in Germany, Stalin was exhibiting the same narrow-minded misanthropy.

In the midst of this growing crisis, Hurley tossed the bombshell of
his resignation. He had been in Washington since the end of September and was becoming increasingly disgruntled, developing a fixation
about foreign service officers who were, he believed, plotting against
him. His resignation came in a ranting letter of violent accusation, an
augury of the McCarthyism to come, which was to destroy, in passing, the careers of Service and many other China officers. He charged
that "a considerable section of our State Department is endeavoring
to support Communism generally as well as specifically in China,"
and named officers as guilty of betraying secret information to the
Communists and misrepresenting American policy. It can be surmised
that Hurley concluded it was hopeless to continue trying to bring the
two sides together, that this was a good time for him to get out, and
to do it in a cloud of dust. He was planning to run for the Senate
from New Mexico.

Truman, anxious to blot out any unfavorable public impression,
asked Marshall, only recently retired as chief of staff, to go to China
as his personal representative. Marshall accepted the thankless as-

signment. The terms of Marshall's mission were the same as those of Hurley's, or of Gauss's or Stilwell's. Again there was a flurry of conferences and discussions; then Marshall accompanied by Byrnes went over to the White House for a final session with the President and Leahy. Marshall summed up the position as follows: he was to try to induce both sides to make concessions toward a truce and the development of a representative Chinese government. If the Communists refused, he was authorized to transport government troops to oppose them. But if Chiang refused, and the project broke down, he would still support the Nationalist government and provide assistance for the movement of its troops, lest abandonment of the Generalissimo mean a divided China and a probable Russian resumption of power in Manchuria, "resulting in the defeat or loss of the major purpose of our war in the Pacific." The President and his Secretary of State concurred that this was exactly our policy. The only difference between Marshall's mediation and the earlier ones was that the civil war was already on, and that he had the authority to control American military movements to lend weight to his mission. Why did Truman and his advisers renew the haggling and exhorting after the many previous attempts had failed? They saw the disaster approaching like a raging storm across a treeless plain, and they could think of nothing else to do. Roosevelt had tied America's fate in the Far East to a rust-cankered machine, and there was no way to disentangle ourselves from the engine of our own devising without abandoning "the major purpose of our war in the Pacific."

While the inner core of American officialdom knew that the Nationalists were standing on a quaking bog, nobody anticipated the complete engulfment that was to come, not Truman, not Stalin, not Mao Tse-tung. Chiang and his crowd thought things were going their way. They had managed to maneuver themselves into the position where the two military powers in the area had crushed Japan for them and were pledged to their support. The United States, under the all-purpose formula of disarming the Japanese, was ferrying their troops to the points of combat, equipping with the latest armament thirty-nine new Chinese divisions plus eight air wings, giving them all manner of help in the struggle against the Communists. Because of American largesse, they had come out of the war with Japan with foreign exchange holdings of $900 million, far more than they had when the war began. The surface appearance was good. Sumptuous parties in the dining rooms of expensive restaurants were in progress again in Shanghai and Nanking where the talk was that the Communists could not stand up against the new Nationalist armies that America was equipping and training. At parties in the foreign correspondents' club atop the eighteen-story Broadway Mansions in Shanghai, where White Russian mistresses mingled with the American wives and black market speculators with embassy personnel, there was the deceptive feeling of a return to normalcy. After all, America was the greatest power in the world, and what America wanted was what would decide the issue.

Initially, as was the case with Hurley's negotiation, Marshall seemed to be making good progress. A "Committee of Three," composed of Marshall and representatives of the two sides, was set up, directing subsidiary truce teams for field investigations. The committee agreed on a truce effective January 13, while a Political Consultative Conference, made up of delegates of the Democratic League and the Youth Party as well as the Kuomintang and Communists, began holding sessions. Resolutions were adopted for an interim coalition government and the convening of a national assembly. This was followed by an accord between the Nationalists and Communists to integrate the Yenan forces into a reduced national army. But the ink was not dry on these arrangements before they fell apart. The same malady that had struck down previous agreements made a mockery of these as well: The formula had not yet been invented for setting up a coalition of a Lenin and a czar. It was not that the Yenan Communists would have been satisfied with nothing less than hegemony over all of China; they were acutely aware of their dangers, and tended, if anything, to overestimate American abilities to direct events in China. But a genuine coalition government was an impossibility given the nature and intent of the Kuomintang. What the Communists might have settled for at this time—autonomous control over sections of Manchuria and north China—the Nationalists could not and would not grant. A concession of that magnitude would have meant for them, at best, the strengthening of the enemy until he was ready to press for complete power; at worst, the immediate discrediting and disintegration of their regime. They went through the ritual of negotiations to please the Americans, but they were confident they could crush the Communists in battle—an estimate that Marshall did not share—and were readying themselves for that engagement.

In early March, the Kuomintang Central Committee emasculated the agreements and rigged the elections for the forthcoming national assembly. By April, heavy fighting had resumed in Manchuria, and the Communists announced they would boycott the national assembly because of Kuomintang violations. At the same time, the United States earmarked an additional half-billion dollars for a loan to the Nationalist government and agreed to transfer surplus stock, with a procurement value of $1 billion, at knockdown prices. By summer, Chiang had started a reign of terror. Marshall's mission, in which he tried to combine the role of impartial mediator and munitions supplier to one of the contestants, became untenable when "Hands Off China" and "Americans Go Home" became popular rallying cries.

Marshall and Truman were disturbed at the turn of events. The President in August sent off a long appeal to Chiang taking note of assassinations and oppressions. He warned that "unless convincing proof is shortly forthcoming" of progress toward a peaceful settlement, we would have to reexamine our policy. Chiang unperturbedly replied that it was all the fault of the Communists. American support was sewed up. What did he have to worry about? On September 13 Marshall reported to Truman that he was stymied. On October 2 he reported that his mission was at a complete impasse. On October 5 he reported that he ought to be recalled. On November 15 Chiang convened the rigged national assembly, which, in the face of the boycott of both the Communists and the Democratic League, was just a renamed Kuomintang reunion, and Chou En-lai boarded a plane back to Yenan. At the end of the year, Marshall returned home. His mission had failed. Stilwell said, "What did they expect? George Marshall can't walk on water."

For the next two years, while the Nationalist armies were getting entrapped in the north, and the country sank under an inflation more ruinous than a plague, when entire armies defected to the Communists with their expensive American armaments, Truman's administration had no active policy except to continue to ship money and supplies. The Cold War with Russia was on in earnest and the managers were in the grip of assumptions that ranged from the half-true to the false. They thought the Western powers that had dominated world history for 400 years, would determine again the international course when rehabilitated by, and in alliance with, the United States. Once economically and militarily revived, this bloc would shift the balance back to the West and assert its supremacy, as of old, in every section of the globe. It took the disaster in China, and other disasters thereafter, to pound it into their heads that while the old powers retained importance, the pre-1939 balances and relations were irretrievably gone. The outright erroneous assumption was that revolution could be treated as a subhead of the Russian problem, so that if Russia was effectively contained, regional disturbances and civil disorders would die off of inanition or be easily broken. Since Russian troops had left Manchuria and Korea and been kept out of Japan, and Stalin's expansionist thrust seemed directed at Eastern Europe and Germany, the predilection to view Europe as the main battleground of the Cold War was reinforced.

When the full dimensions of the China disaster struck America in 1949, made more horrendous by coincidence with Russian acquisition of the atom bomb and the developing spy scare, the administration was subjected to a merciless assault that kept it on the defensive for the rest of its term. The attack inaugurated a witches' Sabbath whose principals could be recalled from their orgies only after four years of travail; which threatened to create a police state, and left a lingering odor of police-state deviltries. For Taftite Republicans, never enamored with Vandenberg's bipartisanship on foreign policy, the China debacle was the perfect issue to tear up the party truce and discredit Democratic administrations back to the New Deal. After the 1948 defeat, they—and before long, most Republicans—had concluded that past electioneering methods would not do, that they needed a new tactic and method if they hoped to return to office. Their frustration, added to their many setbacks, made them reckless and their politics irresponsible. They seized on the earlier controversy between Hurley and junior foreign service officers to blame Truman and his coadjutors for the Communist victory; to charge them with a policy opposite to that they had been pursuing. They pretended that the administration attempt to tame the Communists through a coalition represented a scheme to enthrone them, broadening the charge that Communist traitors inside the American government were the reason for our "losing" China.

The Republicans had no policy to counterpose to Truman's. The only basic alternative was to dispatch a full-scale expeditionary force to China. No important Republican had the temerity to propose this, even when the Taftites were flirting with MacArthur before and after his dismissal, although that was the implication of many of the philippics, spelled out more candidly in the envenomed harangues of Joseph Alsop, General Claire Chennault, and the China Lobby coterie. The Republicans were not primarily concerned with devising a counterpolicy. The business of an opposition, Taft said, was to oppose; and it was their hour of glory to bury Truman and his predecessor in the ruins of their own policy.

In April, senators called for an investigation of the State Department, hurled accusations that China had been "betrayed" and that the Secretary of State had "sabotaged" the Nationalist struggle. Press criticism grew lurid. Thinking to forestall the political explosion that would come with Chiang's final defeat, Acheson proposed to Truman that a thorough account of relations with China in the past five years be prepared for publication when the collapse came. Truman told him to go ahead, and a group of scholars headed by Dr. Philip Jessup went to work. On August 5, with the end in sight, the White Paper, an impressive 1,054-page compilation of policy summary and documents, was made public in support of the administration's rationale. As put by Acheson in his introduction, "The unfortunate but inescapable fact is that the ominous result of the civil war in China was beyond the control of the government of the United States. It was the product of internal Chinese forces, forces which this country tried to influence but could not." The only alternative policy was a major intervention which "would have been resented by the mass of Chinese people, would have diametrically reversed our historic policy, and would have been condemned by the American people."

Acheson imagined he would still the angry waters with this display of erudition and bureaucratic solidity; instead the waters surged higher, lapping at his own legs and shoulders. Anyone who had any connection with China policy was marked for extermination. Every explanation, regardless of its nature, was the occasion for a new outburst of epithet and indictment. Senator Hugh Butler of Nebraska, one of Taft's stable, roared, "I look at that fellow, I watch his smart-aleck manner and his British clothes and that New Dealism, everlasting New Dealism, in everything he says and does, and I want to shout, Get Out, Get Out. You stand for everything that has been wrong with the United States for years." Hurley came back to life to describe the White Paper as "a smooth alibi for the pro-Communists in the State Department who had engineered the overthrow of our ally, and aided in the Communist conquest of China." The China bloc called it a "whitewash of a wishful, do-nothing policy which has succeeded only in placing Asia in danger of Soviet conquest." After Taft decided to go for broke with McCarthy, he attacked "the pro-Communist group in the State Department who surrendered to every demand of Russia at Yalta and Potsdam, and promoted at every opportunity the Communist cause in China." Senator Wherry, now Republican floor leader, said Acheson was a "bad security risk" who had to go. The Republicans of both houses caucused and demanded his dismissal. When Truman offered a bill to name Marshall Secretary of Defense while permitting him to remain a five-star general,

Senator William Jenner of Indiana denounced Marshall as "a front man for traitors" and "a living lie."

Truman was righteously indignant that he, the Cold War leader, should be calumniated as "soft on Communism," and that his aides should have to wade in the muck of McCarthyism. What neither he nor his aides could grasp or would admit was that they had broken the ground for the emergence of this kind of opposition. For years, they had reiterated to the American people that insurgency was a conspiracy emanating from the Kremlin to subvert decent governments for the sole purpose of satisfying the expansionist lusts of a grasping, godless cabal. Just as the old open-shop employer used to protest that his happy, satisfied workers would never strike but for outside agitators who stirred them up, so in the mythical kingdom of Victorian virtue and cliché concocted by the administration, there were no angry peoples wanting to eliminate governing cliques who were making life unbearable for them. The world would bloom like a garden if Communism could be conjured away. Even in his statement releasing the White Paper, Acheson insisted that the Chinese Communists were working "in the interests of a foreign power," to be shortly strengthened into, "They were completely subservient to the Moscow regime."

Once one accepted the premises—and there were very few in the early Cold War years who were unaffected by the relentless propaganda—that revolutions, civil disorders, nationalist turbulences, and social struggles were the work of Communist agents, and that because of our incomparable wealth and virtue we had the responsibility to set things right internationally to protect our way of life, then a major question arose. What were the American officials doing while the Communists were overrunning China? Either they must have been stupid, or gullible, or were themselves in league with the Communists.

Moreover, in the pursuit of a major international policy there is an interaction of social elements as when a cue stroke sends billiard balls colliding. It had been pointed out at the time of the Truman Doctrine that containment required taking on for allies and clients all sorts of factions and juntas without inquiring too closely into their habits and dispositions. It was further necessary to whitewash and idealize them to justify the connection and the expenditures. If, at the next juncture of the play, the client was threatened by his own people, then the demand would inevitably arise to turn containment into intervention to safeguard the position. Did Truman and Acheson believe, when their policy collapsed in a decisive area like China, that the rhetorical attack they had perfected against Cold War dissenters would not be employed against them? That they could for the occasion discard their own demonology in favor of historical social forces?

The administration's plan to disentangle itself from an unprofitable and compromising alliance, and to move cautiously before fixing on its next strategy, disintegrated in the heat of the Washington furnace. The National Security Council, fearing early in 1949 that further shipments to Chiang would fall into the hands of the Communists, advised suspension pending clarification. Acheson let his literary talents get the better of him when, in the course of trying to convince a group of Republican congressmen of the wisdom of holding off further aid for the moment, he said, "when a great tree falls in the forest one cannot see the extent of the damage until the dust settles." The roar of anger that greeted his imagery could be heard all the way to Shanghai. The next day Senator McCarran introduced the China bloc's grand solution—a $1.5-billion loan to the Nationalists with customs collections in the major ports to be taken over by Americans to guarantee repayment. Acheson managed to get this screwball proposal tabled, but after the formal proclamation of the Communist government in the fall, he mollified the bloc by promising that the government would not be recognized. With the next turn of the screw America found herself resoundingly recommitted to the Nationalists. At the beginning of the new year, Senators Taft and William Knowland, dubbed by the press the "Senator from Formosa," joined by Herbert Hoover, demanded that a naval fleet shield Formosa from the Communists. Truman emphatically rejected the demand, stating that he did not intend to use American forces "to interfere in the present situation" and would "not provide military aid or advice to Chinese forces on Formosa"; only economic aid would be continued. Six months later, with the start of the Korean war, he dispatched the Seventh Fleet to Formosan waters. The China bloc had won its point. The retreat before the Republicans was on. The following year Marshall testified at the MacArthur Senate hearings that Formosa "must never be allowed" to come under the Communists; Acheson pledged that he would never consider recognizing Communist China or agree to her admission into the UN; Dean Rusk, the Assistant Secretary of State, declared that the United States recognized the refugee Nationalist regime as the government of China, that the Communist government was not Chinese, that American aid and military shipments were going to Formosa. The course was set for decades.

16

Intervention
in
Korea

June 24, 1950. A hot, humid Saturday ushering in the summer. Truman was home in Independence on personal business. The telephone rang—Acheson calling with the startling news that the North Koreans had attacked across the border. He had already arranged for an emergency meeting of the UN Security Council to call for a cease-fire. Truman approved the action, said he could return to Washington right away. Acheson saw no need for a night flight; he would report again the following morning when information would be more complete. By next day it was evident that a full-scale attack was in progress heading for Seoul and the Kimpo airport. That evening a grim session got under way at Blair House attended by the President, his State and Defense secretaries, service secretaries, the Joint Chiefs, and others. Without any hesitation, the President and his advisers decided to involve this country in the struggle of two factions in a small peninsula 7,000 miles away.

After they heard reports of battle developments, Acheson read the recommendations of the State and Defense departments: (1) Arms and equipment were to be rushed to the South Koreans over and above those already allocated under an existing program. (2) The Air Force was to protect Kimpo airport by attacking North Korean troops and planes approaching it. (3) The Seventh Fleet was to move into adjacent waters to prevent any attack on Formosa. Acheson also urged more military assistance for Indochina. What impressed Truman in the ensuing discussion was the unanimity of all present, "the complete, almost unspoken acceptance on the part of everyone that whatever had to be done to meet this aggression had to be done. This was the test of all the talk of the last five years of collective security." Dulles, who was in Japan working on the peace treaty, had an identical reflex. His message to the State Department read: "It is possible that the South Koreans may themselves contain and repulse attack, and, if so, this is the best way. If, however, it appears that they cannot do so then we believe that US force should be used even though this risks Russian countermoves. To sit by while Korea is overrun by unprovoked armed attack would start a disastrous chain of events leading most probably to world war." Governor Dewey sent along a statement solidarizing himself with the administration's actions.

Within a few days, the terrifying machinery of the world's mightiest establishment went into high gear. The program of intervention had been broadened, as news was received that the South Korean army was crumbling, to include the transfer of American ground troops from Japan to Korea, air and naval missions against North Korean targets, a blockade of the Korean coast, acceleration of military aid, and the dispatch of a military mission to the Philippines. Truman wanted to employ Chiang Kai-shek's troops in Korea as well; he was dissuaded from doing so by Acheson who thought the political cost and entanglement unwarranted, and by the Joint Chiefs who said the troops were useless for strengthening the South Korean forces and would become a drain on American resources.

What accounted for the almost instantaneous decision of the administration to set the wheels of war in motion before the military or political situation was clear? To reverse policy on Formosa, which was not immediately related to the Korean events? To buttress French colonialism in Indochina, 2,000 miles from the area of combat? And to draw the distant Philippines into the vortex of military decision-making? Truman, Acheson, and everyone else in the councils were convinced that the North Korean decision to move troops across the 38th parallel had come from the Kremlin, that the Korean battle was another inning in the contest between Communist Russia and Free America, that Stalin was testing American resolution and nerve as he had done before. If America failed to meet the test, horrific consequences would follow: disintegration of the Western alliance, the swing of Asian nations to neutralism, development of power vacuums, more audacious thrusts of aggression, and, finally, the inevitable world conflagration. In Truman's mind, this was a replica of the inter-war aggressions in Europe, Stalin's "Rhineland occupation" or "Austrian anschluss," so that unless set back in Korea, he would, like Hitler, become emboldened for more dangerous adventures. General Omar Bradley asserted the line ought to be drawn now, and Truman answered emphatically that it would be drawn now. It was not that Korea was necessary for our security or strategic position; it had not been included in our Far East defense perimeter. The decision to reverse strategy by commiting military forces to Korea came from fear of inaction. We could not let the other side have its way. It was a test of wills, and we had to demonstrate that ours was the stronger. Otherwise, the moving finger of fate would write of our descent to disaster.

None of the wise men had any doubts about this reading. There was no one at Blair House to interpose a cautionary word, because the reading fitted the political gospel of received wisdom. Just as militarists are said to plan the next war by fighting the last one over again, so our political leaders could interpret the unfolding events only by means of the Churchillian gloss of the 1930s. The Cold War brought on the stage the children of light and the children of darkness; put its imprimatur on sanctions against heretics; produced an exegesis based on misplaced analogies, and a sociology of the Stalin regime that was questioned by the author of containment himself. Kennan, who believed, like others, the North Korean attack had been triggered by the Kremlin, saw it as reaction to our readying a separate peace with Japan, not, as others maintained, arising out of the congenitally evil, expansionist nature of Communism. He also thought no one in Washington knew what it was all about. "Never before," he wrote, "has there been such utter confusion in the public mind with respect to US foreign policy. The President doesn't understand it; Congress doesn't understand it; nor does the public; nor does the press. They all wander around in a labyrinth of ignorance and error and conjecture, in which truth is intermingled with fiction at a hundred points."

On the governing fact: Did Stalin give the signal, or approve the decision, for the North Korean attack? No one knew then, and no one knows now. It remains one of the missing pieces of the Korean war puzzle. What should have prompted further investigation was that a military movement across the borders of an American ward was at variance with Stalin's generally cautious foreign policy, particularly where the United States was concerned. In the Berlin crisis, which he had precipitated, Soviet troops never attempted to move into West Berlin or to halt the airlift. A former member of the American occupation government in Korea concluded that the North Korean Communist leaders jumped the gun to entrap the Soviets into backing them. Whether that is so or not, it was something the United States government should have probed.

The invasion was not a bolt out of the blue. Every American official connected with Korea knew its volatile elements might explode at any moment. The division of the country at the 38th parallel had no justification on topographic, economic, or cultural grounds; it was especially objectionable for a poor, backward country because it thwarted natural exchanges between the relatively industrialized north and food-producing south. As in Germany, what was to be a temporary military occupation line was transformed, with the developing Cold War, into a permanent partition to which the Koreans would not be reconciled. Roosevelt's scheme for a four-power trusteeship over Korea, agreed to by Stalin at Yalta, and reaffirmed by Molotov, Byrnes, and Bevin at the December, 1945, Moscow foreign ministers conference, melted away in the rising heat of nationalist vehemence; the projects to set up a unified government disintegrated under the pressure of the East-West conflict. Again as in Germany, the Koreans in the north proceeded, under Russian aegis, to sweeping agricultural reform, nationalization of industry, construction of a Stalinist-type state. In the south, the American military government sponsored a Chiang Kai-shek type of regime based on rightist forces, headed by Syngman Rhee, a Princeton graduate, a Methodist, and a fascist fanatic.

After having set up their respective regimes, and armed their clients, the Russians and Americans pulled out their own troops, the Russians at the end of 1948, the Americans six months later. They were aware of the tinderbox they had left behind. The two halves of the country resembled Missouri and Kansas during the Civil War. Border raids, guerrilla forays, retaliatory killings were the order of the day. Both sides issued savage broadsides threatening to unify the country with the sword and mobilized their troops to lend credence to their threats. What precise miscalculation—an expected uprising in the south, or American noninterference, or both—led the North Korean Communist leaders at this moment to commit their colossal blunder, we do not know. That the invasion was the climactic stroke of three years of growing civil strife, and might therefore have come from North Korean initiative, was no secret to the Americans.

The White House people had no need to pursue this question because they had a doctrinal chart that informed them that insurgencies were part of the Kremlin's master plan to make trouble for the West in order to conquer the world; that like a spider, the Kremlin sat at the center of its cunningly constructed web, now pulling this thread, now that one, in order to entangle and undo its victims. "The attack on Korea was part of a greater plan for conquering all of Asia," Truman informed the nation. Walt W. Rostow, a high priest of the Cold War, intoned the familiar litany years later (after the master plan theory had been generally discredited among scholars):

> Stalin, working through the Cominform, launched an offensive in the East, which can roughly be dated from Zhdanov's speech of September 1947. It involved guerrilla warfare in Indochina, Burma, Malaya, Indonesia, and the Philippines. And after the Chinese Communists came to power, the offensive in Asia reached its climax in the invasion of South Korea.

American intervention in Korea was powered by the Cold War excitation, which had built up cumulatively its own dynamic, to which our prestige was tied. It gripped the minds of intellectuals as well as political leaders since it was homogenized with liberal liturgy. Isolationism and appeasement were the villains that made possible the rise of Hitler and brought on the Second World War. Had we rallied behind Wilson to join the League of Nations, had we signed up for collective security, then Hitler could have been stopped during the Rhineland crisis, and the calamity of the "unnecessary war" would never have overtaken us. Now, with Stalin cast in the role of the new Hitler, it was necessary not to repeat past mistakes. Internationalism, which had been for liberals a totem rather than a program, became a slogan that included and justified anything from a multinational conference for geodetic surveys to roaring imperialism.

Those who took solace in the belief that the Korean intervention would build up the UN as a peace-keeping agency could do so only by ignoring the realities in favor of legal forms and pretenses. The UN moves were the thinnest of façades for what was an American action peripherally supported by Britain. General MacArthur, the UN commander in chief, to the extent that he obeyed instructions, was under the direction of the American Joint Chiefs and State and Defense secretaries. The decision to throw in American naval and air forces, as continuing crucial decisions, was made unilaterally, with the UN then falling or being pushed into line. The "Uniting for Peace" resolution hustled through the General Assembly by Acheson and Dulles violated the UN's own statutes. It gave the assembly power to employ force which the charter had lodged exclusively in the Security Council. Although sixteen nations nominally contributed to the United Nations forces, the United States provided half the ground forces (and South Korea most of the rest), 86 percent of the naval power, 93 percent of the air strength. "Collective security" became a pseudohumanitarian mantle with which America, with a dependent Britain and France in tow, clothed her intervention, and sought to transform the UN into an anti-Soviet mobilization. Far from bolstering the UN, the action nearly ripped it apart. Law, international or otherwise, cannot transcend, much less overturn, the power realities from which it is derived.

At first it seemed as if Truman's decisiveness and confident assertion of American power would bring him back the popularity he had following the 1948 victory. The country's mood was reminiscent of the exaltation in the first hours of the First World War when crowds in London, Paris, Berlin, Vienna were waving little flags and cheering on their boys to the battle fronts. Joseph Harsch, Washington bureau chief of the *Christian Science Monitor*, wrote: "I have lived and worked in and out of this city for twenty years. Never before in that time have I felt such a sense of relief and unity pass through this city." When the President's statement was read in the House, the entire chamber (with the exception of Vito Marcantonio) rose to cheer. In the Senate the few grumblers were quickly put to rout by Knowland who shouted that in the Far Eastern intervention, Truman "should have the overwhelming support of all Americans regardless of their partisan affiliation"—whereupon the Senate broke into cheers and applause. Even Taft, who in his speech carefully prepared the record for the subsequent opposition, insisting that the President "had no legal authority for what he had done," and reiterating his demand that Acheson resign, made clear that he approved of the actions taken, and that if a joint resolution of support was introduced, he would vote for it. Truman, however, never sought congressional approval—a tactical mistake that was to haunt him. He feared that even in this hour of triumphant approbation, the submission of a joint resolution would provoke a nasty debate with a die-hard minority delaying a vote, all of which would damage his standing, and might lead to efforts to circumscribe his freedom of action. To escape the interference of a refractory Congress, Truman upheld presidential authority for dispatching the armed forces—the legal theory and historical precedents for this constitutional arrogation were set forth in a special State Department brief—employed by successor Presidents in subsequent crises.

Truman's early nervousness about committing ground troops to Korea was assuaged by a gratuitous Russian assurance. To the American note requesting her to disavow responsibility for the attack, and to influence the North Koreans to withdraw, the Soviet government replied on June 29 that the responsibility for the war was with the South Koreans "and upon those who stood behind their backs." Moreover, the conflict was an internal Korean affair, and Russia opposed foreign intervention in the domestic concerns of other nations. Acheson was scarcely surprised by the Soviet refusal to disavow an ally, but the real significance of the note, he pointed out to his confreres, was that Russia would not intervene. The Russian note obviated caution for another reason. Operating on the "Communist master plan" theory, Truman and his aides worried that the attack in Korea might be a diversionary tactic, luring them into this Far East pocket and then unfolding the major attack in Europe or the Near East. The Russian note was interpreted as dispelling these uncertainties. The way thus clear for the commitment in Korea, Truman gave MacArthur authority to employ all the troops stationed in Japan.

The battered, retreating South Koreans, reinforced with American troops, established and secured a beachhead at Pusan on the southeast tip of the peninsula facing Japan across 200 miles of water. In the middle of September, after weeks of preparation and the arrival of additional troops and transports from California, MacArthur, in an audacious movement, made an amphibious landing at Inchon, 140 miles up the western coast, behind the North Korean lines. As the forces at Pusan moved northward and those at Inchon fanned out southward, the North Korean army was trapped in a pincer. The Communist force was shattered; many killed or captured, the rest fleeing northward. By the end of the month, MacArthur had reached the 38th parallel, and Syngman Rhee had been reinstalled in Seoul—a brilliant military stroke. It should not be imagined that because the campaign lasted no more than three months, it was sparing of death and destruction. The introduction of a modern host with immense firepower into a primitive territory is a devastating experience. R. W. Thompson, reporting for a London paper, found the campaign "profoundly disturbing." He said that the slightest resistance brought down a deluge of destruction, blotting out the area and thousands of civilians. Korea was to become the grisly charnel house that formed when one side tried to overcome with manpower the other side's firepower. Seoul was a shattered city when the Marines finally fought through nests of snipers and suicide squads to plant the Stars and Stripes over a metropolitan inferno surrounded by hills blazing with napalm. "The coolness of the welcome received by the liberators is understandable," read a United Press release. "Despite communiqués that Seoul was spared, there is evidence everywhere of the pummeling it took from United States planes and artillery."

According to *Brassey's Annual* for 1951, the British armed forces yearbook,

> The war was fought without regard for the South Koreans, and their unfortunate country was regarded as an arena rather than a country to be liberated. As a consequence, fighting was quite ruthless, and it is no exaggeration to state that South Korea no longer exists as a country. Its towns have been destroyed, much of its means of livelihood eradicated, and its people reduced to a sullen mass dependent upon charity. The South Korean, unfortunately, was regarded as a "gook," like his cousins north of the 38th parallel.

The North fared no differently. Within a year, General Emmet O'Donnel was to testify that "everything" was destroyed. "There is nothing standing worthy of the name. Just before the Chinese came in we were grounded. There were no more targets." To pit the death-dealing superproducts of American engineering and industry against the technological poverty of the Orient was to produce lopsided casualty statistics. American casualties, at the end, stood at 142,000 out of a total of some 4 million; 1.3 million South Koreans, including civilians, 1.5 million North Koreans and Chinese, 1 million North Korean civilians.

The United States was in a position, when it regained the parallel, to close the dangerous operation, declare the war won, the Seoul government reestablished, the lesson taught that aggression would not be tolerated, the status quo restored. The continued existence of two Korean governments would have meant that new outbreaks were possible, but if Washington was resolved to send troops to every area of the globe where trouble was brewing, an army of 20 million and a war budget of $200 billion would not suffice. It had been stated the objective of American intervention was to push the Communist troops back to the 38th parallel. Acheson had so defined the task after the outbreak of the war: "Soley for the purpose of restoring the Republic of Korea to its status prior to the invasion from the North." This had been accomplished, and with the North Korean forces badly mauled, an armistice very likely could have been concluded. Unfortunately, the administration grand viziers got greedy. Now that the North Korean army was broken as an effective fighting force, why should they not rid themselves of the canker of the North Korean Communist regime? Truman had in mind the midterm elections, and that Knowland and others had noised it about that failure to cross the parallel would constitute appeasement of Russia. Truman and his advisers decided to press their luck.

The Joint Chiefs' instructions to MacArthur on September 27 were a study in bureaucratic canniness, an effort to push off on him responsibilities for decisions that Washington should have faced. He was to move across the border to destroy the North Korean forces "provided that at the time of such operations there has been no entry into North Korea by major Soviet or Chinese Communist forces, no announcement of intended entry, nor a threat to counter our operations militarily." After MacArthur's battle plan was approved by Washington, Marshall sent him an "eyes only" telegram saying, "We want you to feel unhampered tactically and strategically to proceed north of the 38th parallel," to which MacArthur replied, "Unless and until the enemy capitulates, I regard all Korea as open for our military operations." On October 1 he demanded that the opposing forces unconditionally surrender, and a week later, the UN General Assembly, reminding itself that it was theoretically running the show, weighed in with its resolution for military pacification in order to set up "a unified, independent and democratic government." MacArthur on October 9 issued his second pronunciamento that unless there was a prompt North Korean capitulation, he would "at once proceed to take such military action as may be necessary to enforce the decrees of the United Nations." The assembly, which according to the chartered laws, had no executive powers, was by now, in the escalated public relations rhetoric, issuing "decrees." An interim committee created by the October 7 resolution authorized MacArthur to take over the civil government of North Korea pending elections. Unification was to come, after all, by the terrible swift sword, the North Koreans cast as the victims rather than the executioners.

By now warning signals were not lacking from the Chinese. They were massing divisions at their border with Korea at the Yalu River. On September 31, Chou En-lai, in a speech celebrating the Communist government's first anniversary, said that China would not "supinely tolerate the destruction of its neighbor by the imperialist powers," a warning repeated several times thereafter. On October 3, Chou formally called in K. M. Panikkar, the Indian ambassador, informing him that should American troops enter North Korea, China would come into the war, but would refrain if only South Koreans crossed the parallel—a message duly passed on to Washington. The Chinese Communist government had just exchanged at Peking its treaty of alliance with the Soviet Union, an alliance that Chou pointedly referred to in his speech. But the Americans decided that these warnings and threats were just bluff, probably nothing more than an attempt to sway the vote at the UN. Their evalutation, sustained by four hundred years of Western contempt for Orientals, was that China lacked the ability to challenge the American force. As one official inelegantly put it, "I don't think China wants to be chopped up."

Truman was not one to neglect family obligations because of political crises. He planned to fly to Missouri on October 11 to attend exercises installing his sister as worthy grand matron in the Order of the Eastern Star. While glowing from this warming touch, the press suddenly learned that he was going on from St. Louis to Wake Island for a conference with MacArthur. Acheson begged off from accompanying him. "When the President told me of his intended pilgrimage and invited me to join him, I begged to be excused. While General MacArthur had many of the attributes of a foreign sovereign, I said, and was quite as difficult as any, it did not seem wise to recognize him as one."

There have been speculations concerning the purpose of a meeting that could not have been pleasurable for Truman. General Courtney Whitney, one of MacArthur's staff acolytes, wrote that MacArthur saw no sense in the conference, there was not a single thing discussed on which Washington did not already have his views. He concluded that the real purpose must have been to gather support for the administration before the midterm election from a personal association with the dashing victor of Inchon, as well as to build up an alibi in case Communist China decided to intervene—a "sly political ambush." White House staffers shared the former opinion; they thought it was "good public relations." Others surmised that the conference related to Truman's nervousness about MacArthur's inciting intervention by the other side with his high-and-mighty provocations. There had been Chinese protests over American air attacks. On October 9 two American F-80 jets strafed a Soviet airfield 62 miles inside Russian territory. Russia's protests had been ignored. It was only after the Wake conference that MacArthur acknowledged such an attack occurred due to "navigation error and poor judgment," while the State Department apologized to the Soviet government, offering to pay damages.

Whether Whitney's reasons, or the air attacks, explained the conference, to which can be added, for good measure, Truman's own inane explanation that he and his field commander ought to get to know each other, Truman accomplished one thing. He received solid assurance that there would be no counterintervention, and that the war was all but won. MacArthur told him that formal resistance would end by Thanksgiving and that he hoped to withdraw the Eighth Army to Japan by Christmas. To Truman's question about the chances of Chinese or Russian intervention, he answered: "Very little. Only about fifty to sixty thousand could be gotten across the Yalu River. Now that we have bases for our air force in Korea, if the Chinese tried to get down to Pyongyang, there would be the greatest slaughter."

With serene confidence, MacArthur moved his forces northward for the mop-up. On October 20 Pyongyang was taken with no resistance offered; the defenders had fled. The first captured Iron Curtain capital received its baptism of looting and witchhunting. When MacArthur arrived at Pyongyang airfield, he inquired genially, "Any celebrities here to greet me? Where's Kim Buck Too?" On October 24, when informed that he had ordered his commanders to utilize all their forces in the northward drive, the Joint Chiefs timorously pointed out that this was not in accord with the September 27 instruction to employ only South Koreans in the immediate area bordering on Russia and China. Back came one of MacArthur's imperious affirmations. He had lifted the restriction because of "military necessity." He called attention to Marshall's subsequent telegram and claimed the entire matter was covered at the Wake conference. The Joint Chiefs subsided. MacArthur's Tokyo headquarters had already announced that there was no intention of establishing a buffer zone that would constitute a new 38th parallel behind which the North Koreans could reorganize. Truman at a press conference on October 26 said it was his understanding that only South Koreans would approach the northern frontier. From Tokyo came the MacArthur response that "The mission of the United Nations forces is to clear Korea."

The march north was not to be a victory parade. Our boys were not to be home by Christmas, or the Christmas thereafter. A regiment of the South Korean Sixth Division, on its way back from the Yalu, after completing its mission of filling a bottle with water from the Yalu River for Syngman Rhee, had run into a trap at Unsan and been wiped out. To the west, a task force was set upon. At the end of four days of savage battle, the South Korean II Corps was no longer an organized force and the American Eighth Cavalry had lost half its strength and most of its equipment. Clearly some Chinese forces were on the scene, but MacArthur was slow to admit that his evaluation had been wide of the mark. On November 4 he cautioned Washington against "hasty conclusions which might be premature." Nevertheless, he ordered Lieutenant General George E. Stratemeyer to use all his airpower to knock out the Yalu bridges and all North Korean facilities and installations. Stratemeyer informed the Pentagon of the order three hours before his planes were due to take off. Washington officials doubted that bombing would halt traffic across the Yalu and saw danger in bombing Antung, across the border in Manchuria. Truman was reached in Kansas City. He agreed that the action should be postponed until justification for it was submitted, but said he would authorize anything necessary for security of the troops.

The Joint Chiefs thereupon reaffirmed their order against bombing within five miles of the border, stated that the United States was committed not to take action affecting Manchuria without consulting the British, and asked MacArthur for his reasons for the bombing order. MacArthur's rejoinder was sizzling: "Under the gravest protest that I can make, I am suspending this strike and carrying out your instructions. I cannot overemphasize the disastrous effect, both physical and psychological, that will result from the restrictions which you are imposing. I trust that the matter be immediately brought to the attention of the President as I believe your instructions may well result in a calamity of major proportion for which I cannot accept the responsibility." MacArthur was clearly engaged in an offensive against Washington as well as against the North Koreans. He violated a canon of military command relations by holding over the heads of his superiors the threat of the destruction of his troops in order to force a change of strategy. Truman backed off. Since MacArthur "felt so strongly" about it, he told Bradley to give him "the go-ahead."

When the Joint Chiefs informed MacArthur in this crucial week that the September 27 directive to destroy the North Korean army might have to be reexamined in view of Chinese entry into the war, MacArthur issued another blast that this would represent "the greatest defeat of the free world," that "to yield to so immoral a proposition would bankrupt our leadership and influence in Asia," that he meant to keep on going until he got to the border. Again the Joint Chiefs retreated. Neither they, nor Acheson, nor any of the others, had the temerity to take on the general. "I have an unhappy conviction," Acheson reminisced later, "that none of us, myself prominently included, served him [Truman] as he was entitled to be served." This is the technique of disarming criticism by irrelevant concession. Truman was no innocent bystander in the exchanges between the Joint Chiefs and the area commander; he knew what was going on. What inhibited him and his associates was fear of an open break with the proconsul in Tokyo. And added to this was awe of the MacArthur mystique. He had pulled off an unlikely coup at Inchon which the Joint Chiefs had opposed. Maybe he was about to work his magic again. Could they risk interfering with an offensive that might be the prelude to a conclusive victory? Irresolution and a gambler's hope combined to permit the march to disaster.

On November 24, MacArthur flew to Chongchon to launch the offensive. His magisterial communiqué read: "The United Nations massive compression envelopment in North Korea against the new Red armies operating there is now approaching its decisive effort. The eastern sector of the pincer has steadily advanced in a brilliant tactical movement and has now reached a commanding enveloping position, cutting in two the northern reaches of the enemy's geographical potential. This morning the western sector of the pincer moves forward in general assault in an effort to complete the compression of the vise. If successful, this should for all practical purposes end the war." He said to Major General John B. Coulter, "Tell the boys from me that they are going to eat their Christmas dinner at home." Within the next few days, his dream was shattered. The Eighth Army's offensive had scarcely started before massive Communist counterattacks exploded around its columns. The right flank disintegrated, and by November 28 the entire army was in flight. After the Marine division had to save itself by breaking out of the Choisin Reservoir area, the badly mauled X Corps had to be evacuated from Hungnam by a fleet of over a hundred ships. The campaign was over, the greatest defeat suffered by American arms since the Battle of Manassas.

Despite later intimations to the contrary, up to this time MacArthur had followed administration policy in the main. His manner had been insufferable, his contempt for the President and his associates ill-concealed, his rejection of tactical suggestions haughty—and he had been guilty of a number of provocations. But the decision to conquer North Korea had been the administration's, and so was the decision to send the fleet to Formosan waters and to resume aid to the Nationalists. Having only South Korean troops occupy the immediate zone adjoining the Manchurian and Russian borders, and the suggestion of the British and others to establish a shallow demilitarized zone in the north were distinctly second-rate questions preoccupying worried UN delegates who wanted to hunt with the hounds but avoid the risks of the chase. It was clear that the Chinese were concerned about the military presence of a hostile superpower on their borders. Deploying only South Koreans in the immediate zone or the creation of a shallow demilitarized zone while American forces were in command of the entire area would not have altered the basic military equation. The decision that counted was whether to cross the 38th parallel to wipe out the North Korean regime, or not to cross and retain the prewar demarcation and division. Once the decision for forcible unification was made, tactical variations left unaffected the substance of the risk. The later insinuation that the decision had been based on MacArthur's false advice at Wake was equally self-serving. Truman, Acheson, Marshall, the Joint Chiefs, knew the Chinese had armies massed behind the Yalu. Whether the Chinese would choose to use them was a political estimation for which they were not dependent on MacArthur. Though his omniscient pose was afterward an embarrassment to him, they had made their decision independently before the Wake conference. They suffered from the same malady that he did. "They [the Chinese] really fooled us when it comes right down to it, didn't they?" Senator Leverett Saltonstall asked Acheson. "Yes, sir," the Secretary acknowledged. Where MacArthur was vulnerable to criticism was in his special domain of expertise: in separating the Eighth Army from the X Corps with a huge gap of trackless mountain terrain open between the two forces and the flanks of both exposed, and in rushing ahead so recklessly after he knew that Chinese forces were in the battle area. Excessive self-confidence had grown into blundering foolhardiness when he permitted his technically superior army to be trapped into fighting on the enemy's ground and on the enemy's terms.

Now his raging ego dictated his further conduct. He was under the double compulsion of rewriting recent history and transferring the blame for the disaster onto other shoulders. His occasional pinpricks and provocations he now integrated into a systematic campaign to overturn administration policy, his scattered policy differences, he now built up into a counterposition. Press statements gushed from the Tokyo headquarters as water from an overladen mountain stream. The orders forbidding him to strike across the Manchurian border put his forces under "an enormous handicap unprecedented in military history." He told the Joint Chiefs that he was opposed to a defensive strategy, that "unless some positive and immediate action" was taken, "steady attrition leading to final destruction" was in the offing. Truman's patience wore thin. He ordered all military commanders to halt direct communication with publicity media on military or foreign affairs, and sent General Lawton Collins to the Far East to find out what was going on.

Truman himself added to the panic of that week with a rash utterance to the press that use of the atom bomb was under active consideration. His statement followed two earlier sensations. In August, Navy Secretary Francis Matthews had called for preventive war, thought by newspapermen to be a trial balloon of a cabal that included Defense Secretary Louis Johnson. This was followed by the announcement of General Orville Anderson, commandant of the Air War College, that the Air Force was ready and willing to bomb Moscow. Truman's statement set off a nervous debate in the British House of Commons and Attlee's hurried trip across the ocean to confer with the President. Collins returned with the report that it was MacArthur's position, or conditions, that if he was to continue under the restrictions imposed on him, the war was lost, evacuation was inevitable, and it was unnecessary to seek an armistice since our troops could disembark without one. If, however, we would accept full-scale war with China, MacArthur would be willing to combine the X Corps with the Eighth Army to hold a position across the peninsula as far north as possible. The British took a diametrically opposite stand. They wanted to grant Communist China recognition and a seat in the UN, negotiate a cease-fire around the 38th parallel, and liquidate the conflict.

The American planners decided on a course midway between the two positions. They were not going to negotiate; they were not going to recognize Communist China or admit her into the UN; they were not going to let Formosa go; but they would seek to stabilize a line in Korea, and avoid, if they could, a wider war with China. At the end of December, MacArthur was sent a new directive to defend "in successive positions" a line across Korea. If the Chinese committed great forces "with an evident capability of forcing us out," it would be necessary to withdraw to Japan. Until his dismissal a few months later, the tug-of-war went on between Washington and Tokyo, with MacArthur's peremptory warnings and threats keeping the Washington officials jumping in and out of crash conferences. But by January Matthew Ridgway, the new commander in Korea, had stabilized a line below the Han River. After a second inspection by Collins, MacArthur's influence on Korean events dwindled; the Pentagon's consultations thereafter were with the battle commander. MacArthur would not reconcile himself to the solution. He continued issuing statements, or inspired newspaper accounts, demanding the employment of Chinese Nationalist troops, complaining of the "inhibitions" forced on him, suggesting that under the given strategy the best that could be hoped for was a stalemate and an endless drain of blood.

In late March, when Seoul was retaken and allied forces were again moving up to the parallel, MacArthur was informed that a presidential announcement was to be issued to the effect that we were prepared to arrange a cease-fire. It was then that MacArthur perpetrated his major piece of sabotage. Without any notice to Washington, he broadcast his own demand on the Chinese in the form of an ultimatum. He threatened that if the Chinese did not accede, allied action "would doom Red China to the risk of imminent military collapse." He was ready to confer in the field to realize "the political objectives of the United Nations in Korea." With his message he had torpedoed the government's project. He also sent to Congressman Martin a letter of oblique attack on the administration: "Here we fight Europe's war with arms while the diplomats there still fight it with words; that if we lose this war to Communism in Asia, the fall of Europe is inevitable. As you point out, we must win. There is no substitute for victory." Martin read the letter to the House on April 5, after which newspapers carried sensational stories throughout the country.

Hurried consultations began, and the following week, to a group assembled in the President's study, Marshall announced that the Joint Chiefs had unanimously recommended that MacArthur be relieved of all his commands. The President concurred, and the draft orders for the recall were drawn up. Truman claimed that he had reached his decision earlier, but had moved circumspectly to obtain the unanimous agreement of the Joint Chiefs; essential reinforcement, Acheson thought, because "If you relieve MacArthur, you will have the biggest fight of your administration." In truth, MacArthur, in his manic imperiousness, had pushed the contest to the point where the President's constitutional authority was under avowed challenge, and his hand was forced. The issue had to be settled whether policy was to be determined in Washington or in Tokyo. It was ludicrous for the United States to set itself up as mentor to the world when it was not in control of its own government apparatus. In reasserting civilian supremacy, however, Truman, ironically, needed the authority of the Joint Chiefs—so thoroughly had decision-making become enmeshed with the military services, with the increment of prestige shifted to the latter in the minds of Congress and the public. The cord holding Damocles' sword was now cut, in whatever direction the weapon would plunge, and whoever would be its victim. At a Cabinet meeting, in response to the President's invitation to give his impressions of the last few days' events, Acheson said it reminded him of the story about a man who had a beautiful daughter. "All her life," he related, "the father took pains to protect the girl from any harm. He saw to it that she led a sheltered life and went with the right people. Finally, when she was eighteen, the girl came to him weeping and said, 'Father, I have to confess something to you. I'm afraid I'm pregnant.' Whereupon the old man threw up his hands and shouted, 'Thank God, that's over! I've been fearing something like this all my life!'"

The President now braced himself for the ordeal. MacArthur returned, not like a disgraced functionary, but a conquering hero. Taft, Wherry, Martin, and other Republican dignitaries caucused, then informed reporters that they had decided to invite the general to address a joint meeting of both houses of Congress, and intended to conduct a full investigation into the administration's foreign policy. In addition, Martin added ominously to the reporters, "the question of possible impeachments was discussed." The Democrats did not dare resist the Republican demands; they had to content themselves with bickering over procedural arrangements. On the Senate floor, Jenner charged that "this country is in the hands of a secret inner coterie which is directed by agents of the Soviet Union." Nixon thundered that MacArthur's recall represented appeasement of Communism. The Republican Policy Committee wanted to know whether the

Truman-Acheson-Marshall triumvirate was preparing for a "super-Munich" in Asia. McCarthy, to get himself heard above the din, called the President "a sonofabitch" who must have made his decision while drunk on "bourbon and benedictine"; that unless "Operation Acheson" was called off, "Asia, the Pacific and Europe may be lost to Communism," and "Red waters may lap at all of our shores." In San Gabriel, California, the President was burned in effigy. In Los Angeles, "Oust President Truman" stickers appeared on automobiles. The Illinois, Michigan, California, and Florida legislatures passed resolutions avowing their unqualified confidence in MacArthur. Enormous crowds ecstatically greeted the general in San Francisco, New York, and Washington. Seven and a half million people were said to have turned out for the parade in New York, compared to 4 million for Eisenhower when he returned from Europe. What is more decisive, according to the city sanitation department, 3,249 tons of litter were dumped on the streets as against 1,750 tons after Lindbergh's return from Paris in 1927 (although for a strictly scientific finding, it would be necessary to take into account the increase of the population in the interim). In his first public appearance after dismissing MacArthur, when he threw out the first ball at the opening baseball game of the season, Truman was roundly booed. The Gallup poll reported that only 29 percent of its respondents favored the President.

How account for this fantastic response to a general who defied the orders of the civilian authority? Didn't people care about the Constitution? Some have explained the public's bizarre behavior by the widespread dissatisfaction with the administration's limited war strategy, frustration with containment that did not contain, the shock of unexpected reverses. But the public had no specific feelings or fixed opinions, as was quickly apparent, on strategic concepts; the defeat in North Korea could have been blamed on MacArthur as easily, or more easily, than on Truman; and the general was crusading not for peace, but for a bigger war. The public's emotional spree had to be explained in the total context in which McCarthyism was flourishing. However, like a tropical deluge, its intensity was matched by its evanescence.

As the MacArthur hearings ground along day after day, and week after week, people got bored with the general's mystique, and his God-bless-America oratory. Talk of MacArthur-for-President died down. When he attended a ball game at the Polo Grounds, a recording of a seventeen-gun salute was played, and the general stood up in his box decorated with the Stars and Stripes and a five-star flag, to inform the crowd how overjoyed he was "to witness the great American game of baseball that has done so much to build the American character." Afterward, as the MacArthur party trooped out before the rest of the audience, walking across the diamond toward the centerfield exit to the strains of "Old Soldiers Never Die," the crowd roared with laughter when a voice of purest Bronx vintage cried out, "Hey, Mac, how's Harry Truman?" In two months, the spell had been broken. MacArthur had lost his gamble. He did not get the opposition party nomination; the Republicans picked another military hero.

The MacArthur hearings conducted by the Senate Armed Services and Foreign Relations committees started May 3 and went on for two months, during which time 2 million words were spoken, with complete transcriptions (very lightly censored) distributed daily to the reporters. The hearings were the climactic explosion of the Great Debate on foreign policy that had begun to billow after Truman announced on December 19 that he was sending more troops to Europe to fulfill the NATO program. The midterm elections had resulted in Democratic losses, the appearance of new ultraconservative faces in the legislative halls, the retirement of some prominent liberals through McCarthyite onslaughts, and the emergence of Taft as the unchallenged Republic leader on Capitol Hill. Since the line of betrayals-at-Yalta-and-Potsdam, Alger-Hiss-and-Communists-in-the-State-Department, and the loss-of-China had proven its worth, Taft and his cohorts were primed to press the battle home. National unity around the Korean war was of shorter duration than MacArthur's victorious advance. The war was exacerbating all the tensions, divisions, and frustrations of the postwar society. One had to go back to the Civil War for political struggles of equal ferocity conducted in the midst of war.

The debate opened with Hoover's introduction of his "Fortress America" thesis, to be followed by Wherry's submitting to the Senate a resolution that no ground troops be sent to Europe without congressional authorization. Taft rose in the Senate on January 5 to make his major speech. Time and circumstance were in his favor. By the very act of setting himself up as a critic of the administration and of the war after the Chongchon disaster, he occupied the position of a people's tribune voicing the growing disillusionment. He was unable to rise to the occasion. He could not construct a working opposition platform for two reasons: because his own inconsistencies and muddle mirrored the situation in his own camp, that the gripes and maledictions issuing from the country clubs were more useful for chamber of commerce harangues than for serious policy positions; and because he could not drive his major propositions to logical conclusions because the Republicans were split.

The emphasis on land war in Europe, he declared, was strategically ill-conceived, politically disastrous, and financially ruinous. NATO would create the very conditions it was designed to forestall. Russia, in fear of a coming invasion, would be incited to a war that she might not otherwise undertake. Not only was the policy provocative; it was self-defeating. Administration strategy would fight the Communists on their own terms. The Russians could atom bomb the ports on which our troops depended for reinforcements and supplies, precluding even another Dunkirk. It was an illusion to think that NATO with its projected 60 divisions could succeed where Napoleon with his Grande Armée and the Germans with their 240 divisions, had failed. Financially, the policy was equally foolhardy. There was practically no limit to the size or expense of such an army. Even with the President's present program of 25 divisions, obviously insufficient to control the land areas in Europe and Asia, the costs were at the very limit of, or beyond, our economic capacity. If we continued in this reckless manner to overuse our economic strength, bankruptcy and collapse would inevitably result. The entire present trend was to ever bigger government, proliferating bureaucracy, increasing controls, higher taxation, stifling of individual initiative, and restriction of individual liberty, the very totalitarianism or socialism whose destruction was the purpose of our efforts. The solution was building up our air- and seapower into an irresistible force for the control of the Atlantic and Pacific (with one frontier, as spelled out by Hoover, on Britain, the other on Japan, Formosa, and the Philippines), while preserving the Western Hemisphere inviolate. As for the European nations, they had the manpower, industry, and resources to establish strong forces of their own. We could help, but the initiative and forces had to be theirs, and our own main attention was to the areas which our air- and sea might could dominate.

In the light of world realities and subsequent experiences, this was an alternative strategic variant for pursuing the Cold War, neither as fantastic nor as fatal as administration spokesmen made it out to be. But as the debate went on with mounting intensity, the Taftite offensive lost its policy cutting-edge. It became a grab bag of irresponsible changes of front, contradictory demands, demagogic assertions. The Great Debate was reduced to electioneering oratory. Taft pulled the rug from under himself, and from under his crucial charge that the administration was taking the country to bankruptcy and disaster when he offered his own budget: $20 billion for the Navy and Air Force, $20 billion for the Army, $25 billion for all other purposes. This contrasted with Truman's budgetary request of $41.5 billion for the military, $7.5 billion for foreign aid, $23 billion for the rest. The difference of $7 billion was by no means a negligible one, but to propose a $40 billion military budget and a $65 billion total government budget as a return to frugal, limited government, was farcical. He was no less cavalier with the principle of land warfare. At one point he wavered in his opposition to NATO by saying he would not object "to a few more divisions, simply to show the Europeans that we are interested." Marshall seized on the opening. How many divisions was "a few more"? The administration was proposing to send four divisions in addition to the two that were stationed in Europe. "A few" was certainly more than two, three anyway. The Great Debate over strategy was thus a bickering over one division. In the end, the Senate resolution stated that no ground troops beyond the four divisions should be sent to Europe without further congressional approval, and that was passed merely as an expression of the sense of the body, while approving and implementing the administration course by the appointment of Eisenhower as NATO commander and plans to rearm Germany.

Some have tried to glean out of Taft's dispersed attacks and fugitive asseverations an attachment on the part of Republican stalwarts to the nineteenth-century ideal of limited government, a weak Executive, a dominant legislature, to illustrate how out of touch Republicans were with the times. Taft and Company ideas were not that well thought out; their interest in statecraft more fleeting, opportunist, and dictated by momentary partisan needs. The subsequent Eisenhower and Nixon administrations were no less traders in Big Government and an overriding Executive than those of Truman, Kennedy, and Johnson. It would have been a rash prediction to have maintained that had Taft, a man of pronounced elitist temperament and habits, reached the White House, he would have resembled Buchanan or McKinley, rather than Roosevelt. Major struggles for greater congressional authority in relation to the Executive have invariably been waged not for abstract principles of governance, but in the pursuit of opposing political aims. When, later, faith in the Cold War declined, when the strong Executive's power for lightning interventions had lost its glitter, Fulbright, from a different vantage point, and for different reasons, took up the Taft argument for a return to the constitutional balance between the Executive and Legislative branches.

Even during these dog days of the Truman Presidency, when the McCarthy cabal was calling into question whether traditional constitutional processes would continue, the President was making the foreign policy and war decisions. He was spat on and reviled, but the scepter remained in his hands. Congress, as an institution, was not a partner in forging the changes that were revolutionizing American society. Congress could be querulous and noisy, it could make life difficult for administrators, it could block projects and force through appointments; but it did not have the will to assert countervailing power. It was split into a dozen parts on what it wanted, because its machinery for decision-making was antiquated and inadequate for the formulation of policy, because most of the politicos were dependent on patrons who were more interested in Congress as a vehicle of obstruction, stalemate, and special favors than as a creator of the national design. The initiative, the big prestige, and with it, much of the power, had passed to the Executive.

17

Troubles
on the
Home Front

Taft helped make the MacArthur legend and cult. His faction had made its own the call for a wider war on China as soon as the general went on the offensive against the administration. In the second round of the Great Debate, begun after his recall, MacArthur became, during the Senate hearings, the opposition's spokesman. The opposition program was wrenched from its Hoover moorings and tied to MacArthur's geopolitics in which "the whole epicenter of world affairs rotates back toward the area whence it started." It was not a drift to uncharted waters; Taft, Knowland, and others had always believed Asia was the decisive battleground.

Both administration and opposition partisans tended, under the compulsions of the debate, to make the differences more orderly and definitive than they were. Both sides started with the same premises: There was a Communist conspiracy to conquer the world; the Korean war was a single engagement of that battle; it was necessary to contain and crush Communism. The immediate issue was whether to wage a limited war, as the administration was doing, or to promote a wider war with China, which MacArthur wanted. MacArthur denied the validity of the administration concept. You go to war after exhausting all other means. Once at war, you use all means at your dis-

posal to crush the enemy. You cannot fight a "half-war." The administration has introduced a new unheard-of concept that "when you use
force, you can limit that force—the concept of appeasement." The administration aim to go on fighting indecisively with no mission except
to resist meant that our cumulative losses would be staggering, with
no results achieved. Better to end the war on the enemy's terms than
to continue this bankrupt course.

The Joint Chiefs, in rebuttal, easily knocked down MacArthur's
specific proposals—blockading China, destruction of her industrial
capacity by naval and air bombardment, employment of Nationalist
troops in Korea and on the mainland. They demonstrated that neither
a blockade nor bombardment promised conclusive results, and recalled that MacArthur himself had recognized that use of Nationalist
troops would be a liability. It was a debater's point they won, however, made possible by MacArthur's deliberately piecemeal formulation of his war-with-China strategy. They understood that if these
proposals were accepted, others would follow once America was committed to an unlimited war. As Bradley testified, "If you go to an all-
out war with China, I think you would have to do something like the
Japanese did. Go in and try to get a decision. I do not believe you
could get any decision by naval and air action alone. We have only
to look back to the five long years when the Japanese, one of the
greatest military powers of that time, moved into China, and had almost full control of a large part of China, and yet were never able to
conclude that war successfully. I would say from past history one
would jump from a smaller conflict to a larger deadlock at greater expense." What has been considered the resounding refutation of Mac-
Arthur's position was contained in Bradley's winged phrase that it
would "involve us in the wrong war, at the wrong place, at the wrong
time, and with the wrong enemy." This sounded persuasive and
clear-cut, but administration theory and practice were not in perfect
alignment. While the administration was rejecting MacArthur's proposition, it was shipping arms and supplies to Chiang Kai-shek, had
sent in a training mission, instituted a partial blockade of the China
coast, vetoed her admission into the UN, and given Ridgway secret
orders that in the event of air attacks from Chinese bases, or other
unrevealed contingencies, he was to strike at China outside Korea. At
the least, the difference between the two positions was not absolute.

Much was made of the belief that MacArthur's course would lose
America her allies and possibly break up NATO. When asked
whether we should proceed without support from other nations, Mac-

Arthur said that he hoped others would see the wisdom of his proposal, but if they lacked the sense to see where appeasement led, we would have to go it alone. At this, the self-proclaimed internationalists raised their eyes heavenward and exclaimed, "Can such things be?" Here was the ugly recrudescence of isolationism in a new guise. It was a forced issue. MacArthur was accurate in maintaining that our European allies were far more dependent on us than we on them, and the formal sixteen-nation alliance waging the good fight in Korea did not gainsay the reality that America and her South Korean client were shouldering nine-tenths or more of the burden.

Nor were Truman and Acheson disposed in actuality to show greater solicitude for the wishes of the allies. In the "collective security" UN venture, the Americans made decisions and then asked the UN to adopt ratifying resolutions. When Attlee pleaded for a less stiff-necked policy, Truman and Acheson would not give an inch. Truman said we were going to stay in Korea and fight. If we had support from others, fine; if not, we would stay anyway. When Attlee asserted that nothing was more important than retaining the good opinion of Asia, Acheson observed acidly that "the security of the United States was more important." He then lectured Attlee that the American people would not tolerate a vigorous policy against aggression on one ocean front while accepting defeat on the other. The last thing that Britain and France wanted was a full-scale war with China, but they would not and could not break with the United States or abandon NATO. No, reading into the MacArthur controversy a division over first principles was as arbitrary as MacArthur's harping on the enemy's "privileged sanctuaries," with no mention of America's "privileged sanctuaries" in Japan, Okinawa, and Pusan.

If an unlimited struggle with China was the wrong war at the wrong time, what was the right war and the right time? Here it came out that the administration was rejecting MacArthur's fantasy of an easy victory over China for the NSC-68 fantasy of its own. The right war was with Russia, the putative center and powerhouse of the Communist conspiracy, and the right time was on completing NATO's and our rearmament. That was why it was necessary, in the midst of the difficulties of the Korean war, to park troops in Europe, to assign a disproportionate part of our resources for strategic airpower for the test of wills to come. The statistics were impressive, if irrelevant. Western Europe had more steel capacity, more industrial plant, more shipbuilding facilities, more skilled personnel, more technical prowess, than the Soviet Union. Conquered by Russia, it would double her capacities. Allied with America, preponderant power was with the West. "I believe," asserted Admiral Forrest Sherman at the hearings, "that if we lose Western Europe, we would have an increasingly difficult time in holding our own. Whereas if we lost all of the Asiatic mainland, we could still survive and build up and possibly get it back." Since Western Europe was not like a pocketbook that one could lose or find, but consisted of a number of nations with their egotisms, ambitions, interests, and structures not invariably aligned with ours, and since they did not believe Russia was planning to attack, was Acheson's perspective more substantial than MacArthur's? Its major superiority was that his plunge was scheduled for the future while MacArthur's was immediate.

MacArthur replied, in effect, to his critics, "Look, I realize the contest is global and Europe is important, but here is where the Communists have elected to make the fight; consequently, here is where we must seek a military decision." When McMahon asked whether the Kremlin was the locus of the conspiracy, he answered, "One of the loci." When McMahon said that they were both agreed the Soviet Union was the main enemy, MacArthur rejoined, "I didn't agree to it. I said that Communism throughout the world was our main enemy." In the light of what Truman was doing at this time in Indochina and the Philippines, in China and Korea, in Greece and Italy, the difference here too was more in verbalization than either contestant, in partisan zeal, understood. At the focal point of the conflict, the administration was set to fight a limited war to keep inviolate its total war perspective—for elsewhere. Korea was a diversion from the main battleground. China would be a greater diversion. Two and a half years later, when both the United States and Russia were armed to the teeth and had the hydrogen bomb, instead of the grand testing of wills there was the grand stalemate. In the Senate debate, each gladiator was more successful in punching holes in the other's position than in advancing his own. It was not because they lacked ingenuity. It was because they had set themselves illusory goals.

In his initial announcement committing American air and sea forces to Korea, Truman included directives to redouble military assistance to the Philippines and Indochina. This was not fortuitous. Both countries were beset by armed rebellions led by Communists. In the Philippines, Truman helped the native oligarchy to put down a rebellion that was hampered by a lack of outside support. In Indochina, however, the decision makers stepped into a quagmire that proved more perilous than the Korean one.

During the war, Roosevelt played with verbal anti-imperialism, an historic strand of American Far Eastern policy. He wrote Hull, "France has milked it for one hundred years. The people of Indochina are entitled to something better than that." He offered the same nostrum as for Korea, a long-term, four-power trusteeship. It was not a working policy, however. Wrote the Pentagon Papers researchers, "Despite his lip service to trusteeship and anticolonialism, FDR in fact, assigned to Indochina a status correlative to Burma, Malaya, Singapore, and Indonesia: free territory to be reconquered and returned to its former owners." At Potsdam, America agreed that the British and Chinese Nationalists occupy Indochina, preliminary to the restoration of French rule. The State Department thereafter ignored Ho Chi Minh's many appeals at the conclusion of the war and after fighting broke out between the insurgents and the French.

By the time the Indochina war got hotter toward the end of 1946, the United States was arranging a $160 million credit for France to purchase equipment for use against the Vietnamese. American officials continued to assume the Ho forces were puppets of Moscow though a State Department intelligence report said that was unlikely. The attitude that underlay this and other suppositions like it came out during the conference with Attlee in a discussion on China. When Attlee observed that opinions differed on the extent to which the Chinese Communists were Kremlin satellites, Truman told him he was convinced of it. It was all part of a pattern, he assured his guest. After Korea, it would be Indochina, then Hong Kong, then Malaya. By now Acheson was not so sure of the Kremlin satellite theory; but that made no difference to him. He really was not concerned whether the Chinese Communists were satellites or not. He had concluded that they would act the same way in either case.

In the summer of 1949, with the collapse of the Chiang regime and the movement of Communist troops to the Indochinese border, Indochina took on new importance for Washington as a dike, a levee, to contain the Communist flood. Moreover, after the administration "lost" China, if it "lost" any more countries to Communism, it is doubtful that it could have carried on. The State Department set up a review committee headed by Philip Jessup, which Acheson supplied with the following instruction: "You will please take as your assumption that it is a fundamental decision of American policy that the United States does not intend to permit further extension of Communist domination on the continent of Asia or in the Southeast Asia area."

Concomitantly, he was aligning American and French policies by calling on France to ratify an agreement handing over internal authority to the puppet government of Bao Dai. At the end of the year Truman approved NSC-48/2 "to block further Communist expansion in Asia by providing political, economic and military assistance to governments facing threats from Communist aggression, direct or indirect." The French parliament passed the ratification act a month later. Within a matter of days, the United States and Britain recognized Bao Dai. Peking and Moscow had already recognized Ho's government. In February, NSC-64 directed State and Defense to prepare "as a matter of priority," a program to protect American security in Indochina. The die had been cast. Indochina was locked into the Cold War—even had Korea never been interposed.

Three weeks after Anglo-American recognition, France requested and received military and economic aid that amounted to over $500 million. At the conclusion of the Truman term in 1952, the French, bleeding in the savage struggle with a foe who refused to bend the knee, pleaded for American volunteers and more finances. The United States was then carrying 40 percent of the war costs, and France had spent, since the struggle began, twice the amount she received in Marshall Plan aid. In briefing the incoming President, Acheson reported that Indochina was "an urgent matter upon which the new administration must be prepared to act." By mid-1954 America had put out $2.6 billion on Indochina.

The American people had no stomach for the kind of crusade into which it had been thrust in Korea. Within a few months the initial approbation had given way to grumbling, the enthusiasm to disenchantment, the crusade against Communism had become "Truman's war." Some attributed the rapid disintegration of popular support to Truman's lack of talent as a public tribune, to his inability to explain the reasons for sending out young men to die in the forbidding hills of that far-off land, to a communications gap. Eighteen years later, employing identical logic, cousins and younger brothers of this tribe of commentators, attributed the popular disillusionment with the war in Vietnam to President Johnson's communications difficulties. The explanation was akin to blaming a salesman's failures on his humdrum sales pitch rather than his shoddy product. The President had no need to rely on his own powers of persuasion. Being an orator would have been an asset; but it was no fatal weakness that he was not. An army of editorialists, newscasters, commentators, White House spokesmen, had been exhorting, inculcating, arousing, the American people, with every argument, through every medium of communication, on the morality and necessity of the Cold War from the time of the promulgation of the Truman Doctrine. If the country's most expensive journalistic and ideological talents could not sustain popular support, the fault was either with the war, or with the American people—not with the experts' hortatory efforts.

Truman's problem was of a different order. The American people had been educated to an anti-Communism both stereotyped and demonological. Balance-of-power considerations as well as Communism as an expression of immanent social struggles were muted in favor of a caricatured conspiracy whose agents imposed their will on unsuspecting peoples by force and fraud. Most people saw no relation between destroying the Communist conspiracy and spilling American blood to seize and hold worthless parcels of property where the "gooks" of the south greeted them with not much more warmth than those of the north. Kennan and others of the realist school had long ago criticized the Wilsonian tendency to depict America's purposes in foreign wars in terms of moral absolutes. The shortcoming of the realists' criticism was that it was not very realistic. Did they think that in the twentieth century it was possible to mobilize a literate and assertive people for balance-of-power wars by doing less than pointing to the stars?

The difficulty was compounded by the American state of mind at midcentury. It was not that the country was rent by class animosities. These had been reduced to subsidiary discontents, defused of social danger by conventional legislative, trade union, and other processes. It was that advanced capitalism had nurtured a consumer-ridden society of other-directed groupers. A voracious thirst had been bred into the public. An individual's worth, status, success, happiness, was established by the things he owned and intended to buy. The brave new world was a Huxleyan society whose individuals revolved around chrome-plated automobiles, split-level homes, well-tailored clothes, speedboats, and cameras, and an ever-expanding stock of gadgets for housekeeping and play. The surge was on for the good life of privatism, the suburbs, the cookout in the backyard, the enjoyment of leisure, and for those who lacked the wherewithal, as yet, of planning and preparing to partake of the sweets. The Korean war, therefore, had to be fitted into a life style that advertisers were convincing Americans was their mark of distinction. The government impresarios had to try to keep up the interest of a commercial society characterized by grab, by money lust, excessively materialistic in its wants, and not a little cynical about the motives of leaders.

In the Korean mobilization, the Truman administration displayed again its broker's proclivities with a marked listing to the conservative side. The President had the same essential attitude toward the problem that he displayed in his first two years, except that measures were taken from the reverse end, since he was mobilizing for war, not demobilizing at the conclusion of one. On July 19, in announcing a partial mobilization, he called for tax increases, credit restrictions, and allocation of scarce materials; he did not call for price and wage controls. The omission was noted and pointed to on all sides, since he had been belaboring Congress for the preceding years with demands to control prices. "Why did he seek price control in 1948 but not in 1950?" asked Lubell. "Could it have been that in 1948 he requested legislation which he knew would not be enacted so he could blame the Republican-controlled Congress for whatever happened, while in 1950 he feared that price powers would be given him, leaving him no alibi for failing to check the rise in living costs?" Congress, no novice at political maneuvering, included on its own initiative some discretionary price and wage controls in the Defense Production Act that became law in September. But this authority went unused for another five months. Leon Keyserling and other economic advisers were urging reliance on indirect controls; Keyserling, particularly, favoring an expansionary policy even if accompanied by some inflation. Truman, as a journalist reported, was an economic illiterate and did not have an inquiring mind. Indirect controls suited his predilections and natural bents because they appeared to interfere as little as possible with the free market, and avoided bringing into play the complicated, obtrusive bureaucratic machinery of direct controls.

Fiscal and monetary measures adopted were ineffective. The war and escalated government procurement set off a roaring economic boom. Employment shot past the 62 million mark, accompanied by an explosive buying spree in anticipation of shortages and higher prices. A second buying wave was set off at the end of November after the Chinese attack. By the time Truman put through his general freeze, prices of raw materials had gone up 50 percent. Marshall told Congress in the spring that rising prices since the Korean war had added $7 billion to procurement costs. Although Truman subsequently did his share of tub-thumping for stronger controls, and his congressional opponents handed him legislation leaking like a sieve, he was never to regain his standing on the issue. His failure to provide leadership in the initial seven months when inflation was at its worst had shaken public confidence that he could or would do anything about prices.

After MacArthur's disaster, when it was evident that the system of indirect controls was falling apart, the President, in mid-December, declared a national emergency. He set up the Office of Defense Mobilization headed by Charles E. Wilson, president of General Electric, who was given broad powers theoretically analogous to those held by Byrnes under Roosevelt. There were further weeks of vacillation and disputes among the experts; finally, on January 26, Truman issued his general freeze order to hold the line on prices and wages. That the controls worked very poorly is universally acknowledged; that they did any good at all is debatable. To the inherent difficulty of administering controls over an economy in which basic decision-making is in the hands of private corporations and banks, was added the aversion of the President and his entourage to another descent into the bureaucratic labyrinth of economic supervision. If the housewife was indignant about high prices, they feared she might be more indignant were there a return of rationing, disappearance of cheaper products, brand-name manipulations, tie-in sales, black marketeering. The limited nature of the emergency, the unpopularity of the war, Truman's lack of prestige, the vitriolic opposition attack, all militated against securing the measure of unity that Roosevelt had elicited a decade before. Patriotic exhortations to sacrifice for the commonweal dissolved with little trace in this political ether in which nihilism combined with apathy.

Truman initiated controls with the dedication of a man who starts looking for a job Monday morning hoping he will not find one. After he issued his hold-the-line order, the wage board ruled that increases of more than 10 percent above the January, 1950, base period required its approval. Labor representatives felt shortchanged. Prices had risen far more than wages, they said. No allowances were being made for substandard conditions or gross inequities but the price board was permitting increases in food prices, they added—and they walked out. The United Labor Policy Committee broadcast a condemnation of the 10 percent decision and a denunciation of Wilson and all his works. "Virtually the entire program has been entrusted to the hands of a few men recruited from big business." The labor leaders wanted more representation and an equitable policy affecting wages, prices, rents, and taxes. Truman had to list a bit to their side. He appointed several union officials as assistants to the mobilization heads, and reconstituted the wage board with additional authority to make recommendations for settling wage disputes involving defense workers. Two months after their leavetaking, the labor representatives trooped back to a board that in practice had vitiated its 10 percent ruling. The year before, the auto union had signed a five-year contract containing provisions for productivity improvement and cost-of-living raises, as well as allowances for health and pension funds. The board now converted this key bargain into national wage policy. Since Eric Johnston, the new economic stabilizer, was approving such wage and ancillary increases, he was all the more outgiving with industry's price prescriptions. The Capehart amendments of that year to the Defense Production Act tore additional holes in price regulations. They put the finishing touches to the unstrenuous playact.

The board avoided at its inception a confrontation with John L. Lewis, who had won a substantial wage increase, by ruling that contracts negotiated prior to the freeze order did not require board approval. But Truman was fated for another brush with the rail unions. Fallen behind prevailing standards of other major industries, they had been seeking a 40-hour week with no reduction in pay for a year to no purpose. The railroad workers were handicapped by the industry's deterioration and their own antiquated organization, split up as they were into almost two dozen craft unions led by a case-hardened officialdom. In June, 1950, the members rejected a presidential emergency board's recommendation for an 18-cent increase; they figured 31 cents was needed to maintain weekly pay. With an August strike date set, Truman seized the industry, placing it under nominal Army administration.

The ranks, greatly aroused, disrupted service with wildcat actions. In February, 1951, there was an outbreak of "sickness" in the Trainmen's union. Truman ordered them to return to work or lose their jobs, at the same time instructing the Army to put into effect part of the workers' pay demands. He angrily said at a press conference that the union officials acted "like a bunch of Russians" in breaking their agreement with him; to which charge the officials responded that their members had simply "exercised their democratic rights by rejecting an undesirable proposal in open voting." Government attorneys went into court with a motion for the imposition of fines of $1.5 million, and the union was fined $75,000 for criminal and civil contempt, and an additional $25,000 by a Chicago judge for its defiance in an earlier December strike.

In April, Johnston approved a cost-of-living settlement that the fifteen nonoperating unions had negotiated, so this section of rail employees was out of the battle. A month later, the Trainmen settled their two-year dispute. The Engineers, Firemen, and Conductors held out for another year. The last major stoppage occurred in March, 1952, when members of these three organizations tied up the Midwest lines, returning to work only after the government obtained an injunction against them. Finally, in May, they won their demands, in addition to a $100 million lump-sum settlement for back pay, ending the long controversy. The lines were formally returned to the owners.

It was the blowup in steel, however, that finished off the control setup and revealed the rickety structure behind the administration façade. The steel contract expired at the end of 1951, and since the companies would not agree to new wage and other demands, and the union was set to strike, Truman referred the dispute to the wage board. The board made known its findings on March 20, proposing that the workers be granted 12.5 cents an hour immediately, 2.5 cents more on July 1, and another 2.5 cents the following January. Nathan Feisinger, the board's new chairman, defended the award on the ground that the steelworkers needed to catch up with conditions in other major industries. The industry members on the board dissented from the recommendation; the steel officials turned it down, and began a brassy offensive against the administration, in which they were joined by most of the press. At the very least, they intended to hold up the government, as they had at the conclusion of the war, for a hefty price increase. If, in the process, the government control machinery was wrecked, and the administration suffered a loss of face, they would shed no tears.

After conferring with the President, Wilson began to sound out industry officials concerning the kind of price increase they would settle for in order to accept the board's ruling. The industry was talking in terms of another $6.60 per ton. Ellis Arnall, the new price administrator, convinced Truman that the industry's demands were unjustified, since profits were higher than lush profits of the year before. He could not see where more than $2.86 more per ton was in order, and that, after increased costs had been incurred, not in anticipation of them. Wilson was a spokesman of big business; he was against the wage board's ruling and had publicly said so; now caught in the crossfire between the industry and his price agency, he solved his dilemma by resigning. The strike was only ten days away. To escape a shutdown in the midst of a war, and to escape labor's opprobium in an election year when it was the steel industry that was resisting the government's rulings, Truman decided to bypass the Taft-Hartley eighty-day injunction road. He took over the steel mills under his authority as Commander in Chief, authority supposedly validated by the Defense Production Act. Now began the second series of misadventures.

The task of formally administering the steel industry he assigned to Charles Sawyer, his Secretary of Commerce. Why Sawyer? There was Oscar Chapman in the Cabinet. Or he could have turned it over to an amenable general or admiral. Aside from his lack of moxie, Sawyer was more reactionary than Snyder, had publicly opposed all controls, was himself a corporation lawyer and officer, and had no intention of resisting industry pressures. If Truman had passed up Chapman in favor of Sawyer because he thought Sawyer would be more acceptable to the steel masters, it was a pathetic lapse of judgment. Within one week after the seizure, a tactic was devised at the White House to force both sides to settle. The steel administrator was to put into effect that part of the union's demands to which the men were automatically entitled under the board's cost-of-living rules. Concurrently, he was to ask the price controller to grant the amount of price relief to which the companies were entitled under the Capehart provisions. At that point he would announce that was all he would do, on the theory that both sides would thereupon conclude that they had more to gain from a settlement than from continued government direction. Whatever the merits of the tactic, and the situation in steel was different than on the railroads—Sawyer did not play his assigned part. He did not refuse to act, he did not resign, "he managed to immerse himself in preparations," as Richard Neustadt wrote. The President, who had just seen the departure of his Mobilization Director and had fired his Attorney General, was not anxious to lose his Secretary of Commerce at this time, as well. Once the case was in the hands of the courts, Sawyer was relieved of further embarrassment and inconvenience.

All this time, a public campaign against Truman was blazing. Clarence Randall, Inland Steel head, accused the President in a radio and television address of seizing the steel mills to pay a political debt to the CIO. Congressmen gleefully joined the revelry. In legislative halls and newspaper offices, loud calls were heard for the invocation of the Taft-Hartley law. Taft said that Truman's action was grounds for impeachment. That the steel corporations, which were earning bonanza profits, were refusing to carry out recommendations of a government board while demanding additional large price increases, was a fact lost in the hurricane of public rhetoric that branded Truman a dictator, a usurper, a tool of the union bosses, whose illegal action would set off a new round of inflation.

The coup de grace was delivered by the Supreme Court in a 6 to 3 vote in which it incredibly declared the seizure unconstitutional. The six majority justices gave their decision in a set of opinions both diverse and abstruse, the only instance in the national history when the Supreme Court failed to follow the leadership of the Commander in Chief in a war period in a matter of this sort. It is doubtful that the court would have been this precipitate in taking the case, and ordering a freezing of wages pending its decision, but for Truman's poor repute. Judges have certainly not lacked ingenuity in discovering grounds for upholding the authority of the President when they wanted to do so. In the railroad case, Truman had invoked statutory powers under the National Defense Act of 1916. When the Switchmen's union argued that the seizure was unconstitutional, the trial court granted the government's motion for an injunction on the ground that the Second World War was still on in the absence of peace treaties with Germany and Japan. Though the court's contribution in *Youngstown Sheet and Tube v. Sawyer* remains in dispute among constitutional lawyers, there was no question that the decision tore brutally into Truman's diminishing public stature. What the judges lacked in legal illustriousness, they made up for in political clout.

Truman had maneuvered inexpertly, probably misled by his relative success in the railroad controversy, and by legal advice that precedent indicated a government victory should the companies challenge his seizure order. It was unwise to seize the steel industry at all unless he intended to put through his board's recommendations. If he did not dare to do that, he should not have dared to seize the industry without statutory authority. Beyond the customary bumbling of his staff aides—a constant in both his administrations—lay the reality that when the steel industry wanted more money, the government had to accede substantially to its demand. The industry had demonstrated that to Roosevelt, to Truman in the reconversion period, and now again during the Korean war.

An exasperated President returned the mills to the corporations and 600,000 steelworkers hit the picket lines immediately thereafter.

He would not invoke the Taft-Hartley law, as Congress continued to call on him to do, because the imposition of an injunction would only postpone the crisis for eighty days, and there was every likelihood of widespread wildcat strikes. It was the steel corporation officials who warred on his board rulings and presidential rights. It was the Republican-dominated Congress that refused to support his seizure decision. Let the onus of a cutoff of steel production be on them. The strike was a long one—fifty-three days to July 24 and a settlement. The contract embodied roughly the terms approved by the wage board four months earlier. In return, the corporations were granted a price increase of $5.65 per ton, which Truman approved "with a reluctant heart, for I was convinced that it was wrong." There was nothing else to be done. "If we wanted steel—and we wanted it very badly—it would have to be on the industry's terms."

As if to make sure that the mortally wounded patient was really going to die, Congress, in the 1952 amendments to the Defense Production Act, stripped the wage board of further authority over labor disputes, and made its members subject to Senate confirmation. It also eliminated price controls on numerous additional items, halted price rollbacks on beef, weakened rent controls, continued the Capehart "pass-through" provisions. In the circumstances, Truman decided to administer extreme unction by overruling the board in the bituminous coal case. When he approved the $1.90 daily wage increase plus 10 cents-a-ton added royalty that John L. Lewis had negotiated with the coal operators, the board chairman and industry members resigned. Two months later, a new President ended controls by executive order.

The Korean war dogged Truman right to the end, demoralizing and disintegrating his administration. It had been easier to start the war than to finish it. At the time of MacArthur's recall, the allied forces were dug in just above the 38th parallel. In April and May, the Chinese resumed offensive operations with the Eighth Army giving way. Then the Americans counterattacked, chased the Chinese back across the parallel, and reoccupied their previous position. As matters stood, all sides—the North Koreans, the Americans with the South Koreans, the Chinese with the North Koreans—had failed in their attempts to unite Korea by force. The war was stalemated. Consequently, both sides had a common objective of recognizing politically the military reality.

When on June 2 during the MacArthur hearings, a senator asked

Acheson whether his testimony suggested "the possibility of a cease-fire at or near the 38th parallel," Acheson gave a guardedly affirmative reply. It was July 10 before the preliminaries were cleared away and representatives of the two sides met, first, at Kaesong, subsequently, at Panmunjom. Newspapermen speculated that the talks might go on three to six weeks. It was two years, during which time 63,000 American casualties were added to the 79,000 already accumulated, before an armistice was concluded. In the Cold War chronicles of the period, it was customary to attribute the long-drawn-out agony to the treacherous character of the Communists, who cared nothing about using up their "coolie troops" and "slave hordes" so long as it served their propaganda purposes. In contrast, our own negotiators were pictured as long-suffering Jobs who continued to reason with their opponents in the face of insults and calumnies. That the North Koreans and Chinese were tenacious, grim bargainers was obvious. But in Truman, Acheson, and the generals and admirals, they were not confronting a group of Quakers or Gandhians. That they deliberately dragged out the discussions, despite the cost to their own side's lives, cuts across the record. Revolutionists, because of the nature of their trade and experience, are inclined to ruthlessness and conclusive solutions. That is not the same as callousness concerning the lives and welfare of their troops.

The maneuvers that spun out the Korean talks at such heavy cost came from the American more than the opposition side. There were pressures on Truman that militated against a fast armistice. What outraged the Americans was not the Communists' maneuvers, but their aggressiveness and abusiveness. Our State Department had lined up the UN to condemn the North Koreans and Chinese as aggressors, and the judgment had been pronounced just by all major statesmen and publications of the free world; still, the Communists conducted themselves as if the Americans were the criminals. How could you do business with people like that? Admiral Turner Joy, commander of our Far Eastern naval forces, who headed the so-called UN delegation for the first year, wrote a book about the chamber of horrors he entered in negotiating with the Communists. As well read the Earl of Clarendon on Cromwell and the Puritans. The worlds of Cavalier and Roundhead are always incomprehensible to each other.

What was inhibiting Truman was that the armistice negotiation was caught up in tricky political crosscurrents. First, the military commanders in Korea still had dreams of a military decision. Bradley had said that Korea was the wrong war, and MacArthur had been re-called, but the MacArthur mirage had not been laid to rest. James Van Fleet, Mark Clark, Turner Joy, all thought America should and could go out to win. Van Fleet, the Eighth Army commander for a period, testified before a Senate committee that his army had the Communists on the run in the summer of 1951, that he was "crying" to be unleashed to finish them off, but was ordered by the govern-ment to stop. When Mark Clark took over from Ridgway in May, 1952, he put his staff to work developing a plan to bring victory. The total costs in lives, planes, ships, equipment, widening war, turned out to be not inconsiderable, but Clark was sure the prospective losses "would be far less than losses we would have to take eventually if we failed to win militarily in Korea and waited until the Communists were ready to fight on their own terms." When at one point, the gov-ernment ordered the negotiators to establish with the other side a truce line, Ridgway and Joy both objected heatedly. The American negotiating team at Panmunjom was psychologically not attuned to the idea of a truce. These were not ideal people to call off the war. But Washington had to take their belligerence into account, since everyone understood that whatever compromise agreement was drawn, the Republican opposition would scream accusations of sell-out, capitulation, appeasement, and worse.

Nor was that all. Truman and his advisers themselves had mixed feelings about an armistice. The Korean war was unpopular. It was devitalizing the administration like a suppurative infection. It had to be ended. At the same time, the war was the instrumentality that en-abled the administration to put through the vast rearmament and man-power draft. Would the stilling of the guns halt the wheels of rearma-ment, as well? It was a danger that could not be ignored. As soon as the proposal for a cease-fire was announced, all the main mobilization and military officials—Wilson, Johnston, Harriman, Eisenhower, Sherman, Marshall, Bradley—made speeches or declarations warning against any relaxation if there was peace in Korea. The President bore in with a Fourth of July oration in which he solemnly informed that nation, "We must remember that Korea is only part of a wider conflict. The threat of Soviet aggression still hangs heavy over many a country—including our own. We must continue, therefore, to build up our armed forces at a rapid rate." Earlier he had told the High-way Safety Conference that the "sabotage press" and "Congressional demagogues" were exaggerating Korean casualties; there had been less than 80,000 compared with over 1 million killed and injured on

United States highways the previous year. The voluble Van Fleet, in as Associated Press interview, blurted out what others were hinting at more discreetly: "Thank God for Korea. Where would we be if we hadn't had something like this to shock our people into action?" The administration had become as avid for crises as a junkie for another fix. It was the Greek crisis that enabled it to pass the Truman Doctrine; the Czechoslovak crisis to pass the Marshall Plan; the Soviet atomic explosion and the collapse of Chiang Kai-shek that assured the arms money for NATO; the Korean war that got the wheels of NSC-68 rolling. Could the program survive peace? The administration was buffeted by opposing forces that did not make for expeditiousness in the armistice talks.

From July to November the negotiations were hung up on the question of the truce line. The Communists had assumed that there was to be a restoration of the status quo ante. That had also been the assumption of congressmen and newspapermen. Acheson revealed at a bull session, several years later, that "several of my colleagues suggested that the Russians and Chinese could well have been surprised, chagrined, and given cause to feel tricked when at Kaesong we revealed a firm determination as a matter of major principle not to accept the 38th parallel as the armistice line." The Americans were insisting that the truce line had to be north even of the battle line, which was somewhat above the parallel, to compensate for the cessation of air and naval action that ranged to the Yalu. The ambivalence of attitudes came out time and again as the negotiations dragged, were broken off, halfheartedly resumed, postponed again. In August the disposition was to let discussions lapse until after the San Francisco conference that was to ratify the peace treaty with Japan. The *Wall Street Journal* reported that American strategy was to demand more than we expected the Communists would concede. "Barring a complete cave-in by the Reds, the State Department would prefer no cease-fire deal until after the San Francisco conference ends." Two months later, with the issue still unresolved, Ernest Gross, our UN deputy representative, was publicly voicing fears that an armistice would enable the Soviet Union to launch a "phony" peace offensive at the UN assembly scheduled to open in Paris.

The deadlock was broken at the beginning of November by the Communists giving in to the American demand. They agreed that the armistice line was to be based on the line of battle contact. Thereupon, the American negotiators insisted that their line must include Kaesong, held by the Communists. At this, criticism spread of Ameri-

can negotiating tactics. At their weekly meeting with the State Department, allied representatives were concerned, reported *The New
York Times*, "that after the Communists had made the big concession
on the line, the United Nations officers might be sticking at straws."
Several days before, the *Times* had carried a dispatch from its correspondent in Korea that the way an increasing number of troops "see
the situation right now is that the Communists have made important
concessions while the United Nations command, as they view it, continues to make more and more demands." The impasse was broken on
November 27 with the American proposal that the current contact
line was to constitute the demarcation line provided the armistice
was signed within thirty days; otherwise the demarcation line would
be the contact line existing when the armistice was signed.

What was not being discussed in the press, and came out only
later, was that while the generals and admirals were still thinking of
victory, and sacrificing lives for the capture of hills having no strategic value, the troops were being progressively demoralized. They
saw no sense in continuing the slaughter when an armistice was due
to be signed. In January, 1953, Truman was quoted as saying that
there had been 49,000 desertions, which he attributed to influences
such as the *Chicago Tribune*, the Scripps-Howard newspapers, and
MacArthur. The general replied that the desertions could more plau-
sibly be traced to lack of faith in President Truman's policies of appeasement. Whatever the influences, the desertions were symptomatic
of an army whose morale was shaken, and a more significant indica-
tor than the later sensationalized reports of defections among
American prisoners of war.

The discussions lumbered along all through the winter into the
spring of 1952 at the customary pace and with the usual interruptions
for mutual charges of violations and bad faith, until all items on the
agenda had been disposed of except the exchange of prisoners. On
this, the Americans dug in, a disagreement that prolonged the war for
another fifteen months. The dispute was whether there was to be an
automatic repatriation of all prisoners held by both sides, or whether
the prisoners were to be given a choice of being repatriated or proceeding elsewhere. Truman made the issue one of high principle. He
insisted in a public statement that "Forced repatriation would be re-
pugnant to the fundamental moral and humanitarian principles which
underlie our action in Korea. We will not buy an armistice by turning
over human beings for slaughter or slavery." (At the time, General
Clark was sending in urgent appeals for more troops, reactivating

again MacArthur's old proposal to have Chiang Kai-shek supply two divisions. This time, the Joint Chiefs approved the idea, but after long study, it was turned down again.)

Walter Millis concluded that the prisoners were pawns for both sides in a power game. "If Peking could force Washington to relinquish them, America's prestige and authority throughout the Far East as the major bulwark against Communist infiltration and domination would be shattered. If Washington could force Peking to give them up, thus proving that tens of thousands of Communist citizens preferred the non-Communist to the Communist world, the prestige and authority of Communism throughout the Far East, as the representative and defender of the Asian common man against Western imperialist exploitation, would likewise be shattered." Millis's estimation was a correct representation of the way the issue appeared at the time to the negotiators on both sides. That an analyst as sober and judicious as Millis could accept at face value this hyperbole is an indication of how judgment gets warped in a struggle of the Korean kind. Events have long since reduced the quarrel to an episode of the Korean negotiations, and shown both sets of claims and fears to have been exaggerated out of all proportion to their true worth. The issue should not have been employed to prolong the war for fifteen days, much less fifteen months.

The equities were ambiguous. The civil war had penetrated into the POW compounds and converted them into armed camps, so that it was difficult to determine to what extent prisoners were able to exercise any free choice. And both the Americans and Russians had shifted their positions over the years. The technical legality was with the North Koreans and Chinese. The 1949 Geneva Convention provided that "prisoners of war shall be released and repatriated without delay after the cessation of hostilities." During the debates on the convention, the American representatives had argued for total repatriation because the West, at the time, was seeking the return of over a million German prisoners in Russia; the Soviet delegates, for their own reasons, were arguing for voluntary return. Now the positions were reversed. The Americans were especially loath to agree to a full exchange since the enemy lists contained only 11,000 names, as against the UN lists of 132,000 Communist prisoners. (There was a discrepancy of 53,000 in the Communist lists. They had released great numbers of South Korean prisoners, and then, forcibly or otherwise, reenlisted them into the North Korean army.) Some expressed fear that the uneven exchange might shift the precarious military balance to the other side. Truman and his advisers continued to dawdle, to wax morally indignant, to take refuge behind immutable principles. In the end, the new administration finished with it on a variation of the Indian compromise proposal. Walter Lippmann subsequently summarized the reasons for Truman's behavior:

> [He] was not able to make peace, because politically he was too weak at home. He was not able to make war because the risks were too great. President Eisenhower signed an armistice which accepted the partition of Korea and a peace without victory because, being himself the victorious commander in World War II and a Republican, he could not be attacked as an appeaser. President Truman and Secretary Acheson, on the other hand, never seemed able to afford to make peace on the only terms which the Chinese would agree to, that is to say, which Eisenhower did agree to. [Truman himself admitted as much. "I would have been crucified for that armistice," he said.]

It was a ragged-looking administration in its final year. Beset by an unscrupulous opposition, terrorized by a bullying adventurer and his piratical crew, compromised by scandals and boodlery, scorned and disregarded in its halfhearted attempts to control inflation, rattled by a war that it could neither win nor end, Truman's esteem with his fellow citizens sank lower than in 1946. Three-quarters of the electorate, according to the Gallup poll, had turned against him.

18

Trumanism
and
McCarthyism

In 1917, the night before his war message to Congress, a distraught Woodrow Wilson said to Frank Cobb, editor of the *New York World*, "Once lead this people into war, and they'll forget there ever was such a thing as tolerance. To fight you must be brutal and ruthless, and the spirit of ruthless brutality will enter into the very fibre of our national life. There won't be any peace standards left to work with. There will be only war standards." Wilson helped his prophecy come true by asking Congress for the Espionage Act, used to round up IWW's, Socialists, and other war opponents. He instructed the Civil Service Commission to discharge without any formal proceedings employees whose retention "would be inimical to the public welfare." Soon came the Sedition Act of 1918 providing severe penalties for expressing disloyal opinions, followed by the Palmer raids, the deportations, the vigilante attacks.

The conflict with Russia following the Second World War produced a corresponding intensified concern with domestic radicalism, and unleashed groups and individuals who hoped to pursue their objectives in the wake of a Red hunt. The conflict with Russia was this time a very real thing, not the anticipatory worries over the earlier Russian Revolution. During the war, when the Soviet Union was an ally and was supposedly popular among Americans, the House Committee on Un-American Activities was voted funds, session after session, to investigate, harass, and discredit dissenters and reformers along with Communists and fellow travelers. Even Roosevelt was powerless to quash or sidetrack the congressional witch-hunters who were trying to smear the New Deal with the Red brush. Despite its reckless and unscrupulous methods, the committee under Martin Dies and his successors received generous press attention and was supported by a majority of the public, if the Gallup poll accurately reflected opinion. In 1945, on a motion of John Rankin of Mississippi, Congress voted to make it a permanent committee.

Thus, when Truman became President, both the tradition and instrumentality of the witch-hunt was at hand, distinctly anti–New Deal in its direction, though the committee chairmen up to that time had been Southern Democrats, and the committee researches had been upheld and financed by legislatures nominally under Democratic control. It was still a secondary theme in government orchestration; it was not to become the obsession of American politics until the emergence of Joseph McCarthy; but the conditioning was under way. Americans were becoming accustomed to the idea that free-enterprise orthodoxy and Americanism were one and the same thing, that opposition was equivalent to disloyalty, that government was entitled to proscribe and punish activities, associations, or opinions that it could not constitutionally declare illegal. Once the committee had castigated an individual as a left-winger, or a dupe of Communists, or an associate of such undesirables, it was like a sentence of ostracism in ancient Greece. Even where no contempt citation was made, the individual was left to the press, his employer, and the local patriotic societies for punishment, the more unrestrained because it was extra-legal.

In Truman's first year in office, the essential relationship between the administration and the congressional witch-hunters appeared to remain what it was under Roosevelt, and the committee's antics constituted, for all their sordidness, a sideshow. Roosevelt's wartime record had been better than Wilson's, aside from the atrocity against the Japanese-Americans on the West Coast, and his earlier favor to his supporter, Daniel Tobin of the Teamsters Union, of securing the indictment and jailing of eighteen Trotskyist leaders and union officials under the sedition clause of the 1940 Alien Registration Act. Francis Biddle, the wartime Justice Department head, was a civil libertarian. He went in for no mass roundups, harassments, or arrests. Even so, repressive measures were accumulating on the books. The Hatch Act of 1939, meant to block a Roosevelt third term, had a provision forbidding federal employment to any member of an organization advocating the government's overthrow. In 1940 and 1942, Congress empowered the War and Navy secretaries to dismiss summarily any employee considered a security risk. Roosevelt authorized wiretapping in national security cases limited "insofar as possible" to the investigation of aliens, and in War Service Regulation II he disqualified from federal employment any person whose loyalty was in reasonable doubt. In response to Congress's voting of funds for the Justice Department to investigate federal employees, Biddle set up an interdepartmental committee, one of whose contributions was the Attorney General's list of subversive organizations, which became the foundation for loyalty star-chamber proceedings.

All through 1946 Truman sat on the requests, and did not respond to the pressures, for additional security arrangements, pressures that mounted in intensity both in Congress and his administration after the Canadian government made public Russian espionage revealed by Igor Gouzenko, a defected code clerk in the Soviet embassy in Ottawa. After the Republican gains in the November elections, a panicked President threw caution and restraint to the winds. Now began that indecent competition between moderates and primitives as to who was the best hater of Communism. The liberals moved to forestall the reactionaries by adopting their proposals, only to be confronted with a new set of accusations and demands, which they again rushed to preempt. Once bigotry and hysteria were the order of the day, control passed to a political thug who browbeat Congress and blackmailed the President while a great nation, banners flying and drums beating, was marched back to the fifteenth century when an inquisition enforced right-thinking.

Before November was out, Truman set up the President's Temporary Commission on Employee Loyalty to examine the effectiveness of existing security procedures. The commission members made a halfhearted attempt to determine how serious the security problem was, to be told by Justice representatives that the presidential mandate required the commission to assume a serious problem, not to make a determination. Attorney General Clark stepped into the breach by taking the position that while the problem was not so grave as it had once been, any disloyalty was a serious matter. Admiral Thomas B. Inglis of naval intelligence took a dim view of some of the personnel recruited in the Roosevelt epoch. "As early as 1933," he wrote the commission, "the 'progressive swing to liberalism' which characterized the 'socialized planning' of the next decade in American history, resulted in the introduction into the federal system of large numbers of individuals whose concepts of democratic institutions had been developed abroad." Lieutenant Colonel Byron N. Randolph of military intelligence made the contribution to the discussion that "A liberal is only a hop, skip and jump from a Communist."

After much hesitation, the commission accepted Clark's evaluation. Its definition of disloyalty included not only membership, but "sympathetic association with" any organization on the Attorney General's list, or one seeking to alter our form of government "by unconstitutional means." It decided that existing standards and procedures were inadequate to safeguard internal security, and that a more systematic screening of federal employees was required. Truman hurried to adopt the recommendations and set up the Federal Employee Loyalty Program. He admitted to Clifton Durr, a liberal attorney who was a member of the Federal Communications Commission, that he had signed the order "to take the ball away from Parnell Thomas" (the new Republican chairman of the House Un-American Activities Committee in the Eightieth Congress), to which Durr replied "that the order would be construed as giving presidential sanction to the fears Thomas was trying to create."

Centuries-old procedures of Anglo-Saxon jurisprudence were reversed. The burden of proof was now on the accused, not on the accuser—and for charges based on the vaguest definitions of "loyalty," "security," "subversion." The government need not prove an employee guilty of any specific misdeed; it was sufficient to assert that past or present association or expression of opinion gave grounds for belief that the employee might be disloyal. Worse than the disregard of federal workers' constitutional rights was, as Durr pointed out, that loyalty programs confirmed claims that the government was honeycombed with Reds, whose ferreting out and removal was a major task of the lawmakers. Many liberals were shocked. Carey McWilliams, editor of *The Nation*, wrote, "At the height of the delirium of the Palmer raids, organizations were not banned without hearing nor were citizens deprived of civil rights merely by listing their names in a political rogues' gallery." Philip Murray, the CIO head, wrote Truman asking what grave emergency had made obsolete existing laws against treason and sedition that had afforded sufficient safeguards in wartime. He feared that "the open expression of opinions on public issues may be listed by the Attorney General as subversive or disloyal."

In truth, the entire security issue was a fabricated one. There was no security problem necessitating new regulations. The Soviet Union, like all major powers, had espionage agents moving around the country, and these customary activities were monitored and checkmated by American counterespionage forces in the customary ways of such operations. Certainly no one in the government, no matter how bigoted or backward, believed that loyalty oaths, the Attorney General's lists, or the House Un-American Activities Committee's harassment of radicals and reformers had anything to do with catching spies. Political opposition is another matter: No government tolerates a revolutionary attempt to overthrow it. The problem was exclusively theoretical, however. The American Communist party was never very influential, and confined advocacy of revolution to infrequent doctrinal explanations. It never commanded the support that Communists won in the 1920s and 1930s in Germany, Czechoslovakia, or France. At its highest point in 1938, major Communist activity was not among government employees, but in some CIO industrial unions and among Eastern intellectuals, and there its influence was exerted on behalf of programs well within the liberal orbit.

Some averred that while radicalism was entitled to a voice in the political marketplace, the Communists did not qualify because they were part of a foreign conspiracy. This was not an original thought. Radicals have traditionally been stamped by conservative opponents as foreign-inspired. Jeffersonians were denounced by the Federalists as French Jacobin agents. Populists were attacked as foreign conspirators. The elder Henry Cabot Lodge discovered that Bryan's 1896 Democratic platform was based "on socialistic and anarchistic theories imported from Europe." Unfortunately for American radicalism, the accusation of foreign control was not merely a familiar canard when applied to the American Communist party. Like Communist organizations generally, it had become subservient to the Soviet regime in the Stalin period and had permitted a few of its members to be recruited into Soviet espionage networks. Essentially, however, for all the duplicity, disorientation, and ideological sycophancy of its leaders, it was a regulation radical party enlisting in its ranks individuals of a similar breed, with similar motives, as those in the Debs movement in pre–World War I America, and it was conducting the regulation activities of Marxist-type organizations.

The conservatives' anti-Communist animus was directed less at the handful of Communist lawyers or economists in government bureaus than at those New Dealers who were platonic admirers of the Soviet

Union. It was a rage against the welfare state, with its new arrangements, values, and personalities, translated into security semantics for the same reason that advertisements for soap are attached to sex allure. To imagine that those New Dealers who were somewhat leftist in their thinking, or that the isolated Communist technician could determine or sway high policies would be as naive as to suppose that left-wing writers in the Hollywood movie factories could inject Communist propaganda into their scripts. In any case, by the time the loyalty mania took hold under Truman, the Communist movement was in headlong decline, and popular frontism had become a yellowed page of history. Liberals grew disillusioned with Communists with the signing of the Stalin-Hitler pact, and what remained of popular frontism was shattered with the turn to the Cold War. Anti-Communist drives were in progress in the CIO unions, eliminating remaining Communist strength. When Dies, the burly, back-country Texan with the hog caller's voice, was cracking the whip at the House committee hearings, at least there were New Dealers with popular front inclinations still around and Communists counted for something in unions and uplift organizations. The fact that the loyalty scare went into high when all important New Dealers were gone, liberalism had turned anti-Communist, and the Communist movement was falling apart, signified that it was only remotely related to either security or Communism, so far as its organizers and engineers were concerned.

Truman's presidential order instituted an inquisitorial apparatus that took on a life and vigor of its own, and was sustained by a climate as favorable for security-sleuthing as the Central American tropics are for growing bananas. Neither Truman nor the fixers around him were book burners, and in less stormy days they would not have gone berserk on loyalty investigations, but they had the politicians' mentality that the hullabaloo about security was another problem, like lining up the vote of a congressman who wanted a dam built in his locality, that had to be finessed. Consequently, it was a good day's work when they got Seth Richardson, a sound, impeccably conservative Republican lawyer who had served as Assistant Attorney General in Hoover's administration, to take on the chairmanship of the Loyalty Review Board. Truman accepted the opposition's definition of political reliability as well as loyalty. If one was going to take the witch-hunt away from the witch-hunters, it would not do to appoint a first-amendment fanatic to head the enterprise.

While undoubtedly a splendid person to represent the interests of a bank or railroad, Richardson was out of place at the head of a quasi-judicial board, for he did not believe that federal employees had constitutional rights. It was his position that "the government is entitled to discharge any employee for reasons which seem sufficient to the government, and without extending to such employee any hearing whatsoever. We believe that the rights of the government in that respect are at least equal to those possessed by private employers." (Richardson had not heard of union contracts and grievance procedures.) This was the outlook of the man heading the top board that would oversee regulations of regional and agency review boards to ensure equitable attitudes and fair play. In one widely publicized case, the victim, Dorothy Bailey, an employment service supervisor, was fired for allegedly being a member of the Communist party. In the appeal hearing, her attorney, Paul Porter, charged that the allegations against her were "a result of malicious, irresponsible, reckless gossip which has no foundation whatever in fact and stems from an internecine union controversy." Richardson informed him that the reports came from informants "certified by the FBI as experienced and entirely reliable." When Porter demanded their names, or some identifications, he was told that the board could not disclose the information. The elaborate appeals procedure was only elaborate camouflage.

The investigations and hearings in the departments were of a like or worse character. Most of these boards—there were eventually 150 departmental and regional loyalty boards in operation—were staffed with rabid reactionaries, provincial bigots, and scared bureaucrats. The line between disloyalty and critical thought was effaced. The National Association for the Advancement of Colored People complained to Truman "about an increasing tendency on the part of government agencies to associate activity in interracial matters with disloyalty." Congressman Andrew Jacobs of Indiana inquired why 128 of 139 postal employees questioned by loyalty investigators in his constituency were Jews and Negroes. Employees were queried on their views on the draft, lend-lease, and the Marshall Plan, on how to break the Berlin blockade, and the possibilities of coexistence. In one case this was the bill of particulars:

Confidential informant, stated to be of established reliability, who is acquainted with and who has associated with many known and admitted Communists, is reported to have advised as of May 1948 that the informant was present when the employee was engaged in conversation with other individuals at which time the employee advocated the Communist Party line, such as favoring peace and civil liberties when those subjects were being advocated by the Communist Party.

Since even the casuists cranking the loyalty machine were hard put to explain, in the face of criticism, some of the dismissals for disloyalty on the basis of their own captious criteria, the fine hair was split to create, in addition to "disloyalty," the new category of "security risk," first applied in the so-called sensitive agencies. The surgery for this now skillfully isolated disease, designed to eliminate the unintentionally as well as the purposefully dangerous, required neither explanations nor hearings. Agency heads were empowered to dismiss employees without the safeguards and procedural protections allegedly afforded by the loyalty program.

Truman warded off criticism with glib assurances that the loyalty program was protecting employees' rights while rooting out disloyal elements. Many liberal critics accepted the program, but concentrated on improving procedures. Truman's assurances were gratuitous and the liberals' calls for procedural reforms vain. The methods and biases of loyalty investigators and boards developed inescapably from the nature of the assignment. Once the criteria were no longer conduct and acts, but thoughts and associations, how else was loyalty to be established except by relating these to the norms of right-wing orthodoxy? What other standards could the loyalty boards adopt except those of the House inquisitors? And would any bureaucrat, uneasy about an individual, dare to resolve his doubt except by getting rid of him in the face of formidable congressional pressures from Congress to produce victims? A witch-hunt which by its nature seeks to ward off unreal dangers and resolve synthetic problems necessarily begets its own illusory world of fictitious categories and sophistical distinctions. If witches and wizards are to be unmasked, one must have appropriate tests and sacrificial rites.

When the program was first devised, the FBI was assigned the subsidiary role of gathering information upon request by civil service or other agencies. This function quickly expanded in practice to the FBI's becoming the dominant force when it was directed to screen all federal employees, and if initial checks uncovered derogatory information, to conduct full field investigations. By this time the FBI had become the commanding institution that the present generation knows. When in 1939 Roosevelt added investigations of espionage and subversive activities to its jurisdiction, he opened the door to its expansion into a secret police overseeing the nation's orthodoxy. After 1939, when its budget was $6.5 million with a payroll of 785 special agents, it grew steadily until in 1951 it was voted over $57 million and the number of special agents had grown to 4,600. As with all secret police, the gathering of dossiers, over which it sought exclusive control, occupied an important part of its attention. In December, 1947, the FBI clashed over the issue with the Interior Department. Interior wanted the relevant FBI files because it had promised its accused employees a list of the charges against them and an opportunity to cross-examine their accusers. Justice objected that this procedure would cripple FBI investigations. Truman upheld the FBI, and followed this with his order in March, 1948, that no requests for loyalty reports were to be honored, whether from the departments or Congress, without specific presidential approval.

The FBI's passion for secrecy was a function of its role. Its grip on a mass of secret dossiers gave it access to all manner of information on individuals in and out of government that could be transmuted into power for presenting budgetary requests, neutralizing criticism, gathering allies, and intimidating opponents. Moreover, the loyalty files would not survive public scrutiny as was revealed over the government's strenuous objection during the Judith Coplon trial. Dossiers were loaded with slanderous gossip, unsubstantiated allegations, malicious chit-chat reflecting ultraright prejudices, all included on the rationale that the FBI did not evaluate testimony, and that all accusations and data might prove helpful in future investigations. The FBI's argument that it had to protect its secret sources of information was not well taken: Names and other telltale information identifying agents and informers could have been deleted from the copies provided. But Truman had special reasons for upholding the FBI. The congressional committees and their prowling investigators had to be kept at bay, for their interest was not in ensuring the implementation of the loyalty program, but in using any clues or names they might find in the files to entrap and scandalize the administration. J. Edgar Hoover's need for secrecy combined with Truman's for shutting out Congressional marauders to create the hushed atmosphere of national awe for the FBI and its director. Nominally a division in the Justice Department under the Attorney General, the FBI achieved the status of a sovereign fiefdom, to criticize which was to condemn oneself as a tool or dupe of the Communists. This was a heavy burden on the country, for a secret police is forever discovering new dangers to the country's security that call for new appropriations and increased personnel for surveillance of the enemy within. It never saves the country once and for all from the nefarious encroachments of its internal foes. The country has to be saved anew with each budgetary request.

Truman did not confine himself to the loyalty program to demonstrate his anti-Communist bona fides. Attorney General Clark impaneled a special blue-ribbon grand jury in New York, which handed down indictments in July, 1948, against the top leaders of the Communist party, using the same Smith Act under which the Trotskyists had been jailed earlier. They were not charged with any overt plot or act, but with advocating the government's violent overthrow; and in the subsequent trial, FBI undercover operatives, who had joined the party, appeared as the main prosecution witnesses. Clark was also alerting the country to grave threats against internal security, and comparing the expert ministrations of the Justice Department and the FBI with the partisan, publicity-seeking escapades of the House amateurs. Within the administration, he was pressing for more stringent legislation authorizing wiretapping, calling for registration of Communists, and the like. The spirit of the times was manifest when the Loyalty Review Board denounced protestors who thought its program violated civil liberties, and when the certified liberals of Americans for Democratic Action, who were critical of loyalty procedures, ran newspaper advertisements listing the names of the Wallace party's contributors and the organizations on the Attorney General's list to which they belonged or had belonged.

Anti-Communism was a thriving concern, and the Truman strategy of taking over its control seemed to be working out. The Republicans were unable to make Reds-in-government a major issue in the 1948 election campaign. Truman centered attention on real problems even if he provided an imaginary scenario of a united Democratic host mightily defending the people's interests. Some thought the loyalty program enabled Truman to neutralize the Red issue; others attributed his success to the Wallace third party, which by defecting from the Democratic fold, demonstrated for all to see that Truman was an authentic foe of Communists. At different times, as in the 1948 election, and later, at the height of the anti-Communist delirium, the mass of people were not as engrossed with Communism as were politicians and newspapermen who were trying to ascribe to popular preoccupation their own monomania.

Truman, intoxicated by the 1948 victory, thought he had the problem licked. The committee, he told the press, was "defunct," and he directed Clark to draft a resolution for the Democratic leadership to amend the House rules in order to put it out of business. He would have been scornful if told that to achieve his electoral victory, he had transformed a disreputable printer of off-color literature into a national concern bearing the imprimatur of the White House, which would menace his own administration as well as the public at large. For he had legitimatized the proposition that Communists in government constituted a major security problem; therefore it was proper for government to proscribe organizations, membership in which was proof of disloyalty and grounds for dismissal from employment whether one's job was wrapping sandwiches in an agency cafeteria or running a mimeograph machine in the Bureau of Wildlife and Fisheries. Not only that. He had left the door wide open for the attack to be turned against the Democrats themselves since many New Dealers before and during the war had joined organizations that were now listed by the Attorney General as Communist fronts. The witch-hunt had been anti–New Deal in origin, orientation, and inner character, and the Democrats could not appropriate it without repudiating their recent past. The smart politicians were to be overwhelmed by the furies they had unloosed.

When McCarthy came forward at the beginning of 1950 as the latest Communist-slayer, both Congress and the nation were well acquainted with the breed. A succession of provincials on the make had been aspirants for this role for over a decade. McCarthy produced nothing new in technique, method, or concept from the routine that had been worked out by Dies and others. He himself launched his pseudocrusade simply to create enough stir to justify asking the Wisconsin voters to return him to the Senate. He was as surprised as anyone at the incredible response to his wild, unsupported charges of card-carrying Communists in the State Department, the precise number varying from one speech to the next. Truman and the Democratic directorate in the Senate moved fast to crush the upstart before he could establish another antiadministration center for slander and mayhem. A subcommittee of the Foreign Relations Committee was hastily convoked to investigate McCarthy's charges. As its chairman was selected Millard Tydings of Maryland, another impeccable old-line conservative, a veteran opponent of the New Deal whom Roosevelt had tried unsuccessfully to purge in 1938.

It was soon evident the Democratic counterstroke would not work. The Tydings hearings were enabling McCarthy to raise a hysterical clamor that furnished gory copy to newspapers from one end of the country to the other. No matter that his so-called evidence was the flimsiest mélange of tattle and vilification; as fast as one charge was knocked down, he responded with five new accusations and demands. The effect was to create a national tumult about spies and Communists with McCarthy as Hercules determined to clean out the Augean stables whatever the obstacles and opposition. To the committee's demand that he supply the names of the Communists, he bellowed that the information was in the loyalty files, that the committee should get them from the State Department. When Truman closed the files that month, the uproar in Congress became deafening. What was the administration trying to hide? On March 27, in an attempt to beat back the angry tide, Tydings called as witnesses Attorney General Howard McGrath and J. Edgar Hoover, both of whom testified that the files could not be released for the familiar reasons: because release would expose secret informants, and because the files contained raw, unevaluated data whose publication might destroy reputations of innocent people.

Hoover further testified that in 98 or 99 percent of the cases, the fact that the FBI had not sent a person's file to the Justice Department meant that there was no conclusive case. In the rare exception when that did not apply, it was because the bureau wanted to keep the suspect under surveillance to implicate others. This was one time Hoover's testimony cut no ice. Wherry told the Senate that its inquiry was being "hamstrung by the President's shameful refusal to cooperate in this patriotic effort upon which the security of our country may depend." On the radio McCarthy declared, "The President is afraid to make those files available." Finally, in May, in a vain effort to take the issue away from the Republicans, Truman, reversing himself in an exception to his ruling, agreed to let Tydings committee members examine the files of the 81 accused individuals. That settled nothing. McCarthy brazenly shifted ground. The files would prove nothing, he coolly asserted, because they had been "skeletonized," "tampered with," "raped."

Several days before, Democrats on the Senate floor called McCarthy a liar. Scott Lucas read a statement from John Peurifoy, in charge of State Department security, in which he contended that far from presenting new, sensational information, McCarthy had revived shop-worn charges that had been rejected by the Republican-controlled Eightieth Congress. Matthew Neely shouted that if McCarthy's accusations were disproven, "those responsible should be scourged from the company of decent men." He demanded that the Tydings committee determine "where the truth lies" regarding McCarthy's Wheeling, West Virginia, speech in which he made his original charge that he held in hand the evidence that there were 205 Communists in the State Department, because "some one whose identity is not yet officially determined is lying at the rate Ananias never lied." On June 1 Margaret Chase Smith, in presenting to the Senate "A Declaration of Conscience" signed by herself and six other Republicans, denounced, in effect, McCarthy and his backers. She saw the growth of "a national feeling of fear and frustration that could result in national suicide," said she was "not proud of the reckless abandon in which unproven charges have been hurled from this side of the aisle," did not wish to see her party ride to political victory "on the four horsemen of calumny—fear, ignorance, bigotry and smear." A month later, the Tydings committee brought in its majority report that branded McCarthy's charges as "a fraud and a hoax perpetrated on the Senate and the American people." McCarthy answered with a threat that the Communists "will be dug out one by one, regardless of how frantically Tydings screams for their protection." He gave the senators notice to prepare for a lengthy siege: "The job will be a long and difficult one in view of the fact that all of the power of the administration is dedicated to the task of protecting the traitors, Communists, and fellow travelers in our government."

Neither the hearings, nor the report, nor the tongue-lashing from the Senate floor dented McCarthy. On the contrary. He bloomed like a crocus in springtime. What would have, in different circumstances, destroyed another senator's career, left him untroubled, unscarred. He was clothed in immunities that made a mockery of the accepted laws of political warfare. Without belittling the considerable talents he had displayed for blackguarding, double-shuffling, and demagogy in his five-month campaign, there obviously were new elements in the political mix to account for his run of luck. Dewey had tried the Communist issue on Roosevelt in 1944 without success. The Republicans could not make it a major campaign issue in 1948. Now, two years later, it was working like magic. Some have pointed out that in the interim, the public had been bombarded with spy sensations in the two Hiss trials, the Coplon trial, the arrest of Klaus Fuchs in

England, reinforcing the disquiet caused by the government's own loyalty investigations, so that the idea that Communists had infiltrated into high government positions and were conniving to defeat our projects and plans was given credibility.

The Hiss case especially had a profound effect on public opinion since Hiss had been an important State Department functionary and had attended the Yalta conference. Even if Whittaker Chambers' accusations against Hiss were accepted as accurate—and to this day there remain grave unresolved questions since Chambers changed his testimony on crucial matters between his grand jury appearance and the trials—neither the Hiss nor other spy sensations automatically explain why they should have damaged the government in office. The Fuchs, Pontocorvo, Burgess and MacLean spy exposures in England, of a far more serious nature, never served to discredit the government. When there were suggestions in the British press that the Fuchs case showed security inefficiency, Attlee promptly rejected the aspersion and absolved the predecessor Churchill government of any blame. "I am satisfied that unless we had had the kind of secret police they have in totalitarian countries, and employed their methods, which are reprobated, rightly, by everyone in this country, there were no means by which we could have found out about this man." There was no further discussion in Parliament. There was no public outcry, no government crisis, no mad chase after security risks.

Here the spy cases cast doubt on the administration's ability and sincerity in clearing Communists out of government because—unlike Attlee's exculpation of the opposition—the Republican Old Guard decided to exploit public bewilderment and anxiety. Margaret Chase Smith's sentiment that she did not want the Republicans to ride to victory on the four horsemen of calumny was not shared by Taft or the other stalwarts, or, before long, by almost all Republicans. The 1948 election had demonstrated their desperate need for new talking points to divert the electorate's attention from questions of domestic economics. Ranting about the "loss" of China held possible rewards, but was that enough? Supplemented by a panic about Reds-in-government, it could make a winning Republican platform. So the fateful decision was made to frighten the public to the end that the Republicans could climb triumphant out of the bedlam.

In January Taft rose in the Senate to weave together the loss-of-China and betrayal-from-within themes. "The State Department," he said, "has been guided by a left wing group who obviously have wanted to get rid of Chiang, and were willing at least to turn China

over to the Communists for that purpose." Next month, three days before McCarthy surfaced at Wheeling, the Republican National Committee laid it on the line in a declaration of principles: "We denounce
the soft attitude of this administration toward government employees
and officials who hold or support Communist attitudes." Whatever
hesitation Taft evinced the first few days after McCarthy's opening
foray in the Senate about tying Republican fortunes to this freebooter
("A perfectly reckless performance," he had called McCarthy's ti-
rade), were quickly dispelled when it was evident that the senator was
more than holding his own.

All through the Tydings hearings, Burke Hickenlooper ran interference for McCarthy, calling out protests, making threats, engaging in
rough exchanges with the Democratic members. After the first few
days, Owen Brewster complained feelingly in the Senate about
McCarthy's mistreatment and warned of an impending "whitewash."
When Franklin Roosevelt, Jr., made a speech in the House in praise
of ambassador-at-large Philip Jessup, one of McCarthy's targets for
the smear, his remarks were drowned out by the hoots and jeers of
the Republicans. At the height of the campaign in March, Taft, who
after Vandenberg's removal from the scene because of illness, was the
all-powerful policy maker calling Republican signals, said to reporters that "McCarthy should keep talking and if one case doesn't work,
he should proceed with another." Again, "Whether Senator McCarthy
has legal evidence, whether he has overstated or understated his case,
is of lesser importance. The question is whether the Communist influence in the State Department still exists." After he pronounced the
Tydings report to be "of a purely political nature" and "derogatory
and insulting to Senator McCarthy," the Senate divided in the vote
on strict party lines, 45 Democrats for, 37 Republicans against. Not
even the signers of the conscience declaration had the temerity to
break party ranks. The die was cast.

McCarthy's hocus-pocus and congressional caterwauling would
have availed little without the cooperation of the press. Jack Anderson and Ronald W. May recognized this when, in what was one of
the first full-scale exposés of McCarthy, they wrote, "You can dis-
count his personal ambition; that may have started the McCarthy fly-
wheel, but it was the press that kept the wheel turning. You can dis-
count his native cunning; had it not been for the fourth estate, he'd
have used this talent in a vacuum. If Joe McCarthy is a political monster, then the press has been his Dr. Frankenstein." The Hearst chain,
with its then eighteen newspapers, news wire service, *Cosmopolitan*

magazine, three radio stations, and other subsidiaries, built up the hero and traduced the critics. The other press lord, Colonel Robert McCormick, and his niece, Ruth McCormick Miller, contributed their stable of roughhouse reporters from the *Chicago Tribune* and *Washington Times-Herald* to the cause. The big brass was joined by a supporting section of numerous newspapers outside the major cities, as well as Facts Forum with its public-opinion poll mailed to 1,800 newspapers and radio program carried on more than 200 stations.

The unabashed McCarthy cheerleaders were not his sole, or most important publicists. Virtually the entire press, particularly at the initial stage, joined in to broadcast, and lend credence to, his accusations, intensify the hubbub, popularize his medicine show. Without this gratuitous advertising, the house would never have been filled. This towering, compromising datum has been obscured for several reasons. McCarthy would seize an incidental or mild criticism of his methods to chastise and threaten offending publications. He not only tried to punish by applying the Red brush to them, but would circularize their advertisers to withdraw their patronage. As he gained in power and insolence, he scrimmaged with the *Milwaukee Journal*, the *Madison Capital Times*, columnist Drew Pearson, *Time* magazine, the *Washington Post*, the *St. Louis Post-Dispatch*, the *Christian Science Monitor*, *The New York Times*, the wire services.

It was a sour jest nonetheless that while these and other critical newspapers were rebuking him in occasional editorials, they continued to splash his vilifications as authentic facts across their front pages. Apologists for the press owners explained this singular behavior by McCarthy's adroitness in taking advantage of the press requirement for objective reporting. The explanation went that the American press, schooled in the tradition of impartial presentation of the news, was not equipped to deal with a politician who specialized in the big lie. The newspapers had no alternative but to accept the role of gullible fools that McCarthy assigned to them. In a special series of articles, *The New York Times* admitted that it had misled its readers, but pleaded that it was in no position to ignore McCarthy's charges "just because they are usually proved exaggerated or false." It concluded fatuously that "the remedy lies with the reader." The explanation did not explain. Why were McCarthy's accusations and self-serving announcements "facts" and "news" that had to be reported straight, and his contradictions, failures to supply promised proofs, known falsifications, not equally "facts" and "news"? William Evjue, the editor of the *Madison Capital Times*, documented the systematic selectivity that was employed. Students of American journalism, aware of the formidable techniques perfected by the media to puff or deflate a public personality, will guffaw at the suggestion that worldly-wise press lords were unwitting or unwilling victims of a demagogue's craftiness. After he was censured by the Senate, and expelled, in effect, from the "club," the wires abruptly went dead. Newspapers and press services that supposedly had to publicize McCarthy's charges because they were news, could find no more space for his fulminations.

This is not to say that the McCarthy operation lacked box office appeal. It had the excitement of the chase, the drama of the spy thriller. A nation bred on Mike Hammer and Superman, heroes who ignored criminal statutes and, uninhibited by legal niceties, single-handedly meted out summary justice to Communists and crooks, identified with a roughneck who acted the part of a Hollywood private eye. No sooner did the Tydings hearings get under way than he set up his own counterespionage establishment separate from his Senate office, and called on all patriotic Americans to feed him confidential information without reference to their superiors. One of his cloak-and-dagger haunts, replete with dictaphones and recording machines, was in the basement of the Senate Office Building; another, in the Congressional Hotel on Capitol Hill. Supervising the little Gestapo was Don Surine, just fired from the FBI for fraternizing with a Baltimore lady of the evening whom he had been assigned to investigate on a white slavery charge. Where the funds for the Mad Hatter operation were coming from—like most of McCarthy's finances—was somewhat murky. As his gumshoe campaign gathered momentum, he received big chunks of money from Joseph Kennedy, Texas oil barons, Hearst and McCormick moguls, and many, many others. It is believed that the China Lobby, Chiang Kai-shek's American propaganda arm, supplied him with his initial funds. Then, as the passion play got started, he became the beneficiary, as well, of an outpouring of $1 and $5 contributions from anti-Communist votaries for whom the long-awaited avenger had arrived.

It was the 1950 election that gave McCarthy his reputation that anyone who challenged or crossed him had written his own political death warrant. He had sent his agents into Maryland where they defeated Tydings on his home ground with a political unknown in a scurrilous campaign that featured the use of fraudulent photographs, defamatory literature, and violations of Maryland election laws. He had campaigned against Scott Lucas in Illinois, and Lucas had gone down. What if his vaunted prowess were exaggerated, and other factors figured in the election results? This was no time—when the public was aroused about Reds and McCarthy had seized the leadership of the issue—to tangle with this ruthless character and his private Mafia. Though never the leader of the Republican inner circle, and with only a handful of senators and congressmen for acolytes, he had emerged as an independent power looming over the Senate, goading the body to accommodate itself to his excesses, terrorizing recalcitrants, overawing the club leaders and the administration.

Nine months after the election, a select Senate committee filed a unanimous report that "unreservedly denounced, condemned and censured" the tactics used to defeat Tydings. It suggested that "the question of unseating a Senator" might well include the behind-the-scenes organizer of the election campaign as well as the front man who had been elected. The report rolled off McCarthy as had the Tydings report. He had succeeded in injecting into American politics the special venom of the Renaissance condottieri epoch when the frame-up, the dagger thrust from ambush, the assassin's bullet in the back, were standard reliables of political discourse. One of his agents was convicted by a Swiss court for sending a faked telegram to John Carter Vincent, then American minister to Switzerland (one of the "China hands" on Hurley's hate list), to try to make him appear a Communist. The atmosphere in Washington at the time is conveyed in Owen Lattimore's account of the meeting with his attorney, Abe Fortas (later appointed to the Supreme Court by President Lyndon B. Johnson), during the Tydings hearings:

> He shut his door behind us, looked at me squarely and said nothing for what seemed like a long, long time. Then he said, "McCarthy is a long way out on a limb. The political pressures that are building up are terrific. The report that Budenz will testify against you has shaken every one in Washington. It is my duty as your lawyer to warn you that the danger you face cannot possibly be exaggerated. It does not exclude the possibility of a straight frameup, with perjured witnesses and perhaps even forged documents. You have a choice of two ways of facing this danger. You can either take it head on, and expose yourself to this danger; or you can make a qualified and carefully guarded statement which will reduce the chance of en-

trapment by fake evidence. As your lawyer I cannot make that choice for you. You have to make it yourself."

The rise of McCarthy signified the passage of the witch-hunt into a second, more acute stage. Already far advanced when he discovered its potentialities, he took it and broadened it into a quasisocial movement, or, at least, phenomenon. The Republicans' decision to embrace McCarthyism was given social substance not because isolated millionaires were bankrolling McCarthy, but because an important section of the entire business community resolved to move into camp. Marquis Childs, the columnist, wrote of "the conviction of many businessmen who are Republicans that anything goes in driving the Democrats out. They are sometimes frankly cynical about it." In a later 1954 study in *Fortune* magazine, big-business executives when interviewed showed a cold-blooded calculation for their support of McCarthy ("to keep the albatross hung about the neck of the New and Fair Deals"), said they would drop him the minute he went demagogic, by which they did not mean using good demagogy, like calling the New Deal Communist, but bad demagogy, like advocating a radical social program the way Hitler did in his barnstorming days. There was talk in 1954 that McCarthy was trying to split the Republicans, crush the elements around Eisenhower, reconstitute the party under ultraconservative auspices. Charles Murphy, the author of the study, explained that "for McCarthy to get very far with this kind of 'reform' of the Republican party, he would need, at least at the outset, the support of the business community, whatever diverse political combinations and permutations he might thereafter find it desirable to contrive." He went on to point out that it was a consortium of Wisconsin businessmen that in 1946 helped finance and engineer McCarthy's rise from a county judgeship to the Senate, that "an aura of big business, or at least big money, has enveloped the Senator ever since," and that it was money "contributed by his well-heeled supporters" that helped defeat Lucas in Illinois and Tydings in Maryland.

Naturally, as in all large social developments, there were cross currents, and poll statistics showed at different times large numbers of professionals and businessmen opposed to McCarthy. But the dominant note for four and a half years inside the private clubs, at country club socials, or chamber of commerce reunions, was the hunter's cry of elation when he has bagged his game.

McCarthy's importance to the venture consisted in this: He was not just a more flamboyant Mundt or Jenner; in contrast to the medicine men who had preceded him, he conjured up a substantial following across the country. McCarthyism became a battle cry as well as a by-word. It is difficult to analyze his following since it was without doctrine or organization. There was not a glimmering of program, platform, declaration of aims, avowal of coherent purpose. There was not a scintilla of organization, even informal or decentralized. The movement consisted of the messiah making speeches for four-figure lecture fees to admiring crowds who fed on his slapstick theatricals and periodic press sensations and donated $1 and $5 bills (some of which he apparently used for betting on horses and private speculations). An activist core of the faithful was made up of the Fascist or semi-Fascist groups that had formed in the 1930s and had furnished the Greek choruses for Father Coughlin, Dies, and succeeding demagogues. Another notable section was in the Catholic constituency, particularly among the Irish, many of whom flocked to McCarthy's banner under the tutelage of their priests after Cardinal Spellman and other leaders of the hierarchy espoused the cause.

The massive backing came from traditional conservatives who, even if they never attended a rally or contributed a dollar, lent their moral support when their political leaders and opinion-setters shifted to McCarthyism, and the witch-hunt had become a respectable enterprise among their peers and in their worlds. It was McCarthy's achievement that, in addition, substantial numbers that generally voted Democratic were among his supporters or sympathizers. He made it easier for many at working-class and lower-income levels because, unlike Dies and other Red-baiters, he refrained from attacking labor unions or labor leaders, and unlike Taft and the Old Guard, he never attacked New Deal social legislation. His excoriation of Roosevelt and New Dealers centered invariably on Communist betrayals and betrayers in distant foreign policy fields and matters. In such a mongrel hodgepodge of a following there was the widest variation in individual motivations and aspirations ranging from the cynical to the zany. If there was no coherent structure of positions and political aims at the popular level, the heavy who ran the show, and those who had thrown a mantle of respectability over him, knew very specifically what they were after.

It was not a fascist movement, nor was there ever any attempt made to organize the following into one. McCarthy did not have the temperament or gifts to organize any kind of movement. His personal predilections and lacks were not the decisive reason, however. Others could have come forward or been assigned for the task. No attempt was made nor could it have been made. At the first hint of extralegal military formations, of challenges to established elite institutions, of radical social agitation, the support at the top would have been abruptly withdrawn, and the bulk of the following, mobilized within the framework of respectability, would have melted away. From the first to the last, it was an elitist-controlled mobocracy. America was not in a social crisis in 1950 comparable to the one of 1932; it was in a Republican-induced political convulsion—which was not the same thing. The fever chart registered highest in the Washington pressure cooker, newspaper editorial offices, and political clubs, and dropped abruptly the farther out one moved into the country. In the summer of 1951, after the Democratic electoral upsets, two-thirds of those interviewed by the Gallup pollsters had no opinion about McCarthy, either because they had never heard of him, or just had no opinion. In 1954, when successive Gallup polls recorded a third to a half of those interviewed as favoring McCarthy, the substantial study of Samuel Stouffer laid out evidence that less than 1 percent of the population was worried either about the Communist threat in the country or about civil liberties; nearly one-third could not name a single senator or congressman who had led an investigation of Communism.

McCarthy was the big hit of the 1952 Republican convention, the darling of the galleries; when it came to picking the presidential candidate, no one proposed him; and his ally, Taft, was passed over in favor of the father figure who stood above the fray. The Eastern kingmakers cased the voting public as those election analysts did who wrote after the event: "In view of the enormous furor over internal subversion and the conduct of Senator McCarthy, it is astonishing to discover that the issue of domestic Communism was little mentioned by the public in 1952." All this did not gainsay the potency of the Red issue in certain local and state elections and in certain situations, or its burdensome impact on the political structure. Active minorities, rather than inert majorities, shape the course of politics. But it did demonstrate that politicians and pressmen were creating a false impression of the country's total mood.

Where Truman was earlier contesting for anti-Communist leadership, after McCarthy's advent the Democrats were flaunting their anti-Communist credentials to prevent getting run over. In the summer of 1950, while mobilization was under way for the Korean war, Congress was occupied with the McCarran bill to lock the gates on subversion. The bill had a checkered history. Numbers of alien, sedition, and subversion bills had been tossing about in the congressional hopper, some introduced by the Justice Department, some by congressional Communist specialists. In 1948 the House had passed the Mundt-Nixon bill, which required Communist organizations to register with the Attorney General, set up a board to determine which organizations were Communist, and denied members of such organizations federal or defense employment, passports, and other rights. The Senate took no appropriate action until McCarthy's opening salvos when a companion measure was introduced and placed by the Republican Policy Committee on its "must" list. To head off the Republican bill, Truman sent a message to Congress urging a slightly modified version of an old Justice Department measure that had also originally passed in the House, described by Max Lowenthal, occasional presidential consultant who had been counsel in the old senatorial railroad investigation, as worse than a sedition bill because it depended on determining what was in an accused's mind. McCarran took the updated version of the Mundt-Nixon bill, tacked on a number of other nostrums that had been offered by assorted apothecaries over the past decade, and reported out of his Judiciary Committee the omnibus bill. The Democratic leadership, shaken by the Tydings debacle, begged Truman to accept the measure. "A lot of people on the Hill," he noted, "had been stampeded into running with their tails between their legs." Truman insisted on his counterproposition, introduced only in late August by Representative Emanuel Celler, chairman of the House Judiciary Committee. This was described by David Lloyd, one of Truman's aides, in a vein similar to Lowenthal's earlier characterization of the Justice Department contribution, as "worse than the Mundt bill. All the arguments against a Political Purity Board apply with greater force against the Attorney General as a political purifier."

At this point the Democratic liberals took their stand at Thermopylae. Led by Harley Kilgore, Paul Douglas, and Hubert Humphrey, they offered as a substitute for the McCarran bill a measure for preventive detention of political subversives upon a presidential declaration of an internal security emergency, the "concentration-camp bill," as it became known. This was supposed to block the Republican attack on civil liberties while establishing at the same time the abiding anti-Communist attachments of the Democrats. The potlatch contest was on to see who could give away more of the Bill of Rights. The concentration-camp bill was rejected by the Senate as a substitute for the McCarran bill; then, on the motion of Scott Lucas, it was accepted as an addition to the McCarran bill. Thus, the McCarran bill, as it was finally adopted, included the registration provisions of the wicked Republicans, and the concentration-camp provisions of the virtuous Democrats. They had joined forces to pass the bill almost unanimously, and overrode Truman's veto by 286 to 46 in the House and 57 to 10 in the Senate. The squalid stage business accompanying the passage of the McCarran Act disclosed in a flash the complementary roles of the main actors: the President who vetoed the bill on the lofty grounds that it would "endanger the freedoms protected by the first amendment," while pressing for his own bill whose major distinction was that it would leave the witch-hunt in the reliable hands of the FBI and the Attorney General; the Democratic liberals who decided "to fight fire with fire," and urged the President to veto the bill for which most of them had voted; the reactionaries who were saving the country from evil spirits by ramming through a proposition that invited Communists or those so designated to come in and register as subversives to ease the way for the government to crack down on them.

After the Republican gains in the 1950 election (Democratic panic was out of proportion to Republican gains; the Republicans won fewer seats than in the three previous midterm elections), James Rowe, a former administrative assistant to Roosevelt, wrote to James Webb, the budget director: "It is clear to me and I state it as a fact, not as an opinion, that no Democratic politician in the Senate or the House will undertake to defend the Department of State in the next session of Congress." Rowe's prediction was accurate. As a matter of fact unbridled attacks on Acheson had for a year become as regular as Truman's early morning walks. If a week had gone by with no Solon calling on the Secretary of State to resign for the good of the country, newspapermen would have been on the lookout for a Republican policy switch. There was not very much that McCarthy could add to this ploy. What he could add, he did. In May, 1951, he imparted to the perennial demand his own trademarks of vitriol. "Mr. Acheson!" he declaimed. "If you want to at long last perform one service for the American people, you should not only resign from the State Department but you should remove yourself from this country and go to the nation for which you have been struggling and fighting so long."

Since in all walks of life there is a numerous tribe that mistakes the exploitation of a person's appearance or mannerisms in a propaganda attack for the causes of the attack, it was common talk that Acheson was bringing many of his troubles upon himself. His self-assurance verging on arrogance and his patrician putdown of the Claghorns and Throttlebottoms on Capitol Hill all added up to waving a red cloak in front of the bull. Major General Harry Vaughan, who in the midst of these grim proceedings was tending to his own business of doing favors for the worthy and collecting funds for the Democratic election coffers, related how it looked from the cocktail bars as to what was wrong and how it could be set right. "His elegant appearance and continental manner were against him. I told him he should wear a ratty moustache, wrinkled suit and an American type hat, drop his British accent and make a grammatical error in each speech." What Vaughan and other penetrating thinkers failed to take into consideration was that others, without bristling moustaches or homburg hats, were also targets of the Neanderthal hunt. This was dramatized when, just a few weeks after his attack on Acheson, McCarthy loosed his broadside against Marshall, thought to be beyond the reach of partisan assault, and a five-star general, to boot. "How can we account for our present situation," McCarthy wanted to know, "unless we believe that men high in this government are concerting to deliver us to disaster? This must be the product of a great conspiracy." Nobody took the charge seriously that Marshall was part of a great conspiracy to destroy the United States. Taft even made a feeble attempt to disassociate himself from the attack. But McCarthy demonstrated again the validity of the maxim that if you throw enough mud, some of it will stick. While no one believed the charge, Marshall was torn down from his pedestal. He had become "controversial," a classification sufficiently devastating in those days to push actors, entertainers, newscasters, into the ranks of the unemployed. Several months after the attack Marshall resigned to retire to his farm in Leesburg, Virginia.

Acheson could not be similarly intimidated. He waved away the recurrent attacks with a disdainful fling of the hand. He scorned the opposition when he informed reporters after Hiss's conviction that he did not intend to turn his back on Alger Hiss and referred them to the 25th chapter of the Gospel according to St. Matthew. Then he drove to the White House and said to Truman that, of course, he was ready to resign should that be thought necessary. Truman replied that he understood his attitude perfectly, and reminded him that he had similarly been heavily criticized when, as a mark of tribute to his old friend, he and his wife had gone to Pendergast's funeral. Despite the stiff upper lip and Episcopalian rectitude, Acheson did not avoid running before the shamans. He fired John S. Service on the recommendation of the Loyalty Board although Service had been cleared in six previous loyalty-security checks and three loyalty hearings. (The decision was invalidated by the Supreme Court six years later on the ground that the department had violated its own regulations.) Others were similarly dismissed. The Foreign Service *Journal* protested that the department was failing to protect its employees. The *Washington Post* observed earlier that Acheson "has seemed to be striving to appease the most reactionary elements in the Republican party." Truman himself had to beat back attacks on his own inner household when McCarthy flung out random charges, first against David Lloyd, who had once belonged to the National Lawyers Guild, then against Phileo Nash, another aide. The administration was under siege.

All in all, Truman was able to keep his composure, poise, energy, and health while subjected to ferocious pressures and calumniations. Few Presidents have had to labor in more noxious and cramped conditions. He had learned well from his old mentor how to shrug off the dead cats and barbed shafts thrown at him by the opposition. But he was not a blameless bystander. With his own hands he had set up the nursery in which the rogue politicians had grown. And he had put into motion his own loyalty and security chase. So that if McCarthyism had never come, Trumanism would have been the designation for a more orderly, bureaucratic, administration-led witch-hunt.

19

The
Last
Hurrah

In the fall of 1951 Truman offered Vinson the presidential nomination. Vinson, finally declining for reasons of health, had apparently decided 1952 would not be a Democratic year. Truman also sounded out Eisenhower—according to Arthur Krock who got the story from Justice Douglas—repeating a similar offer of support made four years earlier, and again received a negative response. The canvass of available candidates then led to Adlai Stevenson, governor of Illinois. Stevenson was a hot political property at the time. He had won the governorship in 1948 by a margin of 572,000 votes, the largest plurality in Illinois history, while Truman carried the state by 33,000. He was adjudged by newspapermen to be the head of a brilliant state administration. He came of a renowned political family. He was personable, articulate, witty, considered one of the most appealing men on the political scene.

Stevenson turned Truman down at a January conference, and again at a March talk. Like Vinson, he offered many reasons why he could not accept. And, like Vinson, he did not believe 1952 was going to be a Democratic year. After he returned from Washington, he went over the situation with Jacob Arvey, the Cook County boss who had been his political sponsor. Arvey related:

[He] told me he did not want me to do anything to aid in the movement to make him President, that he was satisfied the way he was. He further said that it appeared that Eisenhower would be the Republican nominee and he did not think that Eisenhower could be beaten, that the American people were a hero-worshipping breed, and that we had been in office—the Democratic party, that is—since 1932, had made many enemies, that our mistakes had been unduly emphasized, and that whoever the Democratic nominee was he would inherit all the criticism that had been leveled at the Democrats for twenty years.

Stevenson's bowing out of the race left Truman in a dilemma. The other major contender, Estes Kefauver, who was going into the primaries, was anathema to the professionals (Truman's name for him was "Cowfever"); his sensational crime investigation hearings of the year before had put many Democratic officeholders on the spot. Briefly, Truman thought of making another run himself. He broached the idea at a dinner meeting with several of his advisers including Frank McKinney, the new Democratic National Committee chairman. All of them, as tactfully as they could, counseled against it. On March 29, he announced at a Jefferson-Jackson Day dinner that he was not a candidate for reelection. This put Stevenson at the eye of the storm. On *Meet the Press,* to the insistent question, he gave the reply he had given before and was to repeat up to the convention: "I am pledged to run for Governor. I must run for Governor. I want to run for Governor. I seek no other office. I have no other ambition." When Lawrence Spivak, the program moderator, asked, "Governor, doesn't this large studio audience give you an indication how some of the people of the country feel about that?" Stevenson answered: "It's very flattering, indeed, and I suppose flattery hurts no one—that is, if he doesn't inhale."

Three months later, at the Chicago International Amphitheater, it was foregone that Stevenson was to be the candidate. He still feebly thrashed about like a fish before expiring, but he knew he could not jump clear of the net. He became the beneficiary of the only draft in the country's history—except for the 1880 call to the colors of James A. Garfield—due to an unusual confluence of circumstances. A by-product of Stevenson's noncandidacy was a weakening of Truman's control. In the decisive preceding months Truman could not issue clear directives to his henchmen. Only shortly before the convention did he settle on Barkley. This was a decision of desperation. The Vice-President could stir no enthusiasm among the party faithful. Upon his withdrawal, the Democrats had their first open convention since 1932. Stevenson was the indispensable man at this particular juncture to hold the South and professionals while attracting the basic liberal blocs. Besides the Presidency, there were the congressional and local candidates to consider. Whether the big steamer made port or not, party leaders hoped it would work up sufficient current to bring in the skiffs and catboats.

By July 24, when nominations were to begin, an authoritative coalition had been cemented, and Stevenson had given his consent. He made a courtesy telephone call to Truman in Washington asking if it would embarrass him if he, Stevenson, permitted his name to be placed in nomination. Truman reported, "I replied with a show of exasperation and some rather vigorous remarks." Anyone acquainted with Truman's vocabulary knew what this meant. He concluded, "I have been trying since January to get you to say that. Why should it embarrass me?" Why? Stevenson's refusal to accept the nomination from him had virtually cut off Truman's power over the convention. He hastily flew to Chicago and persuaded the New York leaders to have Harriman withdraw in favor of Stevenson. He kept the appearance of kingmaking though the substance had eluded him. So it appeared to Walter Lippmann who wrote before the nomination:

> There is no doubt, I think, that from the beginning Stevenson had seen the reality of the situation with extraordinary objectivity and penetration. He has not been coy. He has been wise in realizing what after twenty years in office it would mean to take over the leadership of the Democratic party.
>
> It could be done only under conditions which, if not unique in politics, are very rare indeed. The new leadership had to draw its strength from the mass of the party, not from the outgoing President. There was no value in the kind of nomination for which Vice-President Barkley was, so cynically and so briefly, considered.
>
> The new leadership had to be drafted. It could not be appointed from the White House. A draft, as everyone knows, is almost never genuine. In the case of Stevenson, if he is nominated, there will have been a genuine draft.

He will have been drafted because the party needs the
man more than he desired the office.

The rift between President and candidate widened as Stevenson deliberately put distance between himself and the administration. He
set up campaign headquarters in Springfield, Illinois, to get away
from White House influences and pressures. McKinney was replaced
by Stephen Mitchell as head of the national committee. An imposing
brain trust and team of speech writers, Arthur Schlesinger, Jr., John
Kenneth Galbraith, John Bartlow Martin, Sidney Hyman, John Fisher,
Bernard De Voto—precisely the kind of men Truman could not abide
—moved into Springfield to churn out the verbal and intellectual artillery of the campaign. There was validity in Stevenson's effort to disassociate himself from what the Republicans dubbed "the mess in
Washington," as later researches into voter motivations showed, but
the attempt was futile. Willy-nilly, the Democratic candidate had to
run on the record of past Democratic administrations. He could not
take what he liked and discard what he did not like. His occasional
suggestions that, as the reforming governor of Illinois, he was the
ideal man to run a tight, clean ship were lost in the carnival din, and
led to heightened friction with Truman. When Stevenson and his
aides paid a visit to the White House in August to discuss campaign
strategy, Roger Tubby of Truman's staff related, "I almost had the
feeling that a Republican nominee had come into the house with his
team to discuss the takeover."

The tactic was doomed by the logic of the situation. The Republicans made Truman the main butt of their broadsides. And Truman
was not one to permit the opposition to damn him, his aides, his
works, without giving as good as he got. He took to the hustings to
defend, in his own style, his record and honor. Though tensions between Stevenson and Truman, and poor synchronization of their
speech-making campaigns, exasperated the Democratic stage managers, they did not materially affect the outcome. The character of the
Democratic campaign and the election results were determined by
factors transcending the absence of rapport between the outgoing
President and the new Democratic spokesman.

In crucial essentials, the campaign did not proceed in accordance
with the blueprints drawn up by the strategists of either party. Eisenhower's victory over Taft at the Republican convention presaged a
Whig-type campaign of bombast and platitude set out in the accep-

tance speech his handlers prepared for him. They calculated using the symbol of the military hero to blot out other considerations and questions, to mesmerize the public with parochial folklore and copybook maxims, to create a larger-than-life figure of patriotism and wisdom standing above the squabbles of grubby partisans. Eisenhower slid into the role as if born to it, for he was past master of the opaque, about whom ambiguity gathered like dawn fog on the dunes. At his arranged homecoming to Abilene in June, apotheosizing this living embodiment of the American Dream, the man of destiny said to his admiring neighbors gathered round: "In spite of the difficulties of the problems we have, I ask you this one question: If each of us in his own mind would dwell more upon those simple virtues—integrity, courage, self-confidence, an unshakable belief in his bible—would not some of these problems tend to simplify themselves?"

He was the perfect candidate for the buildup. His outgoing personality, his engaging grin, his enthusiastic greeting of crowds with arms flung out in a triumphal V, his air of geniality, tolerance, and understanding, his note of deeply felt conviction when talking about morality in public life, the gracious, sweet helpmeet at his side—all of this gave the immense crowds that came out to see him the feeling that the hero's reputation was well earned. His attitudes fitted the mood of the times, the weariness with "big questions" and "world issues," the retreat to private concerns, the rediscovery of the homespun virtues of hearth and home. And yet the image, so captivating, so reassuring, would not have lasted out the campaign, much less his two administrations, had the newspapers and networks not protected and perpetuated it, for its relation to this cold, calculating man was that of a court portrait to its monarchical subject.

The influence of the media was all the more telling because the hucksters, this time, were working with the grain and in virtual unanimity. To the section of the press that traditionally supported Republicans were added major newspapers like *The New York Times*, the *Chicago Sun-Times*, the *Washington Post*, whose editors went on the theory, widely accepted, that only an Eisenhower victory would cure the Republican party of parochialism and nihilism, and rid American politics of the McCarthyite incubus. The media did nothing so crude as the *San Francisco Call* did in 1896, when it printed 1,075 column inches of the McKinley campaign to 11 inches of the Bryan campaign; they just accepted at face value the self-serving handouts ground out by the Eisenhower staffs, and added their own superlatives to create the reverential mood of national enchantment. They sought to make the hero not only impervious to criticism; they sought to make criticism sacrilegious, like questioning a national holiday, or knocking mother's home cooking.

By late August the fear arose that psalm-singing superimposed on a Dewey-type campaign would not be enough. The Scripps-Howard chain gave warning in a front-page editorial printed across the country: IKE IS RUNNING LIKE A DRY CREEK. His speeches were those of "another me-too candidate." All through the summer, while the military hero was exuding the aura of middle-of-the-road statesmanship, Republican orators and publications had been blazing away on the themes that had been worked up since 1950. With Ike's invasion of the South in September the decision was made to go over to the offensive. He began hammering away at "the mess in Washington," the inevitable result of "an administration by too many men too small for their jobs, too big for their breeches, and too long in power," a mess the Democratic candidate would be helpless to clean up because he was a captive of the bosses who had handpicked him.

In New York Ike met with Taft, who had been sulking in his tent, and who had let it be known through Edwin Lahey of the *Chicago Daily News* that he would not support Eisenhower without assurances from the nominee himself on basic policy, as well as on the allocation of posts—and that he would want these assurances in writing. At the Morningside Heights conference Eisenhower agreed to and initialed Taft's text. Taft informed newspapermen, with the general's approval, that they were in full accord on campaign issues, and their differences on foreign policy were only differences of degree. Eisenhower cemented party unity by endorsing and campaigning with Jenner in Indiana and McCarthy in Wisconsin, even deleting a favorable reference to Marshall from his Milwaukee speech to avoid antagonizing the chief Communist-slayer. Efforts made by the nominee to keep up the high moral tone with which he had started his campaign, and to affirm his allegiance to stern spiritual values, were more than supplemented by the vice-presidential candidate and the congressional contingent. Nixon called Stevenson "Adlai, the Appeaser," who had shown poor judgment in lining up with the traitor Alger Hiss. He said he was "a graduate of Dean Acheson's spineless school of diplomacy which cost the free world six hundred million former allies." He said that four more years of Democratic rule would bring "more Alger Hisses, more atomic spies, more crises." McCarthy boasted that if he were put aboard Stevenson's campaign train with a club, he might be able to make a good American out of him. A week before the election, on nationwide television, armed with his customary sheaf of "documents" and "exhibits," he linked Stevenson with "the Acheson-Hiss-Lattimore group" that was working to aid the Communist cause. The crusade for morality in government had come a long way from that distant June in Denver when the general lectured delegates confering with him on the need of abjuring half-truths and glib slogans.

The Democratic campaign also changed noticeably from when Stevenson stood before the delegates in Chicago and proclaimed, "Let's talk sense to the American people." Stevenson was a high-minded, upper-classman who, in common with many associates from Chicago's La Salle Street law and business offices, thought originally that it might be healthy for the country if an Eisenhower-led Republican party took over the administration. His initial notion was to conduct a calm, reasonable discourse on the major issues to establish what united and what divided the two parties. What he meant when he made the plea for talking sense, was to try to convince the American people that the Cold War would be a long, grim struggle, with no easy victories or quick solutions, that they had to reconcile themselves and buckle down to a costly, sanguinary ordeal. These were not the tidings the American people were waiting to hear. By mid-September two considerations were borne in on him. His high-level discussion was getting him nowhere. And the national hero employed any expediency to exploit discontents and catch votes. He realized there was an apparent division of labor in which the hero mouthed elevated sentiments while the plug-uglies hurled the mud.

He had also assumed, or hoped, at the beginning, that foreign policy matters would be discussed on the level of Vandenberg nonpartisanship, and that he would be able to exploit, as he tried to do in his September 1 Grand Rapids speech, the division between the general who, "as far as I know, like myself, approves the basic direction our foreign policy has been following," and the Taft Republicans. He was therefore genuinely shocked by the Eisenhower-Taft pact. How could the general stoop so low? Had he not been Marshall's associate? Truman's chief of staff? First supreme commander of NATO? Stevenson was no summer soldier, no sometime fellow traveler of the Cold War. To him, a dedicated, unswerving veteran enlisted for the duration, Ike was sacrilegiously stamping on holy ground. ("Unconditional Surrender on Morningside Heights," Stevenson fumed; and noted that Taft must now be a six-star general since he had dictated terms to a five-star general.)

Consequently, by the time he swung back to the East, his battle plan was drastically revised. He had started out by referring to his rival with deference and promised he was not going to run against Hoover. Now he set out to destroy the Eisenhower myth and get the tag nailed back on the Republican hide as the party of depression. "If I should be elected President in November, I will be President," he belted out to his audience, "I will not be honorary head of a regency." And he described how when the Democrats took over in 1933, the nation was in a state of receivership, and that it was "the great and revered" Roosevelt who led the movement to restoration, reconstruction, and prosperity. Up and down the coast he gave hell to Hoover, Andrew Mellon, and the party of boom and bust. His periods were more graceful, his phrases more apt, than Truman's; the message on both the hero and Republican economics were remarkably similar. The attack began paying off. His campaign acquired momentum, the crowds grew bigger, the sense of purpose increased, and despite Eisenhower's earlier assurances that the reforms were no longer in dispute, the Republicans were here on the defensive. Later studies of the election established that popular fear of another depression was the strongest factor working for the Democrats in 1952, although this was blunted to an extent by indignation against high prices for which Truman was blamed.

Had the election been fought on grounds of depression versus corruption and who was the better fighter against Communism, the various charges and countercharges, pledges and counterpledges, would have largely canceled themselves out, and Eisenhower, profiting from his special status and genuine popularity, would have won in a close election. The electorate would have divided roughly along the lines of 1948 with the Eisenhower mystique supplying the margin for a Republican victory. As the wags put it, "There may not be enough time for General Eisenhower to lose the election." Of the Republican trinity of Communism, corruption, Korea, the first two were igniting the public less than the professionals then believed. Most of them assumed the Communist issue had some potency although no one was sure how much. Stevenson took the offensive against McCarthyism, felt impelled to make speeches on the Democratic record in fighting Communism, and to offer a lengthy defense for his deposition in the Hiss trial. Eisenhower endorsed the Red-hunters (one of them was his running mate), and never disassociated himself from scurrilous attacks against Stevenson or Truman. The most ringing declaration he made deprecating excesses was in his August 23 interview, when, prodded by reporters, he said, "I am not going to support anything that looks to me like unjust damaging of reputation. At the same time I certainly support those persons who will uproot anything that is subversive or disloyal." Later, in appealing for McCarthy's reelection, he permitted himself the feeble aside that the differences between himself and McCarthy "have nothing to do with the end result we are seeking. The differences apply to method." That the outcry against Reds-in-government carried much independent weight can be doubted because McCarthy and Jenner, the two main candidates exploiting the issue, ran far behind the national ticket, and, added Louis Harris, the pollster authority, "there is some doubt that either could have won had Eisenhower not made campaign appearances with them." For those who were exercised about Communism, it was generally the frosting on the anger over the war in Korea, or the two became indistinguishably blended.

Corruption was an issue of another order. The moral fiber of the Truman administration had been called into question by the highly publicized revelations of spoilsmongering. The personal authority of the President had been undermined. Though the Republicans exaggerated the malfeasance, and dealt with corruption on the puerile level of throwing the rascals out and replacing them with good Republican hacks, they were in a position to hang around the necks of Truman and his appointees proven scandals. At the outset of the campaign, Eisenhower brought roaring responses from the crowds when he promised to clean up "the mess" (a hasty pudding encompassing in addition to corruption, Communists, wrong policies, moral laxness, and other unspecified evils; it was the 1952 equivalent of the 1946 slogan, "Had Enough?"). Stevenson's spirited effort to blunt the impact of the attack by calling attention to his Illinois record was vitiated as Truman made himself increasingly heard in his whistle-stop tours around the country.

Truman lambasted the general for all manner of crimes and derelictions from his sellout to Taft to the Berlin blockade because he failed to see that his deputy, Clay, got a written agreement from the Russians on rights of access to the city. In another indictment, he charged the Republican candidate with adopting the Nazi theory of the master race on the ground that the Eightieth Congress had adopted an immigration law based on a national-origin quota system, "a Republican invention," and Republicans had voted 4 to 1 for the 1952 McCarran-Walter bill passed over his veto. When the Republicans countercharged that the bill was sponsored and supported by

Democrats, and that Eisenhower had said he was opposed to discrim-
inatory immigration laws, Truman came back with the assertion that
McCarran "is not my kind of Democrat," and contrasted his stand
with that of Eisenhower, who embraced Jenner and McCarthy. If it
was a contest of brawling, a Missouri politician was on home
grounds. Whatever other effects Truman's protracted barrage had, it
strengthened the feeling that Stevenson was a captive of the Democratic machine who would not be able to do much housecleaning.
After the revelation of Nixon's private slush fund, and the counterrev-
elation of Stevenson's private kitty, the issue receded to a subsidiary
place, to be caught up, like a minor planet of a solar system, in the
gravitational pull of the major star.

Cutting through the usual ambiguities and uncertainties of sample
polls of popular attitudes was the towering proposition that the Korean war was *the* issue of the campaign. All the studies, all the analyses, were unanimous on this score. It was the hegemonic question, the
topic of the first water. The nation was in the first stage of the fever
that a decade and a half later progressed to a convulsion. Where people made other complaints, these became subsumed under the general, fierce opposition to the war. There was an increase of almost 25
percent in the presidential vote over the previous election, a rate of
increase unmatched for a quarter of a century, and most of the newcomers were more in rebellion against the war than smitten by a demi-
god's glitter. It was not that the public knew what it wanted. Confused by the opposition's demagogy, buffeted by contradictory
accusations and demands, it had no clear-cut ideas on what should be
done. Harris concluded from the extensive Elmo Roper–NBC surveys
conducted in the middle of 1952 that the public did not favor any of
the actual policy alternatives available. People were just bitter and
hostile, convinced they had been gulled. Once in this frame of mind,
they were open to suggestions that plenty more must be wrong with a
leadership that had brought them to such an impasse.

That the public was bewildered is hardly surprising considering
the kind of attack that the Republicans mounted for over a year and
a half. It was equivocal, inconsistent, unscrupulous. The deafening orchestration zigzagged among discordant themes. We never should
have gone into Korea, we should withdraw our troops, the Democrats were the party of war, they were bumblers who had permitted
Stalin to entrap them, had given the signal that he could attack with
impunity. As early as January, 1951, Taft declared we had been
"sucked into the Korean war as a representative of the United Na-

tions by a delusion as to power which never has existed under the
Charter"; Jenner found that Truman had "blundered, tricked, betrayed us into a war"; Frank Carlson inveighed against Truman's
"snap decision"; Alexander Wiley was convinced that "Korea was a
trap for us and we fell into it"; Harry F. Cain introduced a resolution
calling for the withdrawal of the troops. The pseudopeace program
coexisted without embarrassment with the MacArthur militancy of
cleaning up in the Far East. The same Taft argued in April that if a
peace was negotiated in Korea on the previous line of division, it
would mean that "we have wasted 140,000 casualties and billions of
dollars." The following January the same Hoover who had called for
withdrawing our ground troops from the Far East attacked the armistice negotiations because "we have retreated from the original purpose of unity and independence for Korea to an appeasement idea of
a division of Korea about where it was before." Knowland was
against the very concept of a negotiated peace. The "peace at any
price" formula would constitute, in his view, "a tremendous victory
for aggressive Communism in Asia." This crude amalgam of pacifism
and jingoism was brought into the election campaign embellished
with new variations and contrapuntal accompaniments. To the furor
over Acheson's inviting Stalin to attack in Korea with his announcement that the country did not lie within our defense perimeter
was added the accusation that it was because of the Truman-Acheson
line of appeasement in withdrawing American troops from Korea
back in June, 1949, that American boys were being killed in a cruel
war. Containment, which abandoned countless victims to "godless
terrorism" was to be discarded in favor of "liberation" of the millions
of captive slaves behind the Iron Curtain. At the same time we would
reduce our military spending and foreign commitments to foil Stalin's
luring us into economic bankruptcy.

Taft's convention defeat at the hands of the Dewey-Lodge-Dulles
international crowd gave some hope that Korea might not become a
partisan issue in the campaign. That seemed to be the tenor of Eisenhower's preconvention remarks. In June he said, "I do not believe
that we can, in the ideological war we are waging, retreat from the
area we occupy. We have got to stand firm and to stand right there
and try to get a decent armistice out of it"; there was no "clean-cut
answer to bringing the Korean war to a successful conclusion." To
visiting delegations he gave the word that trying for a military victory would risk a general war. His managers heard the angry message
from the boondocks, however, no less clearly than had Taft. They had

no trouble convincing the candidate that he must respond, or, at least, exploit the discontent. On September 4 at the rally in Philadelphia's Convention Hall, Eisenhower disenthralled himself. We were fighting in Korea because the administration had permitted America to become weak, had withdrawn American troops from Korea, had not adequately built up Korean forces to defend themselves, had abandoned China to the Communists, had announced to the world that it had written off most of the Far East.

Stevenson was slow in estimating the impact of the attack coming now from the presidential candidate himself, and only responded at the end of the month after Eisenhower had repeated the speech in Cincinnati in more impassioned form. He then answered the general in Louisville point by point. He demonstrated the unacknowledged changes of line and viewpoint and the tendentiousness of the charges. Had it been a college debate on a subject of historical interest, he would have received a good score, but the public was not an uninvolved judge marking points on a score sheet for structure, presentation, sincerity. It was sick and tired of a war that had become a senseless nightmare. Eisenhower had not really proposed anything, but he was against it. Stevenson, in contrast, said the war had accomplished great and wonderful things and he was offering "an opportunity to work and sacrifice that freedom may flourish." Two days later in a nationally broadcast "fireside speech," he said, "How long can we keep on fighting in Korea, paying high taxes, helping others to help ourselves? There is only one answer. We can keep it up as long as we have to—and we will." That settled it. He was going to lose the Korean vote.

Eisenhower's "I shall go to Korea" speech, delivered ten days before the election, was not a shaft of lightning hurled without warning rolls of thunder. It was the climactic stroke in a storm that had been building up for weeks. On October 2, in Champaign, Illinois, Eisenhower said there was no sense in Americans having to bear the brunt of the fighting. "This is a job for Koreans. If there must be a war, let it be Asians against Asians, with our support on the side of freedom." Dulles, in Rochester, elaborated the many advantages of a policy of Koreanization of the Korean war. It would enable us to prove "how Soviet Russia is recklessly sacrificing Asians to win Russia's old imperialist goals in Korea." Dewey added his voice to the chorus on the *Man of the Week* television program. "If you get General Eisenhower as President I will make you this prophecy: the Koreans will be defending nine-tenths of that front within a year." On October 9, in a

major speech at the Cow Palace in San Francisco, Eisenhower rejected the MacArthur strategy and dramatically tossed on the table
his promise, undefined though it was, to end the war. "I pledge full
dedication to the job of finding an intelligent and honorable way to
end the tragic toll of American casualties in Korea. No one can
pledge you more. Nor can there be a more solemn pledge. For this
war is reaching tonight into the homes of hundreds of thousands of
American families. I do not believe that Korea must forever be a part
of our American daily life."

Then, on October 24, in Detroit, came the speech that brought together in coherent form the strays and pieces of the disorderly Republican attacks, made more explicit the pledge to end the war, and
encased it all in the glittering bauble of a trip to Korea. It was a
good speech. It came across. "The first task" of his administration
would be "to bring the Korean war to an early and honorable end."
To accomplish this, a new leadership was needed. "The old administration cannot be expected to repair what it failed to prevent." The
job of ending the war required a personal trip. "I shall go to Korea."
What did Eisenhower and his advisers have in mind? Had they seriously considered a project to Koreanize the Korean war, as the early
October remarks seemed to portend? Or did they have a new negotiating plan? Very likely, they did not know themselves at the time.
Five months later, in the March 20 Cabinet meeting of the new administration, Dulles remarked, "We don't know yet what we're going
to do in Korea." The Detroit speech and the idea of the trip to Korea
had come from Emmet John Hughes, the Luce magazine editor. It
was immaterial that it originated as an ad man's stunt. It was attached to the pledge, and the pledge, once given, became the Sermon
on the Mount. Eisenhower had become both the apostle and prisoner
of the formula.

As soon as he heard about it, Stevenson realized how damaging the
speech was for his cause and he lashed out. The general's "proposal
for a quick and slick way out of Korea" could produce a "Munich in
the Far East with the probability of a third world war not far behind." In other words, let Ike barter away sacred principles for the
sake of votes; he, for one, intended to remain steadfast whatever the
cost. Acheson weighed in at the UN with the admonition that peace
in Korea could not be "purchased at the price of honor." And in
Rochester Stevenson continued to worry the subject. "It is deceptive
and cruel to raise false hopes at this hour. It is a surrender of the
high purpose of collective action to suggest to the Communist aggres-

sors that we plan to let the South Koreans do all the fighting for the principles of the United Nations." Hughes observed, "the indictment proved unwounding." More than that, Stevenson had set himself up as the straight man for Eisenhower's assault. A week later, in an impassioned appeal, he explained again why "Korea was a crucial test in the struggle between the free world and Communism," and concluded in a ringing peroration, "Rather than exploit human hopes and fears, rather than provide glib solutions and false assurances, I would gladly lose this presidential election." He got his wish. The electorate registered a massive foreign-policy protest akin to the repudiation of Wilson in 1920.

Truman was to write that Eisenhower's landslide election was Stevenson's own fault; that he was positive that had Stevenson accepted in good faith the proposition that he had offered him at the beginning of the year the Democrats would have been enabled to make the proper buildup, and Stevenson would have received an additional three million votes. Even if this had not won him the Presidency, the vote would have been sufficiently impressive to rebuke Eisenhower for his "demagoguery." The election data testify against Truman. Had the positions of the two candidates been reversed, and Stevenson been on the right side of the Korean question for the public, he might not only have got 3 million more votes; he might have won the election. With the war around his neck, Truman's buildup would not have helped. It would probably have made things worse. As it was, Truman's careening around the country like a noisy bluebottle during the campaign, while it probably did not subtract from Stevenson's support, did not add to it either. The electorate was not put in the position by Truman or Stevenson where its adulation of the military hero had to struggle with its revulsion against the Korean war. It was able to register both—it was forced to register both—with a single vote—against the Democrats. The 1948 miracle could not be worked again because the majority's sense of the national interest was clashing with that of the Cold War directors.

20

His Place
in the
Pantheon

Truman was an accidental President since he got to the White House because of Roosevelt's death, and would probably never have received the presidential nomination otherwise. It was no accident, however, that a politician of his kind became President. Where the business elite was looking for reliability, not greatness, the political system was weighted to favor the middle-of-the-road trimmer. Despite his growing conceit in his second term—and how many mortals could keep their bearings with such power and acclaim suddenly thrust upon them?—Truman never thought he was another Lincoln or Franklin Roosevelt. His common sense kept his swelling ego within bounds. "Your dad will never be reckoned among the great," he wrote his daughter in the last days of his Presidency, "but you can be sure he did his level best." On two occasions in his final year, to the newspaper editors and in his farewell address, he stated publicly that he was sure there were probably a million people who could have done a better job in the Presidency than he had. It was not entirely coyness, and none among the editors rose to protest. That was the popular consensus at the time. All the more astonishing, therefore, was the result of a poll of historians taken ten years later. In this, Truman won ninth place among thirty-one Presidents, rating as "near great" alongside Theodore Roosevelt and Cleveland. All thirty-one had been assigned to lists labeled as "great," "near great," "average," "below average," "failures."

It would be kind to assume that the academicians were simply extending professional courtesy to an esteemed colleague when they dutifully checked off the questionnaire that the elder Arthur Schlesinger had sent them. In any case, it was an enterprise in triviality. Presidents are America's institutionalized heroes, prophets of a secular religion. Every President is at the hub of national existence when in office, and if not disbarred by incompetence or inanity, the center of a tribe of myth-makers, boomers, and sycophants after he has left office. No President, no matter how mediocre, but has had his Parson Weems. He enters into a quasipersonal relationship with millions more intimate than the connection of the sixteenth-century unlimited monarchs with their subjects. He is part of an intricate governmental and extragovernmental machinery so that what he is and is not able to do is more dependent on circumstances, contingencies, and interactions than on personal exercises of will and assertion. To think, in these circumstances, that it is possible to say something meaningful about American history and national administrations by grading Presidents, like term papers, is to sink into scholastic fatuity. It is to mistake preference and caprice for analyses. It is to reduce history to a parlor game. It caters to the same craving for the banal that has led our modern Presidents to become pyramid builders in order to help along their passages to immortality.

The measuring device employed was made up of a flatulent liberalism rotating around a core of romantic deification of the strong state. The five who made the top grade in the examination—Washington, Jefferson, Lincoln, Wilson, Franklin Roosevelt—"took the side of liberalism and the general welfare against the status quo," according to Schlesinger, "acted masterfully and farsightedly in foreign affairs," and "left the Executive branch stronger and more influential" than when they had taken over. The liberalism under review here clearly demanded little, since Washington—never a battler against the economic or social status quo—satisfactorily passed this part of the test. The other major factors taken into consideration can be generalized under the proposition that the great Presidents were the "strong" Presidents, and by "strong" was meant something not far from what Hegel or Mommsen meant: mastering events, shaping destiny, magnifying their office and power.

There are historical reasons for the presidential cult in the academic world. After the Civil War, Congress became a brokerage house where spokesmen for economic interests adjusted their respective claims to join in despoliation of the public treasury. With the rising tide of Populist and Progressivist dissent came the social-democratic type of President—Theodore Roosevelt and Woodrow Wilson —who pitched their appeals to the masses, were able to gather up a national following, and could act or appear to act as arbitrators between the classes. It appeared to many that the Presidency was the institution within the American scheme of government that had to bear the burden of formulating the predominant national interests and driving through the necessary laws and activities against the interference and foot-dragging of parochial and selfish blocs. Social reform, for many the original interest in a strong Presidency, was secured by the additional powerful strand of Wilsonian internationalism after America's entrance into the First World War, and Wilson's subsequent defeat by the Senate for taking the country into the League of Nations. The conflict of Franklin Roosevelt with Congress from 1938 on, concerning both reforms and war preparations, hardened the predilection into a cult. Historians and political scientists fell into the habit of writing about Presidents in the spirit of court chroniclers to whom the monarch was the embodiment of far-sightedness and virtue. When Schlesinger conducted his final poll in 1962, the outlook of an attenuated liberalism attached to an embattled nationalism was inflamed by the Cold War to which most of the academicians enthusiastically subscribed. This explains why a President who was discredited for most of his administration was included in the second tier of honor in the national pantheon.

The disaster that struck Lyndon Johnson, whose record of liberal reform was superior to Truman's but who brought the country to a state of turmoil and division unknown for a century by the war in Vietnam—unauthorized by Congress like the war in Korea—induced second thoughts about the unrelieved blessings of a "strong" Presidency. In the light of the desolating American experience with two undeclared wars in the past twenty-five years, it might be wise for the experts on the Presidency to recall their panegyrical textbooks in order to issue more up-to-date, less turgidly inspirational, editions. It is as incongruous to become partisans of the Presidency against Congress, or of Congress against the Presidency, as to organize a cheering squad for the Bureau of the Budget against the General Accounting Office. The private citizen, caught up in an era of terror, confusion, and corruption in public life, is called upon to exercise vigilance, wariness, skepticism toward public officials, not to join as a factionalist in the infighting between government bureaucracies.

Though our Presidents cannot be graded, they have to be appraised. They are our national leaders. Our analyses of their rule, our evaluations of their conduct of office, our attitudes toward their traits bespeak our sense of values, our ethical standards, our political aspirations. In political leadership there is a romantic aspect. All leadership partakes of the element of magic, whether supplied by the leader through personal élan, or by the machinery of government through institutionalized ritual. It may be that in the days to come the element of mystery and sacred incantation will have been drained away from the process of government, and the Jacksonian ideal of an association of autonomous, free individuals taking turns in the administration of the affairs of the commonwealth will have become a reality. But that day is not yet here. We still thrill at and idolize the political leader who can stamp his personality on his age, who is able to impose his vision and aim on a people, who by force of will shapes the national course.

It matters little that the phenomenon is an optical illusion, that without the social environment selecting the great man who is enabled to speak with the voice of multitudes, Bonaparte would have ended as a staff officer in the service of some foreign prince, and Hitler would have achieved the status of a Teutonic Gerald L. K. Smith. When the time and the man come together, the hero, the man of destiny, is ignited. Where the godlike leader is an artifact of the repressive state, nourished by public relations humbuggery, and rammed down the people's throat by fiat, as was the case with Stalin, his reputation rarely outlasts his rule. But in our epoch, under conditions of democratic competition and party rivalries, Franklin Roosevelt emerged as a larger-than-life figure in both peace and war, which gave wings to his pronouncements and proposals, and provided him with an independence in manuever not vouchsafed most officeholders. At the start of the Republic, when the franchise was limited to property holders, George Washington, utilizing his unique position as the first President, a war hero, and above-party father figure, established himself as a national deity, modeling his manner on the stylized aloofness of the British aristocracy. Jefferson, without the temperament or aptitudes of a popular leader, enjoyed a vast moral authority in the nation and the Congress to buttress his decisions.

It was Truman's misfortune that he lacked the inspirational touch; the authority he had came from the office, not from what he brought to it. Even at his point of triumph in 1948, he ran behind most Democratic tickets, and evoked popular acclaim as the plucky, peppery little man who would not accept defeat, not as the heroic figure whom smaller men were trying to tear down. His occasional attempts to arouse mass clamor for his proposals were lost in the bedlam of the marketplace. He did not command attention. In this he was not unique. Of the thirty-two White House occupants who preceded him, no more than eight could be said to have possessed enormous authority, because of charisma, or stature, or both; even Lincoln, universally accepted as one of the greats, enjoyed far less admiration during his Presidency than after his assassination and apotheosization; and a defeatist general running against him at the height of the war was able to roll up 45 percent of the popular vote.

Truman was the beneficiary of a grudging affection and admiration in the happier moments of his administration, and these feelings for him have deepened with the passage of years after he left partisan politics for history. Basically, the admiration is that an ordinary courthouse politician could carry it off as President of the United States. His administration was a vindication of sorts of the ideals of Jacksonian democracy. In the American social scheme, an increasingly hereditary money aristocracy has been reinvigorated continually with the fresh blood of vigorous politicians rising from the common mass. It should have produced great talents and bold innovators, but in the prevailing American environment of huckstering and jobbing, it has favored the organizationally dexterous and socially pliant.

On the substantive side of Truman's leadership, he will get no citations for his captaincy on the domestic front. His economic policies in the postwar demobilization and the Korean mobilization effaced the line between conservatism and liberalism; opened wide the doors to inflation, which was to disorder the economy for an entire epoch. In capital-labor conflicts he veered from Hayes-Cleveland strikebreaking to friend-of-labor tub-thumping, all the more disconcerting because the oscillations were determined more by personal pique or election lust than objective evaluation of national need. Much of his Fair Deal program was ignored by Congress. The antireform currents generated by his own administration facilitated the hostile movements of a conservative-dominated legislature to gut his welfarist submissions, many of which were neither energetically pursued, nor seriously intended. The loyalty and security program that he put into operation, after Republican gains in 1946, got out of control in his second term and metamorphosed into the McCarthy witch-hunt, ravaging his administration, demoralizing government personnel, staining the entire society. His most solid achievement was in the presidential promulgations on Negro rights. These were an epoch-making departure for their time, could be considered a precursor of the later, more comprehensive liberal legislation. They were overshadowed by the historic Supreme Court decision that came in the next administration, and the massive black rebellion and white backlash that followed; so that by the late 1960s the entire liberal illusion that the blacks were going to win equal integration into American society through white legislators, judges, and Presidents doling out rights to them piece by piece in an orderly progression, had been punctured.

For better or worse, Truman's place in history will be judged not by his lackluster exploits at home, but by his conduct of that complex of matters assigned to foreign affairs. These dominated his administration; they became the forcing house for far-reaching decisions, even in domestic concerns. That exclusive set, the Cold War managers alumni, who, from their redoubts at law offices, banks, corporation and foundation boards, keep the sacred flame burning, periodically give each other awards, and review each other's memoirs, and who insist their former chief be accorded a place of high honor in the history books, uniformly rest their case on Truman's leadership in the Cold War, from the Truman Doctrine to intervention in Korea, with the bolder spirits throwing in the use of the atom bomb for good measure.

What are reasonable criteria for a judgment? We can say that a President should have a sense of history, or as some call it, a sense of direction. He should have the capacity to cut through the pressures, demands, and complaints, to identify the major issue or issues facing the country and his administration. His aptitude for leadership, his sense of timing, his ability to formulate, articulate, and make public discussion revolve around the burning question, and to carry the nation, or much of it, behind his program; in a word, the talent to use the formidable machinery at his disposal to realize the transcendent task at hand—that is a fair test of his stewardship. Applied to Truman, the paramount issue or set of related issues confronting the nation in his time could be formulated in this way:

(1) The need to organize the peace, to permit bleeding humanity to bind its wounds, bury its dead, and undertake the rebuilding of its homesteads and cities. Given the military and political world reality, given the social character of American and Russian societies, the only

way peace could be organized was by conceding big-power status to the Russians, and by acquiescing, to one or another extent, in their assumption of spheres of influence adjoining their Western borders. Where the lines of conflicting interest were insuperable of settlement, as in Germany, neutralization would have been attempted had a peace settlement been the objective.

(2) The need for arms limitation. With the coming of atomic weaponry, accompanied by scientists' unanimous advice that the American monopoly was to be short-lived, some basic agreement on limitation and control was imperative or both superpowers would be thrust into a ruinous arms race that would inevitably poison all international relations and pave the way for another world war—this time, possibly, of horrendously total consequences.

(3) The need to come to terms with the independence movements in Asia. By the war's end, it was clear that any attempt to aid the British, French, and Dutch in reimposing their rule, or to set this country directly in the path of the erupting national aspirations, meant to involve the American people for years to come in colonial pacifications and wars.

(4) The need to set up a workable economic relationship with the rest of the world. It was not sufficient to call for the "open door" everywhere, and take on the role of the world's prime banker, investor, manufacturer, and consumer. To press a policy of unrestrained multilateral trade meant to contend with our capitalist allies, to wage economic warfare on the Soviet Union and other collectivized regimes, and to appear as the latest and most menacing of the line of despoilers and exploiters to the underdeveloped sections of mankind. Given the American system, the United States was bound to seek an extension of its free-enterprise modalities. These had to be modified and tempered by the circumstances of the day—as the American government eventually had to make adjustments for doing business with Tito's Yugoslavia—if the world was not to be plunged into economic strife and dissension.

Under the tutelage of his experts, Truman decided against a policy of accommodation and making peace. Like William Pitt who matched the finances and arms of the British Empire against Bonaparte, he dealt out the resources of the American colossus to isolate

Russia, put down revolutionary movements, in order to eventually bring down Stalin and his regime. Our leaders did not dare to start a full-scale war with the professed enemy in the Kremlin, and they would not make peace with him. They did not differentiate between the Kremlin regime and regional insurgencies; and, under mistaken assumptions, made common cause with reactionary factions to block popular aspirations. The administration's desires to impose its design on a world rent by revolution, disintegration, and chaos, in a period when militarism was inhibited because of the threat of nuclear annihilation, were out of line with its capabilities—and with each passing year, the gap widened.

In his farewell address, Truman tried to justify his fateful decision to the ages. "When history says that my term of office saw the beginning of the cold war," he opined, "it will also say that in those eight years we have set the course that can win it." That is precisely what history will not say. The course he set, followed with the zeal of knights-errant, under varying battle cries and hallucinatory catch phrases, by four succeeding administrations, and at costs, financial, social, human, too enormous to fathom, has produced no American advantage, much less victory. One cannot even say that Cold War doctrinaires built up American military prowess at the expense of the health and comfort of the citizenry. That the social needs have been neglected, that the fabric of civil organization has been permitted to fray, is attested to by every daily newspaper. But after twenty-five years of the arms race and its consequent dislocation of production and life, with the piling up of armaments and lethal devices sufficient to destroy every human being in the universe several times over, the United States is militarily weaker relative to its Kremlin rival—not that such comparisons mean as much as they used to before the age of nuclear plenty—than it was at war's end. After all the travail and agony and mindless devastation, another President will have to make agreements and recognize historical tides that should have been made and recognized at the conclusion of the great war.

Truman's administration divided Roosevelt's war regime from the returning Republican normalcy when the sons and nephews of the Hardings and Coolidges came streaming back to Washington like an army entering a long-besieged city. Eisenhower's Secretary of the Interior, Douglas McKay, chortled, "We are here in the saddle as an administration representing business and industry," just as the *Wall Street Journal* had exulted thirty-two years earlier, "Never before, here or anywhere else, has a government been so completely fused with business." All the same, though the spirit was willing, the flesh lacked the pristine exuberance of yore. There was to be no simple rerun of the reel of the 1920s. The Truman administration, self-advertised as the inheritor and continuator of Rooseveltianism, had proffered its generous share of normalcy, providing even ornate touches of Harding vulgarity and malfeasance, while exhorting the populace to dedication and exertion. For their part, the Humphreys and Wilsons under Eisenhower were talking of returning to the ancient verities of balanced budgets and "a bigger bang for the buck," while Dulles was crisscrossing the globe with additional military pacts, bawling imprecations and threats, displaying his artistry in moving to the brink without falling into the bottomless pit.

Though the two administrations had numerous interchangeable parts, Truman continued the New Deal tradition in the sense, and to the degree, that the labor and liberal alliance within the Democratic party survived through all the vicissitudes of the postwar years and kept alive the flame of official obeisance to the welfare state. The tradition permitted him to rise like a phoenix out of the ashes in 1948, and for the Democrats to maintain themselves as the majority party despite the Korean debacle and eight years of Eisenhower tranquilization. In a larger sense, he pioneered the postwar crisis Presidency, not only setting the course for the next decades but grappling with all the major problems besetting the country in the wake of an arms race, a Cold War, and a not-so-little shooting war, in the period in which it attained world leadership status. His administration represented the fusion of welfare-state liberalism grown desiccated in the embrace of a voracious militarism. If Franklin Roosevelt, in forging the United Nations, carried forward as the heir of the Woodrow Wilson of the League of Nations, Truman was the heir of the other Woodrow Wilson who invaded Mexico and organized the Versailles system to contain the Bolsheviks.

Harriman, another Cold War luminary who had been present at the creation, in his late seventies watched American cities burning and another Democratic President undone. He ruminated that if Roosevelt had lived, history would have taken a different turn, that American relations with Russia would have been more favorable, that "France would have been denied a return to Indochina and there probably would not have been a Vietnam war." No one can know. History cannot be unrolled in alternative versions. No one can say whether Lincoln's reputation would have been undamaged if he had survived to undertake Andrew Johnson's incongruous peacemaking, or whether Roosevelt would have been able to avoid the extravagances, fanaticisms, and absurdities in this other irrepressible conflict. That Harriman should have come to that opinion was an unconscious recognition of the perniciousness of the advice that he and others had pressed on the incoming President.

In one way the efforts of Truman's cast of Cold War managers to enshroud him in a mantle of greatness—and as a by-product, to vindicate themselves—will be successful. If it is true that a Homeric dimension is attached to individuals who are leaders of, preside over, or are associated with, deeds and decisions that shape the destinies of millions, then Truman will be among that select number, for his postwar operations, of heroic design and titanic proportions, made the ground quake as in an onrush of a race of giants, and hurled entire continents into the turbulence of another age of blood and iron. After he came out of Blair House untouched from the attempt of a group of Puerto Rican nationalists to assassinate him, he remarked to Admiral Leahy, "The only thing you have to worry about is bad luck. I never had bad luck." Yes, his run of luck, once he entered politics, was of the stuff that dreams are made of. It will carry him into Valhalla.

Notes

Author's Note. Because of space considerations, I am not including a complete list of works that I read or checked, or individuals that I consulted in preparing this book. In any case, for the scholar such a list would be redundant; for the general reader it would be of little interest. Students in need of bibliographies will be served by Richard S. Kirkendall, ed., *The Truman Period as a Research Field* (Columbia, Mo., 1967.)

These notes identify only the sources of quotations cited or special data directly referred to by the author. The number preceding a citation indicates the page at which the quotation or information appears in this book.

1   STRUGGLE FOR THE VICE-PRESIDENCY

1, Bundschu, quoted in Richard Wilson, "Truman Is a New Dealer Too," *Look,* June 26, 1945. Drew Pearson column, January 22, 1945.   1–2, *The Journals of David E. Lilienthal* (New York, 1964), Vol. 1, p. 690 (hereinafter designated Lilienthal). Stettinius, quoted in Francis Biddle, *In Brief Authority* (New York, 1962), p. 360.   2, Rosenman and Allen, quoted in Samuel I. Rosenman, *Working with Roosevelt* (New York, 1952), pp. 438, 253.   3, Roosevelt to Hannegan: *Public Papers and Addresses of Franklin D. Roosevelt 1944–1945*, p. 197. Edward J. Flynn, *You're the Boss* (New York, 1947), p. 179.   4, Walter Millis, ed., *The Forrestal Diaries*

(New York, 1951), p. 27.   4–5, Memo from Edwin S. Pauley to Jonathan Daniels, on Events Leading up to Election of Harry S. Truman as Vice-President, Truman Library.   6, *St. Louis Globe-Democrat* and Truman on Hannegan nomination, quoted in Alfred Steinberg, *The Man from Missouri* (New York, 1962), p. 195.   9, War procurement: Walter Millis, *Arms and the State* (New York, 1958), p. 80. New plants: P. A. C. Koistinen, *The Hammer and the Sword: Labor, the Military, and Industrial Mobilization, 1920–1945*, unpublished Ph.D. dissertation (University of California, Berkeley, 1964), pp. 668, 837.   10, Elting E. Morison, *Turmoil and Tradition* (Boston, 1960), p. 496.   11, Hugh Johnson, quoted in Koistinen, p. 71.   12, Harry Hopkins, quoted in Robert E. Sherwood, *Roosevelt and Hopkins* (New York, 1948), p. 280.   13, Confidential Memorandum to President by Clark Clifford, November 19, 1947, Clifford Papers, Truman Library.   14, Jonathan Daniels, *Man from Missouri* (Philadelphia, 1950), p. 235. Flynn, pp. 180–181.   16, Byrnes-Roosevelt conversation: James F. Byrnes, *All in One Lifetime* (New York, 1958), pp. 223–224. Daniels, p. 246.   18, George Meader Oral History, Harry Easley Oral History, Truman Library.   19, Agrees to nominate Byrnes: Harry S. Truman, *Memoirs*, Vol. I (Garden City, N.Y., 1955), p. 190. 20, Byrnes's withdrawal letter and statement to Barkley, quoted in Donald Young, *American Roulette* (New York, 1965), p. 225.

2   EARLY YEARS

24, On guerrilla bands: Darrell Garwood, *Crossroads of America* (New York, 1948), Chapter 4.   25, Martha Truman, quoted in Vaughan Oral History, Truman Library.   26–27, William Allen White, *Autobiography* (New York, 1946), p. 248.   28, Truman accident: William Hillman, *Mr. President* (British edition, London, 1952), p. 131.   28–29, Truman's reply to boy's question: Merle Miller, "Mr. Truman's Home Town," *Holiday*, May, 1970.   29–30, Truman on morality: Hillman, p. 89.   30, John Truman on religion: Bela Kornitzer, "The Story of Truman and his Father," *Parents Magazine*, March, 1951. Solomon Young on religion: Steinberg, p. 18.   31, Music was sissy: Daniels, p. 70. 33–34, William M. Reddig, *Tom's Town* (Philadelphia, 1947), p. 26. 35, Hinde Oral History, Truman Library. Truman's memo to himself: Hillman, p. 154.   36, Remarks to farmers: *The New York Times*, May 6, 1958.   39, Marriage postponed: Hillman, p. 156.

3   ENTRY INTO POLITICS

40, Hillman, p. 133. Henry Bundschu, *Harry S Truman—The Missourian*, unpaged, Truman Library.   41, Footnote: Margaret Truman, *Souvenir*

(New York, 1956), p. 356.   42, Chiles Oral History, Truman Library.   43, Thoroughly scared: Hillman, p. 157.   45, Lady Liberty: Hillman, p. 142.   47, Conversation with Southern, quoted in Edward R. Schauffler, *Harry Truman, Son of the Soil* (Kansas City, Mo., 1947), pp. 59–60.   48, Hinde Oral History, Truman Library. Lincoln Steffens, *The Shame of the Cities* (Sagamore Press reprint, New York, 1957), pp. 20–21.   49, Pendergast interview in *The New York Times*, April 8, 1939.   50, *Kansas City Star*, July 8, 1914, quoted in Lyle W. Dorsett, *A History of the Pendergast Machine*, unpublished Ph.D. dissertation (University of Missouri, 1965), p. 97. Tax abatements: Stark Papers, University of Missouri, quoted in Dorsett, p. 145.

4   JACKSON COUNTY JUDGE

56, Hinde Oral History, Truman Library.   57, *Kansas City Star*, August 3, 1924, Vertical File, Truman Library.   58, Chiles and Truman exchange: Chiles Oral History, Truman Library.   59, Community Savings and Loan: Daniels, pp. 132, 137–138.   60, Steinberg, p. 86.   62, Veatch Oral History, Truman Library. Hillman, p. 152. Charles A. Beard, quoted in Lorin Peterson, *The Day of the Mugwump* (New York, 1961), p. 42.   66, Truman on Pendergast, quoted in Frank McNaughton and Walter Hehmeyer, *This Man Truman* (New York, 1945), p. 69.

5   SENATOR FROM PENDERGAST

69, William Helm, *Harry Truman* (New York, 1947), p. 27.   70, Helm, p. 33.   73, G. H. Force correspondence, quoted in Dorsett, pp. 188–190.   74, Orestes Mitchell correspondence, quoted in Dorsett, p. 191.   76, Aylward to Messall, quoted in Steinberg, p. 125.   77–78, Helm, pp. 7–8.   78, Joseph Martin, *My First Fifty Years in Politics* (New York, 1960), p. 177. Hamilton Lewis remark, quoted widely, also attributed to a Missouri judge.   79, Ike Dunlap, quoted in Dorsett, p. 171. Farley, quoted in Dorsett, p. 176.   82, Messall, quoted in Steinberg, p. 126. On Truman's poker-playing: A. Merriman Smith, *Thank You, Mr. President* (New York, 1946), p. 221.   85, Lowenthal Oral History, Truman Library.   86, ibid. Congressional Record, 75th Cong., 2nd sess., Vol. 82, pt. 2, December 20, 1937.   87–88, Wesley McCune and John R. Beal, "The Job That Made Truman President," *Harper's Magazine*, June, 1945. Samuel Dunn, quoted in Eugene F. Schmidtlein, *Truman the Senator*, unpublished Ph.D. dissertation (University of Missouri, 1962), p. 206.   88–89, On vote for Barkley: Helm, p. 52.   89, William E. Leuchtenburg, *Franklin D. Roosevelt and the New Deal* (New York, 1963), p. 154.   90, Truman I, pp. 151–152.   91, Charlie McCarthy story: Gene Powell, *Tom's Boy Harry* (Jefferson City, Mo., 1948), p. 2.

6   A COCKEYED HORATIO ALGER STORY

93–94, Daniels, p. 197.   94, Jim Pendergast to Messall, quoted in Steinberg, p. 169. Bernard Baruch, *The Public Years* (New York, 1960), p. 395. Truman's luring Milligan into campaign: Schmidtlein, p. 217.   95, Chicago speech, quoted in Helm, pp. 135–136.   95–96, Arthur M. Schlesinger, Jr., *The Politics of Upheaval* (Boston, 1960), p. 426. Roy Wilkins, quoted in William C. Berman, *The Politics of Civil Rights in the Truman Administration* (Columbus, O., 1970), pp. 8–9.   99, Truman to Byrnes, quoted in Samuel Lubell, *The Future of American Politics* (New York, 1965), 3rd rev. ed., p. 33. Truman memorandum to FDR, December 10, 1941, Roosevelt Papers, Official File 25, Franklin D. Roosevelt Library.   101, Ball-Lewis exchange, quoted in Donald H. Riddle, *The Truman Committee* (New Brunswick, N.J., 1964), p. 46.   103–104, Henry L. Stimson diary, August 26, 1940, Sterling Library, Yale University.   104, John Morton Blum, ed., *From the Morgenthau Diaries* (Boston, 1965), Vol. 2, p. 291.   105, Stimson diary, December 20, 1940.   106, Bureau of the Budget, *The United States at War* (Washington, D.C., 1946), p. 182.   108, Letter to Lou Holland, May 1, 1941, Truman Papers, Senatorial File 123, Truman Library.   109, Fulton-Gibbons exchange, quoted in I. F. Stone, *Business As Usual* (New York, 1941), pp. 145–146.   110, Special Senate Committee investigating the National Defense Program, 77th Cong., 2nd sess., Report No. 480, pt. 5, pp. 15–17, 200–206. Forrestal's testimonial letter, quoted in Riddle, p. 157.   111–112, Truman remarks on Sidney Hillman: *The New York Times*, October 23–24, 1941.   112, Truman's record on Smith-Connally law: voted for S796, Congressional Record, May 5, 1943, p. 3993; paired with Tobey of N.H., voted against Conference Report, Congressional Record, June 12, 1943, p. 5795; voted against overriding President's veto, June 25, 1943, p. 6489.   115, "Cockeyed Horatio Alger story": Edward A. Harris in J. T. Salter, ed., *Public Men in and out of Office* (Chapel Hill, N.C., 1946), p. 4.

7   NEW WHITE HOUSE REGIME

117, George Dixon, King Features Syndicate, March 17, 1945.   118, Quotation is that of James MacGregor Burns, *Presidential Government* (Avon edition), p. 87. Remarks to reporters: *The New York Times*, April 14, 1945. Barkley to Truman, quoted in Alben W. Barkley, *That Reminds Me* (New York, 1954), p. 197.   119, James Bryce, *The American Commonwealth*, Vol. 1 (New York, 1959), p. 30.   120, Lilienthal II, pp. 433–434. On Cabinet: Daniels, p. 301.   121, Harry Hopkins, quoted

in Sherwood, p. 882.   121–122, On Biddle: Truman I, p. 325. Opposing account: Biddle, pp. 365–366.   124, Lilienthal II, p. 379.
124–125, I. F. Stone, *The Truman Era* (New York, 1953), p. XV.
125, McKim incident in Marianne Means, *The Woman in the White
House* (New York, 1963), p. 225 and A. Merriman Smith, p. 216.   126,
Rosenman Oral History, Truman Library.   135, Dean Acheson, *Present
at the Creation* (New York, 1969), p. 192 (hereinafter designated Acheson). Rayburn, quoted in Booth Mooney, *The Politicians* (Philadelphia,
1970), p. 39.   136, Joseph W. Jones, *The Fifteen Weeks* (New York,
1955), pp. 63–64.

8   THE COURSE IS CHANGED

140, Joseph C. Grew, *Turbulent Era* (Boston, 1952), Vol. 2, p. 1485.
Winston S. Churchill, *Triumph and Tragedy* (Boston, 1953), p. 486.
145, Footnote: Stimson diary, May 8, 1945.   146, *Foreign Relations
of the United States, 1944,* IV, p. 223.   148, *Yalta Documents,* Matthews Notes, p. 973.   148, William D. Leahy, *I Was There* (New York,
1950), pp. 315–316.   150, Grew Memo, quoted in Gar Alperowitz,
Atomic Diplomacy (New York, 1965), p. 37. Stimson diary, May 11,
1945. Churchill, p. 503.   151, Dwight D. Eisenhower, *Crusade in
Europe* (Garden City, N.Y., 1948), p. 474.   152, Davies, quoted in
Herbert Feis, *Roosevelt, Churchill and Stalin* (Princeton, N.J., 1957),
pp. 651–652.   153–154, Leahy, p. 352.   154, Eisenhower-Zhukov
exchange: Herbert Feis, *Between War and Peace* (Princeton, N.J., 1960),
pp. 141–142. Churchill, p. 605.   155, Reston: *The New York Times,*
June 12, 1945. Lippmann: *New York Herald Tribune,* May 2, May 15,
1945. Grew II, p. 1518. Frederick Lewis Allen, *The Big Change* (Bantam edition), p. 143.

9   CONFLICT AT POTSDAM

162, Stimson diary, October 3, 1944.   163, Byrnes to staff, quoted in
George Curry, "James F. Byrnes," in Robert H. Ferrell, ed., *The American
Secretaries of State and their Diplomacy* (New York, 1965), Vol. XIV, p.
345.   164, Lucius D. Clay, *Decision in Germany* (New York, 1950), p.
18. Eisenhower, p. 442.   165, Stalin on German Communism, quoted in
Isaac Deutscher, *Stalin* (New York, 1949), p. 537.   165–166, *Foreign
Relations: Conference of Berlin,* II (Potsdam Papers), pp.
1478–1485.   166, Stalin, quoted in James F. Byrnes, *Speaking Frankly*
(New York, 1947), p. 86.   166, Feis, *Between War and Peace,* p.
317.   168, Hopkins report: Potsdam Papers I, pp. 41–62.   169,

Byrnes, *All in One Lifetime*, p. 291.   170, Leahy, p. 431. Henry L. Stimson and McGeorge Bundy, *On Active Service in Peace and War* (New York, 1948), p. 642.   171, Byrnes, *All in One Lifetime*, p. 285. Explanation for files, quoted in Barton J. Bernstein and Allen J. Matusow, eds., *The Truman Administration* (New York, 1966), p. 17.   172, Stimson diary, July 21–22, 1945. Allenbrooke notation: Arthur Bryant, *Triumph in the West* (London, 1959), pp. 477–478.   173, P. M. S. Blackett, *Fear, War and the Bomb* (New York, 1949), p. 138. Alexander Werth, *Russia at War* (New York, 1964), p. 940.   173–174, Truman interview, quoted in Len Giovannitti and Fred Freed, *The Decision to Drop the Bomb* (New York, 1965), p. 255. Leslie Groves, *Now It Can Be Told* (New York, 1962), p. 265.   174, Churchill, p. 639. Groves and Leahy, quoted in Giovannitti and Freed, pp. 322–323.   175, United States Strategic Bombing Survey, *Japan's Struggle to End the War* (Washington, D.C., 1946), p. 13. Footnote: Dean Acheson, *Sketches from Life* (New York, 1959), p. 76.

10   TWO HALVES OF THE SAME WALNUT

177, Stimson diary, September 4, 1945.   178, Byrnes, *Speaking Frankly*, p. 109.   179, Leahy, quoted in Herbert Feis, *From Trust to Terror* (New York, 1970), p. 55.   179, Truman, quoted in Hillman, p. 28. Byrnes denial: *All in One Lifetime*, pp. 402–403; *Colliers*, April 26, 1952.   180, Byrnes, *Speaking Frankly*, p. 122.   180–181, Vaughan Oral History, Truman Library.   181, Winston S. Churchill, *Sinews of Peace* (Boston, 1949), p. 104. Joseph Stalin, *For Peaceful Coexistence: Postwar Interviews* (Moscow, 1946), pp. 9, 15.   184, Truman to reporters on Wallace speech: Public Papers of Harry S. Truman 1946 (Washington, D.C., 1962), pp. 426–428.   184–185, Truman Doctrine: Truman Public Papers 1947, pp. 178–179.   185, Jones, pp. 8, 146. *The New York Times*, March 12, 1947.   187, Acheson, p. 219. Vandenberg, quoted in Eric F. Goldman, *The Crucial Decade* (New York, 1956), p. 59. 188, Footnote: George F. Kennan, *Memoirs 1925–1950* (Boston, 1967), p. 358. Walter Lippmann, *The Cold War* (New York, 1947), pp. 12, 21. 189, Vladimir Dedijer, *Tito* (New York, 1953), p. 322. Milovan Djilas, *Conversations with Stalin* (New York, 1962), pp. 114, 164. George F. Kennan, *Russia and the West under Lenin and Stalin* (Boston, 1960), p. 253.   191, Stimson diary, May 16, 1945. Acheson, p. 122.   192, Clayton letter, quoted in Feis, *From Trust to Terror*, p. 230. Boothby, quoted in Howard K. Smith, *The State of Europe* (New York, 1949), p. 88.   193, Jones, p. 253. Department of State Bulletin, June 15, 1947, p. 1160. Truman ("Two Halves," etc.) quoted in Jones, p. 233. Clayton, quoted in Acheson, p. 231.   197, Clay telegram, quoted in *Forrestal Diaries*, p. 387.

11 FROM RECONVERSION TO TAFT-HARTLEY

201–202, Harvey C. Mansfield, A Short History of the OPA (Washington, D.C., 1947), pp. 85, 89.   202, Radio speech: Truman Public Papers 1945, p. 443.   204, CIO News, December 10, 1945.   205, Mansfield, p. 98.   206, Text of original draft reprinted in Cabell Phillips, The Truman Presidency (New York, 1966), p. 116.   207, DNC Clipping File, Truman Library. Taft: Congressional Quarterly, Vol. II, 1946, p. 300.   208, Clifford, quoted in Phillips, p. 125. Saul Alinsky, John L. Lewis (Vintage edition), p. 334.   209, Rosenman Papers, Box 8, Truman Library.   209–210, Harold D. Smith Papers, February 8, 1946, conference with President. Copy in Truman Library.   212, Acheson, p. 200.   216, White House Central Files, Press Intelligence, June 24, 1947, Truman Library.   216–218, Clifford Papers, Box 21, Truman Library.   218–219, Jonathan Daniels Notebook, p. 46, Truman Library.

12 THE 1948 MIRACLE

221, U.S. News & World Report, January 28, 1949.   222, Richard E. Neustadt, Notes on the White House Staff, p. 43, Truman Library. U. E. Boughman, Secret Service Chief (New York, 1961), p. 86.   223, Boughman, p. 85.   224, Acheson, p. 150.   225–226, Marianne Means, pp. 220, 231–232.   227, Margaret Truman, p. 109. Dinner at Blair-Lee House: Hillman, p. 122.   228–229, Truman Public Papers 1948, pp. 406–411.   229, Memo in Rosenman Papers, June 29, 1948, Truman Library. Conference with Taft, quoted in Irwin Ross, The Loneliest Campaign (New York, 1968), p. 137.   230–231, Flynn, quoted in Ross, p. 125.   234, The Private Papers of Senator Vandenberg (Boston, 1952), pp. 456–458. My Name Is Tom Connally (New York, 1954), p. 331. Truman's rejoinder to his aides, quoted in Ross, p. 214.   237, Ickes' private opinion: Michael W. Strauss to Oscar L. Chapman, September 5, 1948, Chapman Papers, Truman Library.   238, PM, December 30, 1947.   240, Vandenberg, p. 460.   240, Lilienthal II, p. 434.

13 SCANDALS, NATO, PEACE TREATY WITH JAPAN

245, Vaughan, quoted in Jules Abels, The Truman Scandals (Chicago, 1956), p. 47. All other references relating to scandals: Abels, pp. 16–20. Senate Hoey Subcommittee on Investigations of the Committee on Expenditures of the Executive Department, 81st Cong., 2nd sess., August 8 to September 1, 1949, pp. 313–315, 535–539 and 82nd Cong., 1st sess., 1951, pts. 3 and 4. King Subcommittee on Internal Revenue Laws, 82nd Cong., 1st sess., pp. 1–10, 255–265. Report of Fulbright Subcommittee, "Favoritism and Influence," 82nd Cong., p. 8. Arthur Krock in *The New York Times*, April 6, 1952; Newbold Morris, *Let the Chips Fall* (New York, 1955), p. 26; Harold Seidman Oral History, Truman Library.   251, Acheson, p. 729. Louis J. Halle, *The Cold War as History* (New York, 1967), p. 284.   252, Dulles, quoted in Robert E. Osgood, *NATO: The Entangling Alliance* (Chicago, 1962), p. 50. Kennan, *Memoirs*, p. 410, and *Russia, the Atom, and the West* (London, 1958), pp. 89–90.   253, Osgood, p. 30.   254, Senate Committee on Foreign Relations, 81st Cong., 1st sess., Hearings on North Atlantic Treaty, pp. 25, 144, 183, 317.   255, Kennan, *Memoirs*, pp. 401, 404. Speech to Congress: Public Papers 1948, pp. 182–190.   257, Acheson, pp. 728, 732.   258, Acheson, p. 126.   268, Kennan, *Memoirs*, p. 382. Acheson, p. 541. 269, Acheson, Department of State Bulletin, April 28, 1952, p. 648.

14   ARMS RACE AND THE BOMB

270–271, Clay, quoted in Jack Raymond, *Power at the Pentagon* (New York, 1964), p. 82.   271, Hanson Baldwin, *Harper's Magazine*, December, 1947. Lippmann, *New York Herald Tribune*, June 20, 1950.   272–273, Walter Millis, *Arms and the State* (New York, 1958), p. 140. Gabriel Kolko, *The Roots of American Foreign Policy* (Boston, 1969), p. 27. G. William Domhoff, *Who Rules America?* (Englewood Cliffs, N.J., 1967), p. 115. Irving Janowitz, *The Professional Soldier* (New York, 1960), p. viii.   276, Stimson and Bundy, pp. 642, 646. Truman to visitor, quoted in William Appleman Williams, *The Tragedy of American Diplomacy* (Cleveland, 1959), p. 168. Footnote: related in Feis, *From Trust to Terror*, p. 98.   277, Tris Coffin, *Missouri Compromise* (Boston, 1947, p. 19). Footnote: Lilienthal II, p. 26.   278–279, Vandenberg, pp. 228–229.   279, Lilienthal II, p. 10.   281, Byrnes, *Speaking Frankly*, p. 269. Lilienthal II, p. 30.   282, Lilienthal II, p. 163.   283, Baruch address reprinted in Department of State, *A Report on the International Control of Atomic Energy: Growth of a Policy* (Washington, D.C., 1946), pp. 138–147.   286, Nourse, quoted in Warner R. Schelling et al., *Strategy, Politics and Defense Budgets* (New York, 1962), p. 137.   287, Quotations in Schelling, pp. 100, 104–105. *Forrestal Diaries*, pp. 536–537.   289, Oppenheimer at White House, quoted in Philip M. Stern, *The Oppenheimer Case* (New York, 1969), p. 91.   290, Acheson, p. 375.

15   CHINA TRAUMA

291, Kennan, *Memoirs*, p. 375.   295, Roosevelt letter to Chiang, quoted in Barbara W. Tuchman, *Stilwell and the American Experience in China*

(New York, 1971), p. 470.   296, Theodore H. White and Annalee Jacoby, *Thunder out Of China* (New York, 1946), p. 189.   297, Roosevelt
message, quoted in Tuchman, pp. 492–493.   298, *The New York Times*,
October 31, 1944. Chiang, quoted in White and Jacoby, p. 129.   300,
On China loan: *Morgenthau Diaries*, May 8, 1945, p. 1535. Hurley, quoted
in Herbert Feis, *The China Tangle* (Princeton, N.J., 1953), p. 302. Mao
Tse-tung, *Selected Works*, Vol. 3 (London, 1954), p. 322.   302, Wedemeyer, quoted in Feis, *China Tangle*, p. 402. Edmund Clubb, *Twentieth
Century China* (New York, 1964), p. 274.   303, Hurley resignation: De-
partment   of   State,   *United   States   Relations   with   China*,   pp.
581–584.   304, Marshall summary, quoted in Feis, *China Tangle*, p.
419.   306, Stilwell, quoted in Tuchman, p. 527.   308, *United States
Relations with China*, pp. XVI–XVII. Butler, quoted in Goldman, p. 125.
Hurley, quoted in Allen J. Matusow, ed., *Joseph R. McCarthy* (Englewood
Cliffs, N.J., 1970), p. 8. China bloc, quoted in Walter LaFeber, *America,
Russia, and the Cold War* (New York, 1967), p. 84. Taft, quoted in Richard
B. Stebbins, *The United States in World Affairs* (New York, 1951), p.
57.   309, Dean Acheson, *Strengthening the Forces of Freedom* (Wash-
ington, D.C., 1950), p. 16.   310, Department of State Bulletin, January
16, 1950, p. 79.

16   INTERVENTION IN KOREA

312, John W. Spanier, *The Truman-MacArthur Controversy and the Korean
War* (New York, 1965), p. 30; *The New York Times*, June 28, 1950.
Dulles, quoted in Courtney Whitney, *MacArthur: His Rendezvous with
History* (New York, 1956), p. 322.   313, Kennan, *Memoirs*, p. 500.
313, North Koreans "jumped the gun": Wilbur W. Hitchcock, *Current
History*, March, 1951.   315, Rostow, quoted in Edward Friedman and
Mark Selden, eds., *America's Asia* (Vintage edition), p. 108.   316,
Christian Science Monitor, June 29, 1950. Knowland and Taft remarks:
Congressional Record, 81st Cong., 2nd sess., pp. 9228, 9319.   318,
Thompson, quoted in David Reese, *Korea: The Limited War* (Penguin edi-
tion), p. 90. *Brassey's Annual*, quoted in I. F. Stone, *The Hidden History
of the Korean War* (New York, 1952), pp. 312–313.   319, Acheson,
Department of State Bulletin, July 10, 1950, p. 46. Acheson, p. 453.
320, K. M. Panikkar, *In Two Chinas* (London, 1955), pp. 108, 110.
Acheson, p. 456.   320–321, Whitney, p. 395. White House staffers: Charles
S. Murphy Oral History, Truman Library.   321, MacArthur remarks:
[MacArthur] Hearings before Armed Services and Foreign Relations Com-
mittees, U.S. Senate, 82nd Cong., 1st sess., pp. 1–8.   322–323, Mac-
Arthur's statements, quoted in Whitney, pp. 411–412.   323, Mac-
Arthur communiqué, quoted in Lynn Montross and Nicholas Canzona, *U.S.
Marine Corps Operations in Korea*, Vol. III, p. 144. Whitney, p. 416, gives

a toned-down version of MacArthur's statement to Coulter.   324, Mac-
Arthur Hearings, p. 3541.   327, Acheson story: Barkley, p. 214. (A
slightly more discreet version in Acheson, p. 524.)   328–329, Mac-
Arthur at ball game incident related in Goldman, pp. 209–210.

17   TROUBLES ON THE HOME FRONT

333–334, MacArthur and critics: MacArthur Hearings, pp. 731–733,
745.   335, Acheson, pp. 481, 484.   336, MacArthur Hearings, p.
100.   337, Cordell Hull, *Memoirs*, Vol. 2 (New York, 1948), p. 1597.
United States-Vietnam Relations 1945–1967, prepared by the Department
of Defense for use of Committee on Armed Services [Pentagon Papers]
Washington, D.C., 1971, Vol. 1, Sec. I, A–2.   337–338, Acheson
to Jessup, quoted in Richard J. Barnet, *Intervention and Revolution* (New
York, 1968), p. 187.   338, Pentagon Papers, government edition, Vol.
1, Sec. IV, A.3 and *Pentagon Papers* (Bantam edition), p. 9.   340,
Samuel Lubell, *The Future of American Politics* (New York, 1965), third
rev. ed., p. 28.   342, Truman Public Papers 1951, p. 144.   344,
Richard E. Neustadt, *Presidential Power* (Signet edition), p. 34.   347,
MacArthur Hearings, p. 1782.   348, Mark W. Clark, *From the Danube
to the Yalu* (New York, 1956), p. 82. See also articles by Van Fleet and
Clark, "You Can't Win if Diplomats Interfere," *U.S. News*, August 20,
1954.   348–349, Truman Public Papers 1951, pp. 330, 372.   349,
Acheson, p. 536. *Wall Street Journal* and Gross, quoted in I. F. Stone,
pp. 299, 321. *The New York Times*, November 12, 18, 1951.   351,
Millis, p. 367.   352, Lippmann: *New York Herald Tribune*, August 24,
1956. Truman admission, quoted in Richard H. Rovere, *Senator Joe
McCarthy* (New York, 1959), p. 15.

18   TRUMANISM AND McCARTHYISM

353,Wilson to Cobb: John L. Heaton, *Cobb of "The World"* (New York,
1924), p. 269.   355–356, Inglis and Randolph, quoted in Alan D. Harper, *The Politics of the White House and the Communist Issue* (Westport,
Conn., 1969), p. 35.   356, Report of President's Temporary Commission
on Employee Loyalty, Charles S. Murphy Papers, Truman Library. Truman to Durr, quoted in Fred Cook, *The Nightmare Decade* (New York,
1971), p. 64. Carey McWilliams, *Witch Hunt* (Boston, 1953), p. 6. Murray
letter in Truman Papers, Official File 252-I, Truman Library.   359,
Richardson, quoted in Edward S. Corwin, *The President: Office and Powers* (New York, 1948), p. 131.   359–360, Bill of particulars, quoted in
Harper, p. 50.   364–365, *The New York Times*, March 28–30, May 4,
May 8, June 2, 1950.   364, McCarthy rejoinder to Tydings Committee:
The New York Times, July 18, 1950.   366, Attlee, quoted in Alan

Moorehead, *The Traitors* (New York, 1963), p. 209.   366–367, Taft, quoted in Matusow, p. 8.   367, Taft remarks to press, quoted in William S. White, *The Taft Story* (New York, 1954), p. 85.   367–368, Jack Anderson and Ronald W. May, *McCarthy: The Man, the Senator, the "Ism"* (Boston, 1952), pp. 266–267.   368, *The New York Times*, January 11–13, 1954.   370–371, Owen Lattimore, *Ordeal by Slander* (Boston, 1950), pp. 111–112.   371, Marquis Childs: *New York Post*, October 31, 1951. *Fortune*, April and May, 1954.   373, Samuel A. Stouffer, *Communism, Conformity and Civil Liberties* (New York, 1955), pp. 59, 86. Election analysts: Angus Campbell et al., *The American Voter* (New York, 1960), p. 50.   374, Truman remark: Spingarn Papers, July 22, 1950, Internal Security memo, Truman Library.   375, Rowe, quoted in Harper, p. 172.   376, McCarthy speeches: Matusow, pp. 51, 59.   377, *Washington Post*, April 28, 1951, quoted in Walter Johnson, *1600 Pennsylvania Avenue* (Boston, 1960), p. 246.

19   THE LAST HURRAH

378, Arthur Krock, *Memoirs* (New York, 1968), pp. 267–269.   379, Stevenson to Arvey, quoted in Edward P. Doyle, *As We Knew Adlai* (New York, 1966), p. 58.   380–381, Lippmann: *New York Herald Tribune*, July 24, 1952.   381, Roger Tubby Oral History, Truman Library. 383, *New York World Telegram*, August 22, 1952.   384, Adlai E. Stevenson, *Major Campaign Speeches 1952* (New York, 1953), p. 142. 386, Louis Harris, *Is There a Republican Majority?* (New York, 1954), p. 32.   386–387, Truman Public Papers 1952–1953, pp. 770, 891. 387–388, Taft, Jenner, Carlson, Wiley, Knowland, Hoover, quoted in Ronald J. Caridi, *The Korean War and American Politics* (Philadelphia, 1968), pp. 116–117, 156, 171, 195.   388, Eisenhower: *The New York Times*, June 6, 1952.   389–390, Stevenson speeches, p. 188. Eisenhower, Dulles, Dewey: *The New York Times*, October 3, 5, 6, 9, 15, 25, 1952.   390, Dulles, quoted in Emmet John Hughes, *The Ordeal of Power* (New York, 1963), p. 73.   391, Stevenson speeches, pp. 303–304. Truman II, p. 500.

20   HIS PLACE IN THE PANTHEON

392, Truman to his daughter, quoted in Steinberg, p. 418. Truman to press conference, April 17, 1952, Truman Library. Farewell speech: Truman Public Papers 1952–1953, p. 1199.   392–393, Arthur M. Schlesinger, "Our Presidents: A Rating by 75 Historians," *The New York Times Magazine*, July 29, 1962.   399, Truman Public Papers 1952–1953, p. 1199.   400, Harriman, quoted in Rexford G. Tugwell, *Off Course* (New York, 1971), p. 304.

Index

Abbott, Jacob, 29
Acheson, Dean, 135–136, 177, 187, 212, 224, 249–251, 253–254, 258, 278 n., 279, 281, 289, 291, 308, 383, 388; China problem and, 308; on Korean War, 311–312, 317, 319, 324, 335, 337–338, 347, 349; McCarthy and, 375–377; *illus.*, 264–265
admirals' revolt, 1949, 275
Agar, Herbert, 226
Air Mail Act, 83
Alanbrooke, Field Marshal Lord, 173
Alexander I, 165
Alien Registration Act, 354
Allen, Frederick Lewis, 157
Allen, George E., 2, 15, 126, 209
Alsop, Joseph, 307
Aluminum Company of America, 109–110, 114
Amalgamated Clothing Workers of America, 238

American Federation of Labor, 96, 108, 112, 238–239
American Labor Party, 238
American Legion, 103, 124
American magazine, 112
Americans for Democratic Action, 230, 263
American Society of Newspaper Editors, 232
Anderson, Jack, 367
Anderson, Gen. Orville, 325
Andrews, "Ham," 287
anti-Communism drives, 357–358, 362–363
Antonov, Gen. Alexei, 169, 296
armed services, postwar problems of, 284–286
arms race, 270–290, 398
Army Air Force, independent status for, 284–285
Army-Navy Munitions Board, 10, 107, 270
Arnall, Ellis, 343

Arthur, Chester A., 119
Arvey, Jacob, 220, 231, 378–379
Atgeld, John Peter, 207
Atkinson, Brooks, 298
Atlantic Charter, 143
atomic bomb, arms race and, 270–290; decision on, 171–172, 397; dropping of, 173, 288; inspection and, 283–284; and Potsdam Conference, 170; power balance and, 176; secrecy on, 276–277; Soviet Union and, 177, 182
Atomic Energy Commission, 289
Attlee, Clement Richard, 225, 277–278, 325, 335, 337
Attorney General's subversive list, 356–357
Augusta, U.S.S., 160
Austin, Warren, 83
Aylward, James, 69, 73, 76; *illus.*, 132

Bacall, Lauren, 117
Badoglio, Marshal Pietro, 146
Bailey, Dorothy, 359
Baldwin, Hanson, 271
Ball, Joseph, 101
Balkan states, 147, 166
Bankhead, William, 97
Bao Dai, 338
Barker, John, 57
Barkley, Alben W., 7, 15, 17, 20, 82, 88; *illus.*, 261
Barkley, Mrs. Alben, *illus.*, 261
Barrow, Clyde, 77
Baruch, Bernard M., 11, 94, 199, 281
Baruch Plan, 276, 281–284
Batt, William L., 108, 231
Beard, Charles A., 62
Bell, Daniel, 104
Bell, Jasper, 66
Bergen, Edgar, 91
Berle, Adolf A., Jr., 243
Berlin crisis, 233–234

Bernstein, David, 96
Berryman, Jim, *illus.*, 259
Beveridge, Albert, 292
Bevin, Ernest, 177, 314
Biddle, Francis, 121–122, 354
Biddle, Nicholas, 234
Biemiller, Andrew, 230
Biffle, Leslie, 207
Bingham, George Caleb, 24
Black, Hugo L., 123
Blackett, P. M. S., 173–174, 281
Blair House, Washington, 227, 313; *illus.*, 261
Board of Economic Warfare, 13
Boettiger, John, 15
Bohlen, Charles, 139, 151, 193
Bolsheviks, 44, 165
Boothby, Robert, 192
Borah, William E., 82
Boughman, U. E., 222
Bowles, Chester, 204
Boyle, William, 61, 247
Bradley, Gen. Omar N., 334, 348
Brandeis, Louis D., 86
Bretton Woods conference, 143–144
Brownell, Herbert, 229
Bryan, William Jennings, 357
Bryce, James, 119
Buchanan, James, 331
Budenz, Louis F., 370
Budget Bureau, U. S., 106
Bulger, Miles, 53, 55, 62–63
Bundschu, Henry, 1
Burch, Jacob, *illus.*, 262
bureaucracy, extent of, 117–118
Burns, James MacGregor, 120
Burton, Harold, 123
Bush, Vannevar, 170, 287
Butler, Hugh, 308
Butler, Pierce, 123
Byrnes, James F., 5, 7, 14–19, 99–100, 106–107, 122, 151, 158, 164–170, 173–177, 199, 249–250, 258, 276, 278–279, 282, 300, 314; ambition of, 7–8; on

Byrnes, James F. (*continued*)
Cold War, 178–180; rupture with Truman, 159–160, 179; *illus.*, 133–134

Cabinet, shake-up of, 121–122
Cain, Harry F., 388
Capehart amendments, to Defense Production Act, 342, 344, 346
Carlson, Frank, 388
Carnegie, Andrew, 22
Carnegie-Illinois Steel Company, 114
Case bill, 207 n., 209
Celler, Emanuel, 374
Centralia mine disaster, 208
Central Intelligence Agency, 271
Chambers, Annie, 34
Chambers, Whittaker, 366
Chapman, Oscar, 216, 231, 344
Chennault, Gen. Claire, 307
Chiang Kai-shek, 167–169, 286, 288, 292, 302–306, 314, 334, 337, 349, 351, 369; alliance with, 298–300
Chicago Daily News, 10, 383
Chicago Tribune, 350, 368, 382; *illus.*, 260
Childs, Marquis W., 371
Chiles, Henry P., 42, 57
China, "betrayal" of, 308; Communist triumph in, 291–310; "loss" of, 307; Nationalist, *see* Nationalist China; unification of, 168–169; White Paper on, 308; *see also* Communist China
China lobby, 196
Chinese Communists, 189; confusion about, 299; growth of, 293–294; *see also* Communist China
Chou En-lai, 302, 306, 320
Christian Science Monitor, 316, 368

Churchill, Sir Winston S., 140–143, 149–150, 152, 154, 156, 167, 172; on atomic bomb, 175 n.; Fulton (Mo.) speech, 180–182; on Polish boundary, 162; on postwar Europe, 191; at Potsdam Conference, 158; rebuffed by Truman on troop dispositions, 151; Roosevelt and, 151; *illus.*, 264
Chu Teh, 301
CIO (Congress of Industrial Organizations), 4, 17, 112, 200, 203, 214, 238–239, 344, 356
CIO Political Action Committee, 13
Civil Aeronautics Act of 1938, 83
Civil Aeronautics Board, 219
Civil Service Commission, 353
Civil War (U.S.), 22, 40, 71, 114, 314, 329, 394
Civil Works Administration, 64–65
Clark, Bennett, 59, 68, 72, 77–79, 83, 94, 97–98
Clark, Champ, 68
Clark, Gen. Mark, 124, 348, 350
Clark, Tom, 121, 123, 206, 355, 362; *illus.*, 134
Clay, Maj. Gen. Lucius D., 164, 197, 233, 255, 258, 270–271
Clayton, William, 191–194
Cleveland, Grover, 119, 207, 393
Clifford, Clark, 13, 95, 120, 135, 183–184, 207–208, 216–219, 229, 231–232, 234, 237, 240, 282; *illus.*, 261
Clubb, Edmund, 302
Cobb, Frank, 353
Cochran, John J., 73–75
Cold War, 137, 148, 180, 184–186, 195, 214, 233, 236–237, 242, 257, 269, 282, 287, 330–331, 339, 358, 384, 391, 397, 401; atomic bomb and, 278; Indochina and, 338; Japan and, 259–

Cold War (*continued*)
267; Korean War and, 313, 347; Marshall Plan and, 194; military caste and, 274; Nationalist China and, 306; NATO and, 251–252; in 1948 campaign, 237–239; in Truman's farewell address, 399
collective security, Korean War and, 316
Collins, Gen. Lawton, 325
Colorado Fuel and Iron Company, 86
Communism, as caricatured "conspiracy," 339–340; defense against, 242; and Korean War, 313–314; liberalism identified with, 356; Marshall Plan and, 256; in 1948 campaign, 235–240; "Truman's war" and, 338; as "world enemy," 336; world revolution and, 188–189; *see also* Soviet Union
Communist China, 189; Chiang Kai-shek and, 298; in Korean War, 320, 322–323, 351–352; MacArthur and, 334; massed armies of at Yalu River, 324; recognition of, 326; rise of, 291–310; *see also* Chinese Communists
Communists, FBI investigation of, 360–362; Popular Front movements of, 147
Community Savings and Loan Association, Kansas City, 59
Connally, Tom, 100–101, 121, 274, 278
Connelly, Matt, *illus.*, 261
Congress of Industrial Organizations, *see* CIO
Continental Can Corporation, 271
Controlled Materials Plan, 106
Coolidge, Calvin, 1, 98, 123, 139, 212, 399
Copper, Kennecott, 77

Corallo, Charles, 92
corruption, as 1952 campaign issue, 386
cost-of-living increases, 343
Coughlin, Father Charles E., 372
Coulter, Maj. Gen. John B., 323
Council of Economic Advisers, 193, 216
Cox, Eugene, 99–100
Crowley, Leo, 149, 191
Crump, Ed, 77
Culbertson, Jerry, 37
Cummings, Homer S., 73
Curtiss-Wright Corporation, 114
Curzon Line, 143
Cutting, Bronson, 76
Czechoslovakia, Soviet Union and, 195, 255, 349

Daniels, Jonathan, 14, 120, 231
Davies, Joseph E., 152, 158, 166
Davis, John W., 89
Davis, Warren, 100
Dawson, Donald, 246
Deane, Gen. John R., 140–142, 296
Debs, Eugene V., 207
Dedijer, Vladimir, 189
Defense Department, U.S., growth of, 273–274; budgets, 287–288
defense production, delays and waste in, 104–106
Defense Production Act, 1950, 342–346
defense program, investigation of World War II, 99–100
Democratic National Convention, 1944, 16–18; 1948, 228–234, 246–247
Democratic party, labor unions and, 200
Denfield, Adm. Louis E., 275
Dennison, Adm. Robert L., 276; *illus.*, 261
Depew, Chauncey, 269

Detmar, Charles, 10
De Voto, Bernard, 381
Dewey, Thomas E., 93, 220, 229, 233–236, 239, 312, 365, 389; illus., 260
Dickman-Hannegan machine, 93
Dies, Martin, 354, 358, 363, 372
"disloyalty" charges, 360–362
Djilas, Milovan, 189
Doheny, Edward L., 243
Domhoff, G. William, 272
Donahue, Richard, 226
Douglas, Paul H., 246
Douglas, William O., 7, 15–17, 123, 378
Draper, William H., 164
Dreyfus affair, 275
Dulles, John Foster, 89, 177, 252, 268–269, 389
Dunlap, Ike, 79
Dunn, Samuel, 88
Durr, Clifton, 356

Earle, George, 284
Early, Steve, 121
Easley, Harry, 18, 65
Eberstadt, Ferdinand, 10, 286
Eccles, Marriner, 219
Eden, Sir Anthony, 142, 162, 250; illus., 264
Eightieth Congress, 241; "do-nothing" stigma and, 233
Eighty-First Congress, 241
Einstein, Albert, 289
Eisenhower, Dwight D., 136, 154, 164, 220, 222, 229, 290, 348, 371, 399–400; on Korean War, 388–389; meeting with Taft, 383; 1952 campaign of, 385–386; as "perfect" candidate in 1952, 382–383; press support for, 382–383; rejects MacArthur strategy, 390
Elsey, George, illus., 261
Elvore, Joseph, 245
Espionage Act, 353

Europe, ancien régime in, 142–143; Communism in, 152; division of, 256; future of at Potsdam Conference, 160; land war fears in, 329–330; NATO and, 252–255
Evans, Tom, 70
Evjue, William, 368
Ewing, Oscar, 216, 231
Ewing, Gen. Thomas, 24
excess-profits tax, 12

Fair Deal, 241, 396
Fairless, Benjamin, 204
Fall, Albert, 243
Far East, Marshall Plan and, 258; NATO and, 291; Soviet Union and, 176, 190
Far Eastern Advisory Commission, 258
Farley, James A., 72, 79–80, 88; illus., 132
Federal Bureau of Investigation, loyalty checks by, 360–362
Federal Communications Commission, 356
Federal Employee Loyalty Program, 356
Federal Reserve Board, 219
Federal Trade Commission, 83
Feis, Herbert, 166
Feisinger, Nathan, 343
Fillmore, Millard, 211
Fisher, John, 381
Fitzpatrick cartoon, illus., 91, 97
"five-percenters," 244
Flynn, Edward J., 3–4, 14–15, 19, 230
Force, G. H., 73
Foreign Affairs, 187
Formosa (Taiwan), Chiang's escape to, 288
Forrestal, James V., 4 n., 10, 110, 124, 140, 173, 180, 278
Fortas, Abe, 370
Fort Leonard Wood, 99

Fortune magazine, 371
France, Communism and, 256; NATO and, 254–255; Yalta conference and, 164
Franck, James, 171
Frankfurter, Felix, 123
Frederick the Great, 292
Frick, Henry C., 22
Fuchs, Klaus, 365–366
Fulbright, William J., 246, 332
Full Employment bill, 199
Fulton, Hugh, 100, 109, 112
Fulton (Mo.), Churchill speech at, 180–182

Gabrielson, Guy, 247
Galbraith, John Kenneth, 243, 381
Galt, Edith, 223 n.
Garfield, James A., 379
Garner, John Nance, 82, 84, 88–89
Gates, George, 40
Gaulle, Charles de, 189, 192, 254, 257
Gauss, Clarence, 295–296, 304
General Motors Corporation, 11, 203–204, 206
Germany, Byrnes' compromise on, 165–166; Cold War and, 314; future of at Potsdam Conference, 162; military budget of, 285; NATO and, 254; postwar treatment of, 162–163; Truman's proposal for, 163–164
Gibbons, G. R., 109
G.I. Bill of Rights, 199
"Goats" vs. "Rabbits," Kansas City, 52–58, 62–63, 72
Goebbels, Joseph Paul, 152
Goldsborough, T. Alan, 208
Gompers, Samuel, 200
Gouzenko, Igor, 355
Graham, Brig. Gen. Wallace K., 219; *illus.*, 261
Great Britain, atomic bomb secret and, 277; military budget of,

Great Britain (*continued*) 285–286; economic crisis of, 191–192
Great Depression, 102, 202, 216, 233
Greater Kansas City Plan Association, 64
Greece, aid to, 188 n., 191; bankruptcy of, 147; Communists in, 300; corruption of, 187
Green, William, 96
Grew, Joseph, 139, 149–150, 191
Gromyko, Andrei, 155, 283; *illus.*, 133
Gross, Ernest, 349
Groves, Gen. Leslie, 171, 174, 276, 278–279
Gunther, John, 30

Hague, Frank, 77, 220, 231
Halifax, Lord, 191
Halle, Louis, 251
Hancock, John, 11, 199
Hannegan, Robert E., 3–7, 15–19, 98, 126
Harding, Warren G., 2, 223, 243–244, 399–400
Harper's Magazine, 87–88
Harriman, Averell, 10, 124, 138–140, 146, 150–151, 159, 167–168, 173, 254, 296, 300, 348, 400; *illus.*, 265
Harrison, Benjamin, 119
Harrison, Pat, 88
Harrison, Gen. William H., 234
Harsch, Joseph, 298, 316
Hassett, William, 226; *illus.*, 261
Hatch, Carl, 82, 101
Hatch Act, 94, 355
Hathorn, Herbert, 245
Hay, John, 292
Hayden, Carl, 82
Hayes, Elihu W., 57
Hearst newspapers, 367–368

Hegel, Georg Wilhelm Friedrich, 393
Helm, William, 69–70, 74, 77–78
Henderson, Loy, 218
Hensel, H. Struve, 10
"Herblock" cartoon, *illus.*, 134
Hickenlooper, Burke, 367
Hickock, Wild Bill, 33
High, Stanley, 113
Hildring, Gen. John, 271
Hillman, Sidney, 17, 20, 105, 111–112, 239
Hinde, Edgar, 35, 48, 56
Hiroshima, Japan, bombing of, 171, 173, 288
Hirth, William, 81
Hise, Harley, 247
Hiss, Alger, 288, 366, 383, 385
Hitler, Adolf, 30, 143, 152, 163, 171, 315, 371
Ho Chi Minh, 337
Holland, Lou, 58, 107, 115
Holloway, Robert, 74
Hoover, Herbert Clark, 117, 185, 202, 246, 297, 310, 358
Hoover, J. Edgar, 364, 388
Hoover Commission, 286
Hopkins, Harry, 12, 64–65, 76, 84, 97, 121, 138, 151–155, 178, 300
Hopson, Howard, 89, 100
House Armed Services Committee, 287
House Judiciary Committee, 374
House Un-American Activities Committee, 354, 357
House Ways and Means Committee, 104, 248
Housing Act of 1949, 241
Hughes, Charles Evans, 235
Hughes, Emmet John, 390–391
Hughes, Tom, 37
Hull, Cordell, 147, 162, 192, 291, 337; *illus.*, 134
Hume, Paul, 225
Humphrey, George, 290

Humphrey, Hubert H., 230, 400
Hunt, Col. J. V., 245
Hunter, Caroline, 26
Hurley, Patrick, 297, 299–300, 303–305, 307, 370
Hyde, Arthur, 53
hydrogen bomb, 289
Hyman, Sidney, 381

Ickes, Harold, 3 n., 120, 182
Igoe, Bill, 73
Igoe-Dickman machine, 73
Independence, Mo., 25–26
Independence Examiner, 47, 70
Indochina, military assistance to, 336–337; outlays for (1954), 338
Industrial Mobilization Plan, 10, 107
Inglis, Thomas B., 355
Inland Steel Company, 344
Internal Revenue Service, scandals in, 248
Interstate Commerce Commission, 83, 86–87, 93
Inverchapel, Lord, 281
isolationism, MacArthur and, 335; Taft and, 213
Israel, recognition of, 218–219
Italy, Communism and, 256

Jackson, Ed, 43
Jackson, Robert H., 100, 123
Jacobs, Andrew, 359
Jacobs, F. L., Company, 247
James, Jesse, 33, 77, 86
Janowitz, Irving, 272–273
Japan, attack on by Soviet Union, 167, 175;
  atomic bombing of, 170–171;
  Communist China and, 291–292;
  democratization of, 267–268;
  ICHIGO offensive by, 294; MacArthur role in, 258; peace treaty with, 268–269; Pearl Harbor and, 292; Soviet Union and, 167, 175, 258; surrender of, 173–175,

Japan (continued)
    301; U.S. occupation of,
    257–267; V-J day and, 199
Jefferson, Thomas, 393, 395
Jenner, William, 309, 327, 386–
    387
Jessup, Philip, 308, 337, 367
Jewish vote, 96, 218
Johnson, Andrew, 211, 400
Johnson, Hugh, 11
Johnson, Louis, 10, 325, 348
Johnson, Lyndon B., 338, 370, 394
Johnston, Alvanley, 96, 207
Johnston, Eric, 342
Joint Chiefs of Staff, in Korean War,
    321–323; on relieving of Mac-
    Arthur, 326–327, 334
Jones, Jesse, 13, 109–110, 116
Jones, Joseph, 136, 185–186, 193
Joy, Adm. Turner, 347–348
Justice Department, U.S., 248, 374

Kaiser, Henry J., 17
Kansas City, Mo., corruption in,
    71–73; Pendergast rule in, 5,
    48–52; politics in, 52–54
Kansas City Journal-Post, 69
Kansas City Law School, 58
Kansas City Power & Light Com-
    pany, 50
Kansas City Star, 26, 33, 38, 50, 70,
    74, 88, 91
Kansas City Terminal Railroad
    Company, 50
Kefauver, Estes, 379
Kelly, Edward J., 7, 15, 17, 77
Kelly, Walt, 234
Kemper, William T., Jr., 73
Kennan, George F., 187–189, 193,
    237, 252, 254, 268, 289, 291, 339
Kennedy, John F., 228
Kennedy, Joseph, 369
Kesselring, Field Marshal Albert,
    137

Keynes, John Maynard, 191
Keyserling, Leon, 216, 340
Kilgore, Harley M., 113, 200, 374
Kilgore-Murray bill, 199
King, Mackenzie, 277–278
Kirk, Adm. Alan, 271
Knecht, Karl, illus., 259
Knowland, William, 310, 333
Knox, Frank, 10
Knudsen, William S., 105
Kolko, Gabriel, 272
Korean War, 168, 225, 235, 268,
    290, 311–322, 391, 394; Ameri-
    can support for, 316–317;
    cease-fire in, 348–349; economic
    policies in, 340; in 1952 cam-
    paign, 387–388; price spiral
    during, 340–341; Soviet Union
    identified with, 335–336; stale-
    mate of, 346–347; Stalin's role in,
    313–315; Taft on, 387–388
Kraft, Joseph, 196
Krock, Arthur, 225, 378
Krug, Julius, 205, 208
Ku Klux Klan, 55–56, 58
Kuomintang government, China,
    189, 196, 305–306

labor unions, excessive power of,
    215–216; in 1948 election, 236,
    239–240; no-strike pledge and,
    202; postwar relations with,
    199–215; and Taft-Hartley Act,
    214–216, 344–346; Truman
    Committee and, 108
La Follette, Robert M., 239
Lahey, Edwin, 383
Lamar, Mo., birthplace at, 25
Landis, James, 219
Landon, Alfred, 10
Landry, Gen. Robert B., illus., 261
Lane, James, 24
Laney, Ben, 230
Lattimore, Owen, 370, 384

Lawrence, David, 231
Lazia, Johnnie, 71–72, 77, 80
Lea, Clarence, 84
League of Nations, 315, 394
Leahy, Adm. William D., 140, 142, 153, 158, 170, 173–174, 179, 401; *illus.*, 134
Lehman Brothers, 11, 271
Lenin, V. I., 146, 157, 165
Lerner, Max, 238
Leuchtenburg, William, 89
Lewis, J. Hamilton, 77–78
Lewis, John L., 101, 112–113, 205, 207–208, 342, 346
liberals, as "Communists," 356
Liberty League, 214
Life magazine, 80
Lilienthal, David E., 1, 120, 240, 243, 279, 281
Lincoln, Abraham, 24, 31, 114, 175, 275, 392–393, 400
Lippmann, Walter, 155, 188, 195, 258, 271, 352, 380–381
Little Steel formula, 202
Little White House, Babelsburg, Germany, 158; Key West, Fla., *illus.*, 261
Lloyd, David, 374, 377
Locke, Edwin, 267
Lodge, Henry Cabot, Jr., 269, 357
London Foreign Ministers Conference, 286
Longworth, Alice, 123
Los Angeles Times, 207
Lovett, Robert A., 10, 124, 175 n., 218–219
Lowenthal, Max, 85–86, 100, 374
loyalty checks, FBI and, 360–362
Loyalty Review Board, 358, 362, 377, 396
Lubell, Samuel, 340
Lucas, Scott, 7, 364–365, 369–371, 375
Luce, Henry, 113

MacArthur, Gen. Douglas, 178, 258, 268, 296, 301, 307, 315, 328, 348, 351, 388; campaign against Administration policy by, 325; dismissal of, 275, 322–323, 327, 329–332; hearings on, 328–332; imperiousness of, 321–322; on Korean War, 317–318; as legend and cult, 333–334; letter to Martin, 326; "offensive against Washington" by, 322–325; on 38th parallel advance in Korea, 319; ultimatum to Chinese Communists, 326
McCabe, Thomas, 219
McCarran, Pat, 76, 83, 310
McCarran bill, 374–375
McCarran-Walter bill, 386
McCarthy, Joseph R., 308, 332, 371, 383, 385–386, 396; Acheson and, 375; appeal of, 369; blooming of under attacks, 365–366; emergence of, 354–355, 363–364; on FBI secret files, 364–365; and 1950 elections, 369–370; demagoguery of, 372, 376; supporters of, 368, 372
McCarthyism, 186, 303, 328, 352–377
McClellan, Gen. George B., 275
McCloy, John J., 10, 124, 145 n., 191, 276
McCluer, Frank, 180
McCormick, Col. Robert, 368
McCulloch, Spencer, 70
McDaniel, Lawrence, 5–6
McElroy, Henry F., 56–57, 60, 63, 65–66, 72, 183
McGrath, Howard, 223, 248, 364
McKay, Douglas, 399
McKellar, Kenneth, 77
McKim, Ed, 125
McKinley, William, 382

McMahon, Brien, 336
McMahon bill, 282
McNutt, Paul V., 17
McReynolds, James C., 123
McWilliams, Carey, 356
Madison Capital Times, 368–369
Mahan, Adm. Alfred, 292
Mahon, George H., 287
Manchuria, Japanese occupation of,
    292; Open Door policy and, 300;
    war booty from, 303
Mann, Conrad, 79
Mao Tse-tung, 300, 302, 304
Maragon, John, 244–245
Marks, Tom, 50
Marshall, Gen. George C., 31, 124,
    140, 142, 169, 186, 218–219,
    234, 249, 295, 303–309, 331,
    348, 376, 383
Marshall Plan, 193–197, 213, 218,
    249, 251, 257, 269, 338, 349,
    359
Martin, John Bartlow, 381
Martin, Joseph, 326–327
Matthews, Francis, 325
Maverick, Maury, 114
May, Ronald W., 367
Maybank, Burnet R., 19–20
Meader, George, 18
Mellon, Andrew, 385
Messall, Victor, 18, 76, 78, 81–82,
    88, 94
Mesta, Perle, 117
Metropolitan Street Railway Com-
    pany, 49–50
Metternich, Klemens von, 257
Metzger, Arthur, 58–59
Middle East, problems of, 187
Mikolajezyk, Stanislaw, 153, 165
Miles, Maj. John, 38, 56
military affairs, civilian control of,
    272–273
military budget, raising of, 273;
    postwar, 287–290

military caste, postwar growth of,
    270–273; rivalry among, 284–
    286
Miller, Ruth McCormick, 368
Millet, G. Van, 34
Milligan, Jacob "Tuck," 59, 68–
    69, 73–75, 80
Milligan, Maurice, 72–73, 82, 91,
    94, 97
Millis, Walter, 272, 351
Milwaukee Journal, 368
Minton, Sherman, 82, 123
Missouri, University of, 65, 75
Missouri Farmers Association, 81
Missouri Field Artillery, 42
Missouri National Guard, 31, 38,
    42, 96, 122
Missouri Pacific Railroad, 86
Mitchell, Orestes, 74
Mitchell, Stephen, 381
Molotov, Vyacheslav, 140–141,
    146, 150, 161, 165, 173,
    176–178, 256, 258, 286, 314;
    illus., 133
Mommsen, Theodor, 393
money changers, New Deal and, 11
Montgomery, Emmet, 55–56
Montreaux Convention, 135–136
Moore, A. Harry, 77
Morgan, David, 37
Morgan, J. P. and Company, 11
Morgan Oil and Refining Company,
    38
Morgenthau, Henry, 72, 104, 122,
    162, 300
Morgenthau Plan, 162
Morison, Elting, 10
Morris, Newbold, 248
Mundt-Nixon bill, 374
Munich Pact, 1938, 143
Murphy, Charles S., 231–232, 234,
    371
Murphy, Robert, 154
Murray, Matthew, 80, 92

Murray, Philip, 203, 238, 356
Murrow, Edward R., 227
Mussolini, Benito, 146

Nagasaki, Japan, bombing of, 171
Napoleon I, 142–143, 330, 395
Nash, Frank "Nelly," 72
Nash, Phileo, 377
Nast, Thomas, 51
National Association for the Advancement of Colored People, 96, 236, 238, 359
National Association of Manufacturers, 210, 233
National Defense Act of 1916, 345
National Guard, Missouri, 31, 38, 42, 96, 122
Nationalist China, 145; Soviet Union and, 296; U.S. support of, 295–296
National Planning Board, 243
National Press Club, 117
National Security Council, 271, 310
NATO (North Atlantic Treaty Organization), 195, 269; and division of Europe, 256; Far East and, 291; Japan and, 259–269; MacArthur and, 334–335; Marshall Plan and, 251–269; Soviet Union and, 330
Navy procurement, investigation of, 110–111
Nazi Germany, threat from, 142; see also Hitler, Adolf
Neely, Matthew, 365
Negro rights, achievements in, 397
Negro vote, 95–96, 236
Nelson, Donald, 106, 297
Neustadt, Richard E., 222, 344
New Deal, 8–13, 69, 78, 81–82, 103, 122, 200, 213–214, 235, 238, 242, 307–308, 364; as bureaucratic leviathan, 117–118; Cold War and, 237; Communism

New Deal (continued)
and, 354, 371; as "disastrous experience," 126; Truman's dislike of, 120; World War II and, 104–106
New Republic, 220
New York Times, 43, 113, 155, 185, 271, 298, 350, 368, 382
New York World, 353
Niebuhr, Reinhold, 237
Niles, David, 14, 231
Nimitz, Adm. Chester, 296
Nitze, Paul, 273, 289
Nixon, Richard M., 247, 327, 383, 387
Noland, Ella (aunt), 40–41
Norris, George, 76
Norris-LaGuardia Act, 208
North American Aircraft Company, 105
North Korea, initiative of, 314–315; in Korean armistice, 351–352; see also Korean War
no-strike pledge, 202
Nourse, Edwin, 286
Novikov, Nikolai V., 224
NRA (National Recovery Administration), 65, 84
NSC-68 arms program, 289–90, 335, 349
nuclear power, NATO and, 253

O'Donnel, Gen. Emmet, 318
O'Dwyer, William, 220
Office of Defense Mobilization, 341
Office of Price Administration, 201–204, 210
Office of Production Management, 102–103, 105–106, 109
Office of War Mobilization, 199, 204
oil company, Truman's early investment in, 37–38
O'Mahoney, Joseph C., 82

O'Malley, Emmet, 51, 92
Oppenheimer, J. Robert, 279–280, 289
Osgood, Robert E., 253

Palmer Raids, World War I, 353
Panikkar, K. M., 320
Park, Guy B., 74
Parker, Bonnie, 77
Parrish cartoon, *illus.*, 265
Patterson, Robert P., 9, 124
Patterson, Roscoe Conkling, 68
Pauley, Edwin S., 3–4, 7–8, 15, 17, 19, 21, 219
peace, need for, 397–398
Pearl Harbor attack, 31, 102, 106
Pearson, Drew, 225, 368
Peck, Mrs. Mary, 223
Pegler, Westbrook, 225
Pepper, Claude, 220
Pendergast, Jim, 33, 35, 48, 52, 94
Pendergast, Mike, 47, 49, 54, 57, 63
Pendergast, Thomas J., 5, 48–50, 53, 60, 66, 68, 88, 167, 376; acquiesces to Truman, 61–62; bribery of, 50; character and rule of, 51–52; continuing relations with, 90–91; death of, 117; downfall of, 79–81, 91–92; estrangement with, 78–79; Negro vote and, 96; Roosevelt and, 79–80; senatorship and, 68–69; in Truman nomination for senate, 75–76; *illus.*, 132
Pennsylvania Railroad, 112
Pentagon, growing influence of, 271–273
Perón, Juan, 225
Pershing, Gen. John J., 271
Pétain, Marshal Henri, 179
Peurifoy, John, 364
Phelps, Nick, 47
Philadelphia Record, 207
Philippines, 292, 336
Pitt, William, 398

Plutarch, 29
PM (newspaper), 238
Poland, Lublin government of, 140; parliamentary democracy for, 141–142, 148–149; partition of, 292; status of at Potsdam Conference, 161; Yalta agreement on, 153
politicians, professional, 244
Polk, James K., 226
Porter, Paul, 359
Post Office Department, 83
postwar trade, 193
Potsdam Conference, 156–175; agenda of, 160–161; atomic bomb and, 275–276; Germany and, 162; *illus.*, 133
Powell, Adam Clayton, 224
Pratt, John Lee, 11
presidency, cult of, 393–394
presidents, "grading" of, 395; social-democratic type of, 394
President's Temporary Commission on Employee Loyalty, 355–356
Price Control Act of 1950, 210
price controls, during Korean War, 340–341
price-wage spiral, 202, 204
professional politician, 244
Pryor, John, 61
Public Utilities Holding Company bill, 89
Pullman strike, 207

Quebec Conference, 296

railroads, seizure of, 205
railroad strike, 1945, 205; 1951, 342–343
Railway Age, 88
Railway Labor Act, 205
Randall, Clarence, 344
Randolph, A. Phillip, 230, 238
Randolph, Lt. Col. Byron N., 356
Rankin, John, 354

Rayburn, Sam, 4, 15, 121
Reader's Digest, 113
Ready-Mixed Concrete Company, 51, 77
Reconstruction Finance Corporation, 84, 246–247
reconversion period, 198–200
Red China, see Communist China
Red hunt, McCarthyism and, 353–370
Reddig, William, 33, 113
Reed, James A., 69, 79
Reeves, Albert L., 91
Reinsch, Leonard, 232
Renegotiation Act of 1942, 111
Reorganization Act of 1939, 117–118
reparations, at Potsdam Conference, 164
Republican National Committee, 248, 367
Republican National Convention (1952), 373
Republican party, anti-Communism and, 362
Reserve Officers Association, 225–226
Reston, James, 155
Revenue Act of 1945, 199
Rhee, Syngman, 314, 317, 322
Richardson, Seth, 358–359
Ridgway, Gen. Matthew B., 348
Riesman, David, 243
Rigdon, William M., illus., 261
right-to-work laws, 215
Roberts, Roy, 2
Robertson, N. G., illus., 132
Robinson, Joseph T., 88
Rockefeller, John D., Sr., 22
Rockefeller Foundation, 86
Rock Island Railroad, 86
Roosevelt, Anna, 15
Roosevelt, Eleanor, 3, 125, 220
Roosevelt, Franklin D., 65, 72–74, 79, 83, 88, 90, 95, 116, 148, 212,

Roosevelt, Franklin D. (continued) 216, 231, 235, 243, 249, 291, 296, 314, 331, 345, 354, 385, 393–395, 399–400; administrative procedure compared to Truman's, 126–135; "balancing act" of, 8, 11–12; as "the Champ," 8; Chiang Kai-shek and, 295, 298; Churchill and, 151; death of, 1–2, 117, 392; defense program investigation and, 99–100; and Economic Bill of Rights, 201; Far East policy of, 337; fourth term of, 13–14; on Morgenthau Plan, 162; Pendergast and, 79–80; Second Hundred Days of, 84; Stark and, 97; Stalin and, 143; and Truman Committee, 103–104; war cabinet of 1940, 9–10; with Truman, illus., 132
Roosevelt, Franklin, Jr., 367
Roosevelt, James, 220
Roosevelt, Theodore, 31, 292, 393–394
Root, Elihu, 249
Rosenbaum, Col. Joseph, 247
Rosenman, Samuel I., 2, 126, 200
Ross, Charles, 126, 135, 231; illus., 261–262
Ross, Mike, 71
Ross, William, 61
Rostow, Walt W., 315
Rumania, Soviet Union and, 146
Russell, Lillian, 34
Russians, confrontation with, 137–157; in World War I, 44–45; see also Soviet Union

St. Louis Post-Dispatch, 17, 19, 64, 70, 74, 76, 91, 97, 220, 368
Salisbury, Spencer, 58–59, 80
Saltonstall, Leverett, 324
San Francisco Call, 382
Sawyer, Charles, 135, 344
scandals, of second term, 243–249

Schwab, Charles M., 22
Schauffler, Edward, 66
Schlesinger, Arthur M., 393–394
Schlesinger, Arthur M., Jr., 95, 381, 393–394
Schwellenbach, Lewis B., 82, 95
Scott, Hazel, 224
Seidmann, Harold, 248
Securities and Exchange Commission, 89
Sedition Act of 1918, 353
Senate Appropriations Committee, 3
Senate Banking and Currency Committee, 246
Senate Finance Committee, 104
Senate Foreign Relations Committee, 363
Senate Military Affairs Committee, 284
Service, John Stewart, 294, 377
Seventh Fleet, in Korean War, 312
Shannon, Joseph, 52, 60, 70, 74, 135
Sherman, Adm. Forrest, 336, 348
Sherwood, Robert, 12, 151, 209
Sienkiewicz, Henry, 29
Sinclair, Harry F., 243
SKF Roller Bearing Company, 108
Smaller War Plants Corporation, 114
Smith, Gerald L. K., 395
Smith, Harold, 200
Smith, Margaret Chase, 365–366
Smith, Merriman, 82
Smith, Gen. Walter Bedell, 271
Smith-Connally Act, 112, 208, 362
Snyder, John W., 122, 126, 135, 204, 209, 223, 286; illus., 134, 265
socialism, wartime, 9
Somervell, Gen. Brehon B., 270
Soong, T. V., 168, 299
Southern, Col. William, 47, 70
South Korea, invasion of, 311–312; see also Korean War
Soviet Union, antithetic social sys-

Soviet Union (continued)
tem of, 156; atomic bomb project and, 172–173, 276, 307; attack on Japan by, 175; "babying" of, 179; Baltic states and, 145; Baruch Plan and, 283–284; cooperation with, 137–157; Czechoslovakia and, 255; economic warfare with, 398–399; in Europe's future, 160–161; expansionism of, 188–189, 242; in Far East, 190; German unification and, 256–257; Germany as counterweight to, 163; "get tough" policy with, 183–184; hydrogen bomb and, 289; as "impotent nation," 188; "iron fist" against, 179; Japan and, 258; and Korean War, 312–314, 317, 348; Marshall Plan and, 193–197; Nationalist China and, 296; NATO and, 251–253; Poland and, 141–143, 161–162; postwar demands of, 143–144; Red hunt and, 352–355; as "right" enemy, 335; veto right in UN of, 154; "worldwide struggle" against, 184–185
Spaatz, Gen. Carl, 174
Speer, Albert, 10
spoils system, 66–67
spy cases, 1950–52, 366
Stalin, Joseph, 141–142, 154, 159, 166, 223, 234, 258, 296, 300, 388, 395; illus., 133; and Chiang Kai-shek, 169; Cold War and, 148; Communist China and, 301; Italian formula of, 147; Japanese surrender and, 301; and Korean War, 313–315; Nationalist China and, 169, 303; NATO and, 252–253; Poland and, 149–150, 161–162; on U.S. atomic bomb, 172–173; Yalta agreement and, 149
Stalin-Hitler pact, 10, 195, 358

Stark, Lloyd, 5–6, 50, 93, 97
State Department, NATO and, 250–257; pro-Communists in, 308; see also Acheson, Dean
Stauffer, Samuel, 373
Stayton, Col. Edward, 58, 61
steel industry, labor problems in, 343; price rise and, 204
Steelman, John, illus., 261
Steffens, Lincoln, 5, 48
Stettinius, Edward R., Jr., 2, 11, 108, 139, 159
Stevenson, Adlai, Jr., 10, 378; Korean War and, 390–391; in 1952 campaign, 378–380; rift with Truman, 381
Stilwell, Gen. Joseph W., 294, 297–298, 304, 306
Stimson, Henry L., 9–10, 105–106, 123–124, 140–141, 145 n., 150, 159, 162, 170, 172–173, 275–276, 284, 300
Stone, Harlan, 123
Stone, I. F., 124
Stowe, David, illus., 261
Strandlund, Carl, 247
Stratemeyer, Lt. Gen. George E., 322
strikes, 1945, 203
subversive list, of Attorney General, 356–357
Suez crisis, 257
Supply Priorities and Allocation Board, 106
Supreme Court, U.S., 83–84, 208, 216; appointments to, 123; in Inland Steel case, 345; Roosevelt and, 8
Surine, Don, 369
Swope, Herbert Bayard, 283
Symington, Stuart, 223
Szilard, Leo, 171, 174

Taft, Robert Alfonso, 202, 207, 212–216, 229, 235, 275, 310, 327,

Taft, Robert Alfonso (continued) 344–345, 372; on Communists in government, 366–367; on Korean War, 387–388; and MacArthur hearings, 329–334; meeting with Eisenhower, 383; budget proposals of, 331
Taft-Hartley Act, 209, 214–216, 233, 239, 344–346
Tanforan racetrack, 245
Tanguay, Eva, 34
Teamsters Union, 354
Teeter Oil Pool, 38
Tennessee Valley Authority, 1
Thomas, Parnell, 356
Thompkins, William J., 95
Thompson, R. W., 318
Time magazine, 368
Tito (Josip Broz), Marshal, 149, 398
Tobin, Daniel, 211, 220, 354
Todd Shipbuilding Company, 111
Trainmen's Union, 342–343
Transportation Act of 1940, 83–84
Trotsky, Leon, 146
Truman, Bess (Elizabeth Virginia Wallace, Mrs. Harry S. Truman), 40–41, 45, 56, 78, 122, 212, 224, 232, 245; character of, 226–227; illus., 261, 264, 266
Truman, Harry S., accepts nomination for Vice-President, 19; as "accidental" President, 393; accommodation policy of, 398–399; Acheson and, 250–253; administrative procedure compared with Roosevelt's, 126–135; aggressive stand of, 141–142; on aid to Greece and Turkey, 191; and Alcoa investigation, 109–110; assassination of, attempted, 401; on atomic bomb, 170, 174, 175 n., 276–277, 397; attitude toward women, 35; with Attlee and King, 277–278; with Ayl-

Truman, Harry S. (*continued*) ward, *illus.*, 132; on Baruch Plan, 281–283; break with Byrnes, 179; as butt of 1952 campaign, 381–382; as captain of artillery, 43; ceremonial duties of, 222–223; childhood of, 26–27; on China unification, 168–169; Churchill and, 150–151, 181–182; on city planning and bond issues, Kansas City, 63–64; Cold War crusade of, 186, 399; compared with Wilson, 157; credibility gap of, 219; criticizes loyalty program, 360; cronies of, 124; on "cutting out" of Russia, 258; "defeat" of by Dewey, *illus.*, 260; depression following 1948 election, 240; and destruction of Pendergast, 91–92; drop in popularity standing of, 183; early reading, 29; early years, 22–39; earthy humor of, 36; education of, 29–30; on Eisenhower candidacy, 386–387; and Eisenhower map-reading incident, 136; election as President, 236; emotional stress in, 225; entertaining of by Washington society, 117; entry into politics, 40–54; evening education courses taken by, 78; exaggerated decisiveness of, 135; and Executive Orders 9599 and 9651, 201–202; as ex-President, *illus.*, 266; eyesight of, 27; as failure in 1946, 211; and Far East problems, 292–295; farewell address of, 399; farm background of, 36; first job, 32; as first lieutenant, *illus.*, 129; folksiness of, 98; with Harriman, Acheson, and Snyder, *illus.*, 265; as "Gentleman from Pendergast," 76; ghost-written anti-Roosevelt article and, 112; his haberdashery

Truman, Harry S. (*continued*) business, 45–46; his honesty, 61–63, 66–67; his humility, 118, 135; illnesses of, 27–28; independence of, 88–89; on Indochina aid, 338; in Inland Steel seizure, 344–346; and interservice rivalry, 284–285; on Interstate Commerce Commission appointment, 88–90; as Jackson County judge, 55–67; with Japanese surrender message, *illus.*, 134; Jewish vote and, 96, 218; at Key West Little White House, *illus.*, 262; and Korean War, 311–322, 347–348, 351–352; labor problems and, 342–345; his lack of inspiration, 395–396; his leadership, 396; leads 1948 parade, *illus.*, 260; and John L. Lewis fight, 208–209; at Little White House, *illus.*, 261–262; in low esteem, 1952, 352; on loyalty and anti-communism drives, 358–360; MacArthur and, 275, 322–323, 327, 329–332; marriage to Bess Wallace, 40–41, 45; Marshall Plan and, 193–194; his middle initial "S.", 25; as middle-of-the-roader, 14; on mission to Moscow of Justice Vinson, 233–234; with Molotov in Washington, 140–141; on morality, 35, 67; national buildup of, 113; in National Guard, 38–39; and nation's needs, 397–399; Negro rights achievements of, 397; and Negro vote, 95–96; New Deal and, 120, 400; at 1944 Democratic convention, *illus.*, 133; in 1948 campaign, 231–234; offhand speeches by, 135; oil business of, 37–38; Oppenheimer and, 289; parents of, *illus.*, 127; with Pendergast, *illus.*, 132; as

Truman, Harry S. (*continued*)
Pendergast candidate for Senate, 61–62, 70–71; as Pendergast's "office boy," 74, 90–91, 96–97; his piano playing, 31–32, 34, 117, 223; his place in history, 392–401; his poker playing, 223; on Poland agreement, 153; populism of, 65; postwar domestic policy of, 198–220; on postwar military outlays, 288; at Potsdam Conference, 158–175, *illus.*, 133; Price Control Act and, 210; with Princess Elizabeth, *illus.*, 264; "radical" speeches of, 86–87; railroad seizure by, 205–206; reconversion and, 198–200, 210; reelection to Senate, 94–98; relaxation and play of, 221–222; Roosevelt and, 15–16, 95, 119–120, *illus.*, 132; his self-assurance in second term, 225; as senator, 75–76, 87, 94–98, *illus.*, 129; his shortcomings, 395–396; his snap decisions, 135–136; Stalin and, 172–173, 179; Stevenson nomination and, 379–380; and strikes of 1945–46, 205–207; Supreme Court appointments by, 123; and Taft-Hartley bill, 212–216; on Truman Committee, 99–115; his Twenty-One Point Program, 200, 208–209; unpreparedness at FDR's death, 118; veto of McCarran bill, 375; of Taft-Hartley bill, 216; as Vice-President, 116; Victorian code of, 35; Wallace and, 184; in World War I, 18, 42–43; on yacht *Williamsburg, illus.*, 262, 264; other *illus.*, 129, 131, 134, 259, 262, 265
Truman, John Andrew (father), 22–23, 25, 30, 35; *illus.*, 127
Truman, Margaret (daughter), 45,

Truman, Margaret (*continued*)
58, 65–66, 227–228; singing career of, 224–225; *illus.*, 261
Truman, Martha Ellen Young (mother), 22–25, 30, 32, 35, 37, 43
Truman, Mary Jane (sister), 25, 27
Truman, Shippe (grandfather), 25
Truman, Vivian (brother), 25, 28, 32, 36–37, 46; *illus.*, 128
Truman & Jacobson Haberdashery, 46; *illus.*, 130
Truman-Attlee-King Declaration, 277–280
Truman Committee, 85–86, 99, 114–115, 123
Truman Doctrine, 186, 188, 192, 195, 213, 237, 249, 252–253, 289, 309, 339, 349, 397
Truman Library, Independence, 26, 36
Turkey, aid to, 191
Tweed, William Marcy, 49
Twenty-One Point Program, 200, 208–209
Tydings, Millard E., 363, 365, 370, 374

United Nations, 154–155, 281–284, 316, 319–320, 326, 350
United States, imperial role of, 292; postwar exports of, 193
universal military training, 285
UNRRA, 194

Vandenberg, Arthur H., 82, 187, 196, 212, 229, 234, 240, 268, 278–279, 281, 307, 367, 384
Van Devanter, Willis, 123
Van Fleet, Lt. Gen. James, 348–349
Van Sant, Tom, 181
Vardaman, Jake, 217
Vaughan, Maj. Gen. Harry H., 31, 36, 125–126, 135, 180, 225,

Vaughan, Harry H. (*continued*)
244–245, 247, 376; *illus.*, 133,
261
Veatch, Nathan, 61
Versailles Peace Conference, 44–45
Vice-Presidency, struggle for, 1–21
Vietnam War, 394
Vincent, John Carter, 370
Vinson, Fred M., 122–123, 191–
192, 233–234, 378; *illus.*, 134
Vinson-Tramnel Act, 2, 102
V-J Day, 199, 201
Vyshinsky, Andrei, 146–147

wage-price spiral, labor peace and,
205
Wagner Act, 215
Walker, Frank, 7, 15–16, 19
Wallace, David, 42
Wallace, Elizabeth Virginia, *see*
Truman, Bess
Wallace, George, 17–20
Wallace, Henry Agar, 4, 7, 13–15,
17, 20–21, 97, 116, 120, 135,
182–184, 186, 236, 238–239,
295, 362
Wallace, Madge Gates, 41–42
Wall Street figures, 9–11, 89–90
Wall Street Journal, 349, 399
War Labor Board, 201–202
War Production Board, 106, 113,
115, 201, 297
War Resources Board, 10
Warsaw Pact, 256
Washington, George, 31, 393, 395
Washington Daily News, 124
Washington Post, 225, 368, 377,
382
Washington Times-Herald, 368
Watson, Gen. Edwin, 4, 78
Webb, James, 286
Wedemeyer, Lt. Gen. Albert C.,
302

Werth, Alexander, 173
Wheeler, Burton K., 84, 96
Wheeler-Rayburn bill, 89–90
Wheeler-Truman bill, 85, 87
Wherry, Kenneth S., 258, 308, 327,
329
White, William Allen, 26, 34, 64
Whitney, A. F., 89, 96, 207, 238
Whitney, Gen. Courtney, 320
Wiley, Alexander, 388
Wilkins, Roy, 96
Williams, Aubrey, 116
Willkie, Wendell, 89
Wilson, Charles E., 297, 341, 343,
348
Wilson, Woodrow, 38, 117, 157,
200, 203, 223 n., 235, 268, 353–
354, 393–394, 400
Winant, John, 15
Wood, Gen. Robert, 11
Woodring, Harry, 94
Woodward, Stanley, 224
World War I, 108, 143, 271, 285
World War II, 270, 285, 353–355
WPA (Works Progress Administra-
tion), 65, 80

Yalta agreement, 140, 142, 149,
153, 159–162, 167, 177, 258
Young, Ada (aunt), 37
Young, Harrison (uncle), 36–37, 45
Young, Laura (aunt), 37
Young, Martha Ellen (mother), *illus.*,
127; *see also* Truman, Martha
Young, E. Merl, 246–247
Young, Sally (aunt), 37
Young, Solomon (grandfather), 22–
24
Yugoslavia, relations with, 298, 398

zaibatsu, Japan, 267
Zhdanov, Andrei, 195, 256
Zhukov, Marshal Georgi, 154
Zionism, 218–219